THE
LIVING LIGHT
DIALOGUE

Volume 1

THE LIVING LIGHT DIALOGUE

Volume 1

✀

Through the mediumship of
Richard P. Goodwin

Living Light Books

This book, the first of many volumes, is dedicated to Richard P. Goodwin, our earth teacher who, through his mediumship and dedication to the Light, opened a church and a school for all souls interested in following his demonstration of the Living Light philosophy.

We also dedicate this volume to Isa Goodwin, Chairman, to the members of the Spirit Council, who guided the activities and counseling of the Serenity Association, and to the Wise One, who first received these teachings from the realms of Light and then shared them with Mr. Goodwin and the students. We are grateful for the privilege of receiving these truths and for the opportunity of applying them.

CONTENTS

ACKNOWLEDGMENT

Grateful acknowledgement is made to the many students, supporters, and friends of the Serenity Association who selflessly gave their interest, energy, and effort in transcribing and preparing the text of the Living Light discourses and classes.

Heartfelt acknowledgement is given to the immeasurable guidance and help received from the realms of Light in bringing to press this first volume of *The Living Light Dialogue.*

PREFACE

The teachings in this book are part of the Living Light philosophy, which was given through the mediumship of Mr. Richard P. Goodwin, beloved teacher and founder of the Serenity Association. The foundation of this philosophy is the Law of Personal Responsibility, which states that we, and we alone, are personally responsible for all our experiences, which are the effect of the laws that we have set into motion, and we establish laws with our thoughts, acts, and deeds. The teachings also state that we, at any moment, have the divine right of choice. The teachings help us to broaden our understanding so that we may establish laws that return more harmonious, more joyful experiences. And thus we fulfill one of the many purposes of our souls' incarnation into form.

The philosophy teaches that we are inseparably united with the Divine. Yet we have lost conscious awareness of our souls. The classes help us to become more aware of our thoughts; through that inward journey, we awaken to our divinity. When we still our minds, we awaken to our own souls.

THE TEACHINGS

The teachings of the philosophy can be grouped into categories. The basic categories are discourses, consciousness classes, church lectures, annual world forecasts, and church questions and answers. Within the categories, each class has a number, such as Discourse 1 or Discourse 65.

The discourses are a series of spiritual awareness classes that were given to a very small group of students between January 6, 1964, and May 29, 1972. The deluxe edition of *The*

Living Light, which is often referred to in the classes as the textbook or the study book, contains all sixty-five discourses, as well as two seminars. The entire text of *The Living Light* is included in this volume. The early discourses were often held at the home of a student or supporter, because Mr. Goodwin's one-room apartment was not large enough to accommodate all the students.

The consciousness classes were given to a larger group of students between January 11, 1973, and May 9, 1985. There are 246 consciousness classes. Early classes were held on Thursday evenings at the American Legion log cabin in San Anselmo, California. Later classes were held at the church office, which was located in Santa Venetia, Marin County, California. During most of the consciousness classes the students were organized into small circles, with members of the circle facing inward. A typical class began with one student reading a discourse aloud. Then students said the "Total Consideration" affirmation aloud in unison. This was followed by a short period of meditation. After that, the one-hour class began.

Both the church lectures and the church questions and answers were given during the church services of the Serenity Spiritualist Church, which were also held at the log cabin. Public services were held from May 1, 1971, through June 9, 1985. The lectures and questions and answers were part of the service and were usually given on the first Sunday of the month. There are 101 church lectures and 57 church questions and answers. The lectures were usually twenty minutes, but it was not unusual for them to go longer.

Annual world forecasts, of which there are twenty-five, were generally given on the last Sunday of the year. Many, but not all, of these forecasts were recorded on audio tape. The forecasts revealed the events for the coming year.

Although not all of these teachings have been published in print, all are available as audio recordings.

MR. GOODWIN

As a beloved teacher, Mr. Goodwin shared his wisdom and understanding with all who were interested. His mediumship allowed a loving angelic presence to manifest countless times. He was the living demonstration of the philosophy by his dedication to the Light and his selfless service to the Spirit Council. Mr. Goodwin was born on February 22, 1927, in South Portland, Maine, and passed to the higher life on February 24, 1989.

THE FRIENDS

When Mr. Goodwin was first asked to open a church, so that the Living Light could be introduced to a wider audience, ever the servant of the angels, he had only one request: that the angels make all decisions of the church and he make none. Through his mediumship, the Spirit Council made all the decisions regarding the operation of the church. All the thousands and thousands of decisions involved in holding fundraising brunches, dinner socials, and bazaars were made by the Council. There are eighty-one members of the Spirit Council, and they are often simply referred to as the Friends.

SERENITY AND ITS CHURCH ACTIVITIES

"The workers win" is a saying in the Living Light philosophy and Serenity provided many opportunities to win. The bake sales, the holiday bazaars, the Sunday brunches, and the numerous church committees all provided opportunities to witness the teachings in action, apply the philosophy, and associate with other spiritually minded people.

THE TRANSCRIPTION

Great effort has been made by the members, friends, and supporters of the Serenity Association to accurately transcribe and publish these teachings. And it is with joy and gratitude that this, the first of many volumes, is presented to the world.

No specific instructions were given by the Friends with regard to the transcription, except for a simple guideline from Mr. Goodwin in the introduction to the deluxe edition of *The Living Light*: "It is presented with a minimum of punctuation to be freer for the individual interpretation of each reader." And yet, even with minimal punctuation, the placement of a period, comma, or colon can significantly alter the meaning of a sentence. Indeed, although great effort has been made to transcribe the teachings accurately, the punctuation may suggest a meaning that was not intended by the Teacher. Thus, to experience the teachings as they were given, free from the influence of the transcriber, the classes are available for purchase as audio recordings.

There is much in the recordings that simply was not possible to transcribe. For example, the volume of the Teacher's voice, whether he whispered or spoke forcefully, could not be transcribed. Nor could the strength and reassurance of his voice or the sound of his laughter be transcribed. The hesitation and uncertainty in a student's voice, as he or she struggled to articulate a question, could not be transcribed. All these things, and more, could not be conveyed in a transcription. And the recordings often include the sounds of the environment, such as the croaking of the frogs that lived in the creek that ran beside the log cabin, a plane passing overhead, the rain falling heavily upon the metal roof, or children playing just outside on a warm summer's evening. There is a sense of immediacy, almost a sense of participation, in listening to the audio recordings that is not available in the transcription. So if a particular class speaks to you, please consider purchasing the audio recording.

It is with joy that the Serenity Association offers more of the teachings of the Living Light philosophy to the world. Great effort, on both sides of the veil, has been made to bring this light to the world. Consider the teachings that are offered. They will serve you well in this world and in any world you have yet to awaken to, for they are divine in origin and in essence.

INTRODUCTION

*[This introduction was written by Mr. Richard P. Goodwin
for the 1972 deluxe edition of* The Living Light.*]*

*Think, children. Think more often
and think more deeply.*

The teachings in this book were given as a progressive series
of lessons to a group of four students who were sitting for
spiritual unfoldment with me beginning in January of 1964.
The communications were regular until October of that year,
when nearly a seven-year silence ensued, and resumed in 1971
to the present. They were received in three ways by me as a
channel. The main text was taped from a direct control of my
voice in deep trance at special sittings of our group, during which
I had no experience of the voice or what was being transmitted.
A few scattered verses were given independently when I was
privileged to see and hear our teacher clairvoyantly. I have also
been a channel for this communicant when speaking from the
podium at church and in answering difficult questions at our
public seminars.

Nearly all we know about our teacher is contained in these
lectures. He reports that he had tried for sixteen years to break
through an interference barrier that the channel had to deep
trance. When our conditions were in resonance with his patient
wisdom, he came through, ready to teach his understanding.
I have seen him as an old man dressed in white, with long,
flowing white hair. He has blue eyes, is slightly smiling and
deeply compassionate. I have always called him the Old Man.
The students liked to call him the Wise One. He is surely one of
those often called a Teacher of Light. I do not know his country,
although he indicated at one time that he was from 6000 B.C.
and a form of judge in his time.

The text is often difficult, but it is complete, having been
transcribed word for word from the original tapes recording the

trance voice. It is presented with a minimum of punctuation to be freer for the individual interpretation of each reader. The lessons given before the long silence are phrased with many allegories, often paradoxical. There are repetitions and renewals of theme, but it is explained that if an understanding is not perceived, compassion dictates that it be said again. Some of the topics have but a simple mention with little development, but all are revealed, we are told, according to merit.

The Old Man is a fine teacher. He has in a hundred ways intertwined his allegories, progressive explanations, unfolding exercises, and timely references to reach a multitude of levels of individual understanding. A notable change is his more direct style of presentation beginning in 1971.

There is an endearing intimacy of person that can be felt through his lectures, a meaningful and loving encounter with a wise friend. Like an old man, he makes a mistake and conscientiously corrects himself a few paragraphs later. He listens often and carefully to our earnest discussions of his words. He consults with a group of experts on evolution and cites their learning in his lesson. His use of the direct address "Children" or "My children" is not patronizing, but infinitely loving and supportive.

A word must be said about the teachings. The Old Man makes clear that his lessons are not dogma, a creed, or a narrow way, but simply his own understanding offered to us as a form of instruction to aid us in our own individual progression. When he speaks of laws, he does not refer to man-made rules or moral traditions, but to the cosmic and atomic way-things-are, the natural world of what-is, the universal laws of life, part of the original creative design and through which creation is fulfilled. These laws are beyond the possibility of being changed, suspended, transcended, or destroyed, but they are ever a tool of mankind, not his master. First, through our awareness of the universal laws and then slowly through our developed understanding, the powers of creation are accessible to us. Not power over men's minds or circumstances, but power over whatever is selfish and imperfect in ourselves is the way up the eternal ladder of progression. When the Old Man cautions us concerning the Law of Responsibility or gives us a thinking exercise to explore the Law of Identity in a dynamic manner, he prepares us to take another step. And all move in accordance with the Law of What Can Be Borne.

Our teacher shows us how the two worlds are drawn together. In his realm, he describes, there is a great diversity of thought, many schools of understanding; but the Light is always known by the Light. Because of the interdependence of the two realms, listening to our discussions helped to clarify his teaching to others on his side of the curtain. His love and gratitude he humbly equates with ours.

The lessons to be perceived are not new: they are very old, but they are new to certain levels of our being. I would personally advise the reader, after reading this volume of discourses in full, to make a daily habit (or when there is a feeling or need) to sit quietly with the book. Open it at random and be guided to the Light by the passage that is there for the day. This technique is still used by the original students who were given the lessons and by many students after them who have studied in unfolding classes with me through these teachings.

Go beyond the words into feeling, into the immediate meanings for you. Touch into the inspiration that flows into the form of this book. It is from the Divine.

RICHARD P. GOODWIN
San Geronimo, California
June 1972

DISCOURSES

DISCOURSE 1 ✣

I am indeed honored to be with you at this time. It is difficult due to the hesitation on the part of this, my channel. I have waited for sixteen of your earth years for this opportunity to speak. We have waited so patiently for we know that all is given to those who give.

I know that your interests lie in the eternal question of life in general. We too are interested and have been for many, many centuries. So much talk is given to the soul, to the forms, and the spirits and to all forms of life as you know on your planet. To the best of our knowledge, the soul potential is form and forms unlimited. By this we mean, in thy soul all things are known. All things that are to be, or have ever been, to thy soul are known. For thy soul is part of Allsoul. And through thy heart thy soul doth speak.

There are many spheres and planets—high or low is only in vibration, not in distance, as you know. Ask wherefrom the soul doth come. How many times we have asked, and to the best of our knowledge we feel and know in our hearts that the soul comes anew from the Allsoul at the very moment of conception.

So often, so many things that are seen are reflections from within. As the soul is given greater expression, the reflections of the senses shall be dimmed when the brightness of the soul shines forth. All things your soul is. You, your form, is the sum total of ages past; the potential of ages yet to come.

> When of thy mind thou seekest to know the truth,
> On the wheel of delusion thou shalt traverse.

For life eternal is not of form but of soul. Know ye not that in form higher yet to be with potential of the soul create all forms—it does and can.

3

Ye, my children, shall never find the light without, for the light can only be known by the light. Therefore, it is thy light within that thou must first permit to shine and this is done through the education of the form in which thy soul is at this moment encased.

As I spoke a moment ago, that thou art the sum total (thy form) of ages past, thou art affected to a degree in thy physical form and thy mental form by the evolutionary processes of those forms. Through the Laws of Heredity, which affect the forms of your planet, the soul is passing. God, the Allsoul, in great aspiration to raise the physical forms to the great and higher life has sent a part of itself, an essence, a Soul into the form, that by its journey it may raise the rates of vibrations of forms that in time, in eternity, they may be of the higher life. And as the soul, like the circle, passes though the forms, millions there are and millions yet to be.

I pray that you do not misunderstand for thou art a soul, a soul of man. Thy form is the highest form known on your earth planet. All forms have soul essence, but only man has self-consciousness, an awareness of this great soul within. For the form of man is composed of all the lower kingdoms. When in the embryonic stage of life, thy form in the womb doth pass through all stages of evolution in that nine-month period. Oh think, my children, think not that soul is form. Think not that God is form, for God is formless—yet God is form.

I wish to stay for but a moment longer that I might speak to you of the reflections of the inner self. When you feel, sense by feeling something by you or near you, do you know why this, in your form, is the most accurate of all your senses? It, my sons, is because your sense of touch or feeling is the original sense and by the process of evolution the most developed. For the sense of sight (physical) and the sense of hearing and your other physical senses are but an outshoot of the original sense of touch.

I must be leaving my channel for I must not tire him on my first journey. I pray that I may come again in this way, though it will take much work to overcome the resistance of my channel. I do pray that you will think not of thyself, for seekers of truth can think only of all life. As I withdraw, I feel a great questioning in the mind. I shall return.

Good night.

JANUARY 6, 1964

DISCOURSE 2 ✣

My dear children, again I am honored to be with you. There are so many things that we would like to discuss with you, my children.

You know, oh, so long ago, so many centuries ago, there's an old, old story, a story about a diamond chariot and an old ox wagon. The diamond chariot was drawn by the fastest of animals, and one day a gentleman, burning with enthusiasm, wanted to know all about all things—now. Not tomorrow, but now.

And he got aboard this diamond chariot and off he sped, looking for the Gates of Truth. And he traveled faster than the speed of light, onward and onward. So fast did he travel that all things he passed were but a blur. Many were the people he passed, but in his ears the sound was but a murmur, for so fast did he travel.

He had heard that the Gates of Truth were off in the far distant universe, and off he had sped to find them. And one day, after much travel, thinking only of his goal to get to the Gates of Truth, he came upon the golden gates, exhausted and tired, his animal spent, and behold, he found that the golden, shining gates were but a reflection from a great body of water. And behold, he looked and there upon the great high and rugged

Mountain of Aspiration were the true Gates of Truth. He had sped in great hurry and found only a reflection.

> My children,
> When of naught desire is,
> In vain doth sorrow speak.

I cannot give you any greater truth than I myself have earned. I too discuss and study and, yea, have I discussed for centuries and centuries past. Oh yes, I could tell you of the many things that I have seen.

How well I remember so many, many centuries ago, when I came from your planet into this other dimension. I was not one of the better of humanity and when I came to this other dimension, I found myself wandering upon a vast desert and, oh, how the sun did burn. Oh, how my lips did thirst for only a bit of water. But I had entered into the realm that I had earned but at that time I knew not. And after much wandering, I came upon a well. Oh, how my heart did fill with joy as I saw that well. I rushed up to the well and behold, as I looked down at the very bottom I saw but one drop of water at that very bottom of the well. Oh, what could I do! So far down to that one drop of water! In despair I cried, "Have I wandered so long to find so little? And yea, I not have the energy to climb so far down even to get it." And in my despair I fell asleep and in my sleep I heard a voice so beautiful sing to me. It was the first voice that I had heard in many, many a year. And the voice sang unto me:

> No one can carry your burden,
> No one can lift your load;
> But Angels of Light wait patiently
> To tell you their stories of old.

We must all tread the path that we ourselves have made. Others may tell of their paths that somehow, someway, someday this will give us the courage to carry us through.

As before, I have spoken of the many spheres and planets. There is so much to learn, but, my children, it is an ever-unfolding glory to God to see the beauties and the planes, the spheres, and planets that await your travels. I may tell you a bit of some of my journeys where the beauty never ceases and where the glory knows no end. We who are wise, or try to be, tarry not in these spheres of beauty. I do not mean to say that we do not enjoy or visit them, but we have learned that it is more perhaps, like you would say, a vacation. We have found that there is much work to do and to be done.

One of the first things upon entering this side of life is the strong tendency for rest, and to the millions who have earned this, unto them is given. But I pray that you will realize that much work is to be done on both sides of the veil. I am so honored and grateful to be with you because of the time I have waited. Like waiting for anything, does it not fill the heart with joy? I have unfinished work that I must do because, though it has taken me centuries to establish this contact, I did not fulfill what was given to me to do, yea, centuries ago upon your planet. I pray, my children, that you will love all life and know the Light.

I should like to speak but a moment longer on the Law of Responsibility. You are making the world and the world is making you. Every thought, act, and deed that you send forth help to build a better world. In these so-called invisible worlds, many journey and many tarry. Do not think, my children, that when you leave the physical body at transition that you go to the spirit world. Oh no, not all do. The astral world, the mental world, how many linger for how long! You, my children, are helping to create the good or the bad in those worlds. Think, think, and think! Are you making these worlds better worlds or are you making them worse?

Now you know there was a time when they said your planet was flat. And then they said it was round, and today they say it looks like a pear. My children, be ever ready and willing to change. Be free like the wind for you are, your soul, eternal. Hold not to form for form doth pass. Mind cannot know soul and mind too shall pass. Will you cross the bridge knowing not where it may lead? Oh, children, cross for life and life eternal is a great and wondrous adventure. How many times will you be tempted to stop and how many times your soul will cry and cry like the voice in the wilderness. You cannot stop progression.

And now, dear children, as I withdraw, I pray to visit with you soon. If you would, tell my channel to rest one hour prior to these sittings.

God bless you all.

JANUARY 25, 1964

DISCOURSE 3 ✣

My beloved children, I bring you greetings from our realms. It always gives me great pleasure to be with you. I would like to speak this evening about some of the things and people I have met on this side of life.

Oh, it is well to be so very grateful for all of the experiences of life for in time we shall see how they have given us a freedom, a freedom well earned, as all freedom is earned.

> As I came upon the mountain
> And felt the glory of my God,
> I looked about in wonder
> At the many paths I'd trod.

Won't you travel with me in thought for but a few moments as we drift through this so-called invisible realm? As you know, there are many spheres and planes, but I should like to travel in thought to the realm so close to earth. For this is one of the first experiences that the children from earth go through. So many find themselves lost but they are only lost within themselves for their thinking had not been clear while yet on earth. I do not wish only to speak of that realm of confusion and of anxiety and regret, but I do wish to point out that it exists, though many stop there for a short time.

It is well, O man, to know thyself; not as we would like to know ourselves, but to know ourselves as we are. Yes, won't you think on that for but a moment?

> For what of our self freely gives,
> In God's love forever lives.
> O seekers doth thou seek in vain,
> Who knows not of patience's pain.

I must be leaving you, children, as my channel was not well prepared, as I had asked before. I pray that in the future he will make a point of resting, as was requested before.

The climb, my children, is never higher than the fall. God bless you and, as I know you are sending forth this higher rate of vibration, I pray that you all may soon see how you are building within and without.

Bless you.

FEBRUARY 13, 1964

DISCOURSE 4 🌿

Greetings, greetings, children. Again I am pleased to be with you. Yes, it is indeed a wonderful thing to be able to come here in this way. I would like to discuss this evening a few things, perhaps, about service and limitation.

What is service and does it know limitation? We have discussed this, along with many other topics, in our school here on this side of the curtain. And we feel that true service is serving through humanity. You cannot serve *to* and serve spiritually. You serve *through* humanity serving the one and only God.

No one limits us but ourselves. We alone set into motion these limitations. All things, my friends, you are capable of. The potential of all things is within you. Whatever it may be that you wish to do or to know or to have, this potential is within you. But it is the limitation of the race mind that keeps these things from you. You know, friends, I wish that you could think for a few moments on the next statement that I would like to make:

> Be ever ready and willing to give
> That which you hold most dear,
> Then, my child,
> You shall know not of fear.

Perhaps this evening you would like to follow me for a few moments and visit, if only mentally, the realm from which I come. I am grateful that you are and have been willing to listen to the gibberings of an old man. Though in my class, I feel like an infantile—just like an infant. However, in this realm from which I come, we are discussing life prior to our earth life. You understand, my children, we're discussing theories. We do not know. We have listened to many visitors who claim they know all about that and we have listened to them and have thought for some time. For we surely would like to know where we came from, meaning the expression of life, if any, prior to the earth life. Because we feel that if we can know of that, we can know yet more of this life eternal.

We have had also visitors from realms who by their discussions are obviously from a higher rate of vibration than ourselves. But with all of the discussions that are made and of all the things that are said, we have found that truly are we closer to God as we become closer to nature, to all life.

One of the students asked, "I want truth. I have been searching for centuries for truth. Can you give me truth?"

And I said to him, "I cannot give you anything that is not already within you though dormant." And I asked him, "What is truth?"

And he said, "I do not know: that is why I am seeking it. I hear it's so wonderful but I do not know."

And I said to him, "You have searched for centuries, seeking something that you have heard about that you know is so wonderful and do not know what it is. Perhaps, my son, it is right inside of you and you have known it all the time; but knowing not what it was, you had not the realization of it."

So many things we seek without, when truly they have to be within in order to be without. Yes, there are many theories, many views; but what has given me the peace surpassing all understanding is when I realized within myself that I was but a channel for the higher life to flow through unobstructed.

As I spoke a bit earlier, be ready and willing to give that which you hold most dear. My friends, when you reach that state, then you have found freedom.

I ask, perhaps, if you would be so kind as to speak to my channel. I have had great difficulty in coming through again this evening and the basic reason for this is because he is not able to go into the unconscious state at these times. This, please tell him, is coming, but he must not analyze so much what is said but be patient to see what grows from the seed before he digs it up.

And now again, my beloved children, yes, I must be leaving you. I was not, dear friends, on vacation or away. But you know, I too am a student and I am so grateful to be a student of life.

Our class has no name and it has no banner. We sit in the vale
with the flowers and trees and we do ponder and think as we
watch the great beauties of nature pass before our eyes.

And now, friends, as I withdraw, think well, think long, for
life here and hereafter is a life of thinking. Be ever ready and
willing to change. God bless you in accordance to the Law.

Good night.

MARCH 19, 1964

DISCOURSE 5 ✒

Greetings, greetings, children. Again it is my pleasure to
be with you at this time. Earlier this evening I was impressing
upon my channel some of the many things that we on this side
of the curtain must witness at these times.

As you know, my friends, this is one of the holy times for
certain types of religious people. And as their thoughts, their
thinking, is sent out into this great universe, it attracts, creates, and draws its kind. How many from the realm of deception
and delusion are drawn to the earth planet at this time! Oh, so
difficult and heavy is the work of those from the realms of light.
For indeed, my children, we witness untold numbers of entities
which are drawn close to the earth planet at this time. However,
my children, it works through one of the many of God's natural
laws and I do not wish to dwell upon the cloudy side of things
at this time. For indeed we are grateful to have the blessings of
light also in the universes.

Now, as I speak to you this evening, I am so pleased to witness the many friends and relatives so close to you who are here
this evening. Yes, it is indeed a blessing, for they have joined
hands and brought many who knew not of the possibility of communication. And oh, how their hearts are filled with joy and
gratitude as they stand here amongst us, sending out their love,

their blessings, and their joy. However, my children, it is not my purpose or duty to go into the personal message at this time or at any time in the near future.

But may I take you this evening with me to some of the different scenes that are witnessed on this side of the veil? As perhaps you already know, we are in a type of school. It matters not, dear friends, who I am or used to be: it matters what I may be able to do to serve my God and humanity.

However, the other day we had come to our school a new student. He had been sent to us from one of the other schools. It seems that his helpers and instructors were having a most difficult time with this student. His problem seeming to be that he couldn't believe his own impressions. He couldn't believe or accept his own intuition. Now, friends, this chap is on this side of the veil and it is most difficult to understand how an individual cannot feel and believe the impressions that they ofttimes receive from within.

Well, my children, he's now with us and he has been giving our group lectures and speeches on what he feels—he thinks—is the purpose of life. Now, friends, do not please misunderstand. We have been listening to this fine young gentleman and we shall continue to listen to him. For he is seeing the world from without and we know in our hearts that as he continues to talk, to discuss, and to express himself, that in time he will draw back to this source of wisdom and of love, of truth that is within all of humanity. Yes, he will in time draw back to the core, the nuclei, the heart from whence all good, all knowledge, all wisdom, all love doth come. But what we are trying to do is to let this individual wear out from without for we know that as soon as this happens, there will be nothing left but to return to the source.

Now I know that there is a great question: Why should this entity be brought to our school? My friends, he is like a fresh fountain of pure water for he teaches us in his way gratitude and eternal thanks to God that we have come so far. And through this blessing which God has seen fit to bring to us, we again are able to serve through another channel.

I pray that you do not feel that we here do nothing but discuss soul and life. My friends, we do live a life. Yes, indeed, we do. We take our little trips and our visits to the other realms. You know, we have and are so grateful for so many friends in so many spheres.

And now, dear friends, especially at this time, won't you send out your blessed thoughts to the higher realms for so many entities hover close—so many from the realm of delusion.

Keep, my children, a mind of logic, a mind of reason. All of life is at your feet. And with the blessings which come from on high comes also its balance: responsibility. No one is ever permitted to glimpse the Light without their share of responsibility. The law that works for me also works for you. So often have I seen you visit these other realms. Yes, my children, indeed we live on both sides of the curtain. And we are indeed grateful to know beyond a shadow of a doubt that the worlds are in our hands.

> As we give, unto us is given.
> I pray each day that my God
> Will show me the way to serve today.

And now, my friends, as I prepare to withdraw, to the doubts and to the fears I must forever say, "Behind thee!" For the secrets of life are for the courageous and for the patient, that they may uplift all of life to the greater life that the Father in heaven has prepared.

And as the beloved angels shed their blessings and as I watch the golden rain here in this very room, oh, won't you think, think, and think of life, my friends, of life eternal not once or twice a week? Won't you consider to think each and every day? There is so very much work to be done.

And now:

> As the frog croaked
> And the wolf howled,
> The ears of Ego heard not
> For the door was locked
> By the key of fear.

God bless you with his love and from these angels from above who are so close beside you—my, there are so very many! In gratitude, in love, good night.

MARCH 26, 1964

DISCOURSE 6 ✦

Greetings, friends. Again it is my pleasure to be with you, children, this evening.

I should like to discuss, if I may, this communication between the worlds. So many have asked for so long, Why isn't more proof, more demonstration given to humanity? My children, as the rain that falls from above must first be drawn from below, we, dear friends, can only give to you in matters of demonstration what we are able to draw from our channels. By this I mean to answer the many questions dealing with the phases of mediumship. So many seek phenomena and these physical manifestations. Friends, we cannot give you what we are not able to draw from you. This is one of the many reasons why we ask that you try to consolidate and to solidify your vibrations. For as you, my friends, grow spiritually, we shall be able to give more to humanity.

Now, as perhaps you will recall, I mentioned once before about describing some of the places and scenes that I have been privileged to visit. I hope that you do not feel that you have been disappointed. I was in hopes, my friends, that you would have been able to attach yourself to the vibratory waves that were present at that time. Therefore you would have been able to witness as a scene in the mind those different places of which I wished you to be aware. However, where this was not possible at that time, I shall try in my humble way to describe some of those places.

If you can but visualize a cloud: you all know what a cloud may look like, but will you try to visualize a cloud that takes the forms that the waves of the mind reflect. Friends, if you will think on this and try to understand, you'll have an awareness of one of the early spheres, the entrance to the spirit realms.

As in our last speaking with you, we gave, dear friends, what is known as a parable. Truly we can give you the answer to this parable. But, dear children, I have not the heart to take from any of you your blessings and joy of growth. When you are able to solve the parable that has been given unto you, you, dear friends, will have perceived into one of the higher teachings. I cannot take away your growth. I cannot.

Now, as I have tried to describe one of the early spheres in entrance to our realms, you may think, dear children, that it is indeed a poor description. But think, my friends, think and think! You have been given the essence: from that you must build.

I know that many entities come and speak through various channels and we are aware of their varied descriptions of our realms. As varied is the mind is also varied the realms of the so-called invisible. No one, no, dear children, no one that we know of has been given a description of the higher, higher realms. For God in his infinite mercy has shown it not to mortals that they may discuss and lower our beautiful, higher spheres. Do you want all of life's blessings in a day or are they to be shared in the many days of eternity?

Like the camera that takes the picture, it can take only what is receptive to its own vibration; and so the eyes of mortals and the minds of men are only capable of receiving and comprehending that to which they have grown. If I see the world a little different than my brother, it is because I am different than my brother; it is because I am different than anyone who has ever been or will ever be. This is the Law of Eternity. The form shall never be the same. It is the soul and only the soul that knows. For what the mind may know today, the heart shall close and know not tomorrow.

And now, dear friends, as I prepare to withdraw, I send my blessings to all. May they reach forth and climb another step on the Ladder of Eternal Progression. As was said before, the climb is never higher than the fall. And I pray that you will, when feeling so inclined, think on the parable that has been given to you:

> As the bird flew
> And the snake crawled,
> The lion said,
> "Of what good are those?"

And now, my children:

> The mouse doth chase the cat.

Think. I have not come to do more than to help you to help yourselves.

God bless you.

APRIL 13, 1964

DISCOURSE 7 ✺

Greetings, children. It is indeed a great joy to be with you at this time. It always gives me great pleasure to visit with you in this way.

I should like to take you with me this evening to a realm of satisfaction and attachment. For nothing brings us more quickly to attachment than satisfaction. Now, children, as we journey on to this realm, you will find millions upon millions of souls who know not that they are in attachment. For it is indeed difficult to awaken the vision within when we are in satisfaction. Does not the child so close to the mother at birth know satisfaction? Oh yes, my friends, we must keep an even outlook on the drawing, magnetic power of satisfaction. Indeed, it holds so many for so long from progression as they lie about in their seeming pleasure and enjoyment.

Now there have been so many questions in the minds about the different planes and universes: What are they like? And who may be there? My friends, this planet earth is one of the younger planets and it has much to go before it reaches maturity. Now I can say that we have and do have visitors from other universes than our own. They all have soul, and the ones whom have conversed with us through the magnetic and vibratory waves, for we do not and cannot communicate with the so-called spoken word. We have been informed by some of the privileged ones who have visited with us of their great concern over the rapid advancement of earth men. For the physical, material advancement is centuries in advance of spiritual growth and understanding. Do you not see, my children, that the realm of which I spoke is the earth on which you now reside?

Think! Oh, think and think!

O sleeper, doth thou wake serene,
Knowing life is but a scene.

Indeed, my children, we are concerned with all of you. Never expect what you are not ready to give. Won't you search deep within, come back to the core, the nuclei? Free thyself from the great war and battle of thy senses. For, my children, you bring the essence of them into these other realms.

It has been a bit difficult for me to enter my channel this evening. I do pray that he shall take heed and rest for it is absolutely necessary to have sufficient magnetism so we may come in this way.

And now, to be always prepared for we go in the blinking of the light; and where might we find ourselves?

I am indeed pleased to say that our wonderful young visitor is now at rest and in his rest, a greater awakening from within is dawning upon him. And now as you continue to walk the wheel of progress, do you duty-bound care for those on either side.

> For as the moon sets,
> The sun can never shine
> Until the stars doth shine.

The little parable that was given before: it is the howling that perhaps will help you to perceive a bit. And now I must be leaving and I do pray to visit with you again. Patience is the only path to truth.

MAY 14, 1964

DISCOURSE 8 ✤

Greetings, greetings, children. Again it is indeed my pleasure to be with you this time for it is my duty to bring you the words and instructions from our realm.

You know, as we have so often spoken about the laws of responsibility, so many have a tendency to ask for more than they are willing or able to carry. For when one asks of these eternal things, they do not fully realize what a great load they are asking for. Now, my children, you must not only be willing, but be able to carry this load. For God will give to you what you are asking, as you yourselves are being prepared.

Now the many differences of opinion that are so evident in your realm are also evident in ours. For there are no two beings on the same step of the Ladder of Progression. Therefore, throughout the many spheres and planets which await you, you shall find these differences. For there are many schools on both sides of the curtain. Then, my children, perhaps we might ask, Who or what am I to believe? What is right for you is not right necessarily so for another. Therefore, keep your right and let the others keep theirs, for you cannot take away the experiences, mistakes, and errors that others have a privilege to have. In other words, my friends, it is well and good to share only to those who seek.

I should also like to speak of this so-called Law of Magnetism. For in these past weeks, my children, I have been watching and in attendance several times when, like sponges, you were being drawn. Before, we have mentioned the necessity for those who are on the paths of Light to protect themselves from this idle thought and chatter. I again speak to you of this for you are holding the progress of another from continuing to permit the magnetic powers to be drawn and depleted. I know that it is most difficult to break a habit. However, I must again bring this to you as strongly as I am permitted to do so.

Now, my children, I am pleased to say this evening that we have been discussing this life prior to earth, as once before we spoke to you. As you will recall, we said at that time we had heard many theories and had talked with many souls who claim they know all about those things. Well, children, we have indeed had a most interesting discussion with some very fine people who for centuries have been giving this a great deal of thought. I should like to pass on to you this, a bit, however, of the discussion that we had.

These friends feel that indeed they have experienced many, many, many lives. They feel that they have experienced but one of those lives on earth. And they feel that prior to their earth-form existence that they had existence and being on another planet than earth. They claim that there are many planets in various stages of evolution (of this we are indeed in accord) and they state that, like the planets, like the animals, and like man, everything is in progression. Now, if their discussions prove to be correct, this means that no one will ever find the so-called missing link between the animal and the human. For, as they state, "the man" entered from another planet. Now, friends, do not, please, be confused. They are speaking of the inner man and not of the form.

We shall be most happy to discuss this matter further with you at another time. However, I must not tire my channel.

You know, your creeds—like your shoes—wear out in time.

JUNE 25, 1964

DISCOURSE 9 ✀

Greetings, friends. I bring you greetings and love from our side of the curtain. I am so pleased to be with you again for indeed there is much to discuss.

As we were speaking before about the wonderful talks and exchange of thought that we have been having with these wonderful people that have stopped at our little center, you will recall, some of you, that we were discussing the possibility and the belief in life in form prior to the earth realm. Now, my dear children, I have been permitted to pass on to you some of this discussion and knowledge. I cannot give you more than you are able at this time to bear.

However, there is life in form on many, many planets. This life is evolving and progressing. There is life on other planets with a higher developed intelligence than the earth people now have. There is also life on planets which you might say is below the present standard of earth man. Now, my children, I can only say at this time that these lives are and that there are planets which are much higher evolved than what the earth planet now is. This I say to you as my complete belief, knowledge, and truth as I now know it.

Now we have discussed before some of the laws that affect the forms and we have discussed the possible purpose of the soul's journey through earth and the many, many forms. I know that I have always been and that I will always be. My children, when I speak of "I," I do not speak of "me," as you have perhaps conceived in your minds.

However, I should also like to speak this evening about the work that is before you and at your very fingertips. You are opening the doors to realms known but by few and what you will do with what you find will affect many, many a soul on both sides of the curtain. I pray that you have chosen wisely and well.

And now I must be leaving for indeed my channel has been tested to the utmost these past weeks and we must keep his strength in order to continue the battle, which is all around and about him. Now, like the leaf in the breeze, I leave, not in distance but in degree. We are closer than your hands and feet. I feel a slight disappointment but I shall come back.

Good night.

JULY 23, 1964

DISCOURSE 10 ✤

Greetings, greetings, greetings, children of the Living Light. Again it is my duty and my privilege to speak with you at this time.

Wise indeed are those who give in such a way that it is not too much for the receiver. Indeed, much has been said about life. Yes, much has been said and there is so much yet to say. However, my

children, I can only give unto you what you yourselves are prepared to receive and just a bit more. I do pray, my dear children,
that you shall continue your investigation and seeking.

Truth to the form is a very personal matter. It is something
that must be perceived from within. There are many schools
of thought of whose purpose it is to help to guide you in this
matter. As before, I have spoken, no one, my child, can give you
truth. Seek, my children, and indeed ye shall find. It is well that
the seekers observe the characteristics of the chicken. Watch
and wait and ye shall see.

As I mentioned to my channel some days past that I would
at some time like to discuss the plane of ozone. My dear friends,
what I am at this moment permitted to grant is this plane of
ozone does exist. It is to the form what the seed is to the tree.
There are those on this side of the curtain who are studying
deeply into this plane of which I now speak. Before the form may
be created, as you now know form, the secrets of ozone must be
understood. Peace, my children, peace; peace that passeth understanding.

How often have I asked that you think, think, and think.
And now, dear friends, I ask that you do this in reason, logic, and, above all, in balance. Overactivity of the mental body
causes a very strong pressure. Some are able to bear this pressure greater than others. Those who are highly tuned and sensitive can bear this pressure only in small doses, so to speak.

Intuition is expressed through reason. There is no other expression of it no matter what seems to be. God is a God of law
and order, a God which is Love. Before, it has been said, "Ye
shall know not thy God, my child, with the vehicle of the mind,
for with the vehicle of the mind your God shall continue on and
on to change." Won't you think on that?

Yes, it is indeed well to think. And it also is indeed well to
feel, to know.

> He who loves the tree the same as he loves me
> Knows that I am I, that thou are thee
> That all is one and one is me.

In regards to the life in form on other planets, I should like to bring forth at this time that, to the very best of our knowledge, their souls have passed through the earth planet of form.

Won't you again broaden your horizons? Know that ye indeed are God. Being gods, my children, ye shall always be, have ever been. Think, my child! God is form, yet God is formless. Won't you consider and meditate upon the great truth that is within you? Can you not feel, my children, that you indeed are in all things?

We know that music is color. We know that color is harmony. My children, you are either in harmony with the universal vibrations of life or you are not. To the child the secrets are given that they may confound the seeming-wise. I again ask, my children, that you send out and forth your love, your feelings, and your truth. Love conquers all for love is harmony perfectly expressed. Look upon all life as your own for indeed, in actuality it is your own.

So often is it spoken—limitation of the form. Ye have perceived that form, destruction doth await. So, my child, limitation shall meet its kind. Free thyself according to the universal laws of life. Know in your heart that I am I. Know within that all things are possible to God. Ye are God. Can you not see the truth that is within thyself?

> Truth is like a river
> For it continually flows,
> Ah, indeed, it flows
> From the Mountain of Aspiration.

I ask that ye take not anything that is said as the ultimate truth. Perhaps you may think and consider what has been brought forth. What is good for me may not be good for you. It depends on your step of the eternal Ladder of Progression.

> Know within and unto thee all shall be.
> Thy will shall be done, O God.
> Not my will, but thy will.
> This will is within thee.
> It is known not by the mind,
> But it is known within thee.

Blessed indeed are those who know the true meaning of the word *perseverance*. God bless you, my children, in accordance to the law. Unto you is given what thou hath earned.

> Slow steps are sure steps
> When they are under the guidance of selflessness.

May I serve well and long, that within thyself peace may be known unto all. God bless you.

AUGUST 13, 1964

DISCOURSE 11 🌾

Greetings! Peace unto you. I grant thee my peace. Greetings, beloved children, and duty bound, it is my privilege and honor to speak again with you in this way.

As you know, if the Light is too bright, it is best that they see it not now. For truly the Light can blind and ofttimes it is mistaken for the night. However, I should like that you bear with me at this time, for indeed I have a message to grant unto all. I have tried in my humble way to serve, being and guided by my feelings from within. And I do pray that the message of which I am about to give forth shall not be too bright for you.

We have been discussing soul, life, life eternal, forms, planets, and universes for centuries and centuries. There are so many schools of thought, my children, on both sides of the veil. And I give forth now some of our little talks, for we too pray that we may serve, for we know that is indeed one of the many purposes that is before us.

We have spoken before of the soul journey through the many, many forms. Also we have spoken of the soul journey in form and forms prior to the earth planet. You will find that life is progressive, and what has been given forth to you before is in accordance to the Law of What Can Be Borne. Now, my children, we feel that you are (and we pray that it is true) prepared to make another step forward on the eternal rung of the Ladder of Progression.

The soul is in the form. One of its purposes—to raise the rates of vibration of the form. As the soul journeys on, these things that you call experiences help to refine the vehicles or forms that the soul may be given greater and greater expression. We have witnessed from this side of the curtain untold millions of entities who hover close to the earth realm awaiting rebirth in form on your planet. Please bear with me, for there is truth in what we are trying to give forth.

Desire is of the form. Aspire is of the soul. The millions of entities of which I speak have been drawn close to the earth realm by the highest form or vehicle in which their soul is now encased. This vehicle being driven by the power, and indeed a great power: it is desire. My dear children, as the soul is given greater expression in the form and its aspirations are sent forth unclouded through a higher vehicle, that soul, if the greater purpose may be served, can and does return to your planet. However, this, my children, is very, very, very rare. For there are so few who have reached that stage of progression who no longer know of self, that have returned. By far, my friends, the greatest masses continue on and on and on. There are many,

many entities who have their soul pass through the earth form who now reside on other planets and other universes.

Have I not asked before that you keep your mind free? Free, my children, like the wind. Do you not see that you indeed are creating the life that ye shall have? Won't you think of this mental world in which you live within. Today it may seem to be within, but tomorrow it shall be without.

The soul knows all. It always has and always will. It is only the form that knows or knows not.

The highest vehicle that the masses of humanity on earth have at this time is a mental body. My children, they can only go to a mental world. In order to function in a world of spirit or higher world, you must have a vehicle in which to travel. It is true that the mental body can and does reflect at times the soul within. At one time I recall having spoken of the glory of the Father in Heaven. Do you not see, my child, that I speak of the glory of the Father in Heaven? It is within you. A dear friend of mine once said to me,

> Hell awaits the form,
> Ah, but Heaven awaits the soul.

We have spoken of the Art of Giving and for my channel I wish to mention a bit about that again. Wise indeed are those who learn the Art of Giving. My dear children, the law has no emotion. If you cannot learn the Art of Giving, you shall hold all things unto yourselves. And the great blessing to the form is you will hold so dearly the things that you would most like to give away.

Free thy mind, my children. Know that God is within, has always been, will always be. As I asked earlier, Can God grow? Love, my friends, is the language of the soul, but not the love of which you know. Is not God in the blade of grass? Does not the blade of grass have soul essence? My dear friends, prepare thyself, for the blade of grass, it too has a soul. Won't you think and think and think!

I must not hold my channel, for indeed his form is so very weary. I would like, however, to express my deepest gratitude to all of you, but especially to my channel. For, my friends, I must serve my God, and indeed he has been so very kind to me of late. Won't you ask him to be patient? He shall see the Light in time. Be free in thought and ye shall be eternally free in life. God bless you in accordance to the Law of Giving. Good night.

AUGUST 24, 1964

DISCOURSE 12 ✳

Greetings, children. Again I am honored and privileged to speak with you in this way.

Indeed we are: our hearts, so overflowing with joy for the Light within is being shared. And truly, this is one of the many purposes of the Light. Much has been said, my dear friends, about life.

May we speak this evening about the processes of communication between the world or realms, so to speak. A great deal of preparation is necessary to bring but one thought from our realm to yours. You see, my children, we must work through the channels that are available to us. And working through those channels, it is so very difficult to mold the matter of the channel.

Often have we spoken of keeping the mind free. My dear children, if you expect to receive revelations from the higher realms, it is absolutely necessary that the mind not be molded to such a degree that the revelation is unable to express itself through the mind. I am indeed aware of the difficulty involved and indeed, my children, a great deal of time is spent on the channels. For it is indeed important to those on this side of the curtain that our thoughts not only are understood, that they are expressed through the channel as clear as is possible.

As you tune yourselves to the thoughts that are brought to you, you will find within a light that is growing brighter and brighter and brighter. The growing, my children, is the educating of the mental body or mind. As the mind grows, the soul within that knows all, always has and always will, is able to express itself more fully.

Discussion, my children, on the higher level of thought is indeed most beneficial to yourselves and to those who are so privileged to hear them. Do you not see, my children, that as you are discussing the seeming mysteries of life, you are helping yourselves and those to whom you are speaking and to the many souls who are here with you at those times. The purposes, my children, of the higher life and the greater good shall be served, for thy will, O God, shall be done.

One of the greatest obstacles to the soul's expression, as we have spoken before, is the mind or mental body. My dear friends, this is why we are trying to impress upon you the great importance of discussion and question. Think, my children, think and think! No one knows all. It is the soul within that knows.

Now, dear friends, I am again privileged and permitted to bring forth to you a bit more about our life and our duty. You have heard it said before that many are called and few are chosen. We indeed are trying to the very best of our ability to plant a seed or two in fertile soil. Do not, my dear beloved children, accept and believe blindly. We are trying to bring to you and to humanity the truth that we have found to be so to us.

My children, the world you find is the world you make. No one can say that this side of the curtain is this way or that way. Don't you see the importance of knowing that the world is just the way that you and you alone are making it? The world, my friend, that awaits you is the world that you are building. Won't you free yourselves from the closed thinking that our side, so to speak, of the curtain is this way or that way?

> The heaven that awaits you
> May be a hell to another.

Think and think and think! How may I best serve my God within today and every day? So very much depends upon the thinking processes of the mind.

I know there have been questions in the minds about the Ladder of Progression. I have so often spoken—the Ladder is, as you know, within you. Wise indeed are those who serve for we are all servants of the higher life. And, my children, the higher life shall be served.

> Let not your deed be your creed.

You know the soul cannot be fed: the soul cannot grow. But as we permit the soul to free itself from the bondage and prison of the form, it can and does create greater and greater and higher forms. The angels have always been pictured with wings. Why, yes, because it is symbolic of the freedom that they now have earned.

And now may I say a bit about what is known in your group as spirit lights. You know that a spirit light may be to you about the size of a pinhead. Yet that is a spirit. Do you think, children, that spirit has form? Yes, it has form, but how, my children, do you think it is able to change its form? Ah, who knows the size or shape of the soul—if it has a size or shape? Children, in truth I say you are the nuclei, the size of a pinhead. Please do not trouble yourselves too much upon that at this time for we shall speak of that again.

Again may I express my gratitude and joy for the wonderful discussions that we have been privileged to listen to. The Light is known by the Light on both sides of the veil. And your discussions that I have been hearing are helping so very many souls on this side of the curtain.

Give, my children, thinking not of return. For those who give and think of return have to learn the Law of Pain of Patience. Give! Think not of return and unto you all shall be given.

God bless you all in accordance to the law. May I return when the need is the greatest.

SEPTEMBER 3, 1964

DISCOURSE 13 ❧

Greetings, friends. I am so pleased to be with you again at this time.

When the child is given a lesson to learn and the child fails to learn this lesson, compassion dictates that the child must again be given the lesson; reason dictates that it must be in different form.

Indeed, my beloved children, you all have been given a bit of a lesson on responsibility. Would you, I ask, willingly wear another's shoes knowing not where they may lead you? The baggage is carried only so far and for so long, then it must be left, for so is the eternal way of progression. Will you continue to eat the chowder before you taste it? Oh, my children, how, how many times and in how many ways we have tried to show many, many how and why they are where they are. Teachers can only carry the baggage so far and the baggage must lighten itself by emptying the useless trivialities that are in it.

It is, I know, so very difficult to broaden one's horizon and see but dimly the greater goal. But, my children, the time has come when it is the greater goal that you must perceive for otherwise progression shall cleanse the path. How often have we asked that you broaden your horizons! Won't you broaden your interest! Won't you try to come outside of yourselves! Don't draw to you another's path. Is it not difficult enough for one to walk their own path without carrying others?

Teachers can only show the way.
It is the student that must go or stay.

How often have we watched the forces in operation and manifestation. You have asked, my children, that the greater doors be opened. Are you to fail in the effort necessary for you to step through? So many of us are so involved in seeming things. Has it not been said, Life is eternal and wise ones act accordingly. Perhaps we might try just a bit more to apply this each day before we act. For so many, so very, very many, react to things and conditions. Have you not, children, perceived that you are so much influenced by the so-called invisible powers? Won't you open your eyes to see the responsibility that is upon you for the creations that you are each moment creating!

You are not alone in your spiritual seeking. Indeed is it difficult to keep unto ourselves things that we believe we see and hear! Do you wish to be another? Do you wish to add to yourselves things that you would not want? Beloved children, this is happening and continues to happen with some. We pray each day that the great God will grant unto you more strength, but even more, awareness of what is being done. Have I not spoken before about that gadget they call the telephone? Oh, if only you could see what is taking place at those times when you linger so very, very long upon it.

I, my children, have come to dedicate, not to dictate. Indeed, the Light is dawning and your responsibilities to God and the higher powers are increasing. It is the weak that need the stronger hand that in time they too, as they are strengthened, may share with the weak. I cannot impress upon you too strongly what has been taking place and continues to do so. Indeed, effort is required. God does not ask that ye be all saints. We are asking those who have been chosen to be more aware of what their responsibility is that they have placed upon themselves according to the law.

> Pride is punishment;
> Humility is harmony.

Broaden the horizon that ye may help humanity to help themselves. The bells of freedom are waiting to toll. Are you the one that is delaying the process? Peace, my children, eternal peace. We ask you to think and think and think.

> Not the way I wish to be,
> But the way I am,
> Is Truth to me.

Open your eyes. The glorious realms await the willing and the worker. God bless you in accordance to the need, for God does not feed greed.

OCTOBER 15, 1964

DISCOURSE 14 ✖

Greetings, seekers of the Light. The subject this evening is cripples, their cause and cure. There is a relationship between the soul faculties and the physical anatomy. The eyes are corresponding and represented with awareness; the ears, perception; the feet, understanding; and the mouth, truth.

We know that when these faculties are in use, they create corresponding parts of the spiritual body; as when the physical legs are not in use, they become distorted and useless. And so it is when the faculties of the soul are not in use, there is no spiritual part created and through lack of use the astral substance is distorted. And this is why we find so many numbers of astral cripples in the flesh and out of the flesh. It has been spoken before that energy follows attention and in order to create anything, it requires energy or attention. Due to the errors of ignorance, man has not put sufficient attention or energy upon these spiritual faculties.

The next faculty to be given is the faculty of reason. Its counterpart or correspondence in the anatomy is the nostrils. I do hope and pray that you will give greater consideration and thought to these soul faculties. There is great truth in the statement that only through service will we find illumination. Remember, my friends, creation is your family and when you truly perceive that, you will find the kingdom of God.

MARCH 4, 1971

DISCOURSE 15

Fellow students, tonight we are discussing man, the great creator. As has been said again and again, the conscious mind is electrical and the inner mind is magnetic. The neutral or superconscious is the odic. Now thought is the first cause and feeling is the second. Whenever thought is combined with feeling, it is given direction and has greater force for creation. We have mentioned the great importance of service and of giving. Now we shall discuss the reasons for them.

Man is indeed a dynamo with a great and limitless energy or power. When our thoughts and feelings are united in selfless service or giving, we release from the inner mind a phenomenal amount of pent-up energy. How often have we experienced the wonderful feeling when we have completed a selfless service. Unless this energy is released, it gives birth, through the idle mind, to many entities in the mental realm. Our thoughts are constantly being created by our emotions and these are the children and the demons that are in our universe. When we selflessly work and accomplish without a thought of return, this energy is released and there is a continuous flow in our universe.

We must ponder these faculties and consider where our thoughts are going, not by the hour, but, my good students, by the moment. In our atmosphere is a multitude of unfulfilled desires, a multitude of senseless creations, and a multitude of war and disturbances. For in one moment we create the good; only in the next, through experiences, create the opposite.

Guard your thoughts and, my beloved children, you will guard your life. Think and think, and when you think you have thought enough, that is the first indication that you have not begun to think. I must not leave until I have spoken a bit on vibrations. It has been said that we cannot walk through a thing without being affected by it. Now, my good students, I would like to try to explain that statement. We are affected by those things and people with whom we have any degree of attachment through the magnetic vibration of feeling. Those who we have a feeling towards we are affected by, until such time as we can rise through the feelings of self that govern our lives.

MARCH 11, 1971

DISCOURSE 16 ✸

Peace, perfect peace, students of the Living Light. Remember, friends, we are permitted to reveal unto you in so-called bits and pieces; that is not cause, but it is effect, according to the Law of Merit. The bits and pieces merit their kind and the wholes likewise. We are indeed grateful and pleased to see the efforts and the growth that is being made in your lives.

Tonight we wish to bring to you clarification on certain points which we have listened with great interest to your concern. There has been over these times several discussions concerning the faculties. Not much has been mentioned concerning the functions.

You will find in creation this great duality known as balance and counterbalance. This energy flows through us and, according to whether it is flowing through the faculties or the functions, it does create. We know that the faculties create the spiritual body and the functions form and deform the astral body.

Now, my good students, we're going to speak for a moment on the second faculty of being and its counterbalance, so to speak, in the functions. All faculties have an equal, corresponding function. All faculties are triune in expression and so are all functions. The second faculty, faith, its correspondence in the functions being material or money; poise in the faculty corresponds to procreation; humility in the faculty corresponds to what is termed ego. As I said, friends and good fellow students, each faculty has its corresponding function. That is the one that we are permitted to give to you this evening.

I listened with great attention to your discussion earlier and it has been and is the teaching from our realm that this so-called God or Infinite Divine Intelligence is a neutral, impartial power everywhere present, never absent or away. We find that when we take all thought, all decision, to the faculty of reason, there is this divine neutral energy directed either into the functions or the faculties. The choice, my good fellow students, is ever and forever within you.

We teach on this side of the veil through the Law of Indirection. Remember that that you desire you already have, for everything you will ever need or have ever needed is right where you are. It has been revealed what the nose or nostrils, the ears, the eyes, the feet, the hands represent. It has also been revealed that the healing power is released through the faculty of humility.

I wish to make a correction, for I find in review on the ethereal waves I have incorrectly stated the corresponding counterbalance on the faculty of faith, poise, and humility.

Faith corresponds, I repeat, to material or money; poise corresponds—and this is the correction—to what is termed ego; humility corresponds or counterbalances in the function of procreation. Please, students, note this correction. I regret the error. I once again repeat, for it is important: faith—money; poise—ego; humility—procreation or sex.

Now, good students, you will understand why and how the healing power flows through the faculty of humility.

There is so much to be discussed and there are so many, many questions in the gray areas of the mind. Consider a little attention to tuning into the Infinite Power flowing through all creation, be it the grass, the tree, or the mouse.

I bid you a short departure to return in divine time.

MARCH 18, 1971

DISCOURSE 17 ✒

Greetings, fellow students. May we be privileged to share with you once again our spiritual understanding.

When the heart feels as the lips speak, words become the savior of the wise. We should like to carry on at this time with a bit more discussion on the functions and faculties, with the first faculty being duty, gratitude, and tolerance, corresponding to the counterbalance of the function of self, pity, and friendship.

Some time ago we spoke a great deal on soul and we do wish to bring forth at this time a statement made so very long ago: "The soul can and does all things create." It is the power that flows through this soul. When the faculties are closed, the power goes down to flow through the functions. It is indeed wise to have a balance in all things. To force or to rush growth of anything will only reap a very poor harvest. Wise is he that does not go beyond his present ability in any task.

We spoke before about perceiving that creation is our family. Choose, my friends, and weigh carefully before creating with this instrument known as mind. When our vision opens and we see the multitude of things and creatures that we and we alone have given birth to, we then truly realize the importance of weighing all things.

We have on this side of the veil a daily exercise which we would like to share with you. It has proven itself to be of great benefit to us. Think of a word, repeat it in the mind three times, then speak it forth into the universe. My friends, the lost word spoken throughout ancient time is only a lack of understanding how to speak forth. And if you will consider this daily, simple exercise, you will find that your word will demonstrate the power which it does in truth contain.

We move and breathe in an atmosphere of our own creation. It is our purpose to share with you the great reality of this atmosphere and how you may change it for your greater peace and prosperity. Think of the word *beauty*, repeat it thrice in your mind, then, my children, speak it forth into the universe. If you do it correctly, it shall be revealed unto you the color that it vibrates.

Good night.

MARCH 25, 1971

DISCOURSE 18 ✿

Greetings, friends. There is a mountain, it is known as the Mountain of Hope and he who climbs to its top perishes in the purifying and illuminating fires below. Hope, my friends, is an eternal thing; therefore do not hope for that to fulfill, for the moment that you fulfill hope, it perishes, unless you once again scale its mountain.

Now we look across and find the everlasting and continuous flow of the fountains of aspiration. Aspiration, my
friends, is without beginning and, being without beginning,
is without end.

Over to the north we find the valley of sorrows. You see, my
children, the things that we are meriting are reflected in this
so-called world of spirit and not only build our abode and our
bodies in which to function, but also the terrain in which we
shall live.

Over to the east we find the rugged cliffs of error upon error
through ignorance, and there you will find the greatest majority
of the masses living.

Then to the south we look and we find a vast and gigantic
city. It has no trees. It has no flowers, no grass; it has no sun in
its sky, nor a moon or stars. But it is a great city of all steel and
glass and it is the abode of the multitudes who, through error,
have permitted material substance to completely dominate and
control their thoughts. Therefore the only thing that they can
see, hear, feel, or touch is that which man has created.

We have spoken that truth is taught through indirection,
demonstration, and example. Each day, my friends, you are being
taught and usually by the one whom you least expect. Remember that the house divided cannot and will not stand. Therefore
it behooves us to unite this house within to let this great power
flow through us, around about us, and encompass us. When we
become united within, we will be free without.

Broaden your horizons: think well where you send forth
your energy. Remember that success and failure are one and
the same thing, for indeed it is only an effect of spent energy,
constructive or destructive: you are never left without choice.

Each and every part of your anatomy corresponds and responds to a soul faculty, a sense function. I have been permitted
to reveal to you a few of those, and when the law permits, for

the law is the Lord, to reveal more to you, I shall indeed be most grateful to do so.

I am pleased to see that you are becoming more aware of the so-called invisible substance and vibrations around and about you. Observe wisely where you go and with whom you spend your life-giving power.

Good night.

APRIL 1, 1971

DISCOURSE 19 ✍

Greetings, fellow students. Again it is our pleasure to be with you.

A bit has been mentioned on the balance and counterbalance of the faculties and the functions, and we would like to mention that it is through the faculty of tolerance that opportunity does flow.

It is so rewarding, so pleasing to see so many students on the path on both sides of the curtain. There are many ways in which to apply the one universal law. There are many laws, and yet it is one law: depending upon how you use this one law does it diversify into many laws.

The mantras that have been given to you were especially brought about long ago to help activate the gland through which your vision peers into this world of ours.

When we strive to go beyond the appearances within ourselves, we begin to see beyond the veil of day-to-day acts and activities. It is our earnest prayer that you, as students, will make, yea, even greater efforts to think and apply the impartial law or laws of life in all your daily thoughts and activities. We find that the meaning, which is but the essence of a thing, the meaning of words in your world has long been lost; and when the meaning of a thing is lost, its power is greatly diminished.

Think and ponder upon the word of your choice until once again you may capture its great power in application.

Many are the guides and teachers that flock to your realm to impress, to guide, to encourage and to help. It is all, my friends, a law of balance. And when you place all things in balance, the great power that is, that has always been, that will ever be, will open new horizons in your life; for in a world of creation there are indeed many, many things to balance.

I would like to mention that if you would make less mental effort in your meditations you would find and receive greater spiritual light. You have come a long way. Try now to remove the activity of the gray matter and just be at peace, for it is through the vibratory wave of peace that all things are harmoniously arranged in your lives. Remember that all of our experiences are effects and never causes. Look wisely at these effects: they are the door back to the cause.

Guardian angels are the inseparable better half of the soul. They are never away from your being and someday in this great eternity you will meet your better side.

Good night.

APRIL 8, 1971

DISCOURSE 20 ✤

Greetings, fellow students.

We are so pleased to see the beautiful growth of the class, and we have listened with great interest to your thoughts and discussions concerning what is offered. In that respect, we shall discuss at this time the one Power, the one Lord, and the one Law. For indeed there is only one Law and that, my children, is the Law known as Love. When this Power, this Law, this God is expressed in equal balance through the faculties and the functions, being a great magnetic power, it attracts and creates unto itself. When the functions and the faculties corresponding are not in balance, then you experience what is known as hate, fear, and all of these varied things. We have spoken before that there is a faculty for each and every function, that there is a part of your body that reflects it. Now when this power moves through balanced faculties and functions, it is the great peace, the great neutrality that passeth all understanding. If you are having experiences which are distasteful to you, it is because the corresponding faculty to that function is not balanced. We have brought to you a bit of this understanding and, according to the Law of Merit, when we are permitted, we shall bring forth more.

Remember, the one and only Law is known as Love and this is why the teaching: Love all life. Then, my children, you shall know the Light.

Listening here with you this evening, I am privileged to bring to you the faculty reflected in your question and that is consideration. I am sure if you will ponder it, you will understand your effect.

Thank you. Good night.

APRIL 15, 1971

DISCOURSE 21 &

Greetings, fellow students. I am again pleased to be with you at this time.

It behooves us not to be concerned with prejudgment, the acts and activities of another, for in so doing we guarantee the experience or experiences necessary for understanding to befall us.

We are constantly moving and being in forces and vibrations. We are constantly bombarded and distracted from the path that we have chosen to trod. The chains and bondage of creation have enslaved so very many here and in the hereafter. Creation is designed to serve a purpose, to ever be the tool of man and not his master.

This wonderful power of neutrality known as love, for love—true love—is neutral. It has no choice and no exceptions: it loves for the sake of love and not for what it may or may not gain. This great neutral power, when the faculties and functions are balanced, flows freely and unobstructed, bringing us the great peace that all souls are seeking both here and hereafter. But we do not seem to spend sufficient time in our thinking for it is, my friends, as we have often said, our thinking that directs the flow of this energy or power.

It is necessary, again and again I repeat, to spend more time concerning one's self with one's thoughts because those are the things that are bringing us disturbance, misery, grief, and mis-understanding. We need, more than just once or twice a day, to think, to bring the mind with all its power back to its home that it may become familiar with itself.

We find so many living on the surface and then when the surface cracks, as it always does, they are lost for they have not made the effort or spent the time to learn who they are, why they are, and what they are. I beseech you, my fellow students, to sit and to ponder. Creation comes and creation goes, only to come again in another form, in another way, in another day. You are not creation, you are only in creation: you are the formless and the free.

Find the purpose of your life. Learn to be free and then you shall know this great God that is within and without. You shall become aware of your eternity, aware that you have always been, that you will always be, that this is but a passing moment that you in your minds call time. There never was a time or a place that you in truth have not been. There will never be a time or a place that you will not be. Think of that, my children! You are one and yet you are everyone and everything. Ponder upon it.

I know that you are moving forward in this illusion of creation and that you are, all of you, swimming against the tide. But remember, only the fool quits before the victory. When we have had enough, we will stop to rest.

Good night.

APRIL 22, 1971

DISCOURSE 22 ✎

Greetings, fellow students. Our hearts are filled with joy as we come at this time. We are so very grateful and will be with you at the opening of this little center of love, life, and light for it has been some time that we have been working on this side for this center to come into your world.

We wish to mention that in functions and faculties that the hands of action also know fear. And do you not recall the ear of ego? We are discussing and reviewing at this time some of the many studies before our class. Remember, students, that the babes are sustained with milk and the men with meat. We await the day when we may share with you more of the meat.

Some time ago we brought forth the discussion and the theory of evolution of the form. We are now permitted to elaborate a bit upon it. You will note that we stated shortly ago that all things you are, have been, and will be. We must learn to separate truth from the illusion of creation. There was a time on your planet that creation was ready for the entrance of the individualized, self-conscious soul to incarnate into form. We spoke some time ago that the missing link in form would not be found upon your planet, for from your planet it did not come. In the evolutionary processes of form, they reached their peak upon your planet and soul individualized, having passed through form on another planet at another time, entered your so-called earth.

Your planet is the fifth in your solar system, representing the lesson to learn in what is known as faith.

Your soul incarnated into form passes through many forms. There are nine spheres and nine planes of consciousness through which you will pass before reaching that from which you came. From that you will be impulsed anew into the next planet at another time and another place. You see, my friends, like the circle, there is no beginning and no end.

The purpose of life in our present understanding is to awaken mind for it is asleep in its dream state, to awaken it by the light of the spirit-soul. And that is why, my friends, when you receive the Light, you are duty bound to share its love.

You students are not new to me, nor in truth am I to you. There is a plane of consciousness which is at this moment within your power to awaken. The pain of patience is only known by the illusion of mind.

Good night.

APRIL 29, 1971

[On May 2, 1971, the Serenity Spiritualist Church held its first public service in the American Legion Log Cabin in San Anselmo, California, with Mr. Goodwin serving as minister and medium.]

DISCOURSE 23 ✺

Greetings, friends. Once again the time has come. I will not be away on vacation. However, compassion bows to the dictates of merit, which declare that you shall be given the opportunity to study, absorb, and apply what you have already received.

Through desire and decision action doth reveal
The merit of our being,
The spirit of our zeal.

Good night.

MAY 6, 1971

DISCOURSE 24 ✎

Greetings, friends. Indeed am I grateful through the law in motion to once again be with you; though expended energy, known as effort, may seem so minute, it has indeed served its purpose.

We should like to share with you our understanding of the creative principle. Before it was spoken that there is one Law, one God, one Power; that man is a law unto himself; that the one Law, the great Law, is Love. Love is the creative principle. From love springs forth belief; and from belief, desire; and from desire, will in action creating all things seen and unseen. We understand that God, known as Love, the one great Law, sustains all things in all worlds; that man is the creator and that this power is the sustainer.

Do not misunderstand, my friends: we are speaking of belief—not that of your conscience-conscious mind, but on the soul level. All things that you experience in your so-called reality is but the image held together by the power of love, shaped by belief, strengthened by desire, and moved by will. This infinite power, known as love, is expressed through creation. Deep within our being we create, through the power of belief, all things in all places at all times.

The question may well be asked, Then who believed and the tree came to be? Who believed and the stars were placed in the sky? I say unto you there is a power. It is known as love. It expresses through what is commonly referred to as Infinite Intelligence or Allsoul.

This belief has and does create all these things. Therefore, my children, it behooves us to realize and to recognize that in miniature this power is within us. Break through the barriers of the layers of mind and you will find these beliefs, some created recently and some of very ancient origin. Without belief, there is no creation; without creation, love does not express itself. This power, properly channeled, brings unto us the great light of eternal truth. And the Light shall be known by the Light.

We are daily given opportunity to serve the Divine, and yet so often things seem to distract us from the only thing that is worthy of our attention. As the light within you shines, it shall call forth from the darkness the souls who are seeking and the purpose of this divine love's expression shall be fulfilled.

My dear children, all things are but belief, image, and this is why it is said that we live in a world of illusion. My children, we are governed by the laws of belief beneath our conscious level. The blind man does not experience the rose unless, through education, he becomes to believe. To the power that is, all things are possible to those who believe. All of our experiences work through the steps mentioned before, which I shall again give to you: love, belief, desire, will, creation. Think about that, my children. I know that if you take it into your silent sanctuary within that it will reach the light within you.

Many in your world and ours are not yet ready for this truth. Good night.

MAY 20,1971

DISCOURSE 25 ✣

We are discussing at this time the Law of Life: Love, its constant application. To those who have a great capacity for love, also have capacity for great problems until such time as the light of truth dawns through their faculty of reason. Love is the magnetic power in all the universes: it is that power which holds things together.

We find that our beliefs, opinions, are held by this power of love. And so without reason we hold and bind to ourselves the limitation of our beliefs because they are held to us by the power of love. Think, my students, how often in discussions you strenuously hold to what you believe is right. Consequently, our problems are given birth.

Learn the power of love in the selfless way and you will be freed from distress, disturbance, and grief. Recognize and realize that you are holding these things in bondage. Free them for they in truth are never yours. Ask for the faculty of reason to shed its light over the many cherished beliefs and opinions that are held in the darkness of your inner being. Cast the light of reason throughout your entire universe and, my children, you shall gain the wisdom of the ages.

I am so pleased to report to you that the plane of purification, a state of consciousness, is awakening with you. The awareness which you realize as odor is to tell you of this awakening. You think that you have sensed it with your physical being, but in truth you sense it with your spiritual being.

There are many planes or states of consciousness and indeed are we pleased with the growth and awareness that you are step-by-step beginning to merit. When again you have an awareness of this plane of purification, be at peace and drift with its odor and you will have a greater awareness than you now realize.

Remember the power of love. Use it, my children: don't abuse it!

> Oh, love divine, a servant be
> Till selfishness imprisons me
> And warps the reason of my mind

Into the madness of the blind,
When truth cries out "Not mine but Thine"
And frees my soul with love divine.

Good night.

MAY 27, 1971

DISCOURSE 26 ✣

Greetings, students of Light. Again it is our privilege to be with you.

We are discussing at this time service, the divine lifeline. For it is service that frees us from self. It is the only thing that separates truth from creation.

I know that you are aware that while yet in your physical suit, so to speak, you are evolving here and now to the plane of consciousness in the world of spirit that is now within you. Most of the people yet on your plane are in the seventh plane of the second sphere. This is the average seen from this side of the veil. You have the blessed opportunity to, layer by layer, enter by way of the divine lifeline into higher spheres and planes of consciousness. For when the flesh goes back to Mother Nature, you will have full awareness of the plane that you have been inhabiting while yet encased in the flesh.

As the hairs upon your head are without number so, my children, have been the paths that you have trod before you ever reached this point.

Remember that he who loves himself more than he loves me shall lose himself to find me. But he who loves me more than he loves himself has found the truth: eternity.

When, my children, this is the type of love you express to the Divine Principle of which you truly are, all of these coverings are but a temporary illusion. They have come and they shall go. But you, my children, have ever been and have trod a limitless number of paths and expressions prior to your present encasement.

There are no magic words that will send you up the ladder of Light and Truth, but there is the Divine Principle that constantly and ceaselessly impresses your heart, your soul, to serve without concern for effect. Place all your attention, my dear children, ever in the doing and, if you will always remember to do that, you will enter the spheres and the glory of peace that is beyond words to express.

Our hearts are joyous to see the numbers who, slowly but steadily, are coming into the Light. I know that it may seem few to some, but when you work year after year after year to be the channel of Light, there is no greater joy than to see if only one or two sincerely enter the path.

You are becoming more and more aware of the so-called invisible atmosphere and that, my children, is very good. The days are not numbered long when your eyes and ears shall open even more and you shall see and ne'er forget. My words at this time are given to all who are present for they are all workers of the one and only Spirit.

Do not be deceived by things. Do not be deceived by emotions. For they shall come and go, only to come again, like the tides of the oceans of your planet.

Be serene and be at peace for you are never, but never, alone. You were brought into this life's expression to fulfill a purpose, and that purpose is the only reason that you have this life's expression. And each day you are coming closer to the realization of the purpose of your being.

Peace to those who know peace. Good night.

JUNE 10, 1971

DISCOURSE 27 ❦

Greetings, fellow students of the Living Light. It indeed has pleased us to see that your faculty of awareness, attention, and appreciation is beginning to awaken. I am also happy to report that two of our students from the other class have been sent to you to help in your daily silence time to inspire and instruct in your study and understanding of what has been and is being offered to you.

The last time that we had a visit we spoke of love, the dreamer, and life, her dream. As you know, my good students, a lesson is never given twice in identically the same way for you are never identically receptive to the teachings in the same way. However, we are permitted to give you a brief review. Life, my children, is but the essence of what dreams are made. All of the experiences and forms, all of the changes, as you know, are created and held in existence by the power of love. This, my children, is but a dream; and you and I and all of us, we are the dreamers. So won't you dream dreams that are pleasant. Learn the laws of the dreams. They have been established over a great length of time. You know, my children, that you have the power to change a dream and that, my children, is what life really is. When you are at peace, in that instant, in that moment, you are totally and fully the Infinite. You are the Eternal Spirit, and then you start to dream.

Learn, my children, the great power of inaction. Learn the great power of silence, of patience. The Divine does its greatest wonders to those who know patience and who understand and apply silence.

I am not, nor have I ever been, concerned with numbers. But I am dedicated to serve wherever and whenever I am guided to do so. For I would rather spend a hundred years with a humble soul who will in turn serve the true purpose of life than to spend an hour with the multitudes who are not ready, willing, or able to make the necessary changes. My dear children, it is not what you need to garner up to awaken. It's what we must learn to give up to serve.

What does it benefit your life to add a multitude of things and experiences, if in the adding there is no light, there is no peace, and there is no lasting purpose? Let the bells of freedom toll. They are waiting to do so in the faculties of your soul.

I know at times it may seem difficult to understand and to apply the bits and pieces that we are permitted to give according to the law. It has never been, nor will it be, our purpose to change you. We only seek to be the channels from which the power doth flow. You are here and I am here according to laws yet to be perceived.

Think, my children. Think well and think long for it is a part of your purpose to think. I am well aware for many centuries of experience of the war within, of the battle in creation. Won't you learn to be the observer and not the observed. View the dream of life in her true perspective. Ye are gods yet to be. And as these students from the other class have merited your vibration, I sincerely pray that there will be a mutual exchange. Please do not ask for names or tags. They bind you to the dream of creation. And that, my friends, we are striving to outgrow.

Good night.

JULY 1, 1971

DISCOURSE 28

Greetings, my good students. We are discussing at this time a review of some of the lessons that have been given: Love, Life, and Light. We understand that when our expression of this power known as Love is not equal to our capacity for it, we have many serious so-called problems.

Now we shall go further with that understanding. You will recall that Love is the law. Love is power. It is energy. And, my children, how many times have we spoken of selfless service! Selfless service is an expression of love in a channeled and a neutral way, releasing through our being this power or energy. The multitude of difficulties and problems that seem at times to befall us is because our expression of love is not equal to our capacity of it. And this is one of the greater reasons for selfless service.

In selfless service you are at the apex of eternity. You are sitting at the peace that passeth all understanding and you are a clear and full channel. Therefore the power known as Love or Energy or God is being expressed. And in so doing, as the water that runs through the pipe leaves its multitude of mineral deposits, so the power that flows through you as a channel deposits its multitude of blessings in your life.

There appears to have been a sincere interest in the little talk that was given a few days ago on divine neutrality, our birthright. It is my privilege at this time to give an essence of that little talk. Divine neutrality: that, my friends, is what we all are seeking and it is what we all shall find in time. These discords and so-called diseases, when placing our thought upon them, direct this love, this energy to them. Consequently we make them stronger.

We have often spoken, my good friends, of the importance of your thinking and your thoughts because what happens in time, the things that you create become your masters and you, losing your divine birthright, become the slave. Won't you please consider well where you are placing your thought or attention? For, my children, indeed are you the creators. God, the power that is, sustains you in all things. But you are the one who directs this power, this love, this energy and consequently build your prison houses here and hereafter.

What can I say or what can I do to make the light within you glow yet brighter than it does? It is my purpose to be the channel and we are concerned only with the soul for that is the only thing that is eternal.

All of life is love and without it, there is no life. All of experience is love and without it, there's no experience. You are the dreamer and you have dreamed a dream. But as was said before, you have the power within you to change your dream, to remain the master and the dreamer before the dream starts dreaming you.

Think on that! Who shall be the captain of your ship, the master of your destiny?

Get all the effects, the experiences. Weigh them out and ever go within and there you will find all causes and all cures.

Remember, my children, you live not in one world but in three. Regardless of your acts, thoughts, and activities, you are not alone, have never been, will never be.

Good night.

JULY 8, 1971

DISCOURSE 29 ✑

Greetings, children of the Light. There has been over the time many things spoken about receiving with the left. But there has not been discussion concerning the reason why the left side of the body is the receptive.

As we stand with arms outstretched, we find that our head faces to the north pole, our feet the south, our left hand the east, and our right the west. This is the governing magnetic and electric vibrations controlling all form or creation on your planet. As the sun rises in the east, you receive its light, its illumination, and life. And as it descends in the west, it has given its life-giving powers to come once again according to the laws governing creation. The head is where the faculty of reason is located and is governed by the magnetic powers of the northern pole. The feet, representing understanding, are governed by the electrical or positive vibrations of the southern pole.

Until of recent date, the normal physical greeting when meeting a friend was with both hands outstretched. The reason being that they were giving their friendship equal to that which they were receiving, and it has changed as man, seemingly, has become more civilized.

However, you cannot change the laws governing creation. That is only an illusion of the senses and of the time. There are important reasons why a form to be in harmonious motion with other forms must be placed in certain positions at certain times. This is the reason why students in their unfolding at times feel a bit strange where they are sitting, standing, or moving. They should learn to pay attention to these feelings and in so doing will find a more harmonious vibration within themselves. It is not necessarily a habit pattern that a person wishes to be or to sit in a certain place at a certain time, though habit pattern could govern it; but not always is that so.

Learn to receive with the proper side of your anatomy, and learn to give with the one which is intended for that purpose.

It has been said that the gift without the giver is of no value. Indeed, my friends, is that true. We must understand the laws governing the gift and the giver. The heart, which is a positive organ in your anatomy, is the one from which all gifts should, and must, be given: otherwise, the gift will be of no value in truth to the receiver.

We are indeed pleased to note the growth steps that you all are taking. They have never been easy for any of us at any time. Do not be discouraged with self for self in truth is not the master. Discouragement faces all students on the path for it is the reluctance of the form to bow to the formless.

Good night.

JULY 15, 1971

DISCOURSE 30 🌿

Good evening, students and friends. Once again we are gathered to fulfill the purpose of our being. At our last meeting we were privileged to have an open discussion. We shall continue for the time with these discussions. However, before that, I should like to speak a moment on creation and procreation.

You know, in evolution there was a time when both the positive and the negative, the male and the female, were expressed in one body and had self-creation. Then along the evolutionary path, ages and ages ago, the split came and today you experience what is termed in your language as sex. But we must understand that its desire is given birth in the faculties, my children, and then expressed through the functions.

There is a great magnetic attraction in that so-called instinct; and that is there for the purpose of building bodies for the untold millions of souls waiting incarnation into your particular earth planet for their expression and fulfillment in that particular realm.

Today you experience one form for which the soul is able to incarnate; but tomorrow there shall be another, for whenever the two poles are brought together, there, under the proper conditions, the spark of divinity shall enter.

Then the question arises, What is it, then: what experience shall I gather that I have merited for incarnation, if my soul is to enter through a so-called test tube mechanically in a laboratory?

Try to understand, my students, that at various ages various types are entered onto various planets for the expressions that they have merited. And so when that day comes, which is now dawning in your earth, there will be those souls attracted magnetically, impartially, according to natural laws to express thereon.

I listened with great interest and intent to your questions this evening and should like at this moment to speak upon them. It was stated, "What is the explanation of ether or the ethereal?"

My dear students, *ether* or *ethereal* is a name that you have given to the element known as air. There are so many explanations and beliefs concerning from what part of the physical anatomy the soul leaves its ethereal body or spirit. You are aware, my students, where the center of air is located in your anatomy and air ever moves through the channel and through the center of which it is composed. *Ether* is only another term for the element *air*. And related to that question was the question "of form and forms and I understood that it in some way had reference to myself."

I do want you to know, my students, that when we have evolved through forms and many forms and have reached a state of consciousness, awareness, that through the power of concentration or will, we are able to clothe ourselves in any form that we are able to image, that we may serve the purpose and intent of the Divine within us; and it is true that I am using this form at this time.

It is also, I know you know, that I am referred to as "the old man." But, my good students, there is a reason why I appear in that type of form. I know that someday you will perceive that. But let it be said and let it be known and if you study and perceive little bits of lessons that have been given, you will find that it was said, "The functions form and deform your astral body. The faculties form your spiritual body." Now do you see the meaning of the word *humility* and what its corresponding function is? Think about that.

There are so many questions from all of those who have gathered at this time. Let us be at peace and we shall try to give forth a bit of understanding unto ourselves.

The question is asked, "Why is it not possible for me to recall the lives that I supposedly have lived prior to this one?" Think, my students. If we were aware of the reason of our being in school and we had the answer to the lesson that was given, there would be no purpose in giving the lesson. This is why in divine wisdom recall is not permitted in your present incarnation; but in time you will evolve to the state of awareness. When you have graduated from form, you will be permitted to return to form with total and complete recall.

And to my students yet in clay, you may feel free to ask a question.

When you have this complete, total recall, would it not be confusing to the mind?

The question is stated from one of our earth students that when you have total and complete recall, would it not be too much for the mind. Indeed, my students, in your present form it would be. But as your mind is expanded and your horizons are broadened and you have graduated through form and forms, then there is no limit and there is nothing that is too much for your mind is no longer limited and imprisoned in the image of the one form in which you are at present incarnated. But there is a freedom and a formlessness in the consciousness and awareness and you become illumined to the truth that you in truth are everything and everywhere, have always been, will always be. Your horizons are so broadened to encompass the allness of truth.

May I ask one more question?

Yes.

Would this be evolving to the point that we have discussed before of returning to the Allsoul and wholeness, completeness, totality from whence we all once came?

The question is absolutely correct in the answer that is within it.

A student has asked, "What is it that I can do to be prepared and to reach this state of understanding? I have been over on this side for centuries."

I can only say, my students, that we must learn this balance and freedom from form and forms of all types and kinds. We must cultivate the vibration of universality, to be universal in our outlook, to not be overly concerned with the flux and flow of the tide of creation.

As our horizons are broadened, we shall receive more; and as we receive more, we become a clearer channel for the divine flow. It is indeed a beautiful thing to witness the changes that are taking place in the minds of the students. The things that were so important yesterday are no longer so important today.

Swim, my children, through the tides of creation. Be free and you shall find the great essence of life herself.

Good night.

AUGUST 5, 1971

DISCOURSE 31

Greetings, students. Once again we are here with our little class to share with you our thoughts and our understanding of life and its eternity.

We shall continue on with the open discussions at this time. And one of our students has patiently waited and has this question to ask: What are the principles and responsibilities of leadership?

I am sure, my students, that we are all aware that leadership is derived from the word to lead and to lead means to know, to understand the path that you are treading and where you are going, its purpose, its service, and therefore the principles. Its basic, primary responsibility is to know where you are going, what you are doing and the reason therefore. Your responsibility is an awareness of where you are taking those who have chosen to follow you.

Leadership is not possible without understanding and tolerance for it is indispensable to leadership to understand those who are following, to know how much they are able to bear at any given time and to be the example for the followers. There are few leaders, my good students, in this world or in your world. There are many who claim to be leaders, but ever judge the trees from what they bear.

Leadership, its principles and responsibilities, are inseparable from goal; and man without goal is drowning in the ocean of creation, for goal, my friends, is the lifeline. And now you may feel free, my earth class, to ask your questions.

From what realm is it that the great teachers such as the Jesus, the Buddhas have come?

In reference to your question on the evolutionary path of the Divine Spirit expressing through creation, it enters what is termed total awareness—there are many names for it—illumination, cosmic consciousness. When the soul has arrived at that state of awareness known as total, it may choose a form to again express itself. It is on extremely rare occasions that an illumined soul returns to your earth planet. When this happens, you may, in your present understanding, term this reincarnation. In truth it is not.

I know this may seem a bit difficult at this time for you to understand, but think of it in this way. Our soul is passing through and has passed through a number of forms. It continues to express in form until such time as it reaches total awareness. When total awareness is expressed, it is the formless.

It is true that souls returning unto form have moments of this total awareness. This is only possible through what is termed the Law of Disassociation. Total awareness or illumination comes when there is no longer identification with self. And therefore it is possible, but rare while in form, to have total awareness or illumination; but because of the tendency of identification or so-called individualization, disassociation from self is very rare.

In reference to the illumined who have walked upon your earth, it is true to our present understanding that they have had a total awareness because of their great evolvement through form. They have managed to learn and to practice disassociation.

If you wish to have a greater light, then it behooves you, my children, to practice disassociation. Learn to be in form and not form. Free this created brain. Let it express itself in creation while you, your spirit, the true one, watches as you watch a play for that is creation. It shall ever be. It is its principle and it will not, because it cannot, change.

Feel free to ask your questions.

You mentioned in 1964 that a soul comes anew from the All-soul. Is this each time a form is incarnated into another form?

The question is, It was mentioned in the year of '64 that when a soul enters form it comes anew from the Allsoul. Bear with me as I repeat your questions in order that my other students may also hear the question. You understand that they hear with their spiritual ears and therefore are receptive to my vibration at this time.

In regards to your question, through the evolutionary processes of passing through forms, the soul returns unto the Allsoul, which is known as total awareness. That soul returns or, if you wish to say, goes out again into form on the evolutionary path. In order to have an understanding of all the forms in which you have passed, you must be in total awareness. As I stated earlier, total awareness is possible through the Law of Disassociation while yet in form. Incarnations into form follow ever in accord and harmony with the Law of Merit. The reason why it is so extremely difficult to have what is termed total recall or awareness is because of the identification with your present form.

A student is asking the question, "I have been with you for many years. Why wasn't I given this understanding before?"

The question is one of deep thought and I can only say that we are permitted to give to you whatever your present growth is able to absorb and yet keep you on the path.

When you have illumination, you go beyond time and space. You go into the eternal moment, the now, and you have awareness of all things seeming past or future for in truth, my children, there is no time. It is the created illusion of your functions. Try to understand that. Rise your being to that eternal moment, to that neutrality.

Do not confuse evolutionary incarnation with the present theory of reincarnation. For it is very rare that a soul returns to your earth planet; and that return is only when it is in the divine plan for the illumination and evolution of the inhabitants of any given planet.

You are free to ask your question.

We understand in our present understanding that there are nine spheres.

Yes.

Have these illumined souls who choose to come back completed the full nine spheres? If so, where else would they have gone? What would have happened to them?

The question is, for the benefit of the other students, We understand that there are nine spheres. When we complete the expression of these nine spheres, where do we go? What happens to us? My good students, the ninth sphere is the sphere of totality. It is the sphere of total illumination and when we reach that sphere, we once again go on into expression. We have a choice and we are never left without it. There are those souls who desire and choose and have merited to return in certain forms for the good and upliftment of fellow man. There are those entering the sphere of totality reabsorbed in the so-called Allsoul or total awareness who then go on the evolutionary path of form to other planets in other universes.

The question is asked, "Do we maintain a resemblance to our present form?"

No, my children, we do not. But as we evolve and reach that totality, we may reexpress ourselves in any given form of our choice that we are able to hold in image. Please do not confuse this teaching with what is termed in your present religious convictions as impersonation. There is a vast difference between the two. There are certain planes where the intelligence is expressed through forms beyond your present imagination. Remember, the forms (physical, mental, or spiritual) are composed of the elements of those dimensions. And this is why we teach, "Hold. Release. Express beautiful thoughts for beautiful thoughts have feelings and colors that are most pleasing and beneficial to your soul."

All form and forms have a color and they also have a number and they also have a sound or vibration. As you look upon the instrument known as the piano and you touch what is known as middle C, that, my children, is the note of that instrument which is the perfect balance. Find your note. Balance your faculties with your functions. Your note, my friends, is your goal and your goal is your lifeline.

Good night.

AUGUST 12, 1971

DISCOURSE 32 ✣

Greetings, fellow students. We shall at this time continue on with our lessons and the questions that have been arising in your minds.

However, before getting to those questions, I should like to speak for a few moments about the expanding universe. We have spoken at times about the laws. The ones that apply in one dimension apply in all dimensions and so it is with the expanding universe. As the macrocosms expand, so do the microcosms expand and so it is with you and your universes. They are constantly expanding and so it is with my universe. This expansion and unfoldment reveals ever new things to our minds; and those things which were beneficial and applied to us in the past are no longer beneficial necessarily to us today. Therefore, my children, it behooves you to keep your minds flexible, ever open for expansion as greater light is revealed to us. Do not stop your growth by accepting anything as the ultimate and only way, but keep your minds open. This is what we are trying to do on this side of the curtain.

It is now again permitted to ask your questions and therefore please feel free to do so at this time.

I have a question about the element of water. It seems to be a conductor of electricity, where we cleanse our hands before and after the healing, and yet it seems to work as a ground for breaking vibrations. Why is this so and what properties does it contain?

The question is well spoken and for the benefit of my other students I shall repeat it. The question concerns the element of water and what it is composed of, its purpose, and is it electrical or is it magnetic.

In reference to your question, try to understand that electric and magnetic are the opposite ends of the same pole. Going in one direction they are electrical, in another direction they are magnetic; and this is why the element water is magnetic and conducts electricity and is also electric. When it is used in its magnetic ways or sense, then it does ground a vibration which is electrical. When it is used in another way, it serves to be the conductor of electrical impulses.

Perhaps we could make it just a bit clearer for you. Water is the life-giving force or power on your particular planet. These properties are necessary for the expression of the Divine Spark in your physical form on your particular planet. Water is magnetic, as I said earlier, depending upon its use. It is also electric, depending upon its use.

I do believe from your question and reading from the records of your aura that you are concerned with its use regarding spiritual healing and communication. When a person is in healing or communication with other dimensions, the pole is basically electrical as they are the channels through which power is flowing forth. They are also, at the same time, magnetic that they may receive these powers. They first must become magnetic in order to become electric. Therefore when a person, having received magnetically, sends forth electrically, they drink water, its element, in order to return them to a grounding or neutral position, balancing therefore the electrical and magnetic poles.

When this element is used, such as in cleansing the hands prior to healing and after, it is an electrical vibration removing from the hands various things that have been attracted magnetically. I am sure upon review of this discussion that you will indeed see the light.

A question is asked by one of my students, "Why is it that truth is not given in its totality so that we do not have to constantly make these changes of acceptance?" It is indeed a good question.

The mind in form is not capable of receiving so-called total awareness or truth. When this total awareness comes, it is through the evolutionary processes, and once returned into form, it may come for moments because of the limitations of the form in which this spark is encased. I do believe, my good students, that we have covered this, basically, in one of our other discourses.

The question is asked, "If the number nine is representative of totality and there are nine planets to a solar system, have I been incarnated in each planet and, if so, what happens when I finally evolve through a particular solar system? Do I go to another or do I return to the source?"

It is true, my students, that nine is representative of the number of totality for it is totality. And to the best of our understanding at this time, we view the soul passing through the various planes and passing through the nine planets of the solar system. Once having expressed through these multitude of forms, we understand the return unto the source to other solar systems in other times.

Remember, my good children, it is an ever-expanding universe in which you have been captured; therefore look to the horizons and see them ever increase and expand. Let yesterday go. Be in this moment in which you have power and that moment, my children, is your eternity, the now, the present moment. This is what you can do something with that is worthwhile.

Good night.

AUGUST 19, 1971

DISCOURSE 33 ✀

Greetings and peace we bring with you, fellow students.

We would like to discuss at this time the science of color. Some time ago we instructed our channel concerning this science and we feel that it is wise to reveal certain things concerning color to you at this time. You have studied the lessons given and the time has come to perceive in greater depth this science of color.

You know that color is vibration and you know that your so-called shield or aura vibrates certain color or colors. If you wish to help another, you must first see and know the color of their so-called aura for their color is the state of consciousness that they are expressing at a given time.

For example, if the color of the aura of the person you are trying to help should be dark or medium green, it would be necessary to change that color or vibration in order to help them. Now you know, my good students, that the color white is the combination of the three primary colors in perfect harmony. You know the primary colors are red, yellow, and blue; divine wisdom in action is spirit. Therefore in helping a person with the vibratory wave or color green, you must first become pure in heart and sound in mind. This will therefore change the color of your aura to white. When your aura of white mixes with medium or dark green, it will change the aura of the person you are attempting to help to a very light green.

For example, a dark shade of green represents human intellect. By casting over that aura or vibration the color white, you change their aura or vibration to a very light green. You know that light green is the color or vibration of conscience. Therefore in order to help the person, you must first recognize the color of their aura; change your aura to white. The interblending would bring it to the light green, revealing to you that you may help that particular person through their conscience.

Now let us take, my students, another example. If a person you are trying to assist is confused, bewildered, you know that the color of that vibration from your class work is brown. Casting the color of purity of your own aura upon them, you would change the brown to the color beige, therefore being enabled to help them on the soul level.

I know that it has been most difficult for most students to perceive the colors and their importance and the time has come that this be revealed to you. Do not be disturbed that my channel was not permitted to reveal it to you before, for there are many laws involved in study and application. Do not underestimate the importance of vibration, which is color. Open your vision, you will perceive, not necessarily in the way you may think, but you will perceive the color of vibration and in so doing you will help many to help themselves.

Do you not see, my children, depending on what your aura is, it may or may not blend with another's? But when you learn to emanate the purity of white, it will blend and change all colors and therefore serve the true purpose of the spirit. The changing of vibration or color does not only apply to persons, but it applies to places, to things, to all creation.

We will once again permit your questions at this time from your realm. Feel free to ask them.

I would like to ask a question about imaging the golden band about the head of an individual while being placed for healing, at the same time emanating this white, this purity. I was asked to envision a golden band by my doctors in the beginning. Is this compatible with this white?

The question for the benefit of our other students is in regards to healing and the visualization by the healer over the recipient of a golden band and what effect, if any, would it have in relationship to the color white.

My good students, gold is the color of divine wisdom and there is no greater purity than divine wisdom. It is completely and totally impartial. Therefore a perfect blending would take place. For when the patient comes to the healer, their color is usually brown. It must first be permeated by the white, therefore bringing about the color of beige (representative of the soul vibration). I know that you are aware that in the aura there are varying colors, some more predominant than others. It is the predominant color of vibration you must learn to perceive and in so doing the white will blend with the color of action and through divine love the healing and the great benefit shall be accomplished.

You are free to continue with your questions.

I have another question about the moral issues and the spiritual responsibilities of an individual to the mundane plane that we live on and how these affect our spiritual growth pertaining to world conflict.

The question has been asked concerning our morals and spiritual responsibilities and also concerning world conflict. Man, like all creation, is in a constant process of evolving. Morals, as you presently know them, concern themselves with form. According to your evolution and spiritual awareness, there bears your responsibility. The man who is blind is not aware of his responsibilities of the things he does not see. Please do not misunderstand, my children. Your spirit is responsible, your soul, for all its thoughts, acts, and activities.

What we are trying to bring to you is, Judge not and condemn not, but go by the moral standards that you and you alone have perceived. The greater your light from within, the greater your responsibilities, the greater your understanding, and the finer your morals shall be. But each has a right to their expression. Each has a right to their grade of school.

We must look within and there find our responsibility and be the living light through indirection, demonstration, and example. We change the world by changing ourselves and when this takes place, my children, heaven shall be on your earth.

Another question is arising in the gray areas. Feel free to speak them forth.

We have discussed the microcosm and the macrocosm. Were churches first formed in the spirit realms and then perceived in the physical? Are the corrections taken first place in the spirit realms and then tuned into by us?

The question is asked, Were churches first conceived in realms of spirit and then sifted down, so to speak, to the earth realm? Yes, my children, all things sift from the source of Light, from the realms ethereal. But in their passing down through form, they ofttimes become contaminated by the functions of form. And sometimes, as we look across the worlds, we do not recognize the original conception. But this is true in all creation or form.

And remember the so-called bad and the so-called disturbances in your world are only undeveloped good. Those things did not sift from a higher realm. They are distortions of the pure Light. These distortions are created by the functions and this is why we ask you to balance your functions with your faculties because your faculties are the expressions of the Light. When in balance, the light of the soul will shine over the functions and all good shall come to pass.

Good night.

AUGUST 26, 1971

DISCOURSE 34 ✁

Greetings, fellow students. I am indeed pleased to be with you again in this way. The time has come to spend and direct a greater energy upon the awakening of your sight and your faculties of seeing, hearing, and sensing. Therefore at this time we bring to you an exercise to be fulfilled at this meeting and in your daily contemplations.

Visualize a fountain before you. Think of a word. Do the exercise you have been given and you will witness the changing of the colors of the fountain before you as you emanate the vibration from within.

Through your powers of concentration you will be enabled to see, to be aware. In this simple exercise a great deal will be revealed to you.

Do not underestimate the value of the exercise you are given at this time. It will increase your powers of concentration and open many doors to many dimensions. Therefore I ask that at this time and for a few moments you visualize this fountain before you. You think the word. You fulfill the exercise and watch the colors before your vision.

I should like to state also that the mantra you were given and are exercising—its color in this order is light green, light blue, and red.

Good night.

SEPTEMBER 2, 1971

DISCOURSE 35 ✁

Greetings, friends and fellow students. It is our pleasure once again to be with you in this way. At this time we are going to share once again our understanding of your spiritual interests and questions.

However, before we come to that time, we should like to speak for a few moments on self-healing. We find this of interest and import at this time to you. We have spoken before on healing and receiving this great power; and there are many forms of healing. We have spoken on the importance of the perfect balance of the mind that it may reach the neutral point through which this healing doth flow.

Now we should like to speak on another type of healing which we feel may be of interest to you. I believe that it was mentioned some time ago that each organ of your body vibrates and therefore expresses a certain color. Now for example, should the hand be hurt or in need of healing, it is possible by discerning the normal vibration or color of that part of the anatomy to visualize that color and therefore receive a certain type of healing. This is not the usual healing of which you are familiar, but it is a proven and a beneficial one under certain circumstances.

Each part of the anatomy vibrates and expresses its color. You may discern this color and combination thereof by becoming more receptive to the little exercise known as the fountain exercise that has been given to you. And in regards to that, we are indeed most happy to see how well that you are doing with it.

Now for a short time we're going to exchange thoughts and to welcome your questions. The class is here from our side, but will patiently be the listeners instead of the questioners this evening. So you may feel free to ask the questions that you have.

I have a question concerning people who have lived on this earth plane that say they believe in absolutely nothing—no life, nothing—beyond this. When they pass across with this complete disbelief, do they stay in that condition or what happens? Do they have moments of spiritual awareness when they can be reached?

The question is, for the benefit of our other students, If a person does not believe in the continuity of life beyond the physical change called death, is it possible for them to be helped in other dimensions or do they remain in that attitude or state of being?

In reference to that question at this time, please ponder and think for a few moments. Belief is a part of creation. If you will recall and study the five points given to you concerning creation, you will find that there is nothing existing in form that is not under the principle ruling of the five steps of creation. Therefore we recognize and realize that a person seemingly stating they do not believe in the continuity of life beyond the changes of form does in truth have belief because their very expression in form has guaranteed belief as part of the principle of creation. Therefore angels from the realms on high, working through the principle of belief, are able in time to awaken them to the truth of this great eternity.

I would like to ask another question about the nine planes of consciousness, the nine spheres, planets, and zones. We have been given seven in a previous teaching. What would be the other two?

I understand your question to mean that there are teachings of seven planes and spheres and states of being and that you have received from and through our understanding that there are nine.

When you look through the history of your civilizations, you will find that it is based upon an understanding of what is termed the mystic or the occult. The seven planetary systems were the first to be received by your past, very past civilizations and they understood at that time that they had grasped the All. Therefore the teaching has come down to your present day of the seven planetary systems and states of being or planes of consciousness.

There are in truth, to our understanding, nine. There are in truth nine vehicles of expression. We gravitate from your so-called earth realm and we lose one of those vehicles. We go from the nine back to the one, to come out again to the nine. From beginning to end to totality is totality. The circle is ever complete. We are only expressing through different vehicles at different times. Therefore it behooves all students to be open and to be receptive to the possibilities and probabilities of more than they are at present understanding.

You cannot go beyond totality and find truth, for totality is truth. It cannot be defended for there is nothing in it to defend. You cannot define that that is beyond the mind at any present time to express or to accept.

We live in a formless world of form. We are the formless and we are the form. We are all things and we are in all ways these things and yet we are not these things. We become them in order to express through them. We are indeed free and we are the totality here and now. Because we may not be aware of this totality is no guarantee that we will not become so at some future time in your dimension of time. We are not governed by your space and time dimensions but we are expressing through them at this moment. It takes power and concentration to do so, but we do it with gladdened hearts, that we may be the instruments of the Light, that it may flow and free the enslaved bondage in which the form has encased so many.

Learn, my children, that there is only one Light; that it expresses through nine vehicles; and therefore, at any given time of your so-called time dimension, you are free only to the extent that you permit yourselves to be receptive to the whole. This is why we teach, Reject not, my children. It may be the very thing necessary to free you.

Learn to understand. Learn to tolerate and you will find the greatest heaven that you will ever know for it awaits your visitation, not tomorrow, not today, but this very moment, this very instant. You have the inherent right to visit it at any time that you so choose, but you must learn patience and gravitate to the heaven of peace that is within you.

There are many theories and many philosophies and religions concerning the purpose of life. We are here to share with you what we have found and our understanding of this moment. We have been aware and are aware of the incarnation of soul through the various bodies and forms and planets. When we speak of the totality of nine, we are speaking of the nine spheres and the nine planets through which our so-called soul does express. You may, through awakening the power within your being, express and be in tune with your nine vehicles at any given moment and in so doing be awakened to the many spheres and planes on which you shall pass and also be awakened of your life before and your life hereafter.

I thank you. Good night.

SEPTEMBER 16, 1971

DISCOURSE 36 ❧

Good evening, students. Again it is our pleasure to be with you in this way.

With your kind permission, the time has come to share with you a bit of my personal history, so to say, for there appears to be a little interest in that direction, and I shall give to you what I am permitted to do. In reviewing the record of my life, it was in the earth year of 6000 B.C. that I wandered in your present realm. As I have mentioned before, I was not one of the better of humanity; but I had a job to do and I was at that time what you may refer to in your day as a judge or magistrate. It was my responsibility to pass the judgment upon those who came before me.

I had no belief in life beyond the physical realm. I had no concern and did not bother to investigate in any way. To me and to my understanding at that time, the law was very clear and many were sent into the nothingness: their life ended because they had transgressed, in my understanding, the law.

When I left your earth realm, I found myself wandering on a barren desert. There were no trees, no water, nothing, for that's all that I had within me and that's what I found when I left.

And then in time I gravitated to another awareness and I met all of those that I had passed sentence upon. And it was indeed a painful experience that lasted for seeming to me an eternity. But out of the darkness comes the Light and the journey has indeed been long and it's far, my children, from over. Take heart in whatever your endeavors may be. We escape nothing here or hereafter. Each judgment that we pass is another prison that we place ourselves in and they are so easy to get in, so difficult to get out. It cannot be overemphasized, the importance of pausing in your daily activity to ponder, to think, to be at peace.

There is eternal joy awaiting all souls, but that eternal joy does not need to be in some far distant so-called time. You may enjoy it this moment, this day, this time. The things which you seek with such effort wait for your recognition as you let the mind drift into the mental realms of its creation and separate your spirit, your soul from all these forms. This great peace and joy is yours and everyone's who is willing to draw within and make the effort to block out the illusions of the mind.

There are so very many who wait to help, to assist and work with you. When you think that you have done enough that weariness has taken its toll, be rest assured, my children, you have yet to begin. Think about the things that take so much of your energy and time. They are of little importance to your eternal responsibility. Think of the frills and fancies that entertain your daily thought, when the greatest thing you may ever gain is lying waiting for your recognition. Duty is so misunderstood. We must ask ourselves the question, "Is my duty a true responsibility or is it a fabrication of the illusions of my mind?"

We have mentioned a bit before on the great power of the great white Light, the Eternal Truth. Now, my friends, imagination is the vehicle of expression of the life force, the prana, the energy that holds all things in space. Therefore image constructively and you shall serve the Light and it shall be good.

Be quick to think and whatever your experience is, the power is within you to shed this great vital energy through this wonderful white light on all things, in all places, and at all times.

I have returned to your dimension by choice. But once having made that choice, the law shall be fulfilled. It has been and is my duty, having made that choice, to share with you our understanding and experience. But, my children, it bears with it a heavy cross and that you have merited, as I have merited. Be of good cheer for the cross is not beyond your capacity to endure, nor is it beyond mine. But we must be about the work we have to do for the Light must go forth into the world; and it is doing so slow, but steady. And to those to whom much is given, much shall be required. We have a few moments left, therefore you are free to ask your question.

It seems difficult to ask a question when we have been given so much! Our channel asked earlier a question about astral surgery. With the penetration of this astral surgery, is there a possibility of air entering, such as in the removal of a malignancy, as in physical surgery?

The question is, Does the element known as air enter the body pierced by physical surgery and psychical (so-called) surgery?

The element air enters wherever an opening is made, be it on the physical or psychical levels. In reference to your question, we understand that it is not advisable to pierce the aura of form without understanding how to properly close it. If we can be assured of this knowledge, then we are free to reach a wise decision. I hope that has helped with your question and I wish to remain a moment longer to speak of energy.

There is no limit to the divine flow of eternal energy. We find a lack of energy when our thoughts are in contradiction with each other; and therefore garner up your thoughts and channel them to the Divine and you will find all the energy and, yea, even more than you could possibly use.

Good night.

OCTOBER 7, 1971

DISCOURSE 37 ⚘

Greetings, fellow students. At this time we should like to discuss with you a little understanding on the different parts of the anatomy and what they represent. We are not unaware of your bit of concern to understand what has been given and we listened attentively earlier and should like to clarify something for you.

You know that we have brought forth that the feet represent understanding and there seems to be some question that the knees are colored green. You understand that green represents human intellect. Stop and think, my students. Understanding is a soul faculty and without human intellect, it cannot express in your plane of awareness. Therefore the knees are intellect. Without them, the feet cannot be moved and could not be lifted.

So we are going to try to explain a bit more to you at this time for the question has arisen in the gray areas of mind, Why are the hands action and why are they colored yellow? Why is the head red? Think, my children. Spend time to ponder. You know that red is action and you know that yellow or gold is divine wisdom. The hands without the head do not create and the head without the hands does not create in your dimension and you know that red and yellow are orange, the color of creation. Think, my students. Think more, think long, and think wisely

Each area of the brain governs certain parts of your anatomy. For example, an area in the brain, through which the faculty of understanding functions, controls and moves the feet and that is why they are termed understanding. The area in the brain governing action controls the hands and that is why they are termed action. An area in the brain, through which reason is expressed from the soul level, is representative and controls a certain part of the anatomy. Think and ponder and put these things to the test.

We'll discuss for a moment anger, temper—its cause and cure. You have been given in your lessons the function of logic, suspicion, and credulity. When they are out of balance, you experience what you term anger, temper. It has a corresponding faculty reason, consideration. Think and you will find the other point.

Study and apply the laws of vibration. Learn the colors of each vibration and you shall in time gain what is commonly termed self-mastery. It is much easier, my good students, to learn it here and now. Make greater effort to break the chains that bind you to self, and if you will do that, you will gain a kingdom that is beyond words to express. That is the natural law that will follow.

I know that it is difficult to give up what we are accustomed to. It has taken me many, many centuries, but I would not exchange the bit that I have gained for all that I have given. For there is no greater purpose in life's expression than to be a free agent of the Divine Intelligence. None of us grow without great payment. But that is the way of creation.

Some may think I have an eternity to do this, and in a sense that is true. But remember, though ignorance may seem bliss, it does not have wisdom; and sooner or later the suffering will become so intense we will gratefully give up all the things we cherish, the things of mind, and be free. For what you hold to, you are bound by; and the longer the duration, the more difficult the freedom.

I can only share with you what I am permitted to share. I cannot and would not tell you what to do for as free agents you are never left without choice. I only try to show a better way here and now.

Good night.

OCTOBER 14, 1971

DISCOURSE 38 ✣

Greetings, students. Again it is a pleasure to be with you. And though you have been given much of the teachings, they are indeed far from complete, though they do contain all that is necessary for your soul unfoldment and for guidance on the path of life.

We are discussing at this time the human anatomy and I am sure by now you realize how the body or anatomy is formed and deformed.

We shall speak now on the heart, the mother aspect of your universe. It is life, light, and love. The solar plexus or father aspect of your universe will be revealed to you at another time. As the heart pumps the life-giving blood through your system, it is important that you understand these parts of the anatomy and their relationship to the areas of your brain.

Now the brain is the vehicle through which the mind or mental body expresses and is activated. It is constantly in motion and therefore it is of great importance that you learn, practice, and demonstrate the ways to calm and to still it.

We have spoken before that the feet are understanding and we have mentioned the hands of action, the toes, the fingers, and various other parts of the body. The human body is composed in vast amount of the element known as water. You know that there are on the triangle the positive (electric), the negative (magnetic), and the neutral (the odic). The odic force—or, properly called, power—is transmitted through the element known as water and it does balance the positive and negative elements in your universe. It is used and has been used for unknown time as a cleansing element. The reason that it has been known as the cleansing element is because it is the neutral point, the great balancer of your universe. I did listen attentively earlier and in reference to the questions that your minds were entertaining, it is true that you may be cleansed or balanced in vibrations through the use of the element known as water.

The Light is everywhere present. The power is ever present. And, my good children, learn to be still and as was said before be ever the observer and not the observed. Indeed we are pleased with the stable and slow growth of the students on both sides of the veil for we know when the Light is held high by one, the many to it shall be attracted. And though responsibility ofttimes seems to be a heavy cross, it is never beyond your capacity to endure. I look forward to the years ahead for all of you, for the day is dawning when greater understanding shall dawn on your horizon and as you study what has been given, your eyes will open, yea, even wider.

Good night.

OCTOBER 21, 1971

DISCOURSE 39 &

Greetings, students. We have brought for our lesson at this time a continuation of the understanding of the human anatomy. Now you have been given several meanings to the various parts of the body and at this time we will continue with this discussion.

You know that the hands represent action, the elbows, conscience; the neck, will; the shoulders, courage; the reproductive organs, desire; in the solar plexus, illumination. Now the color of what is termed the pineal gland, that spot between the eyebrows, is colored yellow; the right shoulder, red; the left shoulder, blue. I know that you understand that the feet are colored purple.

Be patient in your study and investigation. You are coming along well, but do not be tempted to put the cart before the horse. As we have mentioned before, we gratefully give to the limit of the law at any given time. The pattern will be complete before you leave your earthly shell, as complete as is possible to your understanding. Therefore we ask your patience, your continuity of investigation. We are pleased with the efforts that are being made and we are ever willing to share the Light with those who are striving to share it.

Remember that the Light has greater value in the night and this is where our prayers and aspirations ever go: to those in the dungeons and pits, to those blindly stumbling along the paths. For those are the ones, my children, who have the greater need.

We have spoken before on spiritual arrogance and we mention it once again. Balance in all things, balance in your endeavors.

The lips represent aspiration. Think, my children. Continue to study, continue to think. The Light is dawning ever greater in your universe.

If the teachings were too simple, they would not hold the attention and therefore those in the darkness would not be benefited. You understand the truth is simple, but it needs many coverings, that it may attract those who are so immeshed in mind, in brain, that we may, through whatever method legal, bring them to the light of eternal truth.

You are ever testing yourselves and ever tempted to leave the Light; and the greater your soul expansion, the greater the temptation from the worlds of creation. There is but one responsibility and that is the responsibility to the Light, for that is the only thing that is eternal and the only thing that merits responsibility to it. Be not deceived by the creations of mind.

There is a light within all souls that knows its divine heritage. Be true to the Light and the Light shall ever light your pathways.

Now you may ask, Why are the elbows conscience? Why is this and why is that? I am happy to serve whenever the opportunity presents itself and therefore think, my children. Think. Think. What is the very part of the anatomy that moves, directs action? It is the conscience that knows right from wrong and does not have to be told. I know as you continue with your studies you will perceive more and more.

It is true that each organ and part of the body is represented and each part emanates its own color and its own sound. The music of the spheres, my children, is but the celestial sound that is created by all forms in all places. Be then in tune by being in harmony in your own universe.

I have said long ago that I have come to dedicate, not to dictate; and I shall ever try to remain the servant because those who ever seek to be in front destroy themselves in the illusion of their creation. He who serves is served by the greatest servant of all. My children, God is not a master. God, the Infinite Intelligence, the Divine Love, is the servant.

Good night.

OCTOBER 28, 1971

DISCOURSE 40 🌿

Greetings, fellow students of the Living Light. We are indeed pleased to witness another step forward and upward of the class. And for a few moments we should like to speak on the laws governing responsibility.

When our minds awaken to the great truth of responsibility, we find that service begins to be expressed in our lives. For service and responsibility are inseparable and the moment we awaken to what we are responsible to, we do begin to serve.

As the Light can never shine without its so-called opposite of darkness, which is only Light in lesser degree, so it is with our soul unfolding; and indeed our hearts are filled with joy for the steps that have been taken by the students. Be not concerned with effects. Be not concerned with forms. We are working each day in every way to remove from your lives the obstacles on the path. Be not concerned and misunderstand the removal of them for they have become attachments and are no longer valuable to your eternal purpose.

We have spoken much on color and the human anatomy and we should like to mention at this time sound, how to create it and how to use it. Think before the word is spoken for each word vibrates on the scale of expression. Send it forth with the greater power of the spirit within you. See it flow out from your vehicle and accomplish that which you are sending it to do.

Continue on with the raising of your vibrations, the level of your awareness. Indeed, my students, your horizons are being broadened. Free in thought is he who is free in life. We shall be pleased to answer what questions you may have at this time.

I would like to ask about the original sense of touch. Could you elaborate more and explain more about this?

The question has been asked to expand the understanding on the original sense of touch. The sense of touch or feeling is the first sense awakened in form past, present, or future. The sense of feeling is like a pebble thrown in a still pool of water. It creates an ever-expanding circle of ripples. When you feel or sense by touch, you are receptive to the essence of communication. Few people are aware that they sense by feeling, or touch, without ever physically contacting a person or thing. You can sense by feeling or touch a person at a distance of thousands and thousands of miles.

Now, my children, do not limit the sense of touch or feeling to the physical dimension. Learn to sense, to touch the ethereal waves that are passing through all universes at all times. I am here and touch your vibrations. I am here and sense your vibrations. There are many times when I am not here but I feel, I touch, and I sense your expressions.

Through the powers of concentration and visualization, you will awaken to a greater degree your sense of touch and feeling. Close your eyes and feel where you live and what is going on there at this time. This you can do. Practice it and demonstrate it. It is the most accurate sense that we have.

You may ask your other question.

This then ties into intuition, does it? And also about aware-
ness, does awareness spring from the sense of touch?

The question has been asked, Is awareness and intuition related to the sense of touch? My children, in the use of the word
touch or *feeling* or *sense*, we understand that so-called intuition
and awareness and the original sense of expression are one and
the same.

If you will spend a little time each day in the exercise that we
have given at this time, you will become aware of many things
that have blinded you in the past. Feel the city, feel the country,
feel the ocean. I have found in teaching that one of the easiest
ways of awakening to a greater degree the sense of touch is to
feel the ocean for it has motion and it is life herself. Feel its cool
breeze. I touch it at this moment. This, along with your other
exercises, will awaken other dimensions in a more accurate and
concrete way. Learn to feel. Learn to live.

Good night.

NOVEMBER 11, 1971

DISCOURSE 41 ✖

Greetings, children. Once again we bring to you the light that
you send. We are discussing at this time the Law of Harmony,
how to apply it, through which faculty that it flows. We understand that the Law of Harmony flows through the faculty of
faith, poise, and humility. We know that we express through
various levels or attitudes of mind at various times, and it is not
always an easy thing to do to rise from one level to another. But,
my children, through the faculty of faith, which brings poise
and humility, we are enabled to express through more harmonious levels of consciousness.

The mind is an instrument, as you know, that is used by the Divine and it is our responsibility to keep it in as good a working order as is possible. Patterns of long use are not easily changed, but through direct concentration upon the Law of Harmony, which flows through the triune faculties before mentioned, we can and do elevate the expression of our spirit through higher, more beneficial levels.

You have been given, my children, the various parts of the anatomy. And now think, Where is humility in the body represented? What is it that humbles the mind? What is it that bows the pride? The will? Think, my children. I feel that you will be impressed and know.

Of what benefit are all these things, these so-called creations? Of what good is the gathering if the fruit rots instead of serving the purpose for what it was designed? Try to free the mind from its inherent tendency to gather, to garner. Free the spirit that it may flow through the Law of Harmony and then you, your soul, shall be free.

He who bows the head bows the will; and he who bows the will recognizes greater strength. For when the functions are dethroned to their proper position on the scale of balance, you will know a greater light, a greater meaning, a greater purpose.

I had instructed my channel that I would speak on numbers, the key to the universes, and on that subject I would like to say at this time that the number nine is the number of service. Think, my children, what number can you add to nine that doesn't return unto itself? The three to the nine becomes the three again. The five to the nine becomes the five again, and on through the numbers of eternity. And nine to nine becomes the nine again. Nine is the number of service. You know how to find your birth number.

There is no fulfillment and there is no light without the total service of our soul. You each shall pass to this side in years you know not yet. Do not count them long and do not count them short, but count them only if they awaken your mind to what has value in eternity.

Good night.

DISCOURSE 42 🌿

Greetings, students. Indeed we are pleased to come and receive your understanding of the lessons you have been given. And I know that if you will think, the answers will be forthcoming from within you.

And so it is that the first question is, You understand that the feet represent understanding and are colored purple. Now the question is, What is the color of the legs? Now think, my students. What is it that begets understanding? What is it that brings it forth? Think of the colors you have been given, their combinations and their meanings. From whence cometh understanding? That is the question at this time.

Do you want us to answer now our understanding?

Yes, please feel free to answer the question.

I was going to say that I thought understanding would come from experience, but I wonder if it doesn't come from knowledge combined with experience.

Think, my children. Think well and think long. Understanding: from where does it come? And when you perceive that, you will know the color of the legs. From whence cometh all good? For understanding brings all good forth in all experiences. What is the color of divine wisdom?

Yellow, golden, we've been told.

If the color of divine wisdom is yellow, from whence cometh understanding? When divine wisdom is in action we shall know and express understanding. Therefore, what is the color of the legs?

Divine wisdom in action would be orange, but I don't feel that's the color of the legs.

That, my children, is the color. Think! Is there truly any understanding without divine wisdom? Is there any understanding unless divine wisdom flows in our universe? Flowing is action and the combination brings creation, and the color of legs is orange. Now I would suggest a bit further study of the course and class work and we shall now go on to our next question at this time.

The color purple! I don't quite understand how purple comes out of orange unless it's mixed with spirituality. Is that it?

The color purple, which is the color of understanding, is a combination of spiritual action: red and blue. And think, that when you have spiritual action you are expressing divine wisdom and therefore have understanding.

The next question is, In what way is it possible to channel the energy expressed through the function of anger to a creative principle?

Think, my children. Think well. The question will be answered at our next meeting.

Good night.

DECEMBER 16, 1971

DISCOURSE 43 ✖

Once again we are pleased to be with you and to share our understanding of life, her purpose and her meaning. I should like to first thank you for your efforts—your time and energy— that you have spent in pondering the question that was stated at this time before. And so we will go on with the study and you may feel free at this time to give your answers.

We have given a great deal of thought collectively, I know, on this. And it is my thought that the first thing would be to recognize the function of anger and then to quiet the intellect by drawing upon the spirit of peace. And this salvation, peace, flows down bringing forth right action and a quieting and an understanding so that wisdom can flow through in perfect balance guiding the student into selfless service and illumination.

We thank you, student, for your expression concerning the question and we feel that though the question seems to have perplexed the mind a bit, it was not beyond your present understanding. And at this time we should like to express what we have found in redirecting this energy that flows through the function known as anger.

As you will recall, there have been given to you certain parts of the anatomy, their colors, and their meanings. Please follow with us at this time. I am sure that you understand that this energy flowing through so-called anger must first flow through the function known as resentment. You have received in your class work the understanding that when either the line of credulity or suspicion pierce the circle of logic, we express what is known as anger. Think, my children!

Credulity and suspicion are the balancing points of logic and when they are out of balance, we express anger from the function of resentment. You are aware where this function is located in the anatomy. You are also aware where the faculty of understanding is located. In redirecting this energy that we may not express so-called anger, it is necessary to stop and to direct this energy on the downward path to the faculty of understanding. For what is down in one sense is up in another.

The directing of this energy is not possible without some degree of peace. How you are able to accomplish this, you have been given. It is a part of your daily spiritual exercises. It is possible, as has been stated before, to tune in, so to speak, and to recapture that moment of peace that you are attaining to some degree in your daily spiritual moments.

We are pleased at this time to state that the circle of logic and the balancing pivots of suspicion and credulity are located at the base of the head.

My good children, it is not easy for anyone here or hereafter to express fully, wholly, and completely on the highest spiritual level. The patterns established by mind are changed over a period of many, many years. The bondage of creation serves its purpose and in time our soul, our spirit, shall once again be free.

How many times the question is asked, Why, when the spirit is free, must it enter the prison house of the senses, the functions, and creation?

Creation, my children, is form and it takes something, someone to create it. These are known as the nature spirits and there are many, many levels of them. As you, your spirit, make the daily effort to express its light, its peace, its love, these creatures of creation begin to evolve and to change. But they do not do so without their wars. Therefore you are in truth the savior, the peacemaker, the father, the mother, and the creator. If the children of creation are permitted to have their way, they will bind your free spirit, as they have already done so to some extent at this time.

We bear a great responsibility, as was stated before, to ourselves and to all our creations. So often the mind thinks, "What is my creation? My creation is my child or my creation is that that my hands have built." Oh no, my good students, your creations are without number. Because you do not see them does not free you from your responsibility. But the task is never greater than the ability to fulfill it.

It is necessary to spend more time on different levels of awareness. A balance between the dimensions will free your spirit for in balance, my good children, these creations, these creatures are harmonized and fulfill their purpose in creation.

We have at this time a simple question to ask, and I know as each day dawns and as time in your dimension passes that you are step-by-step going up the ladder of light. And so the question is, "In what way can I truly fulfill the purpose of my life? What in truth is my greatest responsibility?"

Good night.

DECEMBER 23, 1971

DISCOURSE 44 ✸

Greetings, students. Again we come to share your understanding of the questions that were stated before. Please feel free at this time to bring forth your answer.

Well, it seems as though the greatest purpose of one's life is to serve selflessly, or that is my understanding. And the fulfillment of one's person is to try and understand how to express through the faculties, instead of their opposites, the functions, as completely as man is capable of doing. At least that is my understanding.

Thank you.

This has been a question that has been in my mind for many, many years. And at my understanding, even though many times I've stumbled along the way, I still hear the voice of White Owl as he said to manifest the divinity within thee and all things shall be harmoniously arranged about you. And my understanding of your classes are designed for this purpose, to help us to understand ourselves, to guide us to a greater awareness that our souls may find greater and greater expression.

Thank you.

My understanding is basically what my fellow students have expressed.

Thank you.

My good students, we are indeed grateful for your words and understanding, expressed and unexpressed. Perhaps we may share a few moments more in discussion on this subject of the purpose of life and man's greatest responsibility.

We understand that Spirit, God, Intelligence, Infinite, is neutral; and that that is neutral neutralizes whatever it comes in contact with. We also understand that creation is dual and is pairs of opposites, or negative and positive poles. Whenever this power, called Spirit, flows unobstructed, it neutralizes or brings into balance this duality of form or creation. When we as students make this daily effort to place God or Spirit in all our thoughts, acts, and activities, we shall indeed balance these poles of opposites and in so doing manifest harmony in creation, bringing, so to speak, heaven in your dimension.

Now, my good friends, this is only possible through greater and greater effort. We do not wish to imply the annihilation of form for we are expressing through form and without the vehicle we cannot express in that dimension. Therefore learn to attune the thought to the source of all thought, to the center, the nuclei, the core, and free it with this great power and bring balance into your lives in all things.

We find the great responsibility to that which is life, the only life, and that is the Divine Neutrality. All forms, as you know, have come and indeed are going. Strive for greater balance through an awakening of your soul faculties. Many, many times we have spoken on the importance of selfless service. Bring balance into form, freeing the spirit that it may neutralize all things with which it comes in contact.

Remember that everything moves and has its being through energy. Use it wisely, my good students, and all things for your greater good shall be made manifest unto you. Strive to serve the true purpose of life herself. Do not be overly concerned with forms and things for you are the creator of things; and if an overabundance of energy is directed to them, you can be destroyed by them.

Good night.

DISCOURSE 45 ✺

Greetings, fellow students. We are discussing at this time the reasons for the delay, the procrastinations, and the seeming difficulties as we strive to find the light of truth.

Why is it that so many take so long to make changes in established patterns that have proven to themselves to be detrimental and not in their best interest spiritually? Why is it such a seeming struggle? Why is it that man speaks forth his desires to do and to be and becomes so very lazy, so to speak, in application? Then of what benefit is any teaching at any time? Think, my children. On what level do we find ourselves grounded? And if so, why do we remain there?

If a man is born without feet to walk or hands to write, ears to hear or eyes to see, nostrils to smell or a mouth to speak, a tongue to taste, what would be the purpose of his being?

Good night.

DISCOURSE 46 ✺

Greetings, fellow students. We are discussing at this time sun, soul, and solar system; and we have spoken at times concerning these matters. You understand that your planet, your earth, is the fifth planet in your solar system. And you understand that the beginnings of all solar systems are governed by the expansion and the contraction principle. Now by that we mean to say that the sun shot off, so to speak, from itself what you call moon. The expansion continued on and you are aware of the nine planets. In time, in eternity, these planets and so-called moon are once again absorbed by the center or sun. Now the sun itself is an offshoot of a greater sun in another solar system. This expansion and contraction is taking place in space at all times. In other words there is expansion in one area while there is contraction in another.

Now the question may arise, What does all this have to do with soul, with life? My children, this is the principle of life. This is the duality of creation: the expansion and contraction.

You are aware of the evolutionary journey of soul and we wish to speak at this time of your planet, the purpose of your incarnation upon it.

Being the fifth planet, it is the planet upon which the souls shall learn and apply what you call faith. Each soul merits varying forms of expression. As you know, to the best of our understanding, there are nine spheres and nine planes to each sphere. For example, if the lessons and applications of the particular planet upon which the soul is incarnated are not learned while yet in the flesh, they shall be learned as they pass through the eighty-one states of consciousness before going ever onward and ever upward to another plane of expression, another lesson, another day, another time.

It has been said that the lessons and applications are easier while yet in material form and indeed is that true for many reasons. For example, a soul incarnated to learn and apply so-called faith who does not learn and apply it while yet in the flesh of the planet of which his form is composed shall learn it in those other forms, in those finer vibratory rates. And when the day comes in eternity that the soul returns to the Allsoul

to come out again and again, the longer it has taken to learn
that lesson, the merit system of incarnation to other spheres
and other planets will not be as pleasant as those who have
learned it while in the form composed of the planet of their
incarnation. And this is why, my children, you see such variety
in form: you see souls entered in wealth, in poverty. They all
have varying lessons that they have merited. But your planet
is faith. Learn it well and apply it that you may be free while
yet in form.

I know that it has not been easy for some to understand
the lessons that have been given. You understand we are but
the channels through which the Power, the Intelligence, doth
flow. When the student is ready for a lesson, then it is easily
perceived and learned. Sometimes it does seem that lessons
come to us a bit premature. Flow with that that you find an
inner feeling to.

I know, as you know, that growth is inevitable. We are
indeed the formless and the free. Why is it that the attachment to the prison house of form seems at times to be so
great? Souls, my children, are never new. They only appear
to be. That which applies without also applies within. The
expansion and contraction principle is universal and universally applicable.

This moment is your moment: capture it and use it wisely.
Unfold. Express the great lesson that you are there to do. A
foundation is the only thing to which your ship can anchor and
there are no foundations without understanding. The entertainment of the form serves its purpose. But never forget that
you are the formless in form. But you are not the covering, for
you are eternal. May we ever act accordingly.

Good night.

JANUARY 13, 1972

DISCOURSE 47 ✄

Greetings, friends. Again we are pleased to bring to your world a bit of our understanding. At this time we are discussing the art of loving, the way of living.

As you will recall, there has been mention of the second faculty of being known as faith, poise, and humility. When the gates of humility are opened, Divine Love flows unobstructed. When we gravitate in our thought, our actions, unto that second faculty, we become the instruments through which the Divine Intelligence, known as Love, doth flow. We then experience this great power that is expressing through all creation. In so doing we become in tune and attract to us through this power whatever we set into motion. This feeling of Divine Love is possible for all and is indeed the way of life that we have found at this time. It is not necessarily easy to rise in thought to that level, but it is indeed beneficial and it is the true purpose of our being.

There is nothing in our universes or in yours that is beyond the realm of possibility. As more thought is generated and directed to the Divine, the Divine begins to awaken within our being. Do not underestimate, my children, the power of directed thought for it is the channel, the avenue, through which this great energy, this love, doth flow. Be universal in your thinking and you will become universal in your acts and activities.

The stage or expression in which you are in at present is such a passing moment. What is there in creation that is so important to bind us to the illusion of which in truth is its essence and its substance? Be ever the captain of the ship: be not the ship itself.

Try to flow with me in thought into the great sea of eternity of which we all are but a drop in an ocean of so-called time. It may seem to some that the light is so small and reaching so few.

I wish in that thinking you could awaken to another level, to another time, another dimension and see the multitudes who are seeking and be assured, my friends, that that wanders from the source can only in time wander back to it.

Remember that it is energy or love. Be the channels through which it freely flows. Learn to direct it to all life for in truth there is no life in any dimension that we are not a part of.

I know that it is difficult to reeducate the identity system in which you are in. My children, it is such a passing thing. Try to ponder the great truth that you are everything, that everything is you. Does one remove the hand because we think it does not serve the purpose that we desire? Can we ever remove a part of ourselves? In truth we cannot. Therefore the light that is the true you cannot be separated. It is not possible. We can only be in a dream, a delusion, for a time.

You have entered your realm according to divine law and have a purpose to fulfill. Remember the thief of all time. You will only escape through effort. Then let your efforts be daily, and moment by moment, for there is in your dimension but one moment you can capture and that is the eternal moment of now. Whatever it is that you desire to do for the good, do it now. Do it with that thought. Do not see the obstacle known as time for you, my friends, are greater than the illusion of time.

You have the power to set the law into motion. Do it with thought, with feeling and with love, but do it in the moment in which you have power. Do not be deluded by so-called impossibilities. Do not be deluded by what you will do in years to be. Do it now in thought, in feeling, and in love; then in order shall it come into the dimension which you are presently aware of.

Good night.

JANUARY 20, 1972

DISCOURSE 48 ✖

Greetings, fellow students. So often things that are given to the world in simplicity and in truth are complicated and changed by the brain. If you will listen and ponder, apply and act, you will be enabled to find your way through this mass confusion of so-called events in so-called time.

Try to think, my good students, of the eternity that we are in truth. Try to rise out of the patterns of conflict, contradiction, and disturbances. You know the laws and how to apply them. It's only a matter of patient and persistent effort; and indeed is it better to be about the business of the Divine each day in every way.

Who is it that desires to feed the things which are passing and in truth of no import in life herself? All these things will pass as they come, only to pass again. Indeed have the wise ones spoken from on high again and again, dear children: Service selflessly applied again and again, again and again, will free us and illumine us from the bondage, the prisons, and the disturbances of conflicting creation.

We have come to the world and have left your world. And that that we come to and leave shall come again in another world and in another time.

Think of the ageless, children. Think that there is but one eternity and that you are this moment. Place your attention ever upon the Light herself for indeed that Light never faileth.

And remember, that that is ever in order for us, let it be. Do not rush and do not push and do not ever think that there is power outside your being. It exists, you know, within. Touch it. Feel it. Learn to use it wisely.

The lessons to be perceived are not new but very old; but they are new to certain levels of our being. Grow through them with courage, with faith. They are not in truth what we all are seeking. We in truth are seeking to go back home, only to wander again, again, and again.

Good night.

JANUARY 27, 1972

DISCOURSE 49 ❧

Greetings, students. Again we are pleased to be with you and share our thought and our understanding. We are discussing beginnings and the laws that govern them.

Wise is he who studies the chicken, its egg, who sees the embryo so protected, encased in shell. And so it is that nature herself dictates the lessons to be learned. Whatever your beginnings may be, guard them and protect them until they are strengthened and strong to weather the forces of adversity that are destined by the law to attack them. Cherish your beginnings. Guard them well. Protect them and feed them on the levels where it really counts.

Now in regards to beginnings, we have spoken before on soul, soul mates or guardian angels. And when we speak of guardian angels or soul mates, we are speaking in truth of the so-called other half of ourselves. It is a law of creation that division is the Law of Form; and the soul is the covering of form, of spirit, intelligence. And so it is that as this Divine Power enters encased in form or soul—what you understand to be individualized soul—the Law of Division applies as it does in all creation.

So as this soul is impulsed into being, it splits, so to speak. A part of it enters your so-called physical world and its other part enters the so-called ethereal world. And that other part, my friends, is what is termed your guardian angel. In time, in eternity, there is an amalgamation as it returns in its way to the

Formless from whence it came. So learn to listen to this so-called guardian angel as it whispers in the stillness of your mind.

Indeed a slow step is usually a sure one. And so it is these steps, each day in every way. The Light is shining everywhere. Rise to that great awakening and see the purpose that is indeed being served.

When the bird flies, the motion is not the air, nor is it the bird; but it is the essence, the true essence, of creation herself.

Good night.

FEBRUARY 3, 1972

DISCOURSE 50 ✻

Greetings, students. We are discussing at this time auric pollution, its prevention and cure. We find in our daily activities various times when we are experiencing what is called a state of being known as tiredness. This experience is caused from an inability on our part to maintain and to sustain an extended span of attention. As we know, energy follows attention; and you have been given the statement that concentration is the key to all power. Also it has been stated that concentration is placing the mind upon the object of your choice until only the essence remains.

When our attention span becomes shortened, the energy moves from one level up to another and causes what is known as a short circuit in our electrical body. When this short-circuiting takes place, this energy is released into our magnetic field or magnetic body. At such time we experience a high degree of sensitivity. But remember, my friends, your electrical or reasoning faculties are not functioning properly because they have been short-circuited.

Now in reference to prevention of this type of pollution into your aura, it is recommended that you practice daily concentration.

This will release this energy through a constructive electrical vibration and the short circuiting will not take place.

Many times students have thought that it is a natural process to require so much rest in so many given hours. This, children, is a fallacy created by the illusions of mind stuff. As long as you permit this fallacy to entertain your thoughts, you will indeed be governed and controlled by it.

I know that many of you experience this sensitivity, these hurt feelings. But it is not necessary, nor desirable, to experience them. You can pause for five or twenty minutes and direct the energy, channel it to one thing and one thing only and in so doing you will be totally, wholly, and completely rejuvenated. In the course of your activities you are absorbing pollution because you have short-circuited your own vibrations. When you feel these various emotions, stop, pause, think, and act. Take the time once or a hundred times in your day and tune into the power that moves the universes. It is not only beneficial, it is sustaining. And when you take control of this power and direct it in its oneness, you need never again be concerned with weariness and all those things.

Try, children, to do something about these emotional realms through directing the power that heals, the power that moves. It is indeed at your disposal.

Good night.

FEBRUARY 10, 1972

DISCOURSE 51 ✼

Greetings, students. It has been spoken before about the levels of mind, the nine states of consciousness, and at this time we are expanding on that understanding.

You know that we have a superconscious, a conscious, and a so-called inner mind or subconscious. We also have what is termed the solar conscious, the celestial, and the terrestrial: the infinite, the cosmic, and the universal. It is within our being and our power to express through any or all of those states of consciousness if we have evolved within our being to those vibratory waves.

I have heard discussions concerning the lessons that have been given on the anatomy and would like to mention at this time that the joints represent uneducated desire or, as many would call, greed.

Now, my children, we are all seeking the Light that we call Truth and it has been given before the way in many times and in many different words. At this time we speak forth once again: "Love all life and know the Light." It is more than a statement. It indeed is a way. And if we are loving all life, we will indeed find the Light. But it is not possible to love all life without the living demonstration of selfless service. As we broaden our horizons and we elevate our spirit to express through higher states of consciousness, we find that these petty, mundane things of creation are not the dreams we should be dreaming. Therefore, as was said so many, many times, "He who thinks in a universal way shall act accordingly."

When we and we alone are ready and willing to make the change within, we shall indeed do just that. We know that no one here or hereafter can or would do it for us. So let us be about the business of the universe for we are indeed all one. And can we in truth enjoy our being when a part of that being is yet suffering in the darkness?

Good night.

FEBRUARY 17, 1972

DISCOURSE 52 ✣

Students of the Light, we bring you our greetings again and invite you to travel with us in thought as that is the doorway through which we all take our journey. Think of this great Intelligence infinitely manifest everywhere and you will awaken the greater possibilities.

You know that there are nine states of consciousness and that there are nine ways or possibilities of reaching the Light of Lights. It has been spoken before of this great solar system, of these various planets; and now we are discussing their direct and indirect influence upon our being. For example, this planet known as Mars is a planet of action, often referred to as the planet of war. This planet is indeed a part of us, for we are indeed a part of it. When this so-called planet of war or action is brought into the influences of the planet known as Mars or Venus—correction, students, when the planet of Venus and Mars are in harmony, you will gravitate to another area of consciousness where harmony reigns supreme. For Venus represents the influence of love.

Now, good children, the reasons we are bringing this to you at this time is to awaken within your being a greater, a broader horizon. The hands are action. They're controlled by the responding planet and so is love. We must consider a greater light, a greater level, a broader horizon. Each and every part of your created form is controlled by the influences that are the causes of creation herself. Do not misunderstand, students: you are greater than creation; but to become truly aware and apply that greatness within, we must have a greater awareness of the tendencies, the possibilities, the potentialities of the forms.

Why does the form respond to certain things at certain times when it does not respond to those things at other times? Indeed the Soul, the Light, is greater than all these things and in understanding these influences you become freed from them. For to understand a thing is to know a thing, and to know a thing grants a possibility of forgiving it; for we cannot forgive that which we do not know and therefore we cannot be free. Think, students. Think more often and think more deeply. You are not the atom, nor are you the molecule: you are greater than them, so strive to understand them.

It was pleasing to note your questions earlier and in reference to them I should like to say our understanding is harmony!

Remember that the sun, the solar, its location is the center, the nuclei. From it all things have come and to it all things shall return. Your solar plexus is the circuit, the center. Do not concentrate upon it but understand it and you will have greater control of your being. We shall discuss at another time more fully on this subject.

Good night.

FEBRUARY 24, 1972

DISCOURSE 53 ❧

Greetings, friends. We are discussing at this time the divine principle known as Light.

It is understood that light is pure energy; that this divine principle or pure energy is everywhere, constant and available to all form. This energy or light is increased in our universes by an expression of the magnetic principle of our being known as love. And this is why the statement has been made to love all life and know the Light.

Now God is called many things, usually known as Love, as Life, and as Light. Wise are those who awaken to a level, a state of consciousness, where there is a greater awareness of pure love; for in so doing, they are able to attract unto themselves a greater light. In expressing this so-called Divine Love, we are enabled to see the Light in all things and in so doing attract through the faculty of choice the greater good into our being. When there are disturbances within the mind, it is possible to redirect the energy by expressing this great magnetic power of love to another level of expression.

Love, my children, is the greatest power we shall ever know for it is the principle which magnetically pulls the Light to us. He who truly loves a thing shall become the thing; so choose wisely, children, what it is you love. Your experiences are revealing to you where your love is being expressed.

Now the reasons why there are so very many distasteful, so to speak, experiences for us is because we somehow insist upon expressing our love in those levels. Most people think of love as the love of a child, the love of a family. That is indeed an expression of love and if it is overbalanced, we shall experience the loss because we have expressed an overbalance of love in that direction.

Expand your universes, broaden your horizons, express your love on universal levels and the Light shall greatly increase in your universe; and indeed shall it fulfill the purpose of its divine expression. Many, many words have been spoken along these lines; but no one, good students, can do it for you. You have the golden opportunity to express this love. Do not hold it to the limits of your programmed patterned habits for they are only imprisoning the Light of your soul.

Good night.

MARCH 2, 1972

DISCOURSE 54 🌿

Greetings, fellow students. We are discussing the Law of Identity.

In discussing this law, we find apparent difficulty with the class in practice and in application. The Law of Identity is revealed through effort. It has been spoken before that words have great power, the power to move mountains when the levels of mind are harmonized, permitting the power of the soul to express itself. And so, good children, we gratefully reveal to you an affirmation to use with the power of your spoken word:

> I am Spirit, formless and free;
> Whatever I think, that will I be.

Good night.

MARCH 9, 1972

DISCOURSE 55 ✺

Greetings, friends. We are discussing spirit, mind, and motion.

Spirit is likened unto the air, and mind, the wind. Without air, there is no wind; and so it is, without spirit, there is no mind. The seeming difficulties that perplex us at times is because this substance, known as mind, has been permitted to blow in any direction without guidance or control. In so doing our spirit is tossed from shore to shore, from level to level.

It has been stated again and again that love is the magnet that holds all things in space. And it behooves the student to learn to use this power known as love wisely. So many times students will express their seeming difficulties in holding the mind firm to one thing. The reason that it is stated that concentration is the key to all power is because when the mind is held firmly (when the winds cease), the spirit expresses itself. Holding this mind to the oneness is done by what is termed love.

That that you love, you create. And many things does the mind love. It was stated that we are spirit, formless and free; whatever we love, that will we be. Remember, students, he who climbs the mountain becomes the mountain. So won't you consider more often using this power more wisely. So many times the things we love destroy us and we have to build again, again, and again.

You have not been practicing daily the exercises that were given to you. We are free while yet in form, if we practice the law and demonstrate it unto ourselves. How many times are thoughts self-related? The importance of selfless service is ever stressed from the realms of light. It is the only thing that frees us from the bondage of our own creation.

Good night.

MARCH 16, 1972

DISCOURSE 56 ✍

Greetings, children of the Light.

Whatever love gives, it also takes. We have tried over these times to share with you our light of understanding and we have found that there are some points of interest to you that do not yet seem to be quite clear.

The purpose of teaching, my good students, is not to tell you the way to grow but to reveal unto you a way that you may find of awakening the light within you. For when the light is awakened, and by that we mean when the mind is still, the light indeed will shine from your universe and guide you on your paths to return to the source from whence we all have wandered.

When illumination truly comes, the need for systems does indeed disappear. But systems indeed are necessary, my children, for they are the ways to find the light within. Many times it has been requested that the horizons of your universe may be broadened; and it is indeed pleasing to note that over these times they are indeed broadening and will continue to do so.

It has been stated that there are many planes of consciousness. It has been stated and it is demonstrable that we and we alone are the captains of our ship, that we and we alone are the masters of our destiny. As you still the activity of the mind, as you continue to practice it in the systematized, organized way that has been given to you, that light will grow, yea, even brighter in your lives and you will know beyond a shadow of any doubt what you in truth really are.

You know already, students, that you are not the form but indeed you are the creator of all your forms in all times. You always have been and you always will be and that is why it is stated that what love gives she also takes. That is why the wise hold not to form and that is why as we think, we love; and as we love, we garner unto ourselves to lose, to gain, to lose again. Do you not see, can you not view, that you are not all these things that you are creating? You never have been, good students, and you never will be those things. Free yourselves even more, children. Learn to be free! From many places have you come and to many places do we go. Find home this moment because if you cannot find it this moment, then that is indicative that you are indeed far from it.

We have come to serve and in serving have we indeed gained. He who does what is to be done without thought or interest in results is ever free to do the work of the Divine. Our love has brought us here and in time our love shall take us away, to come again to serve where service calls. Be free, my students, for I am a student, as you are a student. No one can ever teach who is not ever ready, willing, and able to be taught.

Good night.

MARCH 23, 1972

DISCOURSE 57 🌿

Greetings, fellow students. How many times, in how many different ways, can the eternal Light be presented? That, good students, is a very old, old question.

Now the reasons that we find for different teachers presenting the one Light in so very many different ways is because of the receptivity of the students as they flow through different levels of mind. What at one moment we are receptive to, at another moment we are not.

It seems that there is with so many great difficulty in finding themselves, the true purpose of their being. So many things distract the mind: so little effort is given to awaken it. The patterns are so set, yet we must ever make the attempt again and again to try to change. No one can ever, good students, do it for us. We and we alone must come to that great awakening within ourselves.

The teachings presented to you are a sharing with you of the Light that we have received. We have given and do give them as freely, according to the law, as they have come to us. There is a statement that the end does justify the means. The awakening and freedom of the spirit does indeed justify whatever methods are necessary. For that that is eternal and everlasting has greater value than that which begins and ends. And so it is, if you have convinced yourselves of the difficulties, then the difficulties will indeed be yours.

It has also been said that man is a law unto himself. Ask the question, "What am I doing with the law that I am?" I can change nothing but that which is within me, and that which is within me, I do indeed experience without. He who does not pick the fruit deprives nature, creation, of her purpose.

Good night.

MARCH 30, 1972

DISCOURSE 58 ✖

Greetings, friends. In review of the various lessons that have been brought forth, we find that a discussion of the so-called basic instinct known as self-preservation has not as yet been discussed.

This so-called basic instinct or self-preservation we understand to be the primary level of awareness. It is a function that serves a good purpose. It is destructive and detrimental when it is not in balance with the faculty of service.

It has been discussed that there are nine states of consciousness or spheres of expression; that there are nine planes to each sphere. In discussing this so-called basic instinct of self-preservation, we are discussing the first plane of the first sphere or state of consciousness. This function is absolutely necessary for the form in order that it may serve the spirit, the soul, as a vehicle through which the Divine may express itself on and through that level of form. When this function of self-preservation is out of balance, it becomes distorted and you become aware of self-concern, self-pity, which grows on to greed, to envy, to hatred, and all of those disturbances. The form is designed by Infinite Intelligent Power to be the servant for the soul as it journeys up through form.

Many things have been spoken about service; and it is hoped that you will ponder awhile and give more thought to balance between these functions and so-called faculties. You will find greater peace, greater freedom, greater love, a greater life, if you will consider the daily, moment-to-moment effort to truly become aware of the purpose for which the form is truly designed. Self-preservation for the purpose of serving, not for the purpose of garnering up to itself that those things will destroy, so to speak, the vehicle through which the Light is beginning to shine.

Again and again it is spoken in so many ways and so many days: you are free while yet in form. Enjoy that freedom. Use it wisely. Remember that there is no separation in truth. Be not moved with all these things that your minds encounter from level to level: a greater light is truly dawning within your being. Remember, my good friends, we cannot be aware of levels of mind that we have not yet grown to. Our light is constantly moving through these levels of mind. Let it flow upward, that you may truly see the purpose of your being; that you may know that you are this great eternity; that these forms and disturbances are never, good students, outside of ourselves. They cannot be. It is the delusion created by a lack of awareness that we and we alone are indeed the cause of all things. Be a good dreamer and dream a life of beauty.

Good night.

APRIL 6, 1972

DISCOURSE 59 ❧

Greetings, students of the Light. We are discussing at this time, change: the eternal Law of Progression.

At our last meeting we spoke of self-preservation and the varying attitudes and feelings that it causes. One of the most difficult things for students to accomplish is to change from patterns that have become so-called habits. Change for all of us is difficult, to say the least. We find that on certain levels of mind that it binds us to the things, the patterns with which we are familiar. For that with which we are familiar represents to our minds a type of security.

In reference to change and its difficulties, we should like to give to you at this time a technique which will indeed benefit you and help you to grow from level to level. We have spoken before of the Law of Identity. And with this technique that we wish to share with you at this time, if you will be loyal to its use and practice it daily, you will begin to see the changes within yourself and your spirit will find a greater expression of freedom while yet in form. The mind has identified itself that you are John Doe, so to speak, or Mary Jane. If you will entertain in thought that you are someone else and you will choose as that someone else a person or persons, a place or circumstance that you find to be intolerable, you will in truth come into rapport with that person. You will in truth experience their feelings, their emotions, and in time their soul, their spirit, of which you are indeed a part.

Be honest with this method or technique that is given to you. Use it daily and you will indeed gain greater understanding.

Good night.

APRIL 13, 1972

DISCOURSE 60

Greetings, fellow students.

Many times workers on the spiritual path of light seem to be discouraged and ofttimes disappointed with their seeming progress to find freedom and truth. If we will try to recognize and to accept that the Law of Ascent is also the Law of Descent, that before we awaken to the Light that frees us we must descend through the so-called levels of mind; and when we have done that, we begin to awaken to the peace, the Light, and the life eternal. As we are descending through these various levels of mind, there appears on our paths many obstructions or so-called obstacles and the attainment of this freedom appears to be increasingly more difficult.

That that is hidden shall be revealed and that that is unknown shall be known; but we must, in climbing the ladder, descend on the outer ladder of illusion and delusion that we alone have created. It is not easy, as was said again and again, for anyone to find the Light for the simple reason that we have covered it with so much error and ignorance. To those who are tested and to those who make the effort, freedom is indeed assured. But, good students, there is indeed no easy path in your travels or in mine to return to the source which is our only eternal Light.

Indeed does the mind by its very nature continue to create, to destroy, and create again, again, and again its multitude of illusions of mind stuff. The importance of maintaining and sustaining a balanced or even mind, to be aware of one thing and one thing alone: only in a oneness of mind can we truly find our eternal home.

Good night.

APRIL 20, 1972

DISCOURSE 61 ✳

Greetings, fellow students. Peace I bring to you.

In review of the class work and lessons that have been given, we find that a further discussion of thought, where it comes from and how it affects us, would be of benefit in greater understanding of what has already been given.

In our daily activities we find times when a multitude of thoughts seem to be entertaining our so-called mind stuff. Whenever we think of a person, a place, or thing, through the very process of thinking of them we open our minds to all thoughts that are related to them. We are not usually consciously aware of this happening. But because we are not in peace, we are not in our own vibration, we do indeed become affected by these related thoughts.

You have been given an exercise for greater understanding. Do you not see, children, that you are experiencing each and every moment, to some extent, this exercise that has been given to you? Whenever your mind entertains a thought of a person, a place, or a circumstance (and it does do it each and every day), you are influenced and affected to some extent by those vibrations.

Unless we make greater and greater effort to be at peace, to think of peace from moment to moment, we will not—indeed we shall not—enjoy and experience the freedom of our spirit. Think, children. Think more often and think more deeply.

Good night.

APRIL 27, 1972

DISCOURSE 62 ✼

Greetings, fellow students. We are speaking at this time on inner levels.

We have spoken before on the nine states of consciousness and on the nine planes or expressions of each state, beginning with the first state of consciousness, which we understand to be self; and the second state of consciousness, which is slave; the third, which is servant; the fourth, which is student; the fifth, which is preacher; and the sixth, which we understand is teacher. In regards to these states of consciousness, there are nine ways of expression to each state.

One of the reasons that it seems so difficult to remove self from the light of eternity is because it is the first state of consciousness. Look at all form! What does it reveal to us? Look at the dog with his bone. He does not share it usually. He guards it and keeps it. Some call that the animal instinct. Others would see it as selfishness.

Now, good friends, that that wanders from its source returns to its source in time. The more we are orientated into self, the farther we are from the Light that frees us. As the Divine Light expresses itself through form, it is wisdom that dictates the first state of awareness to be self. For without that awareness, the species is not protected and does not continue to exist. And this is why you find it in all forms in what you may call the lower kingdoms. Even in the tree, the plant, and the rock, it exists. But do not be discouraged for we all shall return to the Divine Light.

It takes daily, moment-to-moment effort and if you will consider ever to remember, "I am only the vehicle of the Light and it is the Light that doeth the work and that is all that is eternal." If you will remember that in thought and abide by it in all your acts and activities, you will in time be free.

At another time, be it in order, we will carry on with our understanding of the many states of consciousness.

Good night.

MAY 8, 1972

DISCOURSE 63 🌿

Greetings, good friends.

When the lessons given in our life are truly perceived, they will never again be repeated. You have been given the so-called steps of creation. If you will consider studying them and applying their inner meaning as well as their outer, you will become more aware of how to protect yourselves from these various forces around and about you.

We can never be affected by anything, good students, that we are not in rapport with. O man, know thyself, that you may protect yourself and be free and fulfill the purpose of your being! Go within, find the cause, and then you are on the way to freedom from it.

Creation, as you know, has two opposite poles and we are in creation; therefore he who has his attention upon it has his energy in it. When the mind, the vehicle which directs the greater power, holds fast to the power, then we will indeed free ourselves from all these bondages that are so destructive to us.

Again and again and again the lessons are given to think, to think, to think! Make it, good students, your moment-to-moment exercise! Become aware by knowing yourselves: by knowing your thoughts, your feelings and how to change them. Do not be discouraged, for that which is loss is gain.

Good night.

Note: What does the heel in the physical anatomy represent? The heel represents the door to understanding and one should keep it closed: otherwise it mixes with the understanding of others and man does not know himself.

MAY 15, 1972

DISCOURSE 64 🌿

Greetings, good students. We are discussing at this time the womb of satisfaction.

In our understanding, as has been given forth before, the meaning and the importance of number, the key of the universes, we once again will express their meaning, beginning with the great number that holds all things together. You know that five has been given as the number representing faith. If you have studied your lessons, then you know that it is the number of balance. Without faith, there is no balance; without faith, there is no creation. Five, the number of faith or balance, is the great cohesive principle that holds things together.

You have been taught that two is the number of creation. And when creation and faith or balance are brought together, you have this great so-called unseen power that moves all obstructions. Therefore, good students, when you find yourselves disturbed or out of balance, call upon the power that brings you back to harmony, to unity, to freedom.

We are speaking at this time on the womb of satisfaction. You know how much the mind enjoys its slumber or sleep! You know how irritated the mind becomes when it is awakened from its slumber! And so it is when the teachers bring the Light to the sleeping students, it is not always appreciated at the time of awakening.

So let us think, bringing a balance into our lives. It has been stated that that which you place your attention upon, you have a tendency to become. Now, friends, that which you have faith in, you are.

Good night.

MAY 22, 1972

DISCOURSE 65 🌿

Greetings, students.

In bringing to you over these past years our understanding of the purpose of life, we have tried to bring to you these lessons ever in accord with your ability to absorb them. For nature herself is not wasteful and so it is in bringing light to the world. You will notice, I'm sure, that the lessons have been brought in ever expanding or broadening your understanding. They are constantly evolving, as you are constantly becoming more receptive to the Light. And at this time we will speak in a broader way perhaps on creation, duality, and freedom.

It has been stated that fear and faith is one and the same! It has also been stated not to annihilate the functions, but to bring them into balance with the soul faculties! When this power flows through the functions or expresses through them, you experience what is known as fear. When this same power flows through the soul faculties, you experience what is known as faith. It is indeed one and the same. When they are brought into balance, you experience what is known as freedom.

This power flowing through the functions with this experience of fear is caused by this so-called self-preservation. Fear is faith; and in expressing fear or faith we indeed not only create but guarantee whatever we have fear or faith in. The reason that this power, when flowing through the functions, is known as fear is because we have faith in the need of protecting our cherished thought patterns. We have need in the functions to hold fast to that which we are familiar with. That is known as self-preservation. When we make the effort to express the same power through the faculties, we bring ourselves into balance and in so doing are freed from the duality of creation.

Fear serves its purpose in the present state of evolution of the masses on your planet. You have fear that when you place your hand in the fire it will burn. Do you not see, students, that what you truly have is faith that this is what will happen?

Think, students, and think again and again! You have the choice in any given situation to express through the functions or through the faculties. When you find your spirit, your power, your energy, expressing through the functions, which are limitation, and when expressing through the faculties, which are limitless, you may choose at any given moment to bring the thought into balance. That, my good students, is known as freedom.

Fear guarantees a reaction. Again and again and again the experience is repeated. When it is balanced (the thought) through an expression of the counterbalance of the faculty, you will be free from the experience and express indeed the purpose of your being.

Good night.

MAY 29, 1972

SEMINARS

Now we find that poverty is not only an attitude of mind but that in the mass thinking and in the average person's experiences it is necessary for it is used as a device to gain attention. We find that this is a deformity or a weakness in the personality; and that through an expression of this delusion of lack, they are able to attract attention to themselves and in so doing find a fulfillment of their basic personality needs. The vibration of lack or poverty is predominate with the masses of people because of a lack of understanding of the spiritual laws governing the universes.

When these spiritual laws are understood and applied, we will find that there is no such thing in truth as limit or lack of anything. Poverty does not only apply to the material dimension but it applies to all dimensions. It applies to poverty of the spirit, to poverty of the physical body and it applies to poverty of the mind. As long as we find a need in our personality to have attention drawn to us, we will continue to emanate, to express, and to experience this so-called lack and limitation.

This adaptability of which we wish to speak this evening is the adaptability to constant change for that that is in form is governed and under the Law of Change. If a person is not willing or able to be moved from various positions that they think they hold in anything, then they are stagnated in their spiritual awakening and illumination.

We find that the needs of people to hold to things is caused from an insecurity within themselves. The only thing that blocks us from awakening the spirit within us is our mind that sees no security because the mind cannot see the spirit that is within and without.

So often we find ourselves governed by devices that we have set into motion; and these devices are not something that we apply or have learned in adult age, but they stem from our very early experiences. When the child cries and it is quickly attended to, it accepts that that is a means of gaining attention. And unless in our growth through life we become aware of the need of the Divine Spirit that is within us, we will find ourselves traveling through many realms of deception, delusion, and illusion.

We have taught that color is vibration and by vibration are you guided and by vibration do you attract all things into your lives. Balance is the keynote for a perfect peace of mind. But balance cannot be accomplished by those who are not willing or not ready to recognize that there is a power flowing through them. That is the only permanent security that they will ever know.

We are conditioned in a world of form, especially on your earth realm, of gain. The mind, the brain, constantly seeks that which it can bring unto itself. Its great delusion is that it is not able to free the things that it brings to itself because it has not learned and does not understand that man is designed to be a clear channel of perfect, harmonious flow. This flow is blocked when our desires of the mind become the greatest, more so than our soul faculties.

In reference to color (its vibration), it not only is vibration, but it is sound and it is movement. Everything that you are experiencing, you are the creator of. There is nothing outside of you that has brought to you the things that you experience and the things that you continue to experience. If it is your present desire to be freed from the bondage and the prison of self, then learn to be a free channel. Learn to let go. Learn to give. Because, my good friends, if you cannot learn to give, then you cannot free yourself from the problems, the misery, and the grief that besets you.

Therefore be not concerned for tomorrow and be not concerned for yesterday but be ye concerned with this moment, for in this moment you have power and you have the greatest power the world has ever known. It is only yourself that is blocking it from full expression. There comes a time in this great eternity when we wish that we had awakened before.

So many words are given to your realm, so many words of wisdom and guidance. The ear hears but it does not listen because the doors of the ear are closed with what is known as self or ego. We do not teach that the so-called self or ego should be annihilated; but, my good friends, unless we make the effort to educate it, to understand it, then we are traveling in the realm of delusion of our own creation.

This is not the first time that your spirit has expressed in form, nor will it be the last time that it expresses in form. Therefore, awaken to the great truth of eternal life. Awaken to this great understanding that you are here in this particular form or forms to serve a purpose. He who learns the path of selfless service frees himself from the bondage of his own thoughts and creations.

When you learn to give as a daily pattern, you will rise out of creation and you will look at its multitudes of experiences but you will no longer be a part of them.

I wish that it were possible to wave some magic wand and awaken your minds to this great truth, but I know that that is contrary to natural law and is not possible for anyone to do.

Stop each day and ponder. Ask yourself the question, "In what way may I serve this Divine Light this day?" And if you will do that in sincerity and honesty, you will find a new life, a new horizon, and a new purpose to your soul's incarnation. The realms that await the form are ever in harmony and in accord with the basic expression of the inner being known as motive.

No one will ever change you, my friends, nor will you ever change another, for the change comes about when the light of your soul begins to cast its healing rays upon the multitudes of functions and creations that you all are swimming through. I tell you these few words not from reading a book or combination thereof, but from many years of traveling those paths.

The tendency of the mind has its effects upon your body, and not only upon your physical body but upon the body in which you are going into when you shed this piece of clay. Each thought and attitude that you hold in mind you create in form; and being the creator of your vehicle of mind, you will find yourself formed and deformed according to what you entertain in your own inner being.

The realms that await so many are not all a heaven, nor are they all a hell. Each effect in your body is revealing to you a basic deformity in what is termed personality, character, and mind. There is a direct relationship between your attitude of mind and your physical body. Someday, to those who become students, each and every so-called disease will be revealed to you in relationship to the type of mind that creates it.

I am privileged to say to you that conditions that attack the area of the throat are directly attributed to what is termed resentment. Conditions which react in the feet are directly connected to suppressed desire. We ask only, my children, that you think, not that you believe or disbelieve.

There are steps to creation and if you will go inside of yourself and come out of the illusion in which the masses of your world are swimming, if you will make that effort and you will be sincere, you will find a peace, a heaven, that no words can ever express.

There is and has been so much concern regarding communication with these so-called different dimensions. Guides and teachers are the mirrors that reflect back to you where you are on the evolutionary scale of spiritual awakening. They are no higher, nor lower, than your soul's aspiration. Most of them are attracted from higher realms under the vibratory waves of compassion for they have trod the path centuries ago that you are treading today.

You cannot put more water into a cup than the cup is capable of holding for the cup then shall runneth over. Therefore do you not see the wisdom of service, of giving in order that you may receive that which you are desiring?

I am well aware of the seeming difficulties of reaching the light within and so many feel that they're not growing because they're not hearing or they're not seeing. Remember, my children, that God's greatest work is done in silence and indeed is silence golden. So when you see not and you hear not, indeed, you are being blessed, for things of the spirit are discerned by the spirit and things of the mind by the mind. If you would only think and learn to accept. Open your faculty of humility and greater gifts than your mind could ever desire will be bestowed upon you.

Things of your world are things of form. They come, they go, only to come again. Learn to use them, not abuse them. They are the tools that the Divine Infinite Power has given to you. Do not let them rule you for they will rob you of the greatest peace that you can ever know.

Each attitude of mind that you entertain releases from your aura a color and that color blends only with colors that are harmonious to it. Therefore if your experiences are bitter, go into the silent sanctorium within and change your color.

Learn to perceive the colors of peace, of harmony, of poise, and then the power will flow through you to serve all mankind; for he who serves another in truth serves himself. That is the Law of Creation. It is universally applicable to all things. Think of those around and about you. Put your thoughts into action. And then, my children, you will fulfill the purpose of your being in form.

The laws of merit apply in all dimensions. Your soul has not entered the form that you are in by accident or by chance, but it has merited the experience that the form has to offer.

You are never left without choice. You may take the experiences and grow thereby or you may try to push them out of your lives and have them return in another way and another day.

Our adversities are indeed our attachments and it is a great truth that intolerance guarantees the thing intolerable.

Whoever enters your life is attracted to your life by a divine law; you may learn from that experience and be free. We are governed by form as long as we are attached to form. We are governed by the world as long as we continue, through attention, to attach to that world. There is no illumination possible outside of the path of selfless service because illumination is truth, love, and wisdom. Do not let the mind reject the very thing that will free you in this great eternity.

Good night.

SEPTEMBER 24, 1971

SEMINAR 2 ✫

Our thoughts emanate color in what is known as our aura. Now our aura is a vibration in which we move and breathe. There is nothing in form that does not have what is called an aura. Each thought that the mind entertains and expresses releases from the inner being a certain color.

Now various colors are harmonious with other colors, and with some colors they are indeed inharmonious. But there is one color that is and will blend with all colors of the spectrum and that color is white.

I wish to explain at this time the meaning of some of these colors: red, action; blue, spirituality; yellow, divine wisdom; white, purity; green, human intellect; purple, understanding; and pink, divine love. Now when we have a pure thought, purity being white and thought being action, we express a color known as pink. For it is the blending of action and purity that is divine love.

Moving throughout this world of creation we find that at various times in our day-to-day activities we are emanating and releasing from our being various colors. For thought is action, motion; and motion is vibration and vibration is color and *is* sound.

This so-called invisible world around and about us is only invisible to those whose sight is yet dense in a physical and material world. Each and every day and in every way we are mixing with many different colors. And as I said a moment earlier, the color white is the only color that will blend harmoniously with each and every color that is emanated in the universe.

Color has its corresponding sound on the musical scale, beginning with middle C, which is the color white. Middle C being the balance point on the scale of sound, it is that neutral point. We can accomplish this neutrality, this white, by becoming consciously aware of the various thoughts that we are entertaining. For example, if we are discussing things with those who are emanating a strong green in their aura (representative of human intellect), by blending that green with the pure white, we will be able to reach that person through what is known as their conscience.

Now, my good friends, you have heard many words and read many things and yet it seems to many of you that this great simple truth continues to escape you. I ask you to pause in thought, to be still for a moment each day, each hour of your day, and I know if you will practice that simple exercise, you will return to the inner being and you will find this great peace.

There are in truth eighty-one states of awareness. They are not something, my good friends, that you're going to find hereafter for they are within us this very moment. And we cannot find in that so-called hereafter what we have not already found while we are yet in the flesh.

When we become aware that we are influenced and directed by so-called invisible forces around and about us, we will begin to realize that this world of color, vibration, and sound is guiding our ship of destiny.

We have spoken many times on the purpose of life and have tried to express, to the best of our understanding, that we are freed from the bondage of creation through the path known as service. And until we begin to step upon that path of service, we cannot and we shall not be freed from the continuous turmoil of our own creations.

I wish so often that I could wave a magic wand and reveal to you that your soul may awaken to the great truth and this great eternity which you are here and now. But the many things that people hope for are like grasping for a star that is ever outside their reach because they see and spend so much time on things outside of their own soul. He who makes the effort to understand the purpose of the soul's incarnation will awaken to the great Light of eternal truth.

You have not been placed in form, my children, to entertain the needs and desires of form at the sacrifice of your divine heritage. This is not the first time your spirit has entered form, nor will it be the last. I do not speak of return, but of eternal progression. For the light within you at this time ever seeks to express itself to fulfill the purpose of its being. There is no way that I know or have found to escape the purpose of life.

There is nothing outside of us that is not within us. Indeed we find in this eternity a Divine Light of peace and joy and we see the passing creation as the great illusion that in truth it really is. The sights and sounds invisible to your dense sight are no less present and are no less with you.

It was expressed before that the unfolding of your soul faculties creates what is known as your spiritual body; that the expression of your functions form and deform what is known as your astral body. Each and every part of your anatomy corresponds and is governed by a faculty and a function. When we perceive the balance between the faculties and the functions, we begin to flow with the great white Light of eternal truth.

But it is not easy to still the mind. Its very nature is to create. But pause and think, my children. How many colors are you creating and how many forms? Are they beautiful and beneficial or are they ugly and destructive?

The plane on which you are at present expressing yourselves is known as the fifth plane of the second sphere. And on your plane of awareness, five being the number of faith and two the number of duality of creation, it is a grade of school in which, through the poles of opposites, you must pass. And only through great faith will you be able to reach the Light. From the source of One we came and to the source of One shall we return.

There is more to life than form, for form is but the covering of the Light. So I ask at this time that you, those who are seeking freedom from creation, strive in your day-to-day expression to pause, to think, to draw the mind within. You cannot find God without until you have first found God within.

Much has been spoken on the Law of Attraction; a bit has been spoken on the Law of Repulsion. That which we send forth daily returns to us. But it is not easy to find the cause because, my good children, the cause is ever within, the last place that we are willing to look.

If we think that we can pass through a plane of expression without learning the lessons that that plane has to offer, then, my good friends, we are gravely mistaken. For we shall find ourselves in forms physical, mental, or spiritual, bound by the grade of evolution until we have passed the test. There is no God that I know that gives these tests to us, but it is the planes through which we are passing and that we indeed have merited. From this world of form you shall pass and, as long as is necessary, you shall continue to express in form.

The Spirit, the one Spirit, is within and without all form. It is the only life: there is no other. So-called evil and darkness is only a state of expression on a certain plane of evolution. All is elevating in time to the source from whence it came.

Many have asked why they were born into certain circumstances and conditions. From what laws or transgressions had they merited their wealth, their health or its opposite? My children, in forms many you have been, but not on the planet in which you are at present expressing. Do you think for a moment that this is the first time that the God within you has expressed itself? It is not the first time, nor will it be the last time.

Broaden your horizons by broadening your thinking. You are in truth this great eternity. And though many forms have come and gone and many forms yet to be, we are all on the eternal rung of the ladder of progression.

Therefore I ask you once again, hold not to form, be not bound by creation. There is a greater world that awaits your view here and now. You cannot crush truth. You cannot keep it from expressing itself no matter what you do.

Ask yourselves the question, What color blends and what does not? Then go inside yourselves and ask the Divine Spirit within you, What thoughts express what color? What sound? What vibrations?

I heard a student once ask, "If I wanted divine love and if I thought of the color pink, would I not experience divine love?" I assure you, good friends, you most certainly would not, unless the thoughts you were feeling and expressing were Divine and that means pure in motive, right in action.

Good night.

OCTOBER 22, 1971

SAYINGS OF THE
LIVING LIGHT PHILOSOPHY

Self-conscious is the ego clothed in the garment of pride and crowned with the crown of self-pity.

Once I was an apple
And then I was a tree
And when I am an apple tree,
I'll no longer be just me.

Dreamer, dream a life of beauty before your dream starts dreaming you.

Be grateful when you ask and receive not, for then you are truly receiving.

By their deeds, not their creeds, ye shall know them.

The uneducated ego hears only the echoes of its own unfulfilled desires.

Man can only be affected by that with which he is in rapport.

❧

What of thy heart freely gives,
In God's love forever lives.

❧

I'm only a witness of time passing on,
A witness of things that have come and gone.
Never the jury or judge will I be,
For I am the witness, the life, and the tree.

❧

What we cannot tolerate in another, we have not educated in ourselves.

❧

He who seeks the praise of man
Loses sight of God's true plan.

❧

O Love divine, a servant be
Till selfishness imprisons me
And warps the reason of my mind
Into the madness of the blind,
When truth cries out, "Not mine, but Thine"
And frees my soul with Love divine.

❧

It is a wise one indeed who knows when his duty is done, so he may go on to another and another and another.

O God, we love the roses,
The weeds and thistles too;
O God, we love the butterflies,
The snakes that crawl are you.
O God, we love the ones who hate,
The ones who live in fear;
We love them more each day we live
For all to Thee are dear.
O God, we love the ones who see
But even more the blind;
For in our love we hope and pray
Their sight may be Divine.
O God, we love all paths to Thee,
For in them we can see
A light that shines to all mankind
In varying degree.
O God, we love the sunshine,
The darkness and the night;
O God, we love the weak and strong,
For in them is Thy might.
O God, we love all things in life,
For in them we find Thee,
A shining light that's dim or bright
For all mankind to see.

'Tis not the help which may seem small
But the motive that answers the call.

Pride is punishment. Humility is harmony.

≈

Indecision is the inevitable path to confusion,
Which in time places us
On the wheel of delusion.
Upon the wheel we continue to revolve
Until such time as the power of will is made manifest.

≈

What is the motive of one desiring to be a master? On the
strength of the soul we aspire; and in humility we lose desire.
Then in truth shall we become master.

≈

Servants come to teach.
Masters come to preach.

≈

We sit to meditate.
We stand to agitate.

≈

When man is chained to dogma and creed,
The soul of reason is ever in need.

≈

With the blessings which come from on high, come also its balance, responsibility.

Be ever ready and willing to share
The part of you that's known as care
For the world is filled with many a creed,
Thinking first of name and seldom of need.

Slow steps are sure steps when they are under the guidance of
selflessness.

Patience is the only path to Truth.

Truth is like a river for it continually flows from the Mountain
of Aspiration.

What we entertain in thought, we create in form.

Accuser, you are the accused.
Forgiver, you are the forgiven.

Ask nothing, want nothing in return.
Give what you have to give.

❦

Babies are blessings with two eyes, two hands, and two feet.
They become burdens when the parents overshadow the
spiritual with the material.

❦

It is the heart that conquers, not the brain.

❦

Criticism is like a cart without wheels: it's good for storing rubbish.

❦

Let not your deed be your creed.

❦

Unto you is given what you have earned.

❦

Emotions, like ceaseless waves, eternally wash the thirsty shore.

❦

If all I give is what you gave,
And what you gave is what they save,
Then those who save will learn to give
Before they know the way to live.

❦

O Compassion of my soul,
Gratitude has shown life's goal.

Be ever ready and willing to give
That which you hold most dear;
Then, my child,
You shall know not of fear.

As we give, unto us is given.

When you have given all, what then shall be left?

When of naught desire is,
In vain doth sorrow speak.

Your creeds, like your shoes, wear out in time.

Seekers of truth can think only of all life.

Wise ones live to serve. Fools serve to live.

The world needs you or you would not be here.

Greater is he who believes and sees not than the one who sees and believes not.

All your experiences you have willed into action: it is a subtle law.

Life is eternal and wise ones act accordingly.

Our problems are companions as long as we love them.

When you harbor a thought, you are feeding a form.

Loneliness is self-pity in poor disguise.

Today I reap the harvest of yesterday and plant the seeds of my tomorrow.

Our world is ever as we are within.

※

Idle thought, like idle talk, is the greatest enemy in your camp.

※

When of thyself thou thinkest most,
Thine heart is closed to angel host.

※

To be master is the desire of the senses. To be a servant is the
wise counsel of the soul.

※

O, senses, know thou not of me,
For I am I and thou art thee.

※

O seeker, doth thou seek in vain
Knowing not of patience pain?

※

It's the wise who walk their humble way
And let the fools talk and talk
And have their way.

※

No one can define and pinpoint our realms. When you understand
yourself, then you'll understand all life's seeming mysteries, not
before.

✿

Thoughts without acts are like seeds without soil: good to see but waiting to grow.

✿

As the bird flew
And as the snake crawled,
The lion said,
"Of what good are those?"

✿

As the frog croaked
And the wolf howled,
The ears of ego heard not
For the door was locked by the key of fear.

✿

As I came upon the mountain
And felt the glory of my God,
I looked about in wonder
At the many paths I'd trod.

✿

You are making the world and the world is making you.

✿

Be ever ready and willing to change.

No one can carry your burden,
No one can lift your load;
But Angels of Light wait patiently
To tell you their stories of old.

Love all life and know the Light.

O man, think humble yet well of thyself, for in thy thinking is
created the vehicle of the soul.

The climb is never higher than the fall.

If man is a law unto himself, what are you doing with the law
that you are?

CONSCIOUSNESS CLASSES

CONSCIOUSNESS CLASS 1 🌿

It states in Discourse 24 that love is the creative principle of the universe, that love is the great magnet. Now as we understand this principle of the universe, we will understand that whatever happens to us has been created by us. It has not been created by anyone else, but it is something within ourselves that we have become in rapport with. Now we get into rapport with something when we are expressing through that level of awareness. Therefore, we have choice at any given moment to change from one experience to another, simply by a change of our thought patterns or our attitude of mind.

Now the teachings of Serenity are concentration—and concentration is placing the mind pointedly and fixedly upon the object of your choice until only the essence of it remains—concentration is one and therefore concentration is the power. We teach that peace—peace is all things in harmonious motion. When we are at peace within ourselves, everything in our universe therefore is peaceful. This peace comes about through an attitude of mind, through concentration. Therefore, by concentrating upon peace we, in time, will become that peace.

Freedom is not something that we attain without effort. Freedom is something that comes to us through control. Until man learns to control thoughts that are limiting, man will never be free. So we find that freedom comes through what is known as self-control. Control of limited types of thinking frees our spirit to express itself and serve the purpose for which it has been incarnated into this form.

Do we use our imaginations or what do we use?

An excellent question! How do we touch, what facility do we use in touching the universal vibratory waves, is that your question? We use the technique of visualization. Now when we visualize anything, by the very process of visualization, we become in rapport with that that we visualize. Every thought that we think has an effect upon us. The extent or energy that this responds to us is dependent upon how much energy we give to the thought. We give greater energy to thought by feeling than we do, for example, if we think of the word *door*. If we just think the word, we've given it so much energy. If we feel the word, if we visualize it, we give it a great deal more energy. So remember, whatever you think, you come into rapport with that thing.

If you want to get into a more receptive rapport with anything, then you must, through the process of visualization, begin to feel it. As you begin to feel it, you become more receptive to it, and this is the reason that we teach our students to concentrate upon peace. Not only to think of the word, but to touch the very essence of it, and you touch the essence of a thing through the doorway of imagination or visualization.

Are we talking about responsibility only to our own soul's development, our own spiritual development, or to ours plus the other spirits on our level? When we take the responsibility, are we to take it just for ourselves or for our levels?

That is an excellent question. When he speaks of responsibility in Discourse 40 and throughout *The Living Light*, he is speaking of the responsibility of one's self to their own soul and to the Spirit, the Divine. When we awaken to our own soul, to the spirit within us, then we will awaken to the great truth that everything, in every place, is one; that there is no place that God the Divine does not exist in all of the universes. Therefore, when he speaks of responsibility, he speaks of the responsibility of our own spirit to itself, which is God within us and God without us. It's everywhere! Yes!

Doesn't our spirit, our spiritual development affect the development of the other souls and spirits around us?

Definitely! A person's unfoldment, spiritual unfoldment, not only affects themselves as an individualized soul, but it affects everyone and everything that we come in contact with. If we awaken to higher levels of awareness, what happens is everything that comes into our aura, into our vibratory wave, by thought or by physical contact, is affected to some extent. See, man is responsible unto himself and to all his creations.

So by developing ourselves, we're automatically developing the others around us.

Absolutely and positively! And remember, those who do not choose to awaken will leave our universes by the very law that like can only be sustained by like.

I have a question.

I'm glad to hear that, because, you see, this is why we have a mind: to ask, to question, to think. And this is why he teaches, "Think, my students, and think more deeply." Because no matter how much we know, there's always something to learn. This is why I'm so happy coming to class, because as I try to express and share with you students what has been given to me, I, in turn, respond and learn from your questions. Yes, ask your question, please.

We were discussing that all things are, in reality, energy.

Yes?

May the touching be considered to be the tuning of one's level of awareness, that is, the raising of one's consciousness point within one's own energy configuration to that point where it is in rapport with the energy configuration of that object or concept concentrated upon, so that an exchange of energy or an actual flow between the two takes place? Is this the touching or the sensing?

That's exactly what happens. For example, he gives an exercise in there, which we will use tonight, to feel the ocean, to feel your home. Everything, every experience is inside ourselves. The only place the experience is recorded is in our own mind. It is not recorded anyplace else; it's only recorded by our own mind. For example, if you wish to be at the ocean, attune yourself to the vibratory wave of the ocean, which exists inside of yourself. You do not have to go anyplace to be home. You are already home. The thing is to awaken to that simple truth. Whatever it is that you want or desire already exists inside of yourself. The moment that you awaken to that truth, then you will become in rapport or on the same energy wavelength, so to speak, as the thing that you desire. Because the experience exists inside of your own mind. It does not, in truth, exist outside of your own mind.

Now, some students get that teaching a bit confused. Then, they go on to say, "Well, if that's the case, then the spirits that I see or I contact are inside of me." My good friends, you are already spirit. You're not going to *become* spirit; you *are* spirit. Now when you awaken to that, awaken your mind to your own spirit, then you will make contact, because you will be on the same wavelength as those spirits existing here in the universe this very moment. You cannot contact or experience any spirit, anyplace, that is more illumined than the energy level that you are capable of tapping at any given moment. And this is why, if you have spirits that are distasteful to you, it is because we are distasteful to ourselves. We are on the level of awareness through which we are having the experience in our own mind. Does that help with your question?

This is why the teaching is that whatever happens to us is caused by us. It is simply one of the eighty-one levels of awareness that we are receptive to at any given moment. God is not a place or something you're going to find outside yourself. You will never find God outside until you find God inside. Thank you.

In our talking about the energy being emanated, you told them that they had to have visualization.

I didn't mean to say they have to. I said, it is the doorway to the world of spirit and it is a way of becoming in rapport with anything that we choose to be in rapport with. Yes.

But in order to touch something, do you have to visualize it also while you're trying to do this?

Ofttimes—That's an excellent question. Now ofttimes we are visualizing things on a subconscious level that we are not consciously aware of, for the simple reason that we are not aware of the thoughts that are swimming in the depths of our own sub-conscious. Yes! You would have to have visualized it on some level in order to have had the experience, whether it's a conscious or a subconscious level.

But you don't have to be conscious that you visualize.

That is correct; you don't have to be. You know, man, his conscious mind is set aside, he goes to sleep, and he dreams many dreams. Those dreams are triggered through the laws of visualization.

I wanted to ask something in reference to what had been asked before. We're on this physical plane.

If we are consciously aware of the physical plane, then we are on it. The only reason we're on it is that we're consciously aware of it. When we're no longer consciously aware of it, in truth, we will no longer be on it.

So that, whatever level we're functioning on here or whatever level we can attain here, are the only experiences we can have?

That is absolutely correct! Heaven is not a place we're going to; it is a state of mind that we're growing to. If we do not grow to it while in the flesh, we will not go to it when we're out of the flesh. Yes.

I was thinking in reference to the ocean.

Yes?

If we're not on that level of consciousness . . .

We cannot experience it.

Now, it is critically important that we awaken while we're here in this mundane world. Otherwise, when we leave the flesh, we'll not be aware of beautiful things if we cannot tap those levels. So if we can touch those levels while yet in the flesh, when we leave this piece of clay, it will be much easier for us. Now remember, we're not going to go to some heaven that we haven't merited, but the meriting is done here and now. Tomorrow's home, you know, is today's labor. So if we labor well while here, then we can be rest assured that we will gravitate to a state of consciousness right here and now that people compute as heaven. Belief does not take us there. Belief is sustained by four other steps.

If the spirit guidance that we attract is on the same level as we are, how can they guide us, if they're on our level?

That's a very good question; that's a very good question. Now, the question has been asked by the student and it is a very important question. If the spirits that are attracted to us for guides and teachers are on the same levels that we are, then how can they guide us? The truth of the matter is that the guides and teachers that we have are on the same levels that we are, but we are not on those levels very often. Our aspirations are there, periodically, maybe for a few moments in a day or maybe for a few moments in a week. Therefore, when we are on that level, those guides and teachers—we are in rapport with them, and they help us and try to inspire us, because we are receptive to that level of awareness.

So they can only come to us when, when we're—

They can only reach us when we are in those levels. Otherwise, we're reached by entities that are on the levels—if we want to know what level we're on, all we have to do is take a good view at our experiences. That is like looking in the mirror. If we're miserable and we're blaming the universe and everyone around us for all of our faults and all of our frailties, then that is nothing more than a mirror reflecting back to us. My dear friends, that's where we are.

I was going to ask about these guides and teachers who are on the same level. Would prayer put us in tune with them immediately, if we're asking for protection? Would this now put us in a higher rate of vibration for that protection?

Does your prayer, through experience, gravitate your soul to a level where protection exists?

I would think so.

Then, for you, it absolutely works. It's the same thing, my good friends, if you believe in St. Jude as a saint of the impossible and your belief is a true belief for you, then all things impossible will be made manifest for you. We may do the same thing with a rabbit's foot.

Now I am not saying that our guides and teachers, and our friends from the worlds of spirit are not present with us. I know better, because I see them and I hear them, and I know that. However, remember that man must take the first step. If we want protection, we must set the Law of Protection into motion. And what is the Law of Protection? The Law of Protection is the Law of Faith: we have absolute, unshakable faith in the perfect outcome of the situation in our life. So therefore, if you are seeking protection, seek first faith, for that is the law that truly works. Does that help with your question?

Very much.

Thank you. Yes.

If you start thinking very loving thoughts, you touch people with your love. And if the people you're sending those thoughts to don't happen to be receptive, that love will stay there and wait for them to be receptive. Where an unloving thought immediately dissipates if it finds nothing to be attracted to?

Yes. Now in reference to the question, I would like to state this: remember, he who has great capacity for love has great capacity for problems. Now love expresses through eighty-one levels of awareness. Remember that, friends. Many people are expressing love, but they are loving and expressing in levels that are not tolerable to us at any given time. Therefore, remember that if you send love to an individual, God's love, divine love, send it in divine wisdom with divine order, because the Divinity knows if it is that pure love that you are sending out. The Divine knows whether the person receiving it is going to use that love on what level, because there are eighty-one levels of awareness through which love expresses itself.

Remember, all things in God are good. The power behind every thought, every act, and every deed is God power. We do not recognize or accept such a thing as a devil or dark forces. We recognize and accept that behind every thought, act, and deed, God is there. Man, having been given choice in creation, is a dual expression. He chooses at any given moment to express God's love in a constructive or a destructive way. We understand Divine love to be pure Energy or Infinite Intelligence. But what man does with that energy is man's choice and man's alone. He uses it constructively or he uses it destructively. Does that help? That's very important that we understand that God is everywhere present in all things, everywhere.

Remember, friends, there are many people who think that a meditation group of this type is not God's work. When God is in our thought, God is in our act and God is present. God is behind all things everywhere. A person might say, "How could God be behind the war? How could God be behind disaster?" We're talking about the power itself; what man does with that power is up to man.

Is this not true, also, of the warlords in the spirit world? They still have this thought—

Definitely.

Of war and disaster?

Absolutely. And so when man has the thought of those things, he becomes receptive to all the universes of them, everywhere present. Now, man has the choice, he can choose peace, he can choose the good things in life if he wants to.

But, don't you see, my good students, that we hold these things through the power of love? We hold to our misery, we hold to our limitation, and we even hold to a little bit of good through the power known as love. Remember that truth is taught through indirection, demonstration, and example. When we become the Living Light, then all those things added to us will be illumined. We won't even have to think about it. It is an automatic thing. It just is.

Our purpose is not to get people to agree or disagree with the understanding of Spiritualism as presented in this church. Our purpose is to share with you the understanding that we have received. Remember that we recognize and respect the divine birthright of each individual to express on any one of the eighty-one levels at any given time. Any questions?

Being a new student, I have a thousand questions.

You feel free to ask as many as we have time for, because we do have to get to our meditation.

Would you define for me your definition of heaven?

The lady has asked, Would I define my understanding of the word *heaven.* Well, I can only say this, Madam, if I attempt to define what I understand to be heaven, you realize, through my defining it, I'm going to limit it, and I personally do not like to limit what I understand to be heaven. So I hope you will bear with me. That's just as if you asked me to define the word *truth:* I'm going to limit it and I'm not going to have truth anymore. So if I try to attempt to define my understanding of heaven, I will limit it, and I will lose heaven in the process of my limitation of expression. Do you understand?

You're saying what Kirster said. I know what I know and that's what . . .

And you will know when you know on that level. Does that help?

Yes!

Did you have another question?

One question, when it said in The Living Light *to "feel," to close your eyes and feel your home and what goes on around you, or feel the ocean. What exactly do you mean by* feeling?

By "feeling," I mean a receptivity to the energy-vibratory wave of the particular thing that you wish to become in rapport with. Now if you wish to be in rapport and sense and have an awareness of the ocean, what that simply means, you yourself are raising your level of awareness to the energy level through which the ocean is expressing itself at that time.

What would you feel thereby?

I would feel the ocean if that is what I wanted to be receptive to. That's exactly what I'd feel.

You would feel what: the motion of the water?

I would feel the motion of the water and I would feel all the expression of the life force that moves it, because that's what the ocean feels.

Well, wouldn't that be, when you feel the ocean, wouldn't that be different from what somebody else would feel?

Now that's an excellent question and that depends entirely upon their processes of visualization. If, through the technique of visualization, you simply trigger a subconscious memory and someone else actually is in rapport with the ocean itself, that could be a different experience to you than to another individual. That depends on what you trigger; what level you trigger yourself.

You can't exactly say what I would feel if I thought about the ocean because it might be something completely different from what you would feel.

It may be, and it depends on what level that you are in tune with. Yes, but it could also be identically the same thing.

If we were both in tune on the same level?

Exactly. Definitely.

[At this point, the recording is interrupted.]

It is the original sense. You see, the eyes deceive and so do the ears, but your sensing, your clairsensing is very, very accurate. When you see a thing and your soul responds, then you will know and you will not have to be told. And you will know beyond a shadow of any doubt. And this is why the first thing we teach our students in our private classes is how to unfold their sense of feeling, their clairsentience, because that is accurate.

Is it the same as first impression?

Yes, it could be called the same as first impression or intuition. You will find first impressions are usually the most accurate. But not always the most accurate, because sometimes we are expressing through a level where the first expression is a mental one and not a spiritual one. Yes. That depends on how much we have the mind in the way of our own spirit.

Well, why is it so much easier on this side to learn?

That's an excellent question! And the question is, Why is it so much easier on this side, while in the flesh, than it is when we're out of the flesh? For the simple reason with this body of flesh we are not aware of the finer vibratory waves. We are not bombarded by the physical vision and the hearing of the astral realms, while we're so often expressing through those astral realms. Now it would be quite a difficult thing if we all had our sight open and we did not have our soul to a level where it is peaceful a portion of the time, because we would truly wind up in the booby hatch. There's no question about it at all.

Now, in the unfoldment processes, many people have had experiences with what the Spiritualists call elementals and the astral realms. Well, we experience those astral realms when we ourselves are expressing through that level. If we do not have a beautiful meditation, friends, it is not the fault of some spirit or God outside ourselves. It's inside us. Therefore, we are strongest while we're here, because we don't see all this astral substance and all these elementals running all around in the atmosphere. We've been given a chance; we're in a physical body that's rather dense. Consequently, through that density, if we're wise, we can gain a little bit of Light and, in so doing, free our own soul.

Well, do you mean thought forms?

I do. I do.

And we create them by what we say and what we think?

We most certainly do. We create all those thought forms, the good, the bad, the indifferent. Every single one of them. So if you have experiences in your unfoldment with those kinds of things, you can be rest assured, take a good look at them, they're your own creations or something you've gotten in rapport with and you say, "Thank you, God. You're waking up my soul and for that I'm grateful."

You spoke before of the God force, God power, the love power . . .

It's behind all things, yes.

So that when we're in that destructive—when a person acts in a destructive way and they're—I think you said—they're acting on the love force.

Definitely!

Does the change take place in their mind?

Exactly. This is where it gets changed, right here. The power is one and the same. It is the same power, the same God, the same Love, the same Infinite Intelligence. Man chooses to use it destructively through an error in his own thinking. Man does that to himself, yes.

That's really neat!

That's my understanding and I'm happy to share it. That's the understanding that I got into rapport with somehow. I would say accidentally, but then again, I know there are no accidents in the universe.

Doesn't the fountain exercise have the same effect upon us as the ocean exercise because it helps to open the clairsentience more?

The fountain exercise and the ocean exercise are two different exercises, in truth, to serve two different purposes. The fountain exercise, which we will come to at a later time, has been designed and is for the purpose of awakening the clairvoyance. The ocean exercise is for the basic purpose of awakening and opening the clairsentience. Yes.

Spiritual progression shouldn't be used—I'm asking the question—for clairvoyance or clairaudience. Spiritual progression should be used to grow spiritually. I mean, it doesn't always follow that we become clairvoyant or clairaudient. Many people progress spiritually without ever seeing anything. Isn't this right?

Yes!

I mean, becoming clairvoyant doesn't mean that you stepped up spiritually?

Not in any sense of the word! Becoming clairvoyant, mediumistic, psychic, etc., does not in any sense of the word reveal a level of spiritual progression. After all, what is a medium? A medium is one through whom intelligences in another dimension are able to express themselves. Now you can be a medium to any level, at any time, to the levels you have merited, that is, that you've grown to. So being a medium, a psychic, a clairvoyant, or all these other things does not reveal, necessarily, spirituality.

Are belief and faith synonymous, according to our definition?

No! Belief and faith are not synonymous in this understanding. You can believe a thing and have no faith in it at all, but you still believe it. Do you believe it's raining outside?

Yes. Well, what are the four steps to belief?

Have you studied Discourse 24?

Discourse 24? That was last week.

Yes. I would recommend that you study it. It is given there and the five steps of creation.

Once again, this doesn't apply to our class tonight, but I'd like to clarify these things in my own mind. What exercise opens up the clairaudience?

The question is asked, What exercise opens the clairaudience? And you have read *The Living Light*, haven't you?

Yes.

Next week, if you do not have the answer, I will give it to the class. It's in there. If you do not find the exercise in *The Living*

Light by next Thursday, I will be happy to give it because it's in that book.

I don't know what clairsentience *means. I don't know what* clairvoyance *means or what* clairaudience *means.*

Clair simply means, clear seeing, clear hearing, and clear feeling. We understand in Spiritualism when you say *clairvoyant,* "a person who is enabled to see clearly into other dimensions."

So how are you using the word clairsentience?

That's how we're using it. We're using it in that sense of *clear*: clear sensing, clear seeing, and clear hearing.

OK, I just got it. So that's what it means.

OK? Fine.

I hear you mentioning the eighty-one levels that are also referred to in The Living Light?

Yes. Now I've been asked by many students, What's the name of each level. When we reach a level, we will know in ourselves what level it is. No one will ever have to tell us.

I've been sitting here wondering about levels. Could they also be defined in terms of where you are in your evolutionary cycle?

Absolutely. Definitely! You are well studied. Someone else have a question?

I still can't get the difference between belief and faith. If you walk through the door, you believe that you can turn on the lights, and the light will come on and you have faith.

We have faith that the light will go on. You don't understand the difference between belief and faith?

No.

How many things have you believed in life that did not work out? A few? How many things have you had true faith in that didn't work out? Faith is a power; the power that moves any and all obstructions, true faith. Now belief is something else. You can believe in something, and it will disappoint you. But when you have true faith, there is no disappointment. Faith is one, not two. Belief is dual. Faith is not.

Is faith an energy that also can deny? Can it be expressed negatively, like faith in earthquakes, faith in failure, faith in . . .

That's belief.

Faith is only—

Faith is one.

OK.

No matter what you call it, it's one.

Faith is love? Isn't faith when you know, and belief is just believing? You know, like things that come to you from Divine Wisdom or Divine Intelligence, it isn't that you believe in them, you know them. You have faith. Your faith is your knowledge.

It's one step beyond knowledge. The Bible says it quite well when it says, In all of your getting, get understanding. When you get understanding, friends, you'll have faith and you will know it.

You often say, "in truth," and I've never quite understood what you mean.

Well, in truth—truth is one. Truth is one. It is not creation. Until man learns to separate truth from creation, he will not be free. Truth is not creation. Creation is dual and truth is one. Remember that we are in creation, but we are not a part of creation. The Spirit is expressing through form, but it is not form. There is a vast, vast difference.

Is creation synonymous with fabrication, then? Or making it up?

Well, that depends on what level the question is being asked from. If you're asking the question from a level concerning your creations, then, yes, indeed, we are making it up. Our minds create it. We create our atmosphere, we create our aura, we create all things that are attracted to us, and we create all things that are repelled by us. And in that sense, yes.

If truth is one and love is one and faith is one, they're all the same one. Are they all the same?

God is called many things, all the way from Infinite Intelligence to Truth to Love to Wisdom and everything else. It depends on which way you want to look at it. Remember that God, or Truth, expresses through everything and is a part of nothing.

I understand truth to be relative insofar as what is truth for me now was not necessarily truth for me ten years ago or will be five years hence.

Definitely, because it's individually perceived, though it is not individual.

Therefore, what is truth for another person, you cannot knock it, because it is their level of awareness at that time.

That is right. And remember this, that that we cannot tolerate, we make an adversity of, and that adversity, in time, becomes our attachment. So as the prophets have said, In all your getting, get understanding. Remember, my good friends, we will never get understanding until we get tolerance. For you can't have understanding prior to having tolerance. How can you understand a thing if you have something you can't tolerate? It's ridiculous! So the first thing that we teach is duty, gratitude, and tolerance.

Could one say that the physical body is to the soul what the soul is to the spirit?

Absolutely and positively. But remember, we are nine bodies, in truth.

What are those nine bodies?

You have a mental body; you have an astral body. Someday, if you don't already, you'll have a spiritual body, and you have a physical body, and you have a vital body. There are nine bodies. There are eighty-one levels of awareness.

Do the bodies take you through each level?

Absolutely! You cannot express on any level without a vehicle through which to express on the level.

I think sometimes people are frightened when it's mentioned that their spirit body or spiritual body isn't ready for them yet. They do go into a covering when they leave this earth plane, but it isn't always a spiritual body.

The covering they already have; it's already inside the piece of clay.

Yes, but I mean the spiritual body is built through our thoughts and selfless service.

It's built through the awakening of the soul faculties and balancing the energy through the expression of the functions equal to their opposites, known as the soul faculties. When the Divine energy is equally balanced and expressed between the faculties and the functions, then man, in truth, is creating what we call his spiritual body. Having a spiritual body prior to leaving the flesh, he will be awakened. And in being awakened, he will not go to sleep when he leaves the clay, but he will step out of the physical clay wide awake and go into his spiritual abode, which has already been created for him prior to leaving.

This is why part of your soul faculties are given in *The Living Light* and they're given in the teachings of this church. First, let us get through the first soul faculty of duty, gratitude, and tolerance. What is our duty? Where is our gratitude? And are we expressing tolerance? Not to tolerate people, but tolerance inside ourselves, that we are, in truth, everything that we see around and about us. Remember that nothing can exist in a human being that does not exist in all human beings, because human beings are part of the human race or creation. They may or may not have in this incarnation expressed what they cannot tolerate another individual expressing, but anything that exists in one human being exists in all human beings. So when we say we cannot tolerate the way that person is acting, it simply means we cannot tolerate that level in ourselves. That's what it means. No more and no less, because it's in us. We're a part of the human race.

Now, remember, we cannot tolerate what we have not educated in ourselves. So when you find something you cannot tolerate, you can stop and think, if you wish to, and say, "That's very interesting. I never educated that in myself," because that is the truth and it is demonstrable. What we cannot tolerate in another, we have not yet educated in ourselves. What does the word *educate* mean? Would someone like to answer that question? What does the word *educate* mean?

All right, "it's to draw out from within." It comes from the Greek word educae *which means, "to draw out from within." You don't get it from without.*

All right, that's fine. Anyone else wish to express on the word *educate*?

Staying in control of one's self. To understand one's self. If you understand yourself, you understand everything outside.

All right.

I think perhaps the key is the word understanding, *as opposed to* learning. *You can learn, you can memorize numbers and since you haven't been educated to them, you can learn (memorize) them, but you must understand them. And by understanding them, you understand their relativity to yourself, and what part of yourself they play, what they are.*

This is why we teach in Serenity, Go beyond knowledge to understanding. It is understanding that we are seeking. And we gain understanding when we have tolerance. So tolerance and understanding run hand-in-hand. You cannot have tolerance without understanding; you cannot have understanding without tolerance. When you have tolerance and understanding, your spirit is free. Now, we must get to our meditation time.

[At this point, there is a break for meditation.]

—to do things that are destructive—and some of them do not have as strong a tendency—but that deals entirely with the evolution of the soul and what it and it alone has merited. That has nothing to do whatsoever with the truth that all forms (the human race) have all tendencies, because, in truth, they do. Some people don't happen to express some of them, but we should have tolerance for everything and everyone, lest we merit that experience in another incarnation, in another day, in another time. Because what we cannot tolerate in another, we guarantee to experience someday in ourselves in order that we may gain understanding and, in so doing, awareness.

Thank you all very much and good evening.

JANUARY 11, 1973

CONSCIOUSNESS CLASS 2 ❦

In Discourse 41 in *The Living Light*, it does mention numbers. And there are certain pieces, so to speak, in this book that may seem to some to be missing. So at this time, I am going to give to those who do not have it, the meaning, as I understand, of numbers. If you would like to write them down, you may.

I am aware, students, that there are some who prefer a longer meditation. Remember, this is only the third class. And our purpose in Spiritualism is science, philosophy, and religion. If you don't have the philosophy and the understanding of the laws, how the science works, then you will remain ignorant and therefore never be free. So we must have balance between our science and our philosophy or we will never find the religion of Spiritualism. So be patient. We have nine classes yet to go.

Number	Meaning
One	God
Two	Duality or Creation
Three	Manifestation
Four	Foundation
Five	Faith
Six	Manifested power or double manifestation
Seven	Psychic or invisible influence
Eight	Infinite security or double foundation
Nine	Totality

The colors are:

Color	Meaning
Red	Action
Yellow	Divine Wisdom
White	Purity
Light Blue	Spirituality
Purple	Understanding
Pink	Divine Love
Brown	Confusion
Light Gray	Reason
Dark Gray	Emotion
Light Green	Conscience
Dark Green	Human intellect
Black	Darkness
Silver	Character

Now we'll go on to our questions. *[During the classes students sat in groups of six.]* Now, friends, it's very important. This is your third meeting. See who's in your group and stay in that group. That's very important for you. Now if someone is sick and misses a class, we understand that. So we should keep their chair for them, because it's important to building up a rapport in your individual group. So tonight, we'll start with our questions, with group six. Does someone in group six have any questions concerning the teachings or any question that comes to their mind of a spiritual nature? Yes.

You did not mention white as a color?

Purity.

And gold?

Gold we understand to be yellow, which is divine wisdom. Does any student know why pink is divine love? What colors make pink?

White and red, a combination of action and purity.

Exactly! Pure action is divine love, and that's why pink is divine love. Why is orange creation? What colors make orange?

Yellow and red.

What's red and yellow?

Wisdom in action.

Divine wisdom in action is creation, isn't it? You have the answers. Group six, please. You just stand up, so all the class can hear, please.

I'm afraid to ask this question.

Why?

Well, not really.

Fear is nothing more than faith directed in a negative way.

Well, I'm not afraid.

I know you're not.

On this faith, poise, and humility . . .

Yes?

What center—I don't—I see here that it talks about them being in a certain center in the body. And I don't recognize this as the center. I don't remember the center.

Perhaps because you may confuse that faculty with another teaching. He teaches that every part of the anatomy has a color, a number, and a meaning. Faith, poise, and humility is a faculty, a triune faculty. In the book [*The Living Light*] it says the opposite of that triune faculty is money, ego, and sex. For example, the teachings—if you will put it to the demonstration, you will find it's true—the teachings of the Living Light are not to annihilate the functions, but to bring them into balance with the soul faculties. If a person is having material money problems, that simply means that they are not expressing equal energy through the opposite or counterbalance soul faculty, which is faith.

Thank you very much.

Does that help?

Yes, I was confused.

He also teaches that humility, which is a soul faculty, is the counterbalance for the function of procreation.

Could you explain a little bit where it says, He who bows the will, recognizes greater things. How can you tell the difference between my will and thy will?

Very simply, because if it is my will, it is self-oriented. If it is divine will, it is selfless. It is not primarily concerned with self. You see, we understand that God is equal to our understanding. If we understand the Divine Power, known as God, to have total consideration, then if it is divine will, it is not concerned just with one individual. It has total consideration. That is a sure way of knowing whether it is my will or divine will. Our conscience, which is a spiritual sensibility with a dual capacity knowing right from wrong, does not have to be told, dictates to us which is divine will, with total consideration, and which is self-will, with self-consideration only. Does that help with your question?

Yes, does group six have any more questions?

This is regarding Discourse 24 which we studied some time ago. It says, "Break through the barriers of the layers of mind and you will find beliefs, some created recently and some of very ancient origin." Well, it came to my mind that if things have always been, we are just tuning into them right now. What is the difference between the beliefs of ancient origin and those of more recent origin?

Man's expression of them. Man does not have an original thought. I'm sorry to tell all of you that, but it's demonstrable. Infinite Intelligence is everything, everywhere, has always been. Man simply becomes receptive, through a level of awareness, to what has always existed and will always exist. The only place that he may say it is original, is that it is original to him.

Truth has no beginning; it always was or it could not be truth. Therefore, we simply become receptive to a level, and as receiving sets, we receive what we call a thought. And we say,

"I just got an idea." Well, it always existed; we just got hold of it. We became receptive to it. Then, we can say, "Well, man nowadays has the airplane. He's sending his rocket ships to the moon." What does man think? That this is the first time that has ever happened? Does man think that he is the originator of the airplane or the rocket ship? The thought has ever existed. Man only became receptive to it at this time.

Any other questions in group six? You know, I understand that it is a great ego deflator to entertain the possibility that we are not original. But believe me, friends, we're not. Yes.

I know to a degree, but what is the function of numbers, the teaching of numbers in a group such as this? Do these tie into the fears? Do they tie into the cycles of life that we go through?

They most certainly do. And I'm glad that you brought that up, because I meant to tell those who are not aware of how you find your birth number, the simple way to find it. If, for example, you're born on the second month and the third day in 1930, you simply add all the numbers together and that gives you your birth number. You may do that now if you wish. You add the month, the day, and the year. Reduce it to the smallest digit; that's your birth number. For example, the second month, the third day is a five [2 + 3 = 5]; and 1930 would be nine and one is ten [1 + 9 = 10, which then reduces to 0; 1 + 0 = 1; 3 + 0 = 3] is three, that's a four [1 + 3 = 4]. You reduce it to the smallest digit.

[*The birth number for a person born on 2/3/1930 is nine. Or 2 + 3 + 1 + 9 + 3 + 0 = 18, then 1 + 8 = 9. Or 2 + 3 = 5; and 1 + 9 = 10, which reduces to 1 + 0 = 1; and 3 + 0 = 3, which results in 5 + 1 + 3 = 9.*]

Everyone have their number? How many nines do we have in the class? How many birth number nines? How many people have a birth date that totals nine? There's two. Anybody else have a nine? I'll ask the nines: When do you feel best, when you're active and extremely busy? Or when you're not?

Much better when I'm busy.

Always for the nines. *[Aside]* We have two. How many fives? There's two, there's three. Any more fives? There are four fives. You have difficulty with faith? You either have difficulty with faith or you're very strong in it. One of the two. There's no in between, if you're a five. How many fours? Lots of fours. You're all seeking security and stability or you already have it. How many ones? You're either first or God is first. No in between. Well, we can't spend all night with numbers. You've already been given them.

What about eight?

Oh, eight? Infinite security. Throughout eternity, you're seeking security.

No. That's—

You're not?

Eight?

That's eight.

That's eight.

I think you understand that.

What about number two?

That's duality. Constant opposition. Bound to creation.

Oh, you're a nine.

I'm a seven, serving my purpose, I hope.

Would you explain about six?

What did six say? Didn't it say it's double manifestation or manifested power? You have great determination if you're a six. A lot of problems with the heart. All right now, class, we must go on. Group six, do you have any more questions? In reference to the numbers, they do reveal a certain awareness concerning the soul's incarnation. I go into that in my private classes and not publicly.

No more questions in group six? All right, we're coming to group seven. Does group seven have any questions, please?

I didn't catch the opposites of the positive states. I heard money and sex.

Money, ego, and sex.

It was ego.

Money is the counterbalance with faith; sex—humility; ego—poise.

I have it written down.

Yes. There are many triune soul faculties. All soul faculties have corresponding counterbalancing functions. If you're having problems with a function, you simply need to redirect the energy to its counterbalance in the soul faculty and you will bring balance and freedom into your life.

When you're using numbers, I would choose to use numbers, using one as God, if I add one to three, which is manifestation—

That brings you foundation.

Foundation. But isn't that a rather good way to use numbers? If you use foundation with God, then you have faith?

Definitely. Because, you see, our only foundation is with God or faith. Five is faith, one is God, and four is foundation.

I wish that you would clarify seven as occult. I don't always understand that.

For example, I want to clarify that five again. When you have faith in God—you have faith in God—faith is five and God is one, that gives you a six, which is your heart. That's the only place you find God. If you want foundation in God, you must have faith. Now you want to clarify number seven, which is invisible influences. Invisible influences could also be termed subtle influences or influences that the physical world is not aware of. They are the more subtle vibrations. That is the seven.

Thank you very much.

You're welcome. That's group seven. Any other questions in group seven? No more questions in group seven? Then let us go to five, please, group five. Would you stand up if you have a question, so the class can hear?

You said there was ego, sex, and . . .

Money.

Money. OK. About ego, if you can balance it out, that means it is good to have some pride in yourself.

It is good. Without ego, we would never bother to brush our teeth or do anything else. That is absolutely necessary in form or in creation. The teachings of the Living Light are not to annihilate the ego under any circumstances; simply educate it, that it may serve the purpose of your soul's incarnation. Ego is what drives us on in creation. Ego is absolutely necessary in order that we may fulfill our soul's incarnation, the purpose of it. But if it is not educated or balanced between the functions and the faculties, if it isn't balanced, it becomes destructive, self-destructive. That means that the energy is grounded in the functions and we're out of balance.

Yes, in group six. Would you stand up so we can hear you, please?

That leads to another question. Can the energy be balanced the other way or overbalanced the other way in the faculties?

Absolutely and positively. That's what happened to India for centuries. It didn't have the ego drive or it wouldn't have been in starvation for centuries. It would have found resources and it would have fed itself. It became—what did it become? Lethargic. It accepted "This is my karma" and that's it. No longer an ego drive to better itself. So you see what happens to creation without ego or overbalanced in the soul faculties. Does that help with your question?

Yes. Very much.

Group six? Just stand up so they can hear you, please.

How does one educate the ego? We do have to educate it. We know that. But how does one actually educate it? We have to have this ego drive; we couldn't go to work in the morning if we didn't have it.

Absolutely.

How does one know this ego to be the God (or the righteous ego) or the ego that is self?

Yes, did everyone hear the question? When man recognizes that he is the instrument, this thing—the ego—is an instrument that is used by a divine Infinite Intelligence. Nothing belongs to this created thing—it is only like an automobile to serve the purpose of the driver. The driver is the Divine, not the self-created form. If it remembers that and recognizes that in all its thoughts, acts, and activities, it will bring education to the ego, balance to the soul's expression. Does that help with your question?

It certainly does.

All right, group five. Did we have any questions from group five?

Relating back to the first class, I have some questions on faith, as regards working within the principle of creation and as regards motivation. I feel that there is a very close tie between them and I wonder if you could elaborate.

On faith in creation?

Faith in creation as related to motivation.

As related to motivation. I'll try my best to elaborate a bit upon that. Many prophets have taught, In all your getting, get understanding. When we get understanding, we have an expression of this power known as faith. The teachings are that faith, the faith of the smallest seed, of a mustard seed, will move the mountain. The only way that man gains faith is through understanding. What understanding brings is an awareness of how the Divine truly works. When you see something work, you most certainly have faith in it. Therefore, the steps are quite simple. First, we must gain understanding, but how can we gain understanding without tolerance? How can we gain tolerance without duty? And how can we gain duty without gratitude?

So we find that the first teachings of the Living Light are duty, gratitude, and tolerance. When duty, gratitude, and tolerance are balanced or the energy of the Divine is flowing through that first triune soul faculty, we move through understanding to faith, poise, and humility. And in so doing, we become aware, and in becoming aware, we know; we don't have to be told. And we know beyond a shadow of any doubt. And in that knowing, we see that creation is temporal, that it is guaranteed poles of opposites, and that it is dual in its expression. Therefore, we separate truth, our soul, our spirit, our being, from the duality of creation. We use the vehicle like we use the car. We are no longer attached to it. We no longer depend upon it. We use it; we don't abuse it. Does that help with your question?

Very much. Thank you.

Thank you. Any other questions from group five?

Could you provide the definition or difference between soul *and* spirit?

The question has been asked for a clarification between the words *soul* and *spirit*. We understand that soul is not spirit. It is the covering of the Divine Power, known as spirit. When this Divine Power expresses through form, when it becomes individualized, that covering we understand to be soul, individualized soul. That is the covering of the Divine Energy or the Infinite Intelligence; it is not the Infinite Intelligence itself.

Remember that whatever we understand at this moment to be individual is constantly in the process of change. You are individualized. Ten years ago, you had an understanding of your individuality. Ten years later your understanding of that individuality has changed, because that that is form is dual. It is not one; it is two. The soul, what we call soul, being individualized, has birth. That that has birth has death. Therefore, the teachings of the Living Light are very simple: broaden your horizons; hold not to form, for form shall pass.

So the only way we're going to have freedom, the only way we're going to find truth, and it is demonstrable, is to separate ourselves from the duality of form and creation. Use it, but do not be attached to it. If you are, you cannot progress, until you're willing to make the changes.

Remember that man has many gods, the gods that he creates in his own thought. And those gods are changing, ever equal to his own understanding. The God of Gods is a God of humbleness. It is the greatest servant ever known or ever will be, for it serves everything in creation that is receptive to it. Creation, being given choice—Choice does not exist in God, for God is one. So how could choice exist? Choice exists in form and that is the only place that choice does exist. The soul, being form, has choice, because it has individuality. It may choose the faculties and free itself in balance with choosing the limitation of the function. There is no freedom in the functions. The opposite of freedom is enslavement. The functions are what enslave us; the faculties are what free us. But if we overbalance our energy, this divine energy, through the soul faculties, we will have no anchor to creation and we will find ourselves flitting off into the void. Does that help with your question? Yes.

I'm very, very interested. I think this is great, but when we go to spirit, do we drop the functions and live in the faculties? Do we take the functions with us, along with some of the faculties that we've developed?

I may answer your question in this way. Do you take your individuality into the world of spirit?

Yes.

Your individuality is form. Therefore, we take functions with us. It is the nature of mind stuff to attach. If it does not attach to something, it loses its balance. You see, man is a triune expression; he is physical, mental, and spiritual. Now on that trinity, he may attach to one of the three points. He may attach to the spirit, he may attach to the mind or the intellect, or he may attach to the physical dimension, known as creation. But his mind, definitely and positively, will attach to one of the points of the triangle in expression. As long as the spirit expresses through form, it expresses through duality. This is why the teaching is that silence is golden. Silence is divine wisdom. Does that help with your question?

To a degree.

You may ask a further question, if you wish.

Is silence always wisdom?

The question is asked, "Is silence always wisdom?" The answer is quite simple. Is silence one or two?

According to the teachings?

Yes. Is it one or two? Is silence a oneness? Or is it a duality? Anyone care to answer that question?

It would have to be a one.

What is it? Would you say silence is void? Would anyone care to say that silence is a void, an absence of everything? What is silence?

Stillness.

Stillness. What is stillness?

A void. A void. Like a nothingness. [Many students respond.]

Like a nothingness.

Many people have been silent on issues where they should have—in other words, I mean, many people—I'm judging. I don't mean to judge, but, for example, many persons are silent when their word may have helped a condition or given affirmation to something. Many people are silent, but their minds are busy with negation or affirmation.

Then, that is not silence. If the mind is active, it is not silent. We are speaking of silence, not just in physical action. We're speaking of silence and stillness of the mind, which is a dual vehicle. The mind is capable of so-called good; the mind is capable of its so-called opposite, bad. Is that not true?

Yes.

We are speaking of the stillness, the silence of the Divine.

If silence is golden, then is silence wisdom?

Yes, silence, we understand, is divine wisdom.

I was just doing a little physics here in my mind. I think also that silence is harmony.

Yes.

But then . . .

Harmony is what? A total, complete balance. All things in perfect balance is harmony and silence. That is the Divine. Yes.

That's not a void.

It is a void to eighty levels of awareness.

What is a void?

The question is asked, What is void? Someone care to answer it?

It doesn't seem like we could know what it is because we've never—doesn't seem like I've ever experienced nothing.

Very good. Anyone else care to express on the word *void*?

A void, to me, in the way that we're using it, is a stillness, a quietness, a peace, so that you're not turning on all of the forces and you become quiet. To me, Divine peace is golden, but, of course, it's a oneness.

Now, thank you. Why does man have such a difficulty in finding God? He seeks God with a dual vehicle, known as mind. We will find God when this is perfectly still and there is void; then, we will find the divinity within ourselves. Otherwise, we will continue on the circle to seek God ever equal to our understanding of the moment, and those are the created gods, built from mind stuff. Think! Yes.

It seems that the mind becomes still and that's the void.

That is the void.

My thought is something.

Something cannot come out of nothing. Is creation something?

Yes.

It did not come from naught. God is the divine sustaining power, everywhere present, never absent or away, known by the Spiritualists as Infinite Intelligence. If intelligence is infinite, is it perfect harmony? Question: Is it? If intelligence is infinite, is it perfect harmony?

Yes. But if you say, "Is it?" I don't feel you can answer that. I don't think you can define that word.

Infinite Intelligence. Because the moment you try to define it, you put it into duality or creation and you've lost it. That is the void.

According to biblical teachings—there must be truth in that, too—first, there was a void and then there was activity and God said, "Let there be Light."

Let there be Light.

That's right.

And Light is energy.

So first was a void and then came Light.

Definitely, absolutely, and positively. It's all in the Bible. Depends on what level you are receptive to when you are reading it.

Doesn't there have to be an idea before there can be Light?

Let me say this—the question is, "Doesn't there have to be an idea before there can be Light?" We understand the Lord to be the law. The universe is the law's meditation and man is an idea of it. As mind is ever one in substance with the idea and the whole idea, so man and the law and the universes are one and the same. That is why we teach that man is a law unto himself. Now the lady has asked the question, Doesn't there have to be an idea before there is Light? Is that not the question? No! For idea comes from Light. Energy is first and energy is one. Without energy, there is no idea; it does not exist.

Does not Love come before Light?

Love, Light, and Life is the trinity of the Divine. And the teaching is, "Love all life and know the Light." Without Love, there is no Light and no Life. Love is the great magnet that pulls unto itself. Love is the cause of creation. And love is dual. When the Divine expresses itself, like the atom, it splits, and when it splits, you have creation. When the atom is split, it releases its great energy, doesn't it?

Right.

The law of physics and the law of numbers is the law of the universe, and numbers, mathematics reveal it. Now we have to watch the time. Are there any other questions?

How can we tell if we are fooling ourselves by thinking that we are very humble, when, in reality, we are on an ego trip?

Thank you; it's a good question. When we're humble, we don't have to think about it. If we are entertaining the thought that we are humble, then we are guaranteeing an experience to bring us this humbleness that we think we have. That that we think we have, we guarantee to experience. Remember that we are spirit, formless and free; whatever we think, that will we be. Man has the choice.

Would you define poise *as it's used in this discourse?*

I will try to express my understanding of *poise.* The teaching is, faith, poise, and humility. When we express poise, we are in the Law of Harmony; we are in perfect balance. And when we're in perfect balance, we are very humble. No one has to tell us; we don't even have to tell ourselves. We just are.

How is the soul faculty of humility related to healing?

Very good question. The question is asked, In what way is the soul faculty known as humility related to healing? This energy that expresses through the soul faculty of humility is identically the same energy that goes through the function known as procreation. In some teachings, it's known as prana. When this prana is directed through the soul faculty of humility, it has a great healing power, for it is the power of life herself. And that is the way that it is related, that soul faculty of humility, to healing.

A couple of weeks ago, a Buddhist monk was called up in connection with myself. I was wondering if this monk is present with me frequently. Is it possible that people come from certain traditions or certain lines before this life and return to that tradition after this life? If they live their life in consistency with that tradition, will it be more helpful to their spiritual development during their lifetime?

Yes, now that's an excellent question. I'm sure all the students heard it. Remember that man is a law unto himself; that what is beneficial to one level is not necessarily beneficial to another and could ofttimes be detrimental. Now if an entity, Buddhist monk or otherwise, is attracted to someone here on the earth realm, then there is a similarity, a likeness of interest and it could be beneficial to both; in this case, the Buddhist monk and the person that he has been attracted to. It could be beneficial. But remember that the individual here in the earth realm must have set some law into motion to attract the individual in the first place. The spirit in and of itself also must have set some law into motion to gravitate to that particular person. They both could benefit. Now if the individual spirit is bound by his own tradition—do you understand?—if he is bound in tradition, his own traditions, then that is limitation; being limitation, it is not progressive. Would you agree?

I agree with that.

Now a person could be a Buddhist monk and yet not bound by the tradition, do you understand? Or they could be anything else.

In Discourse 11 and 31, they speak of the Allsoul. Are our guides and teachers in the realm of the Allsoul to be incarnated again into form or is it possible that they're already on different planets in different universes?

We will discuss that at another time. Thank you very much. We have much to get to before that.

I would like for you to clarify two words for me, and they are to think and to look. What is the difference when I think about a situation—

And look at a situation?

And look at it?

There's a vast difference, in my understanding. When man looks at something, it simply reveals to him the level that his own soul is expressing on. When man thinks, and he thinks deeply, he becomes aware not only of the level he's expressing on at any given moment, but he becomes aware of all of his levels, without identifying with any of them in a permanent or attached way. You can look at a book and have no understanding at all, is that not correct? You must think about it.

Let's say, you go home and you think over your situation or your circumstances involving two people . . .

Yes. You are entertaining them in thought or you couldn't be even thinking about them.

I'm trying to mull over this idea that I have regarding another person. Their idea of looking at it and then dealing with it, brings an awareness of what the situation was about.

There's no awareness without thought. Awareness does not exist without thought.

Are you speaking of objective awareness? Looking at something and looking at it from afar?

Madam, if you put yourself into a situation, you're in personality, and if you're in personality, no matter who we are we cannot be in principle at the same time because they're opposites. We place ourselves in personality with one reason and one reason alone: to understand and learn tolerance. There is no other good purpose for placing our soul in personality.

When you think you are using the faculty of reason, you're reasoning . . .

If you're thinking deeply.

If you're thinking deeply. But it's a faculty?

It's a soul faculty, absolutely.

When you're thinking about a thing, you're expressing opinions. But when you're thinking of a thing you're working something out, you're reasoning.

Yes, you're using reason. Absolutely, definitely.

That lady in group three, would you rise, please? You see, you understand that you are confused.

Yes, I understand. I am truly confused.

Now that is very important, because, you know, there is a law—I am very grateful that it was brought to my awareness a number of years ago—Never leave a person worse than you found them. So we can't finish class until there's some kind of clarification over your confusion, because, you see, it's kind of brown. Do you understand? But at least there's understanding of the state of awareness. Now you are trying to help two other people. You are not?

I am one of those other persons.

You are trying to help them, yourself and another person?

No!

You're not trying to help them?

No. I think they were trying to help me.

They were trying to help you.

They're trying to help me to think and to look. That to look at something was really where it's at, but thinking, well, I . . .

Well, no, seriously, you have accepted that. You see, that troubles you, doesn't it?

I guess it does, yes.

You see, there's a teaching that says that that troubles us, controls us. But there is a better way. If something is not beneficial to us, we have a divine birthright to choose to release it to a Divine Power. Is it beneficial to entertain that level of awareness?

I don't think so, no.

Don't you understand, madam, that you cannot find the answer outside of yourself? Confusion is a total grounding in one's own vibration. And we cannot come out of confusion until we become receptive to a different level. Now we can look in the dictionary and find out what the word *look* means, and we can look in the dictionary and find out what the word *thinking* means, but it will not release that that troubles you. Would you not agree?

I'm starting to understand something. If they want to look at it and they're satisfied with that word to look, *let them do it. If I want to think that and I like that word, then I'll think that.*

Now that is awareness. Don't you feel better?

Yes, I sure do.

I'm so grateful, because I didn't want to take it home with me. I've enough to do. Thank you very, very much. Now, you're free and you've freed yourself. Because you decided you would no longer be controlled by some word. Remember, the only thing that has power over us is that which we give power to. If you give power to a certain person and what they've said to you, then you're controlled by it and enslaved by it. But you have choice. You can say, "Thank you, God, you gave me a right to think for myself." A lot of people do not agree with me or with the understanding that I have received. I recognize and fully accept their divine birthright to disagree. And I also expect the same right for myself, because I am willing to give that right to another. Give them the right of their expression and demand the same right for yourself. Thank you.

Could you clarify for me the difference between the brain and the mind?

Yes, it is my understanding that the brain is a vehicle through which the mind expresses itself in this dimension. Now the brain is composed from the elements of nature. It brings with it, when it is created from those elements, all that those elements contain. For example, everything that has existed in creation in these elements is in our brain, because these elements are from nature right down there, all those cells and everything. Now it is given birth, and that that is given birth has guaranteed a death. The mind is not something that is given birth. Thought eternally exists; it is not given birth. This is why I said earlier in this class, I believe, that man originates nothing. He becomes receptive to anything. When our awareness is expressing through the created brain, which is termed *uneducated ego* and is also termed *king brain*, there is no awareness of our own eternal spirit. The brain is what denies our divinity; it is only the brain that does that to us. The brain brings us limitation. When the brain computes that it originates this or that, it is doing that; by that very law of thinking that way in the brain, it absolutely guarantees its need.

It is our brain that has need. It is not our spirit, it is not our soul, it is not our true mind, but it is the brain. When the brain computes need, it guarantees all of the experiences necessary to fulfill the need. For example, if the brain computes that it has a need for love—and love is something we already have and are constantly expressing—but if it computes that it has a need for love, it guarantees every experience for that brain to receive it.

Now, for example, if a human being says, "I need love," in the brain are all of the experiences from the moment the soul entered form. It has all the experiences of how it got love. Do you understand? When the brain once again, maybe at age fifty, has this feeling it needs love, it has to go through all of those experiences that it has computed in the brain to gain love again. Now if a child is permitted to receive love by expressing its anger or its temper, when the child becomes an adult, it will go through the same pattern to receive love once again. That's the brain.

The mind, the Infinite Intelligence expressing through mind, it doesn't have to go through all those stupid experiences, because it knows it already has it. You see, the moment that we become in rapport with what we think we need, the sadness is, the brain says, "I need this and I need that." The mind knows it already has it. The moment we express through the brain the truth that we have what the brain thought we needed, we immediately come into rapport with the vibratory wave of that particular thing and we experience it. That is my understanding of the difference between brain and mind. The brain is limited. The mind, the spirit, and the soul are aware of their limitlessness. The brain is not and cannot be.

But all things have a brain.

All creation has a brain. Everything has a brain. Maybe a little one, the size of a peanut or a flea, or maybe a big one, you see. That depends on what the soul has merited, you see.

If it's created, it has to die.

Sure, everything goes back to its source. The brain goes back to the elements of nature of which it was composed. Mind to mind, spirit to spirit, and soul to soul. And that's why Emerson teaches the soul returns to the Allsoul and the Old Man teaches it comes out anew.

[End of recording]

JANUARY 18, 1973

CONSCIOUSNESS CLASS 3 ✄

—Before we get to our questions and answers concerning the triune soul faculty of gratitude. It seems to be so misunderstood. Gratitude, to the understanding that has been given to me, means release. When the soul expresses its gratitude, it releases itself from the bondage of concern created by our mind. And so it is that we teach that gratitude is the door through which supply flows. Now many people may say, "Well, I know someone that's extremely ungrateful for anything and yet they seem to have everything." Well, perhaps the things that they seem to have, they're truly expressing gratitude for. Because it must be, for the law is totally impartial.

Now if it is an awakening of our spirit and our soul that we're seeking—and I believe that is the purpose the students have come to this particular course, to unfold their own spirit, to find their own Light. Remember that the Light varies in the sense that we have eighty-one levels in which to view it. It may be bright and sunny for us or it may be very dim; also remember the darkness is Light in lesser degree. And so it is when we find our understanding. If we are wise, we will not say that we've got it, because that statement, in and of itself, guarantees that we will lose it. The soul is ever seeking to return to the source from whence it has wandered. When it stops seeking to return, it is certainly a long ways from it.

But if we express our soul's gratitude for the crumbs that come to us according to the law that we alone set into motion, then someday, somewhere in this great eternity, we are bound to get the whole loaf. After all, friends, if we got the loaf this moment, it just may choke us and we would have what is known as spiritual indigestion; we would not be able to absorb it all. So let us be grateful for the little bits and pieces that come to us, that we may absorb them and make truth our own, and in so doing, free ourselves. And when we free ourselves, we will then be the instrument, an instrument, to free another who is seeking.

Try to remember that our understanding of God is ever equal to the level that we are expressing on at any given moment. It is no higher and it is no lower. What is meant for us in one level is not necessarily meant for another human soul at that particular time. It may be later; it may have been before. Now we can get to our questions and answers.

In Discourse 7, it deals with attachment and I would like to have some clarification. When one is expressing divine love and feeling so much of it in the atmosphere and wishing to share it with others, sometimes there are other elements that come in that do not always seem to me to be as balanced as they should. I felt that my attachment should be primarily to those things that are of the spirit and for the spirit and spiritual endeavors and in that way, I would have been freed from any other law.

From your question, I understand that you have found attachment to the Divine, or that that is free, is the only thing that can free us. The mind, by its nature, must attach to something. So we look out into the world and we see that people want to be free, free from this and free from that. So a wise man stops and says to himself, "I want to be free, yet it is the very nature of my being to attach to something." Then it is a wise thing that one would choose to attach one's self to what one understands to be freedom itself.

Would you shed some light on our understanding of capital punishment?

Yes. Now I'll be happy to share my understanding and my Teacher's understanding of capital punishment in a vein of spirituality and not in a vein of what is right or wrong for any particular country or any particular individual. There is a vast difference and I do not wish to speak in a political vein, which is something that we don't have in this Association. Spiritually, however, souls who have, through the laws of merit, merited the experience of what is termed capital punishment, that is a law unto itself. Souls who have received that have set certain laws into motion, not man's laws, but certain spiritual laws or they would never have encountered the experience. However, we must bear in mind that the giver of life is, in truth, the only taker of life from any dimension. And there have been many laws set into motion by man. Man, being a dual expression of the Divine, makes errors as well as right judgments.

So it is not within the power of man to reach the decision of what is right or wrong for another. Because of a lack of spiritual awareness and in order to have some type of systematized, organized society, man has reached these decisions of so-called manmade laws. When the souls are awakened, the need for man's laws will disintegrate into the nothingness from whence they came. Therefore, you will no longer know of capital punishment. It was prophesied eight years ago by the man who brought *The Living Light* forth that within the coming twenty years the entire earth realm would dispense with what is commonly known as capital punishment. And so that, to me, is indicative of the awakening of at least the souls who are in control of the various governments of the world.

Can you aspire for something which has to do with something on the earth realm or is aspiration only on the spiritual level?

The question is asked, Can you aspire for something that is on the earth realm of creation or is aspiration strictly of a spiritual nature? It is my understanding that it is the soul that aspires, that it is the mind that desires; that aspiration is a soul faculty.

When you were describing the numbers, you mentioned that the number two is duality, but you also said it was balanced creation.

Number two is the number of duality. Number two is also the number of creation. Do not misunderstand that those with two destiny numbers are destined to creation. No soul is ever lost and creation, believe me, is lost unless we have a little awareness, because it's the poles of opposites, back and forth constantly.

Can we use these numbers as given for unfoldment of our soul faculties?

You most certainly can. The numbers reveal the destiny of the individual soul in this particular incarnation. You see, my mind did not choose to be born February 22, 1927, but my soul set a law into motion that I could not be born any other day on this earth realm at this time. I did not haphazardly drift into the earth realm on that particular date through a particular family known as Goodwin. The law was set into motion. Man is a law unto himself, eternally a law unto himself.

But how do you use this number for a higher rate of vibration? How does this number apply to your life?

Well, I could perhaps give you an example. I happen to be a destiny number of seven; that's the number that I was born under. Seven is the number of the occult, of the invisible forces. I'm doing my best to try to serve them for thirty-one years; that is my destiny. You're a number one?

Eight!

Number eight, eternally seeking security. The number eight is the infinite security. And I am sure, if you search your conscience, you will find that that has been all of your life your great search. Is that not helpful and beneficial to know? Yes, they can be used in your day-to-day activities if you will use them spiritually and not use them like—what do they call those things?—tarot cards.

I've got some questions. One is in relation to numbers and one is in relation to the Living Light.

I think you'll find some numbers in *The Living Light.*

Is there any significance to the number of letters in your name and how you use it in your daily life?

The question is asked, "Is there any significance to the number of letters and how you use it in your daily life?" Let me answer that in this way: there are many books printed on the vowels and the different meanings of numerology. That's not our basic purpose of this class. But I will say this, when you use a name, you set a law into motion. For example, if a person has been called Robert for a number of years and he suddenly decides to change his name to Bob, he comes under a different rate of vibration. Now that rate of vibration is caused by the individual himself. For example, the reason for changing the name is what's critically important. Say, for example, you were called Bob for twenty years and you decided to change your name to Robert, you must ask yourself, "Why did I make this decision to change my name?" Remember that if you've been called a certain name, you have certain experiences in your inner being recorded with that name, and if you change your name, you open the door to new experiences along the level of the law that you, as an individual, set into motion when you changed the name.

On page 124 of Discourse 45, it says, "If a man is born without feet to walk or hands to write, or ears to hear or eyes to see, nostrils to smell or a mouth to speak, a tongue to taste, what would be the purpose of his being?"

What would be the—

What does this mean?

I'm asking the question. You're asking me a question that warrants a question. What does that mean to you?

I don't know. I haven't been able to perceive anything.

How many hours have you spent studying it?

I know I spend about twenty minutes a day.

On that question?

No, not this question, but The Living Light.

I only want to ask one question: How many hours have you spent seeking the answer to that question?

Oh, about thirty minutes in the last week; not very much.

Thirty minutes in the last week. If you are willing to spend three hours on that question alone, I'll be more than happy to share with you my understanding. I am a firm believer in the Law of Effort. I will be happy to answer it, if you are willing to make the effort to give it at least three hours contemplation and study. That's entirely up to you. I'm not asking you to do it, but if you wish my understanding, that is the law that I set into motion for myself.

In Discourse 11, which we just read, the second paragraph says, "As you know, if the Light is too bright, it is best that they see it not now. For truly the Light can blind and ofttimes it is mistaken for the night." Now that one sentence: how can the Light be mistaken for the night?

Because the night is the Light in lesser degree. Many people mistake what one person understands to be their Light or God as the opposite. Does everyone agree with your spiritual understanding?

No.

Do they consider it their Light? Do you consider everyone else's understanding your Light?

No.

That's the answer to the question.

Could you decide that although the other person didn't agree and you didn't agree with their Light and they didn't agree with your Light, that you could know that theirs was Light?

Absolutely and positively! There are eighty-one levels of awareness and having experienced that level of awareness, you would know that that is Light, only in varying degree.

Then you wouldn't call that darkness?

I most certainly wouldn't. But how many people express their Light and someone else agrees that that is a Light in varying degree? If the whole world thought the way you just spoke, there would only be one complete harmony and unity; there would never be any discord left in the world. The religions would not be fighting amongst themselves, because they would all know, beyond a shadow of any doubt, that they're all seeking the same God. They're only on different paths.

Earlier you said, Love, my friends, is the language of the soul. Now I heard you say that inspiration is from the soul, too.

More than one thing is of the soul. I believe I stated that aspiration is a soul faculty; a soul faculty, like duty, gratitude, and tolerance. Faith, poise, and humility are soul faculties. Love is, indeed, divine Love, the language of the soul. It breaks down all barriers because it knows no barriers.

I have a question with regard to: Does not the blade of grass have soul [Discourse 12]? Because I think perhaps that the word soul is being used in a context which may appear confusing. Is this the same soul as man's soul?

Yes. The statement is made in *The Living Light*, in so many words, that soul is a covering of the spirit, that Spirit or God or Infinite Intelligence is formless and free. The moment it becomes individualized, it has what is known as soul. Now the blade of grass is individualized. I question any scientist to prove to me beyond a shadow of any doubt that two blades of grass are identically the same. A blade of the grass is individualized. The individualization is termed soul, which is the covering of the divine spark or spirit. In that sense, yes, the blade of grass, it too has soul.

Remember that our soul differs, not in quality; it differs only in quantity. Now I know that many will disagree, for they all have their own understanding, but it is my firm understanding and conviction through what has been demonstrated to me over the years that the soul of the tree, the soul of the mouse, the soul of the dog, and the soul of the human are one and the same soul. It only differs in quantity, not in quality, for it is God's and God is all the same.

Is soul the life force, then, of all things?

Yes, soul is the life force. It is the covering of the Divine Spirit, known as God. Why is the statement said for untold ages that you may view a man's soul in his eyes? The eyes are representative of awareness. This is why all creation responds to what is known as love, for love is the great magnet. It is the language of the soul. The soul is expressing itself through form, constantly garnering up experiences and, in so doing, raising the rates of vibration of form.

I know that is much to ponder. I don't ask that you agree or disagree with me. I express my divine right to my understanding and respect your divine right to misunderstanding or understanding. I share with you equally.

He talks about breathing, an exercise about breathing. He didn't explain any further what exercise should be done or how to breathe.

You're asking a question in regards to breathing and spiritual meditation, is that correct? Now there is a certain cleansing breath that I do give in the public classes and we will get to it in this course, but I do not give all of the breathing exercises publicly. I do give those in private classes and it isn't as though we are trying to keep something secret. There are the laws of responsibility. You don't give a four-year-old child a stick of TNT because he won't know what to do with it, you would agree, wouldn't you? It's the same in all teachings. But we will go into the cleansing breath at a later time. Yes.

When a person, looking at the light, sees a small, dark spot or a large, dark spot, what would be the difference? What would be the meaning of one over the other?

Well, now that deals with interpretation. Now some people see a light that has no dark spot in it at all. Some people see a light that has a dark spot in it. We see many different things when we open our vision and our view to these other dimensions. Now what is meaningful to one is not necessarily meaningful to another. Seeing a light with a dot in it or the absence of a dot has no particular meaning to me. It may have someday, I don't know, but I have not had the experience of having it have a different meaning to me. Therefore, I could not answer your question on whether there's a different meaning concerned. All right?

How can one use the knowledge of the number six in practical application, such as a choice of occupation?

The question is asked, How might one use the knowledge in the number six—is that the question?—in practical application. What is your understanding of the meaning of that number as it has been given in this class? Would you like to stand up and share that with the class, considering you asked the question? That's known as being the father of an idea.

But I don't see how the two would relate to a particular occupation.

You don't see how the occupation and the destiny would relate?

No.

If man has a destiny of a power number, he already has that power, do you understand? He already has it. He's not seeking it: he potentially has it. All right? Now, knowing and becoming aware that he potentially has it, he bears a great responsibility in using it wisely, for he can either be extremely constructive with it or destructive to himself and to those with whom he associates. You see, it can send us on the downward path or it can send us on the upward path; it depends on what we choose to do with it. I think you understand that, don't you?

Yes.

And always remember, friends, when we hit the bottom in anything, there's no place left to go but up. So be grateful when you reach the bottom; the next step is up to the Light.

Could you give me an idea of suitable occupations for a person who is a number six?

You're a number six. You should be, because you're a very deep thinker. Well, now I don't want to get into the private counseling at a public class meeting, but a six has to be aware of fulfillment. It cannot do a job just for the sake of earning bread and butter. You understand that, don't you? Therefore, it would behoove someone under that vibration to choose some type of occupation in which they may express their creative talents, no matter how hidden they may be. And besides, you work very well with your hands and I'm surprised you're not a carpenter.

Are there certain benefits derived from meditation in the lotus position, when the legs are crossed, that aren't derived from meditation in a position where the feet are flat on the floor?

If you believe that, that's all you will receive. The lotus position is one designed for the Eastern world. It is not one that was designed by the Western world for the Western world. Therefore, the meditation positions that have been designed for the Western people were designed by Western people to fulfill their purpose. That does not mean to imply that the lotus position and the meditation postures of the Eastern philosophies are not beneficial, but the Western world is not basically geared, so-to-speak, for them. They are not. They haven't been conditioned and trained over the centuries for them. We live on a different diet, we live in a different pace, and we're under an entirely different rate of vibration than India and what its culture has to offer its people. Does that help with your question? But remember, there's good in all things and we can derive some benefit from study and application of it.

I should like an explanation of the Law of What Can Be Borne.

I knew that question was going to come before this day ended! The question has been asked for an explanation of the statement, the Law of What Can Be Borne. He says in *The Living Light*, If the Light is too bright 'tis best that you see it not now, for the Light can and ofttimes does blind. Therefore, if a person shares an understanding with an individual and the individual is not on a level of receptivity to the understanding that is being expressed, it can and ofttimes does cause the recipient what is known as a state of confusion. Therefore, the teaching is to leave a person better than you found them. If you open the door to share an understanding with an individual, you bear the direct responsibility of not leaving that individual in a state of confusion. Any teacher that has taught for any length of time at all knows that you bear a responsibility as a teacher, you bear a responsibility to your own spirit. And this is why we teach unsolicited help is to no avail, and this is why he teaches the Law of What Can Be Borne. In other words, a drink, not a flood, is the wisdom of receiving. Because if you give too much and you go far beyond their willingness or ability at any given moment to receive, then instead of doing a justice to another soul, a grave injustice has been done.

Now there's another law involved and that law says that whatever happens to us is caused by us. So we can say, "Well, I merited the confusion that I got. Now knowing that—and I don't feel well about my confusion—I will start changing my merit system." But that does not exempt an individual from expressing their understanding to the point of causing a state of confusion in another soul. Now I can sit here and have twenty or thirty students tell me that in this course in many areas they are confused. All right, so I have to say, What is the balance? Are they 50 percent confused and 50 percent enlightened? If

so, we have a balance. Hopefully, they might be 51 percent illumined and only 49 percent confused. It is the Law of What Can
Be Borne.

*I'd like to know about the art of giving. It says that the law has
no emotion. I'd like to know, what does govern the art of giving?*

The question has been asked, What governs the art of giving? The art of giving is the law of living. Man cannot truly
live until he learns the art of giving. He is constantly within
his own universe, in his own body, in his own being, living this
art of giving. Different parts of the anatomy give to other parts
of the anatomy. The law of nature is a constant demonstration
of the art of giving. Everywhere you go, you see nature reveal
this divine law, which is the law of living. The tree gives of its
leaves to the ground to fertilize it, so that the tree may grow,
yea, even greater. Everywhere throughout nature the art of giving is being demonstrated. And so it behooves a man to learn
more about the art of giving, which is the law of living, that he
may live a more balanced life.

You see, friends, it is not what we must garner up to free
our souls. It is what we must learn to give up to free our souls.
It is the art of giving. We must learn to give up all of the error
that we have garnered up into our heads and into our minds. We
must learn to give up all those preconceived thoughts and ideas
that we have been entertaining. There's another living demonstration of the art of giving. Remember what Ralph Waldo
Emerson said: "The things that I hold are the things that I lose,
but the things that I give are the things that I have." A wise
philosopher!

What is the meaning of, There is no emotion?

Now the question is on, There is no emotion. Emotion is self,
emotion is an expression of the self, the individual self. There is
no emotion in the law of living, which is the art of giving. The
tree feels no emotion as it sheds its leaves to fertilize the soil.
There is no emotion to it. In other words, my good friends, there

is no preconceived thought in the art of giving. It is an automatic expression of nature herself. You do it because it's right to do it. You don't have to think about it; therefore, there is no emotion.

Does that also work into gratitude? Because when people give, and you find yourself giving all the time, as you certainly do, and as everyone, I think, wants to, you may sometimes have an error of thought. "Well, I'm always giving and I'm not receiving." But at the same time, you're always receiving to give and you're always feeling gratitude about it.

Absolutely! The law is very clear. He who helps another, in truth, has helped himself. And this is why the philosophers have taught that God helps those who help themselves. Because if you cannot help yourself, you can never help another. So in helping another, in truth, you're helping yourself. But you do not do it with that kind of thinking, because if you do, you're going to be constantly disappointed and bound to creation.

There is no thought in the art of giving. You never question; you just do. It is pure motive. And if the motive is pure, the manifestation is inevitable. The motive of the tree bearing its fruit is a pure motive to serve the purpose for which it has been designed. And so it is with a human being. We are a vehicle of expression of the Divine. We have been designed by Infinite Wisdom to serve a purpose. So when we are serving the purpose for which we have been designed, then we're going to be free, because we will be demonstrating the art of giving.

Now each form has its various talents. The souls have merited those forms. I wasn't born with a silver spoon in my mouth, like some people think, nor was I handed it on a silver platter. Somewhere along the line I must have merited some of it. There is no such thing as a God that hands to one and takes from another. It is all equally done.

Well, then, in other words, there are no spiritual gifts, because God does not give a gift. It's all faculty and soul and Light.

There are no spiritual gifts, to my understanding. There is no such thing as a God that gives to one and takes from another. The only way one might say a spiritual gift, is that they have merited that particular talent in this particular incarnation. Now we all have the potential. Everybody has the potential to play the piano if they have two hands and fingers and a head to move their hands, you know, and a little bit of thought. And so it is that we all have a potential, but a wise man chooses what is his basic talent and then he sticks with it. We don't scatter our forces, for a jack-of-all-trades masters none. So when man goes inside of himself and he finds out what his basic talent is, what he has been incarnated for, what purpose he has to serve, he doesn't say, "Well, I don't like that. I want this over here." Because that's what he's merited. See, nobody did it to us. We did it to ourselves.

And you merited this, that's true. You came into this—

Well, good, bad, or indifferent, I accept that I merited it, yes.

No, I mean your spiritual powers, is the way I'd like to put it, and what you are doing in this class. But you did come in with more of it than many of us who have to struggle so hard.

Well, because others have other talents that are just as needed in God's world as what little talent I may have.

During the Renaissance, so many souls were incarnated in the musical and artistic fields. Do these people merit this or do they come with this in consciousness?

The soul merits its incarnation. Did that help with your question?

I'll have to think about it. I daresay, yes, I have to think about it.

[The Teacher laughs.] It is my understanding, and I accept that understanding, that whatever happens to us has been caused by us; that we just don't come out of the blue. And here you are, you've got that body and that experience. The law that is demonstrable today is demonstrable tomorrow, and demonstrable yesterday and throughout eternity, for it is divine law.

This I accept.

The Law of Merit is the law of the Divine.

You spoke of a person coming here with a thing to do. How is a person to know if he is doing his service?

He feels fulfilled and complete. That doesn't mean that he or she does not have their struggles. But the searching, you see, there's an inner knowing that you're doing what you came to do. No one has to tell you. Your inner being knows it. And knowing it, it has all the willingness necessary to complete the job. That is my firm conviction and understanding.

Regarding the art of giving, I just want to clarify something. When you give your understanding, and very lightly indeed, because you really wouldn't want to rob the person—

Of their own growth.

Yes. And when I read about the art of giving, what struck me was that no matter how much you wanted to give to the person, and you were aware of the risk of confusion, even if you knew you could clarify the confusion, but you thought you would rob that person of their own growth.

Absolutely. Everything in its season and a season for everything. The tree does not shed its leaves haphazardly. It sheds its leaves at a certain season, according to the laws that it has set into motion. The apple tree sheds its leaves at a time, another tree at another time. And so it is with the human being. We have been given, because we have merited, discernment. We know within our inner being when we should share our understanding, where we should share our understanding, and how much of it we should share. We, our soul knows. And if we listen to the still, small voice within our inner being, that inner being will never fail us. It will say, "Time to stop. Time to go," and though you may not hear it as a voice, you can feel it as an inner feeling and it's absolutely accurate.

In this discourse, we're taught that spirits incarnate. I believe that I've become aware of previous incarnations of my spirit. I believe this to be on the earth plane. Could it be that it wasn't the earth plane? Could the previous incarnations have happened on other planes, other universes, rather than repeatedly on this earth?

It could well be. There is no limit to the Divine. And why should we entertain in thought that this is the only planet in all the vast universes, which there are no limit to; or that there is no intelligence higher evolved than man himself? That's not a very broad way of thinking, but it is a good horse-and-buggy way of thinking.

Let us broaden our horizons, for to God, all things are possible. If all things are not possible to God, then it's a very small god that we're entertaining in thought. Let us not limit the Divine. Remember, there have been many before us who have limited the Divine and found great difficulty in adjusting to what is known as the space age, to rockets landing on the moon, and different things.

So that it seemed to me that the incarnations were on earth, because of the scenery and whatnot, but that doesn't necessarily mean that it was on this earth plane.

No! Not necessarily so. Could be anywhere in the universes; there is no limit to the Spirit. You cannot limit the Limitless.

A teacher once said that she thought that she'd been reincarnated as a princess here and a queen somewhere else. And she said there was an Egyptian—she was almost convinced that it was a spirit guide—who was showing her these things and that's why she had what she thought was memory. But it wasn't memory at all. It was a spirit guide who had lived in this time and was showing her his life on the earth plane.

That is also possible, definitely.

I'd just like to say with regard to reincarnation that my main desire is to look toward the future and looking toward the future, I don't really look forward to coming back. I would rather think that I would move on to better things and so consequently, I direct the attention there.

Very good. Remember that this is our eternity. This is the only moment over which we have power. It is the only moment over which we have control. So let us become aware of the eternal moment of now, so that we may become aware of our true self. Man can never be free until he becomes aware of himself, and he has to be aware on more levels than just this old conscious brain in order to be free. Because it is not just the old conscious brain that's keeping us in bondage. It's all this computed stuff we have back here that holds us from progressing forward, onward, and upward. So let us be aware of the eternal moment of now and let us be aware of what we are, here this moment, so that we can be free.

Now, my good friends, we have time for one more question and then it's refreshment time.

One school of thought teaches that prayer, meditation, and dreams are the only tools that we need to guide us through the earth plane and I wondered if you would comment on this.

I'd be most happy to.

And also, would you tell us how dreams are authored?

The lady has stated that there is a teaching that all one needs as tools in this life are prayer, meditation, and dreams. Well, being a firm believer in doing, I totally, wholeheartedly, and completely disagree that the only tools I need are prayer, meditation, and dreams, because I believe that this is a world for the doers. And I believe that we are here with a purpose to serve; that we're not here haphazardly or by chance or to fill up a part of the space in the universe; that the Divine has placed us here according to the law set into motion by ourselves; and that here we have the great opportunity, through effort, to grow. And in growing here and now, we stand a better chance hereafter.

In reference to dreams and how they're authored, dreams, to my understanding, are caused by the suppressed desires of the subconscious mind. Sometimes there are occasions when one will have a spiritual vision during a dream state. There are times when one will even have communication and proph-ecy during a dream state. But usually, dreams are a release of energy, of desires that one has entertained in thought during the course of a day.

Now I stated once before that there is no form that doesn't dream, whether it's the man or it's the lion or it's the cat or it's the tree. All forms dream. It is a release of energy. Man does not release, in truth, one-tenth of the energy during his con-scious, waking hours. The reason that man gets so tired and so exhausted is because we're grounded at those times in our own vibration. It is a short circuiting. We can be receptive to this great power and utilize this great energy. But when we're grounded in self, that's when we become tired and we require so much sleep so we can release all that energy.

Do you realize that man is dreaming all the time he's sleep-ing? If man didn't dream and release all that pent-up energy, then man would lose the balance, the sanity, of his own mind. A great deal of research has been done at the New York Dream Institute. There have been several books printed on it and the scientists have found, through their various mechanical appa-ratuses, that by depriving an individual of sleep in order that he may dream—they found whenever a person is dreaming that their eyelids start flickering, and they would awaken them when-ever they started to dream. They soon found out that the test cases they were working on began to lose their sanity. We must release that energy. We are not releasing the energy that we are receiving in the course of a day. And so it is, that people with all of this energy, they toss and they turn and they throw the covers everywhere and they have their nightmares and they have their dreams, because they can't be at peace. They have too much energy. They're not working hard enough. That's my understanding.

Thank you. Let us go have coffee.

JANUARY 25, 1973

CONSCIOUSNESS CLASS 4 🌿

Soul may be likened unto the captain of a ship. If the captain is awake, and not asleep, then the ship will reach its destiny; the one it has set out to reach. But if the captain is asleep, the ship comes under the control of the influences of the weather and the conditions around and about it at any given time. And so it is with our soul and our body. When we awaken these minds of ours to the great truth of this eternity, this soul that is within our being this moment, then we will become the masters of this ship of clay and it will serve the purpose that it was designed to serve.

So would you ask any questions that you have this evening, please? Would you please rise?

I would like to know why meditation should be done at a certain period of time.

A very good question. The question has been asked, Why is meditation kept at a certain period of time? One of the first things a student learns on the unfoldment of one's own soul is discipline, self-discipline, spiritual discipline. System and order is the first law of the universe. Without system and order, we have chaos, and man cannot find himself, his own divinity. That is why we teach the students to choose wisely the time you're going to sit for meditation and, once having chosen that time, be honest and sincere with it.

For example, you are setting, so to speak, an appointment, an appointment with your own soul, with your own spirit, and with the levels that you are attracting at that time. If you're going to make an appointment with a friend, you don't tell him seven o'clock and show up at eight-thirty. If you do, you set a law that's most unreliable into motion. And so it is, if man cannot treat himself wisely with system and order, then he is not going to receive any beneficial result. You see, it must mean more to us than the things that distract us in this mundane world of creation.

I was thinking about the time involved in meditation itself. Why do they say not to meditate longer than twenty minutes?

Yes, in the beginning. The reason that we teach the student not to exceed a maximum of twenty minutes in any given meditation period and one meditation period per twenty-four hours is really very simple. The first thing that we have found that happens to the student is they go into a type of self-hypnosis, that they block out their conscious mind, and the thing that takes over is their own subconscious. Now remember that the faculty, the soul faculty of reason, is in our conscious mind. It is not in our subconscious mind. We teach, therefore, to keep faith with reason, for it is reason that will transfigure you. And if we are not able, you understand, to keep a conscious control over the so-called subconscious, then our emotions and suppressed desires will become the governing, ruling factor in our lives.

Many, many students that get interested in the metaphysical and in meditation and things of this nature, they think that all they've got to do is just give way and God will take over. Well, remember that God is in all things and God is in the subconscious as well as the conscious mind. And so it is that we try to train our students not to get into types of self-hypnotic trance.

Is this usually the case? Has it been proven that when people do go into a meditative state for a period of more than a half hour, they do go into a hypnotic trance?

It has been my experience over the past thirty-one years to find that most people who sit in meditation for an hour, two hours, three or four times a day, do break down the barrier to the subconscious and do become controlled by their own subconscious. Yes. That has been my experience with many, many, many students who will not listen and try to organize it in a systematized way that is without discipline.

My question is stimulated by the previous questions. Because I'm really expecting the—because I don't know . . .

Well, you check it out. I'm still checking it myself. Not that I think I know more than he *[the Wise One]* does, but God gave me a reasoning faculty. I try to exercise it.

As we sit and meditate, can we rise above our environment? Does it have to be sitting in a quiet, dark room?

Absolutely not. Positively not. Once the student has risen to a level of peace within themselves, they may use and exercise that level in anyplace at any given moment. The reason that a person chooses a quiet place in which to meditate is simply because they are controlled and brainwashed to a multitude of distractions by their own mind. You see, it is very rare that a human being in this world today spends twenty minutes in silence with God. It is a rare thing. I don't say that it is a normal thing. I say it is a rare thing. That once having attained that level of awareness, you may exercise it anywhere, anytime, at anyplace. Does that help with your question?

I have a question on Discourse 49, the second paragraph, where it states, "Whatever your beginnings may be, guard them and protect them until they are strengthened and strong to weather the forces of adversity that are destined by the law to attack them." I don't understand that.

The lady is speaking in reference to the discourse that speaks on the laws of beginning. Cherish them and treat them wisely, until they are strong enough to weather the storms of adversity, which are destined to attack them. That that is beginning is creation. That that is creation is under the Law of Duality. There is nothing in creation or beginnings, which are creation, that is not dual. Therefore, everything that has form or beginning is subject to and destined to experience the law known as adversity, its opposite.

So when a person, having a beginning, especially of a spiritual experience and a spiritual unfoldment, and speaks it out into the atmosphere, they are, in truth, feeding the Law of Adversity, which is destined to attack it. This is why the teaching is that the secrets of the universes are never given to the blabber-mouths. God's greatest work is done in silence. Because when you speak it out into the atmosphere, you are pouring energy out into creation and the adversity to your beginning will come back much sooner to you and possibly destroy what you're try-ing to set into motion. This is why I teach the students, What-ever comes to you, at least have the strength and the wisdom to keep it between you and God—for you are a majority—at least for seventy-two hours.

Is it possible that by the time the adversity catches up with you, or reaches you, that you could be at another level, so there-fore you wouldn't feel it?

That is very true. That does not mean that your creation will not feel it. Because, you see, the Law of Creation is immu-table. Man cannot change what is divine law. And the divine law is very clear and it is demonstrable: that creation, or form, is dual. Remember that God is one in essence and three in mani-festation; that is the trinity of truth.

In Discourse 48, the very last sentence reads, "We in truth are seeking to go back home, only to wander again, and again, and again." Could this be construed to mean that when you reach the eighty-first level that you might go to another planet and start all over again?

It could be. The eighty-one levels of consciousness, or the eighty-one levels of awareness—there are forty levels of soul fac-ulties, forty levels of sense functions, and one God. And so it is that we did not come from nothing and we shall not return to nothing. Man's divine spirit comes from something and every-thing returns to the home from whence it came. The leaf falls from the tree, only to come up through the tree again, to pro-duce another leaf in another day and in another time. And that is the divine law.

And we look out at nature. If we look at it wisely and we're patient and we're peaceful, we will see that nature herself is demonstrating the infinite universal cycle of constant evolution. Evolution is everywhere present amongst us. We are evolving in thought, we are evolving in form. And so it is that our soul is expanding constantly or evolving.

The soul's journey is to garner up these multitude of experiences, that it may, in time, as it returns to the source from whence it came, deposit those and evolve the form. That is the Law of Creation.

You mentioned a level of awareness.

Yes.

Could you elaborate a little more on that?

It is my understanding, in speaking on the levels of awareness, as has been stated, there are eighty-one that we are aware of. A level of awareness is—the soul rises to various states of consciousness that are within us this very moment. Some people are aware of this physical, mundane world; let us say, most people are that are in it. Some people are aware of a finer vibration of another world that is also here. They're also aware of a cosmic world; they're aware of the cosmos itself. This is because their soul has risen to varying levels of awareness that is possible to all mankind here and now.

Now when you find a person that you are in rapport with, it simply means that you are both vibrating, or expressing, on the same level of awareness. That doesn't mean that you are agreeing in your conversation, but you can be in rapport with a person. You don't know why, you just have a natural feeling for that person, even though they have an entirely different philosophy or different understanding than yourself. It means that you are on the same level of awareness, at least at that moment.

Due to your soul evolution?

Due to your soul evolution. Now remember, people think that the soul has evolved to a certain state and here we are on the earth realm. The soul, we must realize, has the ability to rise to any level that it has experienced throughout all eternity.

Therefore, a person may rise to a level of awareness within a
second inside of themselves, because they have already experienced it. What the soul has once experienced, it can repeat. Is
that intelligent to you?

Does that also apply to déjà vu?

That would apply to all things.

You said that reason is in the conscious mind.

That is my understanding, absolutely.

Now are you saying that the subconscious mind is of no value?

Absolutely not, positively not. I don't mean to imply that the
subconscious has no value. It's the memory bank. God speaks to
man through man. The superconscious speaks to the conscious
mind and the subconscious reacts or expresses. I am aware that
most teachings teach that the superconscious flows through the
subconscious. It is not my understanding or experience that the
superconscious or this divine speaks to the subconscious. To me,
it speaks to the conscious mind and the subconscious expresses.

Is it expressed through the subconscious?

It is expressed by the subconscious, yes.

By the subconscious.

Yes. The subconscious definitely serves a purpose and it has
value.

*Is it only through selfless service that a person can obtain
peace?*

A question is presented within the question. The question is
asked, Is it only through selfless service that man may obtain
peace? Now we must ask the question, What is it that robs us of
the peace that passeth all understanding? So I ask the question,
What is it that takes the peace from us that we are seeking? Is it
because our thoughts are self-related? I think we will all agree,
if we will stop, ponder, and think, that when our thoughts are
grounded in self, when they are self-oriented, we are robbed of the
peace that passeth all understanding, because we are grounded
in creation and in form. When our thoughts are concerned with

something outside ourselves, not related to ourselves, then we are freed. This energy flows through an unobstructed vehicle and deposits its divine blessings. And so he has taught that self- less service is a path to spiritual illumination.

Now a person may say and set a law into motion, "Fine, I'm going to serve selflessly in this particular area; consequently, I'll become illumined." You might as well forget it, because you've already set the Law of Self into motion. Selfless service is doing an act and entertaining a thought without concern for self. It is when the soul is serving its own divinity, which is the Divine or God, not concerned about form, that there's no thought thereof. So any time we entertain the thought that by doing selfless ser- vice we're going to be spiritually illumined, we've already set the Law of Self into motion and the Law of Self is the Law of Limitation. And the peace that passeth all understanding is not a limitation. Does that help with your question?

Thank you for that.

Thank you. You're welcome.

During meditation or dreaming or other individual experi- ences which a great many of us have had, is there any way that we can screen and select these visions or inspirational messages that we get, to determine which are the important ones and which ones are not very valid? Sometimes there seems to be a wealth of things going on and it's difficult to try to wonder, Is this an exten- sion of my own subconscious, or is it a dream, or is it just a bunch of nonsense, or is this really an important thing? Is this one of my spiritual guides, or is this just a bit of indigestion?

That's a very good question. And a very valid and a very im- portant one to anyone seeking to know themselves. And so it is in the very statement itself. When we are in the processes of un- foldment, many stop to experience a vision, a thought just drifts into the mind. The question arises, "Is this a suppressed desire of mine of about thirty years ago, or is this some thought pass- ing through the atmosphere from someone I know, or is this a guide and a teacher trying to impinge a thought upon my mind, or is this my own soul going through a different experience of who knows what time or era?" Now how can man learn spiritual discernment? Because it is spiritual discernment, the only thing that's going to free us from that hodgepodge of all these different experiences. As we begin to unfold, we start to unlock levels within ourselves in the depths of our own subconscious. The things that have been suppressed come out in symbology. They come out in visions.

Now in order to be a free channel for our own spirit, it is absolutely necessary that we empty the garbage can known as the multitude of experiences that we have had in this short earth journey. We do that through a process of daily concentration, meditation, with certain types of breathing exercises. As we start to unfold, all these experiences start to well up. Now some students, they don't see the visions and they don't hear any voices, but they start to have different emotional experiences. Some of them become highly sensitive and they can cry at the drop of a pin. What they are really doing, in truth, is they are going deeper inside themselves to reach their soul. You must go down in order to go up. Believe me, I wish I knew another way. But I only know of going down inside the self and cleaning out all of those suppressed desires, all those hopes, all those fears, all those daydream wishes until you find yourself.

And when you find yourself, you will know your path, you will know your destiny. You will know why you came to earth. You will know what you have to do. You will know where you are going and why you are here. And once you know that, you won't have to put it on television, because knowing it, you will just do it.

That's the only way I know of going through those different levels. I don't know of any other way. Maybe some other teachers have another way. I just haven't found one. But, you see, all this must come up. You know, it is very difficult for people investigating and studying Spiritualism as presented by this Serenity Association, because one might say, "Well, now, Lord, what do I credit to the spirit and what do I credit to my own subconscious? And what do I credit to something else?" This is why we have to first find ourselves. Once we find ourselves, we'll know right where to put it.

You see, it isn't God's fault that we wandered out into the wilderness and all those things are distracting us. But remember this, if you want to entertain the thought that it's my subconscious that is experiencing this or that, fine and dandy, but remember, everyone else has a subconscious, too, so you're not alone, friends, on any level.

Don't ever think you're alone on level ten or level two or level eighty, because you've got millions of other entities in the flesh and out of the flesh that are expressing on the same level. So you've got a lot of help. So that's why it's so critically important that we guard our thoughts. You think these bummer thoughts, you open the door to a whole universe of bums. Who wants to entertain that foolishness? So think good thoughts and then you open up your door to your own home, to your soul, to a multitude of angels on the same level that are willing to help you. And in so doing, of course, they'll help themselves. Thank you.

I'm just not sure about that adversity thing.

An adversity?

I can understand how in meditation something between you and God is observed in a silence and gains strength if it's shielded for seventy-two hours. But I don't quite understand how the adversity comes in. I don't really understand that.

May I ask a question of the class? Would you agree that beginnings are attachments? I ask the class: Are beginnings attachments?

Yes, the moment you're born, you're attached to creation. There's either truth or creation and we're not in truth yet.

Therefore, all beginnings are attachments. I question any-one to prove the opposite, because it is a law that is personally demonstrable. Attachment, its opposite is adversity. That is cre-ation. And this is why we are teaching, Do not be attached: you guarantee adversity. Do not be adverse: you guarantee attach-ment. Don't you see you're getting hit from both sides? And this is why many philosophers throughout the ages have taught, Be nonattached. Be in the world and not a part of the world. Be with a thing and never a part of the thing. The moment you attach, you set into motion the Law of Adversity, because that is the Law of Creation.

Could you clarify the difference between attachment and in-difference?

Yes, the lady has asked the question, What, we feel, is the difference between attachment and indifference? When a per-son becomes attached, they set into motion the Law of Creation. That attachment becomes their child. Man is responsible to him-self and to all his creations. Well, all man's creations are all his attachments and he is responsible for them. If a person has a house, they're responsible for their house. A person has a pair of shoes, they're responsible for the shoes. If they marry a person, they're responsible for the person. If they bear a child, they're responsible for the child. So man is surrounded with a multi-tude of responsibilities simply because of desire. He desires this, he desires that, he desires something else.

When a person awakens their own light within themselves, they see, "I have everything. I've always had everything. There-fore, I have no desire. Having no desire, I have no need. Hav-ing no need, I am fulfilled." That is, to me, indifference. What is there to be different with, when you've got everything? And that's what God is, to my understanding.

Man's sorrow is simply his insistence upon entertaining the thought that he needs something. Ask yourself, in the course of twenty-four hours, how many of your thoughts have stated, "I need this. I need that. I need a glass of water. I need to eat. I need to go here. I need to go there." Usually, the thought is entertained, "My God, I need more money!" Well, tax time is coming up, that's the usual procedure. You know, go right into that level of awareness, along with the masses. Start crying, because if you cry loud enough, you'll get more attention. If you get more attention, you'll get more energy. If you get more energy, you might feel better. And so it is that we continue on this insane merry-go-round of need, need, need, need, need. The longer we say, "I need this and that," then the more we're going to need.

God has given us everything. If God has not given us everything, then the god that we entertain in thought is a very stingy god and I refuse to accept that type of god in my universe. But if we entertain the thought of this divine, limitless Infinite Intelligence that takes care of everything everywhere and we entertain that type of thinking, then you can be rest assured, that kind of God will just flow through our lives and no matter what happens, to the degree of our faith, it shall ever be manifested unto us.

You see, if we have faith that we're going to get five dollars, well, God's not going to bring us five million; he's only going to bring us five, because that's all that we've accepted. We've said five dollars and so five dollars is what we're going to experience. When we could just as well have said five billion. You know, if you're going to use the energy, why not make it big? Why go for this little petty stuff? You are going to use the same energy, the same emotion.

That was a good lecture.

I didn't mean to give a lecture. You know, you speak of fulfillment, you have fulfillment.

But when these money problems come up, seemingly at tax time . . .

That's creation. Man's creation.

We just think, without giving it any consideration, "I hate to pay this" or "Gee whiz, they're asking for something again." In other words, we become the doer without thought of the reaction.

That's right and we just flow. Whatever is to be done, it is best to be done quickly. Remember, the longer we entertain a thought, the more difficult it is to escape from it. But it was your own choice.

All right, now I'm going to have to get this out of my head. What's the difference, then, between the law of opulence and the illusions of grandeur? Some people think they can do an awful lot and they go way beyond anything intelligent or sane to build these castles in the air, rather than having this law of opulence.

Yes, the difference is very simple: it is a level of awareness. One is a level of awareness created by brain and mind stuff and the other is a level of awareness of the Light itself. There's a vast difference between daydreaming and reality, a vast difference.

Is there any profit in being a creator and creating and attracting adversity and working through the adversity?

Yes, indeed, there is profit and indeed it is great wisdom. For example, the soul enters creation and as it experiences and unfolds itself, the creation through which it is expressing, its vibrations begin to be refined. For example, man today is not the man of fifty thousand years ago; he's been refined. He's constantly in a process of refinement, as the souls are constantly unfolding and evolving. You see, as the soul unfolds, the body benefits. We don't need twenty hours of sleep. That depends on our level of awareness, that depends on what we've accepted in thought. Yes, there is great benefit.

I was wondering, then, beginnings and creation and attachment are not in themselves . . .

Absolutely not, certainly not. You see, man can have all kinds of beginnings, but he can stay on a level of awareness where he is not controlled by them. Now, you see, when the tools no longer serve the worker, the worker begins to serve the tools. This is the great sadness. If we don't awaken our own soul, then what we're really doing, we're the worker serving the tool; the tool being the body, creation. We're not serving our own divinity; we're serving this piece of clay. This is what we're trying to help the students to awaken to. This thing came from down there, and down there, it's going back home to; but the soul comes from the great Allness.

When we were talking earlier, in this talk of creation and all this junk that we get, then I wondered what the purpose was to be here if we couldn't learn how to handle it?

We do learn how to handle it, when we awaken. We learn to use the tool wisely. What good is a hammer to a one-year-old who's never been trained how to use it? First thing he'd probably do is hit himself on the head. He becomes destructive.

So in all our getting, as is often said, let us get understanding. Understanding in all things in all ways. But, you see, we can't give what we haven't gotten. So we first must get understanding for ourselves, free our soul, and then we can give it. But let's get it first, because if we don't, we're in very, very deep water. Wouldn't you agree?

I think you stated that we'll never be on the same level twice or in the same place twice. I'm not sure if I misunderstood this or not. Is that to mean the soul is on level nine and it rises to level eleven and never falls back to level nine?

No. I believe, if I checked the tape, I said exactly the opposite. I believe I stated that a soul, having once arisen, for example, to level eighteen, may reexperience level eighteen at any given moment in any given era. Any time. Once the soul has experienced something, that is indelibly recorded. Nothing can or does remove it. Therefore, we may recapture it at any given moment.

OK.

You see, when a man starts to recapture the many levels of awareness, that's when he knows, beyond a shadow of a doubt, that he has forever been, and having forever been, he will forever be. There's no concern about birth and death and all that creation, because we are forever. We don't have to believe it. It's truth and it's demonstrable to every soul.

Are the eighty-one levels of awareness the nine times nine spheres that people go through?

Nine spheres and nine planes to each sphere.

I have a suppressed desire that, if I put it into action, will have a negative effect. Is there any way to get rid of that desire without putting it into action?

Absolutely. Now remember that all suppressed desires won't have negative effects by being put into action. After all, people have desires that, you know, are quite good, I would think. I have some myself, being human, you know. However, there is a way to release the energy, the pent-up energy, known as desire. There is a way. Is that what you want?

Yes. I'd like you to describe it.

When man declares the truth, the truth manifests for him and he is freed. Now, it is in *The Living Light* and the teaching is quite clear: gratitude opens the door to supply. How does man express gratitude for that that he does not yet see, for that that he does not yet hear, for that that he does not yet know? I ask you the question. Through what principle does he express that gratitude?

Through faith?

Through faith. And that's the power that transfigures us. So you want to release the energy? You know the way now, don't you? Duty, gratitude, and tolerance, faith, poise, and you'll be a humble free spirit.

I see our time is up. Thank you very much, class. Let us go have refreshments.

FEBRUARY 1, 1973

CONSCIOUSNESS CLASS 5 ✒

We will begin this evening with your questions. Does anyone have a question this evening?

Credulity and suspicion are the balance points of logic; and when they are out of balance, we express anger from the function of resentment. I don't have too much difficulty seeing credulity and suspicion as the balance points of logic; however, getting down to anger through the function of resentment—I would appreciate a little clarification.

Yes, certainly, I'll be happy to share with you our understanding. It is a characteristic of the human mind to resent that that it is suspicious of, or to resent it when it is easily imposed upon. Whenever someone imposes upon us, it causes the mind to begin to be resentful. Now this resentment takes place in the depths of our inner mind and it comes out into the conscious mind as anger. And this is why he states in that particular discourse that this anger is given birth in the function of resentment. Now, as I said, when we are of a suspicious nature and we're suspicious about this or that and that is not balanced with the credulity, which is logic, then we do have this resentment beneath the conscious level. But it does express as anger, because it is an emotion, as we all know.

[A student asked a question, but it was not possible to transcribe it.]

In the practice of meditation, the more often you do it, does that make it easier for you to reach a level known as peace? Yes, that that we practice, like playing the piano, it would come easier to us in time. However, I am sure that this class especially will note one particular thing. The meditation periods are very short. In the other two courses, they were much longer. We had different vibrations.

Now a person, when they need to tap this great power, when they have the need, they have the need that moment, not two hours later. Consequently, we're trying to help these students in this particular class to be able to touch the spirit, the spirit of spontaneity. So that when you need peace, you speak the word forth into the universe, knowing that it shall not come back to you void, but accomplish that which you send it to do, and that the reaction will be spontaneous and instantaneous. Now, it is a known fact that whenever we set a law into motion, the sooner it comes back to us, this reveals to us our level of awareness. The more aware we become, the sooner the reaction bounces back to us. And so it is that we're trying to teach these students in this class the spirit of spontaneity. You shouldn't have to take an hour to get into a state of peace. If you need peace, you need it in that moment; you don't need it an hour later. Consequently, when you sit down into your meditation, if you train yourself, you will be able to touch this great power in that moment and in that instant. And when you think "Peace," then peace will manifest for you. So it is a matter of practice and demonstration to one's self. We do not recommend that you do meditation more than once a day.

You can go into a silent period at any time throughout the day and night. What happens when you go into a silent period and you think of peace? You will touch that moment of peace that you are establishing in your daily meditation.

In my daily meditation, which is early in the morning, I find that peace, because nothing disturbs me. I need peace at work, where I'm disturbed all day, and just the minute I get it, somebody wants me and I'm running back and forth and all over. Do we just put our mind on peace, if you're walking or talking? I mean, you can close out—

Absolutely and positively. The moment you think and speak the word "Peace," then you are, at that moment, in that level of awareness. Absolutely. If you have established in your daily meditation, this awareness to this level of peace, which is the

Power itself or God, and you speak that word forth into the atmosphere and your minds are united, that is, your conscious and your subconscious mind are in harmony, you will touch the peace that passeth all understanding the moment that you speak it. That is the purpose of these spiritual awareness classes. Because we need peace during the course of all these day-to-day acts and activities. We're constantly being triggered, if we want to be triggered, to the level of people that we are associating with. You see, we're going up and down through all these levels, not day by day, but moment by moment. You can be miserable in one moment and you can be joyous in the next moment. So you see, it's all taking place inside of us. It's from a matter of losing self-control that we have become brainwashed and influenced by people and circumstances around and about us. We automatically react, we don't stop, we don't pause to enter that level of peace.

In Discourse 17 of The Living Light, *it states that the faculty of tolerance corresponds to the function of friendship. Could you clarify that for me?*

Duty, gratitude, and tolerance.

And the one that goes with tolerance is friendship? The function of friendship. Is that right?

What was stated the other week? This is very important, you know. God gave us a mind to think with. It's in Discourse 17 the lady says. Now let us check. Read the part in reference to the faculty.

"We should like to carry on at this time with a bit more discussion on the functions and faculties, with the first faculty being duty, gratitude, and tolerance, corresponding to the counterbalance of the function of self, pity, and friendship."

Exactly. Thank you very much. Now everyone now knows that it's in Discourse 17. Duty, gratitude, and tolerance; self, pity, and friendship. Fine. Now the question is, What does friendship have to do with tolerance? Is that the question? I'm sorry to take so long with this particular question, but it's very important, because the answer is given in *The Living Light*. But if we do not study the book and find it, then it's not going to benefit us.

Now the statement was made by this particular teacher that true friendship, being use and not abuse, respects the right of difference and will weather any storm. Now without tolerance, you understand, there is no friendship. It does not exist. Because if you don't have tolerance, you cannot respect the right of difference. Man cannot respect any differences that he views without tolerance inside of himself.

For example, many people feel that they have great trouble with being tolerant. The difficulty is not being tolerant with others: the difficulty is being tolerant with our own levels, because the levels that we cannot tolerate in another person we have not yet educated in ourselves. So the process is a self-education and a self-discipline one.

Now the lady has asked, Why is the function friendship? Do you have a clearer understanding of why that function is friendship? Go to the other two points of that faculty.

Duty and self, and gratitude and pity.

Gratitude and pity.

I was thinking that in friendship, there is tolerance, but then it came to me that I have been a friend, and had friends, and there hasn't been tolerance, but still we have been friends. This has confused me.

There is friendship because you tolerate the right of difference. If you do not tolerate the right of difference, there is no friendship. Do you respect their right to be different?

Oh yes.

Therefore, then, you have friendship.

But when I was thinking about it, it came to me that there are cases of friendship where there isn't tolerance. There's great abuse and still there's friendship.

But is that friendship? [Another student asks.]

True friendship, being use and not abuse, respects the right of difference and will weather any storm.

Would you clarify that neutrality is a law of love in operation? I carried that with me all week.

Neutrality is a law of love in operation. Absolutely and positively. Because God, the Divine, is the greatest servant of all, totally neutral. It's not partial in any way, shape, or form.

That really gave me an anchor all week. I love that.

Thank you very much. Any other questions this evening?

Going again to the first faculty, is it possible to dissect the triad? In other words, do you have to take the three as three?

Absolutely. They are inseparable. All faculties, all functions are triune and they are inseparable. They are manifestation in the three. They are inseparable. Duty and gratitude cannot be separated from tolerance, no more than tolerance can be separated from duty and gratitude. And it is the same thing with the function, which is its opposite. I'm sure that will help clarify things to the class, with a little bit more study. Anyone else?

Talking on the function of pity, I was aware that pity is a function. Pity on one side and compassion on the other. And there is a difference. And compassion is a faculty.

And pity is a function.

A negative. In other words, compassion is positive and pity is negative.

Absolutely. Definitely. Now when you read that function, you read pity and what else?

Self.

And?

Friendship.

Pity, self, and friendship. Think about that, class. It's very, very important. It will broaden your horizons. When you think of friendship, think of pity, and think of self. They are inseparable. Give it a little thought. We'll discuss it more next week, unless some of you have questions on it at this time.

Remember what faculty is its opposite. Why does man seek a friend? What is the motive? What is the motive for seeking friendship? Anyone have the answer? The motive, if we look at friendship, is exactly what friendship is: use and not abuse. Friendship is a mutual sharing, with a responsible respect for the right of difference for the friend to share or not to share at any given moment. That is my understanding of true friendship. There is an exchange of energy that doesn't take place twenty-four hours a day. In fact, if you want to lose a friend, just live with them a while. All right, class, let's go on now. Please give it some thought. Any questions?

I would like to ask for some clarification on the law of karma on cause and effect. We're taught here, As you sow, so shall you reap. Is this a literal kind of saying? For instance, if I steal a book, could I expect someone to literally steal a book from me?

No, but you could expect a fulfillment of the Law of Stealing. It wouldn't have to be a book. The law would be equal to the energy that was taken from you. For example, if you stole a book from someone and that caused that person 50 percent energy release into the emotional realm and disturbance, you would receive an exact 50 percent drain of your energy in some area through the Law of Stealing.

How does this relate to where we finally wind up when we pass over to the spirit world?

How does it relate to the location or where we would—what we have done here and now? Yes, what we are doing here, this moment, is not only affecting our physical life in this material world, but it is affecting our mental plane, our mental life, and our spiritual life. And it's doing that here, now, this very moment. Things of the spirit are not only discerned by the spirit, but they are composed of spiritual substance. When the faculties—When the energy, this divine power, is expressed through the faculties, there goes out into the atmosphere a spiritual substance. This spiritual substance builds, so to speak, our abode in the world of spirit. Therefore, the teaching is to balance these faculties with the functions, because you're going to go to another dimension.

You can go there this instant, you understand, if you will open your eyes and your ears and your senses and you will see whether or not you're on some desert someplace, where there's not even a drop of water, because that's all the energy that has flowed through your soul faculties. So a wise man says, "Fine and dandy. I'm going to get myself into balance and I'll put 50 percent energy into this world that I'm aware of, this gross physical world, and I'll put the other 50 percent into this other dimension that I don't see right now, but I'm destined to see at any moment." You know, we're going to see it either by awakening our spiritual sight while in this flesh or by leaving this flesh, you understand, and then we're going to see it.

Now why is it that when we leave the physical body, we view this mental dimension or astral or spiritual world? Well, it's very simple. This thing, known as the brain, is the cloud that's over our vision. The longer we entertain thoughts that are self-oriented, the longer we entertain thoughts of this gross material world, that is the difficulty in us piercing into the other dimension, sensing and feeling these finer vibrations. And so it's up to us to make the changes. But what we're doing here and now is building not only our material world around and about us, but right here and now we're building our spiritual one. Let's hope we're all building in both dimensions.

There's a statement in The Living Light *that God is neutral. It's a very fascinating thing, because when I was a little boy in almost all organized religions it taught us that God is over here and hell and the devil are over there. And there's a big battle going on all the time. And lately, everybody said that God was dead, because He would not allow all the terrible things that go on in this world. And* The Living Light *says that God is neutral. It's very fascinating.*

Yes. One of the greatest things that ever happened was when *Time* magazine came out on its cover and said that God was dead.

Because the god of the past and, unfortunately or fortunately, of many people of the present, is a god of duality. Now duality we understand and know, and it is demonstrable that duality is creation. And so if we entertain in thought a god of duality, what we are, in truth, doing is entertaining a god of creation that we have created in our minds. Now that's a mental god. Having a beginning, those mental gods, they're going to have an ending.

And so now, here in this age of light of the Aquarian Age, we've come to an understanding that God is neutral. The first understanding I had of a neutral God was when the Old Man brought it about in those discourses. I've yet to read it anyplace else, but I'm sure that it must be somewhere, because truth is one. Remember, if God is neutral—and that is the teaching of the Living Light—if God is neutral, and we are neutral or balanced, then we're going to be in God. And so it stands to reason that if we balance our lives, we balance these faculties and these functions. We don't annihilate them: we balance them. Then we're going to be flowing in God and God is everything. So we'll have no obstructions in our path, if we will just remain neutral. Does that help?

Yes.

I'm sure, you see, as long as man entertains created gods, a god that's good has to have its opposite, of bad. A god of joy has to have its god of sadness, and on through the entire spectrum of human relations. So let us be more neutral and then we can be at peace. And being at peace, this power will just flow unobstructed and accomplish its great good.

Yes, it is the understanding of Serenity that God is neutral. God doesn't start war. God doesn't end war. How can He end what He doesn't start? God didn't begin creation, and God doesn't end creation. The law is totally impartial. The electricity flows through the light bulb. It doesn't care whether it's red, green, purple, yellow, or white. It is not concerned; it has no concern. The Divine Power, known as Infinite Intelligence, just flows through form.

Why is man good, if you can call it good? Remember, one man says, "I'm very good." The person over there says he's an SOB, because good to one is bad to another. And so we go through all this insanity of duality. We can't find peace that way. Millions and billions of people have tried to find God through creation. You don't find truth, or God, until you can separate truth from creation.

And then, you look and see that the Divine Power flows through everything, everywhere, at all times, in all places. It had no beginning and by that law of no beginning, it cannot end. So remember, our God is ever equal to our understanding at any given moment. And when all of religion comes to that awakening, there will no longer be any battles in the world, for there will be nothing to battle. We've always been, we'll always be, so what's the sense of fighting about it?

One final question.

Now remember, finality is beginning.

Will there ever be this understanding of religion?

"Will there ever be this understanding of religion?" It's on its way. In fact, it is taking place in many areas that are not seen by the physical sight and the physical hearing or senses. Yes, the God of neutrality has come to man and it is here to stay. Absolutely. But remember, the understanding of a divine neutral Power can be most detrimental to anyone who does not have a degree of self-control, because the first thing they do with that great understanding is to put it into license, instead of freedom. And when you put it into license, you guarantee bondage and destruction.

I can say, from what has been given to me over the years, that the understanding of a Divine Neutrality that is totally neutral, was one of the basic causes of the sinking of Atlantis and Lemuria. Because it was abused, instead of used. But remember, it's like electricity. If you don't use it according to the law under which it operates, it will electrocute you; it will destroy you.

You made a reference to the Age of Aquarius coming in.

It's already here.

The law or the science of astrology, is that part of the cause and effect or is it a science that is truthful throughout the universe?

The science of astrology, when properly understood and applied, is the science of mathematics, and mathematics is the key to the universe. Whether they call it astrology, astronomy, or some other "ology," it doesn't make any difference. If it is used correctly and understood, it is the key to the universes. Yes.

What is the meaning of this being the Age of Aquarius, instead of the age of something else?

The meaning of the Age of Aquarius, instead of something else, has to do with astronomy or what you want to call astrology. Either one, it doesn't make any difference. The planets are in space and they're revolving in certain ways. It is a mathematical calculation, and each age offers to this particular earth realm at any given time certain vibrations. At the present age for man, this is the age of air. This is the age of communication, because it is the Aquarian Age. All things dealing with the element air will be revealed to this earth plane in these coming centuries.

Is air like the mind?

Yes. Thought travels through what you call air or space.

Someone said to me, "I don't concern myself with these people who have passed on through accident or holocaust or whatnot. I just don't speak about it." And I said, well, compassion is a faculty, and you must have compassion, because these people will awaken in the spirit world and they will be so confused. Our feeling compassion for them—sending out a prayer for their enlightenment and being put on the path—will help them. Is this not so?

I'd like to make some clarification in regards to your statement. Compassion, being a soul faculty, does not interfere with the divine Law of Cause and Effect. Now for example, compassion sees the law that has been set into motion, do you understand? It is a soul faculty. The soul faculties are Light; the sense functions are darkness. Now for example, you cannot have compassion, true compassion, without consideration. Would you agree? Do you agree that you can't have compassion without consideration?

Consideration, to me, would be compassion.

All right. Now you can't have consideration unless you have reason, because how can one consider something that they cannot reason? And you cannot have reason without total consideration or compassion. Therefore, if someone has what appears to be an accident, number one, there are no accidents in the universe and reason knows that. Reason knows that there is a cause for all things, would you not agree?

Yes.

Reason knows that if we had what appears to us to be an accident, it is nothing more than the effect of a law that we have set into motion somewhere along our path. Would you not agree?

I do agree to that, yes. I know that what happens to me either way—

Has been caused by you. And therefore, that law applies to you and would you not grant that divine, just law to every form?

I would, but I still feel compassion for them.

One can have compassion without interference. That's the difference. If we interfere with the effect of a divine law, then we're in the function; we're not in the faculty. That's not quite clear to you yet? I have a lot of hands raising.

Is it that we should or shouldn't have compassion?

Oh, God forbid, I do not teach that you should or shouldn't have it. We all have it, if we want to express it. That is our divine right of choice.

I don't understand what you are getting at.

I can have compassion for two animals killing each other, one killing the other one, and I can have reason not to interfere and get myself torn up in the process. What I am saying is, if you have true compassion, soul compassion, then you have consideration. And if you have consideration, you have reason.

Now, for example, if you see two people out there murdering each other, do you go up there and interfere and say, "Just a moment! You don't do that!" and get killed yourself in the process? Now if we have pity, we'll just zoom right in there. If we have compassion, we'll have the reason, and reason will tell you what to do. Keep faith with reason; she will transfigure you. Reason will show the way. Reason is the light of the soul. The God I understand is a God of reason, which is total consideration.

Will flows through the functions on a particular level, as I understand it. So if we look at something, a situation or a so-called accident or whatever, on the physical level, through the functions, then we are, in effect, imposing our will on another.

Absolutely, definitely, and positively. Thank you very much. I'm sure that will help many.

It seems that the faculties are of a consciousness higher than the functions.

The question is, Are the faculties of a higher consciousness than the functions?

No. It seems that.

It seems that.

It seems that. And that the faculty overcomes the function or that it's better to use the faculty than the function. And then, how do you get a balance?

No! No, that is not the teaching. The teaching is not that the faculties are—what did you say, a greater, a higher?

They are the soul.

They are of the soul. But remember, our soul, our spirit, is encased in form in the soul and in the mental body and in the physical body, the astral body, and all those other bodies. So remember that a man uses balance in all things if he is wise. We have functions in which our soul may express itself in a physical dimension.

The teaching is not to annihilate or downgrade the functions. The teaching is to balance each function with its corresponding soul faculty. Now for example, procreation is a function, but remember, its birth is in the soul: to procreate the race, the species. So you see, the functions serve a good purpose, if it is under the light of reason, which is the corresponding soul faculty.

Now if you will study the faculties and functions that have been given in *The Living Light,* in order that you may not become controlled by creation, which is form—each function has a corresponding soul faculty. So if you'll direct your attention, which is your energy, equally through the corresponding soul faculty, you will have balance while yet in creation. You will be in this world and you will not be a part of this world. You will be with things, and you will never be part of things, because 50 percent of you is in the function and 50 percent is in the counterbalance of the soul faculty.

At the same time that you are going through the faculty, if you're putting forth the function, a part of you is still in touch with—

Absolutely. It's known as divided attention. When they split the atom, you have power; when the attention is divided, you have balance. Think of it.

Yes, I have to agree.

If you have meditation without concentration, you're out of balance. If you have concentration without meditation, you're out of balance. You see, this is why he teaches the students to have concentration, meditation, and manifestation. There you have your trinity. There you have your creation.

And so it is with your functions and soul faculties. Divided attention. Divided attention keeps you unattached. And the teaching is to be with all of these things and not be a part of them. And you cannot be with them and not be a part of them unless you have your energies split or your attention divided at the time of expression. Otherwise, you're going to become attached. That's man's problem: he's attached to one emotion after another.

I thought we had decided it was all right to be attached. That we needed attachments in order to work through them.

The only thing that we decided, to my recollection, last Thursday, was we were discussing that attachment guarantees adversity and adversity guarantees attachment. So why be attached? Because you're going to be adverse. And why be adverse? Because you're going to be attached. Don't you see?

No, I don't, because I thought the purpose of our being here was to free ourselves from attachment.

That is our purpose.

Well, then, if we don't have attachments, we can't learn to be free.

My dear friend, the moment the soul incarnated into form, the attachment was guaranteed. We're trying to get out of it, not to stay in it. We're trying to serve the purpose of the soul's incarnation in form. We set a law into motion that zipped us right into them. Yes.

We have them. The thing is, we don't have all the attachments, but we take on some more.

Every moment of every hour, we're garnering up more attachments. It isn't what we have to put into the mind that's freeing it. It's what we have to get out of the mind in order to free it. And so it is that we're constantly bombarded with attachment upon attachment and adversity upon adversity.

He is trying to teach the student the path to freedom, not tomorrow, not in eternity, but this moment, this eternity, this instant. And so he's trying to teach balance and counterbalance, to keep us on the neutral path, so that our spirit may flow freely at all times in all things. He does not teach good and bad. He does not teach, for example, that you shouldn't do this or you shouldn't do that. He's trying to teach divided attention in all things. Keep your soul on the soul level and keep your spirit on the spirit level, your mind on the mind level, your body on the body level, but keep them all in balance. And by keeping them in balance, you will soar freely through time and space.

The only reason that we're not aware of the great solar system right this instant (because we are a part of the entire solar system) is simply because we have not risen our soul to a solar consciousness right here and now. We can do that, but we first must let go of this bondage, this attachment that we have to this physical creation.

Now a person might say, "I'm not attached to this physical world. All my thoughts are way out there in space." But how long have they been out there in space? Maybe six months out of sixty years. No. It's a daily practice. We spend how many hours and how many moments thinking about this mundane world? How many moments, in truth, do we really spend thinking about the universal consciousness?

You see, the point is not to have meditation once a day and think about this universal consciousness at the time of your meditation and then go out into this material, mundane world and never think about it again until the next morning. That's ridiculous! You think about it moment by moment.

You're out on a mundane job—I have just as much mundane work as anyone in this room. I know that is an absolute fact. If anyone questions me, I wish they'd come to the office and go through one of my days with me. I have exactly as much mundane work, if not more, as any student here, and yet I make sure to keep my conscious awareness divided. Otherwise, this other part would go, it would disappear, simply from lack of use. You know, lack of use is abuse. If you're a pianist and you don't play the piano for years and you get up to play it again, well, you hardly know how to play because lack of use is abuse of the talent that you have. So whatever your talents may be, use them;

don't abuse them. If you don't use them, they're not going to flow and they're not going to improve.

You see, that's what we are trying to teach: to be universal in your thought and you will be universally expressing your own divinity. Don't think of this type of an understanding just once or twice a day. You want a job doing bookkeeping? I do bookkeeping seven days a week. You want a job doing typing? I do typing seven days a week. In fact, I learned to type in this Association. Coming right along! But my thoughts are not on that typewriter all the time and they're not on all those figures all the time. They don't have to be. They don't have to be.

You can be aware of more than one dimension if you, and you alone, will make the effort. But you've got to make the moment-to-moment effort. Just learn to be still, so that you can hear. Learn to disassociate. He says here in his book [*The Living Light*], you want to awaken your clairaudience? You want to hear? Then, learn to disassociate. Learn the Law of Disassociation. Disassociate from all of the stuff and then you will hear. After all, I'm hearing on several dimensions. It's possible for everyone, but you've got to make the effort every moment. Now we must get on to these other groups.

How can we hear better our . . .

How can you what?

Hear better our conscience.

How can you hear better—Are you referring to hearing in other dimensions?

Either way. Both.

All right. Now that's a very good question. Now remember that energy follows attention. Again and again, the teaching is the same, for truth is one, not two. And so the teaching is whatever you place your attention upon, you have a tendency to become.

If you want to sharpen the hearing, you want to learn to hear better, direct this energy, through this power of will, right here, direct it to the hearing. I just happen to be hearing the ocean's roar. It sounds like I have a shell up to my ear, but I directed it to my ears. Now everybody can do the same thing, but you have to blot out all of this stuff in that instant, by directing your thought, your energy, to your ears and you will hear much, much better.

Any questions over here? I can tell. I see the question mark jumping up and down. Kindly rise.

I'm going to learn while I have the chance.

Well, I see that little question mark jumping up and down in front of you and I said to myself, "I wonder if that's a guide or just a question mark?" And my spirit said, "Richard, that's your mind."

I just wanted to talk about attachment again.

Attachment.

I seemed to get an impression as I was sitting here. It seems that families are attached and yet the Bible says the sins of the father are visited upon the children.

Unto the third generation.

Yes.

And why is it the third generation?

The trinity. The three.

The manifestation. We are physical, mental, and spiritual and those three levels must be worked out. And so unto the third generation are the so-called sins, which are nothing but errors, invested unto the children. But remember that the children have merited that experience through laws that their souls have set into motion.

I can understand how we want to work away from attachment, but I've always heard that one of the most important principles of Spiritualism has been learning the interdependence of the Allsoul.

The interdependence of the Allsoul. Now, we're talking about form now.

*Well, I'm not sure. Now are you talking about attachment in
relation to form and I'm thinking of interdependence in relation
to spiritual forms?*

Form is form, regardless of what dimension form is expressing on. The first thing that we try to do, in regards to attachments, is to refine our attachments. Did you ever take a man
who drinks or smokes and all of a sudden, you tell him, "You
stop that. It's an attachment"?

It's known as the Law of Transmutation, the Law of Re-
placement. So the first thing that Spiritualism tries to do for
the masses and the people is to refine their attachments. Not to
say, Get rid of all your attachments, because the people won't
do it anyway. They've been in them too long. So what we have
to do for them is to refine them and replace them with a higher-
vibration attachment.

You see, instead of attaching to this physical substance, well,
now, let's grow and be attached to a spiritual thing. You see? It's
still form, I admit that, but you can't change them any other
way. A slow growth is a healthy growth. So the first thing they
start to do, they attach to the science of communication. They
attach to guides and teachers and these other dimensions, etc.
Then, in time, we grow on and then we attach to universal consciousness. Don't you see? You cannot just take attachment. It's
too gross. It's too locked in.

When you move into Spiritualism—What pulls the people
to Spiritualism? What is the Light? What is the magnet that
attracts them out of the atmosphere to Spiritualism? It is the
science of Spiritualism. Without the science, we would not have
the philosophy, for the philosophy came to Spiritualism through
its science. However, if a person, coming into Spiritualism and
its refining process of their own attachments to the material
world, moves up to attachments to the spiritual forms and does
not go beyond that to the philosophy, to the laws that govern all

form, then we have spiritists and spiritism. We no longer have Spiritualism and you cannot find the religion of Spiritualism unless you balance its science with its philosophy.

Because, you see, it is one thing to communicate with another dimension, but it is a much wiser thing to understand the laws that you use to communicate with those dimensions. So we must gradually refine our attachments.

And remember, when we see the All, we will find the One. And when we find the One, we will be free because we will be All. So let us gradually, as we refine our attachments and we lose them, go to the oneness of the Divine. And having done that, we will be free in all things at all times.

Thank you. Good night. Our time is passed. Let us go have refreshments.

FEBRUARY 8, 1973

CONSCIOUSNESS CLASS 6 ✀

Before our questions and answers this evening, I would like to speak about a thought. Now, you know, according to the teachings that everything, in truth, is triune, and so it is with thought.

Very few people realize that thoughts are either neutral, electric, or magnetic. Now I'll try to explain a little bit about that at this time. For example, it has often been stated by this particular teacher that the longer you entertain a level of awareness or thought, the more difficult it is for you to get out of it. The reason why it is difficult, the longer you entertain it, is that you entertain it in length of time according to how much you believe in the thought that you are entertaining. And so a thought which is coupled with belief, that type of a thought is magnetic. It is like a great magnet that attracts unto itself.

Then you have the type of thought that is neutral. For example, you have the thought, "It's a beautiful day." That is a neutral type of thought. You don't believe it's a beautiful day, that's another level. You know it is a beautiful day. Why do you know that it is a beautiful day? Because you have been educated that it is a beautiful day. That is a neutral type of thought.

Then you have the type of thought that is electrical. That type of thought comes from the depths of your own spirit. It doesn't only come with knowledge, it comes with wisdom and it comes with understanding.

And so it is in the course of any moment in any day that we are constantly releasing from our aura one of three types of thought: magnetic, electric, or neutral. And therefore it behooves us to go deeper inside ourselves and find out from what level the thought has originated. And in finding out what level it is originating on, we will know exactly what will happen to us, the longer we entertain it.

You may feel free to ask any questions that you have on any of the subject matter.

If it is true that man's soul sets into motion the laws affecting himself, then is it not the soul that determines where and when it will incarnate into form, whom it wishes to use as a vehicle or mother in which to incarnate, the place, astrological aspects, race and so forth, lessons to be learned here, when it will shed its clay body, etc.? And if so, then does it follow that the soul expresses to our guides and teachers how to guide us? There are all levels of guides and teachers and somehow despite their varying levels of awareness they all manage to help us in a direction consistent with that which the soul wishes to go.

And that is, indeed, a very deep question. The statement has been made in the teachings that whatever happens to us is caused by us; that man is a law unto himself. The lady has expressed her interest that if that is a true statement, then does it not stand to reason and to logic that the soul chooses its incarnation and its various experiences? Well, to a certain degree. Let me put it this way: perhaps some light could be shed over that. The soul, by laws that it has set into motion, propels itself, like a great magnet, out into the universe. It does not, to the best of my awareness, pick a particular parent named so-and-so in a particular city. But it does, from laws it has set into motion, go along a principle whereby the experiences necessary for its own unfoldment will be guaranteed.

And so it is, as we step here from day to day, we are never left without choice. But the choice that we have is the moment that we have control of. If we make a choice this moment, we set a law into motion. Now remember that is one of the minor laws, for we have a major law governing us from all eternity that we're constantly passing through.

So man stands ever at the threshold between postponing or fulfilling what he has set into motion. Now if he is ever postponing his own destiny, then that is the destiny that he alone has set into motion. Now by this teaching we don't mean to imply total predestination. After all, we can make a choice at any given moment, but we must choose within the ballpark that we alone have created. For example, some people may have 50 or 60 different variables that they have to work with at any given moment because that is what that particular soul has set into motion. Someone else may have 120, and someone else may only have 30 or 40. Does that help with your question? Anyone else?

I do TM meditation and I don't concentrate on peace, but I receive peace. And I was wondering if that would be better than your meditation for me?

Well, that is a very interesting question and I would be an absolute fool to say that was better or that was worse. I try to remain neutral in these types of things, recognizing for myself, as I do for all others, their divine birthright of choice. However, are you aware that you are not concentrating, or are you concentrating and not aware that you are concentrating? You see, that's the question that must be asked. Because, you see, many people are in the process of concentrating and they're not aware that they are concentrating at all, because they think that concentration is forcing the will.

I happen to see a white rose in front of me that is caused by the powers of concentration. Now, you see, the first thing is to become aware of what concentration really is. If a person is entertaining the thought of peace during meditation, to some extent they are concentrating, because they're not entertaining the thought of its opposite, or war. Therefore, a type of concentration, to some degree, is taking place.

And so I do not see any question in reference to whether or not that particular type of meditation you are doing, or the meditation that is being taught here, is better for you or not. Remember, what works for a person is usually the best thing for them at any given moment. But I would not go so far as to say that concentration is not taking place during your meditation. Many people think that they're just meditating when they're concentrating and they really think they're concentrating when they're really meditating. We understand meditation to be a complete absence of all thought. So if you are experiencing peace during meditation, that only reveals to me as a teacher that, in truth, you are concentrating. Does that help with your question? Thank you. Anyone else?

We really haven't talked much about animals. I wondered if you would be good enough to discuss their purpose on earth, their relationship to man, how man can help them in their incarnation. And does the positive acceptance of an animal on the earth determine where it goes after life or whether it stays in form after life? And would you explain the difference in the relationship between man and animals, with respect to their vibrations?

Yes, you have about eighteen questions in one and I'll do my best to share my understanding with the students this evening. I believe the question is in reference to animals, their purpose in creation, and man's relationship to them and their vibration.

It is my understanding at this time that man, his form, is the highest-evolved animal on the earth planet. I presume that you are speaking, of course, about the "four-legged people." In reference to these so-called creatures or four-legged animals, they all serve their purpose, like the animal known as man serves his purpose. The soul is incarnated into all forms on this earth planet. The soul, its essence, is in the blade of grass, the tree, as well as the human animal and the four-legged animal.

Now it is a known fact that animals have certain instincts, like self-preservation. They do not have concern for their brethren, whether they eat or don't eat; they only have concern for themselves. And so it is that many times when that tendency, I guess you could call it greed, is expressed in the human animal, people call that the animal instinct.

Now when we recognize and accept that the Divine Intelligence, God, this Allsoul is expressing through all forms in all universes, when we rise to that level of awareness, we will not be able to see any difference between the ant and the angel, because no difference, in truth, truly exists. It would be like saying that one man wears a suit and another one wears a pair of dungarees and therefore there's a difference. The only difference, my good friends, is the covering that the Divine is expressing through at any given moment.

The animal has a degree of intelligence. It has emotions. It has a degree of memory. And it does carry on after it leaves this physical earth realm. The tree has intelligence; even the rock has intelligence. There is nothing in form that intelligence, which is God, is not expressing through anywhere, at any time, in anyplace. Infinite Intelligence is just exactly what it says it is: it is intelligence infinitely manifest throughout all form.

It has been stated that love is the language of the soul. If you wish to communicate with another form and you express love from your form, then you will be able to communicate, whether it is a four-legged person or it's a two-legged one. It won't make any difference. Science has recently proven what the Spiritualists have tried to teach for over a hundred years: that the plant and the tree have emotion; that they have senses and feelings, just like the two-legged animal has senses and feelings. So, in truth, there is no difference in any form, anyplace, at any time.

Now how long does the form of an animal stay in the spirit world? We understand that the animal stays in form as long as there is love emanated to the animal, the creature, the insect, the whatever-it-is. But be rest assured, my good friends, there is no animal, no insect, nothing in creation that someone, someplace doesn't love. Whether it's a little pebble in a brook, or it's an ant or it's a snake, it doesn't matter. There is love emanated to that form.

In The Living Light, *it says that the Divine Light expresses itself through form. Does this mean that when we all are evolved high enough and return to the Divine Light, that will be all imaginable activities, shapes, forms, and expressions?*

It most certainly does. All things the soul can and does create. Absolutely and positively. Remember, what we are, in truth, is Light. The question was, Do all things imaginable—can they be created? Is that the basis, the essence of the question? Absolutely and positively! What man usually does not realize is that he is creating all of these shapes and forms and things here, this very moment, this very instant. He doesn't see them with his physical vision simply because he has not created them into a physical dimension as yet. That does not mean that they do not exist.

And this is the great importance of what you entertain in thought. Now again, again, and again, it's been stated that imagination is the doorway to the world of spirit. It is not the world of spirit, but it is the doorway through which we must pass to enter this world of spirit. Now for example, when you do your exercises as have been given in your study book, like the fountain exercise and the different exercises, you will start to use the creative principle and that is what it is all about.

Now a person says, "Well, I don't want just an imagination. I don't want to *imagine* that I'm contacting the world of spirit." My good friends, what do you think all this form is in this physical world? This is all imagination. What has created it is the Divine Principle, the creative principle expressed through imagination. That is why imagination is the doorway to the world of spirit. You must imagine something different, so that you can be receptive to something different. You cannot be receptive to something that you cannot imagine. You have to open the door, and the door is opened through imagination.

For example, we try to teach the student to concentrate upon peace. Well, if they can't imagine peace, then they cannot be receptive to the level known as peace. That is why imagination is the door. And so it is, I happen to see an elephant in front of me. I just imagined him. I didn't consciously do it, but I triggered the level known as creative, the creative principle level, and in that level, all things can be imagined and created. This is the creative principle: imagination. And so when the world imagines that there is a world of spirit, they will step into that world of spirit. You can't expect a dire materialist to accept a world of spirit, because he cannot imagine anything except the imagination of his own materialism. Does that help with your question?

I would like an explanation of the second state of consciousness, which is slave. What is it a slave to?

Thank you very much. The question is in reference to the second state of consciousness, which is slave. If you will recall, he has stated in *The Living Light* that the first state of consciousness is self-preservation. When we express this level known as self-preservation, the next state of consciousness is to be a slave to that which preserves us. We make a master out of anything that helps us to stay in the level that is satisfactory to us.

Therefore, we move from self-preservation, to preserve the self, to becoming a slave to the things that we compute preserve us.

You see, whatever you have faith in, you become. And so does all creation. Whatever you believe—do you understand? If you believe that you need such and such, and such and such, and such and such to preserve you the way you wish to be, you become a slave to that very thing. And this is why a wise man chooses the formless and the free. If he is not aware of the bondage while yet in form, he will most assuredly be aware of the bondage when he leaves this physical dimension, because then he will see the mental world of his own creation. And so we are a slave.

That's why he said, in a very short way, in a little statement, when he said, "When the tools no longer serve the worker, the worker begins to serve the tools." And so it is that our soul is serving creation, instead of the formless and the free, which is its divine birthright. If our soul were not serving creation, then we would not have faith and fear: we would have freedom. But let us move gradually up the ladder and let go of one attachment for a finer one. Thank you. Any other questions?

In the same discourse, the other states of consciousness, the third, fourth, fifth, and sixth, are these regarding how you evolve through?

Absolutely. How you evolve through, from level to level and on up through. Absolutely and positively. Remember that it is certainly not the easiest thing in the world—the things that are beneficial to the soul are not usually appealing to the mind because the mind is a dual instrument and it is magnetically bound by creation. And therefore, things of the soul level, things of the spirit, which are formless and free and universal, do not often appeal to the mind. They appeal to the heart. They appeal to the feelings, the inner being. They don't appeal to the mind.

It is better to have a small class of quality, interested in the soul and the spirit, than to have hundreds packed into this room that are only interested in intellectual entertainment of the mind. We could go either way, you know. It just so happens that I chose some time ago to go this way. Quality, not quantity, is the keynote of Spirit. Thank you.

Do you always sit when you meditate? Is there any difference when you are sitting or lying down?

Yes, there's all the difference in the world between sitting and lying down for meditation, to my understanding and experience. The divine energy, often called prana, this fluid that flows in the being and in the body, when we are lying down, this fluid is also still. It does not reach the base of the brain and awaken the psychic and spiritual glands that are located in the head, in the forehead. And when a person is in the prone position of lying down and going into any type of receptivity or meditation, they become receptive to what is known as the animal vibration.

Now, by that, I don't mean animals are bad. I happen to like them very much myself. But they do become receptive to what is known as the animal instinct. They become receptive to those vibrations. Therefore, a person in meditation should keep the spine erect for many good reasons, that being one of them.

It is the nature of animals, which are in the level of self-preservation, to express what the mind computes as greed, or selfishness, because they're trying to protect themselves in a dog-eat-dog world. And so it is that it is most advisable to be in a sitting position during meditation. Thank you.

It stated that there are nine levels of consciousness and six are given. May you give the other three?

Six have been given in *The Living Light* and that's all I have been permitted to give publicly. However, I am sure if you get through those six levels, you'll reach divine love and be well on your way to divinity and freedom. Thank you.

I was just wondering if you could talk about fear and faith? You said they're the same.

Yes. Fear and faith, it's given in *The Living Light* that they're one and the same power; that when this energy is expressed through the functions, you experience what is known as fear. When identically the same energy is expressed through the soul faculties, then you experience what is known as faith. One we understand to be negative, destructive, and the other to be positive and constructive. Now the truth of the matter is, as I just said, it is one and the same power.

Now they say that the fear of God is the love of God. Well, it couldn't help but be, because it's faith, don't you understand? So the prophets have taught in the Old Testament, "Ye shall fear the God, your Lord, above all things, because in so fearing him you shall love him." And so it is, my good friends, that fear and faith are identically the same.

Now some person says, "I have a great fear of that." Well, what they're saying is they have a great faith in that. That's what they have, but they're calling that fear. Now the key is to rise out of fear and faith and go to freedom. And we get to freedom through understanding. And, of course, we get to understanding through tolerance and duty and gratitude, because we cannot get to understanding, friends, until we open or awaken the first soul faculty.

You see, the moment that we entertain in thought that we have it our way and this is the way we understand it, and that understanding doesn't grant the same right to another soul, then what we're in is the first level. We're in self-preservation. We're trying to preserve what we call our understanding, and therefore we have no tolerance for someone that comes with another type of understanding. You know, the dog doesn't have any tolerance for the needs of another dog that needs to eat also, because it doesn't have understanding. The understanding does not exist in that form, in that way.

Look, we look at an animal and we say, "Such an understanding dog." He understands when it's the hand that feeds him, usually. Now this is the way it is with many two-legged animals. You know, understanding, they have all that you could possibly encompass, if they have a need. Then, of course, the moment the need is fulfilled, oh my, they're on their way, only to return another day, in another time, in another way. Because, you see, that wasn't real understanding away. Don't you see?

That's what Spiritualism has experienced for over 125 years. It has shared again and again and again and again, its light, its understanding. Multitudes of people have touched its light and gone on and out about their way, to stumble, to fall, to bring some new idea into the universe and into the world, which is their divine right. But what I'm trying to say, my good friends, is when we have true understanding, we indeed have tolerance while someone else is expressing their understanding, because otherwise we don't have understanding, not yet. We have opinion, but not understanding, and there's a vast difference between opinion and understanding. You see, opinion needs preservation for its survival. It has nothing to stand on. Opinion is out of the brain. It has no foundation. So recognize and realize the difference between opinion and understanding. Anyone else?

I'll let someone else ask. I seem to be asking all the questions in this group.

Now I don't want to express this evening what self-conscious is. You want me to express what self-conscious is?

Well, we have been taught that we are part and parcel of God. The soul is part of God and approves of all we do. The soul approves of all we do. I think you know what I'm talking about.

Yes.

All right. Who is the chooser for the soul to come into creation if it is part of God? God chooses, then?

I'm happy to share with you my understanding in reference to that. An affirmation has been made that, "I am part of God and he approves of all I do." The Living Light does not recognize a masculine God. It does not recognize a feminine God. It does, however, state a neutral God. Because in these particular teachings, whenever you're teaching and trying to express a light of understanding, if it is on a level of duality, then it's going to guarantee its opposite. So God, to my understanding, is not masculine, and God is not feminine. God *is*.

The soul is a covering for the Divine Intelligence or Spirit. The Spirit or Divine or Infinite Intelligence, call it what you will, is totally neutral. It is a power—an energy is the best way that I can express it. Being an intelligent power, it expresses itself through form. Now the first form that expresses itself is what man calls soul, that's the covering of the Spirit. It is the soul that chooses. It is not the Divine Infinite Intelligence. If God were a God of choosing, then God would be a God of partiality. And if God were a God of partiality, he would be a God of duality. And if he was a God of duality, then he would be a God of creation. I understand God, the Power, to be beyond creation, expressing through creation.

Yes, it says, "I am a part of God and he approves of all I do." I know He didn't approve of things I was doing, but . . .

Well, if a statement is made, "I am part of God and he approves of all I do," well, he couldn't possibly disapprove or approve, if it's just a divine power. If man chooses to accept that God approves of all he does, well, of course, that is man's choice. But I do not personally, nor does the Living Light, imply a God of choice or a God of partiality in any way, shape, or form, because these gods of choice and partiality have caused one war right after another. And they all have clay feet. Any other questions?

The Spirit is the God part and the covering is the soul. From what does the soul come?

From the Allsoul.

Is the Allsoul God?

God is form, yet God is formless. The moment we put God into form, we put God into the mind, where we can express God. You cannot express God without creating a duality, because the moment you express God—that's like asking, What is truth? The moment you define truth, you no longer have truth. So the moment I try to define God, I've lost my God. You cannot define the indefinable. You cannot limit the limitless.

I understand what you're saying and that God is Spirit and we have to consider Spirit.

Yes, Spirit is known by Spirit.

Right. And this would be beyond words. It would be beyond our minds, really.

Absolutely, because our mind is dual and God is not a dual thing.

It would be in our heart, not our mind?

Yes.

I still have to ask, Where does soul come from and what is the Allsoul?

Have you studied the entire textbook?

No, I haven't.

Perhaps that's the reason. After you study *The Living Light* thoroughly, then perhaps we can have a different discussion on it. Yes, I would recommend a thorough study of it. You cannot define truth and you cannot define God and still be expressing either one. It is not possible.

They try to do that, but in this teaching—

No.

You don't think so?

Please, tell me the page and I'll be happy to discuss it.

In Discourse 24.

All right, class, let us turn to Discourse 24 and read from *The Living Light*. Be kind enough to read it, considering you mothered the idea. Discourse 24, please.

[At this point during the class, the student reads Discourse 24.]

Thank you very much. Thank you.

I can give my understanding of that, in that love, as a noun, is not exactly the same thing as a verb. Love as a noun, as expressed in this particular discourse, is the matrix of the universe, the master law of the universe. The master force, the master power, which one might think of as a matrix, a mold. And through the steps of creation, as given in the discourse, that man or the individual completes the steps of creation. Man does not actually create, but man completes the steps of creation. The steps are already there. And he simply follows them. But belief, as stated in this discourse, is the soul coming into being through the fact that it does believe. If it does believe, it is then duality. It is the beginning of duality. Because to simply be aware that it is itself is to believe on that level that it is itself. And being itself, it is then apart from God or in duality. The desire is the next step down. To simply believe that man has a soul doesn't mean he has done anything about it. But to desire is thought. Or man forming his own matrix mentally. And so with that step, man is a mental being. As man gives energy of this being that he now is, he then goes on to complete creation through the will.

Thank you very much for your expression of that particular discourse.

Would anyone else like to express on that discourse? This is a very important discourse. Remember, friends, we can only understand what we're receptive to. So that's why I'm asking the class to express on that discourse, because we cannot understand anything that we're not on a level of receptivity to. Would you like to express your understanding of it?

This means to me that when we come into being as individual souls, that it is our responsibility to do God's work. He doesn't want to do it: it's up to us. That's why he gave us this ability and our love, our knowledge. And that's why God is neutral. So that if we say, "This is a lousy world, God. Why did he make such a lousy world as this? Look at all the wars and everything," what we're talking about is what we're doing. It's our responsibility, not God's. That's what this means to me. That if people are starving to death, why don't we do something about it? God made us with our will and our knowledge, so we're perfectly free. We are God, all of us. And if we get enough of us together, we're a bigger God. That's what it means to me.

Absolutely. Definitely. Thank you very, very much. Anyone else like to express on Discourse 24?

Where it says, "The question may well be asked, Then who believed and the tree came to be? Who believed and the stars were placed in the sky? I say unto you there is a power. It is known as love. It expresses through what is commonly referred to as Infinite Intelligence or Allsoul." In reality, are we not Infinite Intelligence? Is Spirit itself not? If we have the power to create and if it expresses through form, and yet Infinite Intelligence—isn't this a paradox, where it expresses through what is commonly referred to as form?

Thank you very much. Let us try to be receptive to an understanding that everything that is, has always been. There is nothing new in the universes. There never was; there never will be. We only became newly aware of it. For example, so we can say that, fine, the rocket ship is new. But the rocket ship is not new. Neither are the planets in space. They have always been somewhere in some dimension. A chair is not new. It has always been. What I'm trying to say is that man does not originate; there is an Infinite Intelligence. There is a dimension in which all things exist. All things that will ever be, all things that have ever been, exist in a dimension. Man simply becomes aware of them at various so-called ages on this earth realm.

If God is Infinite Intelligence and man is a part of this Infinite Intelligence—if this Infinite Intelligence is expressing through man, then it is within the realm of possibility for man to tap the Infinite, the Divine, at any given moment that he so chooses, if he's willing to get his "big bloated nothingness," as Emerson said, out of the way, so the Divine Intelligence can express itself.

Now we understand in Serenity that God expresses *through* man, not *to* man; that we find God in everything, if we choose to seek God in everything. Our God, remember, is ever as small or as large as we permit that God to be at any given time. Now we may curse him when things don't go well and we may bless him when things are going beautifully. What we're doing is cursing and blessing ourselves. We're cursing and blessing our inabilities or abilities at any given moment to be receptive to the Infinite Intelligence, to which all things are possible, if man would only accept it. Now that is entirely up to man and so we find throughout history that the gods of man are constantly in a process of change, because they're all created gods and anything that's created is going to go through change.

So if we will consider being receptive to God, if you wish to call it God, Infinite Intelligence, if you prefer those words, let us just be peaceful and let that great power do its work and its work is infinite and intelligent. Think: they say that God does this or God does that. Well, if God is going to do anything, what is God? If God is Infinite Intelligence, then it's simply intelligence infinitely manifest and that's God. And so we are expressing intelligently, at least to some degree (we hope), so God is working.

When man works, God works, and when man stops working, God stops working. And if things go bad, it's because we denied our own divinity. God didn't do it to us, couldn't do it if he wanted to, for the simple reason that it's just a plain old Divine Infinite Intelligent neutral power. And the only time it works is when man works. So let us work with God in the sense of just go to work and we will express our divinity.

Then the words that Jesus left us, "Thy will be done on earth as it is in heaven," is the law of noninterference?

Absolutely and positively! When we get ourselves, the little self, out of the way of the Divine Intelligence, then heaven will manifest on earth. That is heaven, all things in harmonious motion, if that's what they want to call heaven. Certainly.

Remember that all of our problems are self-created. The teachings of Serenity are whatever happens to us is caused by us. And the sooner that a person will recognize and accept that great truth—it's not John Doe's fault and it's not Mary Jane's fault. This is the great difficulty in getting the mind to accept the Divine Neutrality: that whatever happens to us is caused by us. It's not someone else's fault.

Now remember, if you have an emotional reaction to change, to the degree of your emotional reaction to change, that reveals to you, my friends, how attached you are to your own level. If you have great difficulty with changes coming to you, it's very simple. Say, "Thank you, God. I can see I'm 90 percent attached to this. Isn't that fantastic? That's how bound I am." Don't you see? If we're so attached to our opinions and to the way we think that life should be, all we have to do is pause a moment and, depending on how emotional we get when change comes about, that says, "There you are, friend. You are bound by those many chains." That's exactly what the law is teaching us. Yes, does that help?

I had an experience of being in a very lucrative job. And when I lost the job, I had this feeling of being completely crushed. Until I went home and realized I had to spiritualize it because it was getting me down. I realized that there was a reason for this and there was a higher law in operation. It was something I had done and had created. I didn't like it. I had done it, but nevertheless I had to release it and I was working again.

Thank you very much. Remember, students, there is no freedom as long as you entertain in thought that anyone outside of you is causing you joy. There is no freedom as long as you entertain in thought that anyone outside of you is causing you misery. There is no freedom if you insist on giving power to another human soul. I don't care whether the human soul is in the flesh or out of the flesh. If you insist on giving power to something outside of you by saying that this one causes me joy and that one causes me misery, every time you entertain that type of thinking, you are binding your soul to creation and you are guaranteeing to experience the opposite.

If we cannot find God inside of ourselves, we will never find God outside of ourselves. It is impossible, because the Light is known by the Light. And we cannot find the Light without, until we first find the Light within. So whatever you are seeking, find it first inside yourself, because if you don't find it first inside of yourself, you will never find it outside of yourself. And that is why the Bible prophets said, "O physician, heal thyself." We cannot help another until we can help ourselves. That's why the statement is made that God helps those who help themselves.

So I can only stress to you, students, try to become more aware of what you're entertaining in thought and try to stop giving this life-giving power to people, to things outside of yourself. Then you will express this so-called divinity, then this peace that passeth all understanding will manifest in your lives. But you are denying the possibility every time you think that someone else is doing this or that, and that is disturbing you. You're giving away the greatest power that you will ever have in that kind of thinking.

Thank you.

FEBRUARY 15, 1973

CONSCIOUSNESS CLASS 7 ✣

This evening, we'll start on our questions and answers.

I had a question on a discourse. I'd like your explanation. The discourse says, Please do not look for names or tags. They bind you to the dream of creation for that's what we're striving to outgrow.

Absolutely. Would you like an expansion on that?

I would.

The discourse says, Please do not ask for names, because they are tags which bind us to creation. For example, if you started entertaining in thought what you did when you were five years old, and your friends, your associates, what you would be doing, in truth, is going backward into an experience that has already passed. You will get no benefit from it. You've already grown through it.

And so when we leave this physical clay, we go on to other dimensions. The very first thing that we lose, as we evolve into the spiritual realms of light, is our last name. This is why it is so difficult for mediums to get full names of people from the world of spirit because, depending upon what level the medium is contacting, depends on whether or not you can get full names. Now those entities who are still closest to the earth realm can give their first, middle, and last names, their full names. But those who have evolved to the higher realms of light, they retain their first name. That is the name that they are known by. Their last name is something that they inherited. As they go on, yea, even into higher realms in the world of spirit, they're known then by a symbol. Now that symbol is given to them under the laws of merit; they merit the symbol that they're known by. And so it is, as they evolve in these other dimensions, they don't want to be held by these name tags. Does that help with your question?

It does, indeed. That's just a created thing, isn't it?

That's just a created thing. They lose all those titles as they evolve. The closer you stick to the earth realm after passing, you have all the earth's memories and all of its attachments. But you must realize, friends, that when we go on to other dimensions, there are broader horizons. There are times that the spirits do come to contact the earth realm. There are certain reasons for that. They have come because they're here to help others to awaken. That's the reason some of them return. The reason that others return is because of the emotional attachment. And then there are other reasons why they return to the earth realm.

If we have been given the name of a guide, that doesn't mean that he is still on the first level of awareness, does it?

No, I wouldn't say so. But we must realize that most entities who hover close to the earth realm have the best recollection of their last name. Now remember that there are many realms of the astral. There are the close, dark realms to the earth realms. There are the higher astral realms. Then, there are the Summer Lands, what the Spiritualists call the Summer Land, the beginnings of the areas of light, where they still have their names. Yes. That doesn't mean because you happen to know a person that's communicating, who's given you a full name, that they're earthbound or that they're in the astral realm. I did not mean to imply that at all. But you must realize that if it is an awakened spirit, which is a guide, then they're bringing that name for a reason. Some channels need a full name. Some guides recognize that and will accommodate their channel in order to get the work accomplished.

How can we tell which part of our anatomy corresponds with which soul faculty?

Now that is an excellent question. How can we tell which part of our anatomy corresponds with a soul faculty or a sense function: is that your question?

Yes, I know that the heel is understanding, but other than that . . .

The heel is the door to understanding. Now if you will study *The Living Light* that you have, you will begin to perceive which parts of your anatomy correspond to certain functions and faculties. Once having understood what is already given in the book, you will be able to perceive the other parts of the anatomy. If you are not, I will be happy to answer, to the best of my ability.

OK. I have another question. In Discourse 19 and in Discourse 34, it mentions mantras that have been given to us. Is this mantra the peace, the meditation of peace, or is that something separate?

The mantra that was given to a few of my students, that is something separate. Yes.

I have a couple of questions, one of them relating to this week's discourse and another one relating to some time ago, when I was asked to spend three hours meditating on a subject.

Yes.

I think that I have accumulated the three hours in meditation on that particular passage.

Wonderful.

However, I would like to ask the first question regarding this discourse.

Yes.

This is, "Won't you learn to be the observer and not the observed." That doesn't seem to follow with bearing the light. The torchbearer is never the observer. He's the observed. And how do the two sharing the light with others relate to being an observer?

Because the Light is ever known by the Light. And so when he says, "Learn to be the observer and not the observed," I understand that statement to mean to first look, think, and listen before acting. So many people act—they think they act and what they really are doing is reacting. So what he is trying to say is, Learn to be the observer and not the observed. The observed are those who are constantly reacting. But those who are truly acting, those, in truth, are the observers. Do you understand?

Yes, I think so.

So, for example, if you sit here and you just observe, there are so many things going on in this room at this instant. Instead of reacting to all of the emotions, the impulses, the thoughts, etc., sit back and observe all of this taking place.

What is it that happens in students' unfoldment? All of a sudden they see something and they react. And when they react, the thing that they see disappears. Well, it hasn't disappeared. What the individual student has done is, they have reacted to what they saw, and in reacting, they have lowered their level of awareness and, consequently, can no longer see the spiritual vision. Do you understand?

Yes. I think so. Yes.

So if we're wise, we'll be the patient, peaceful observer with a heart of gratitude for that that we are able to observe. We will weigh it out in our mind and then act. Now in reference to the discourse that you were to spend three hours on, what did you come up with as your understanding? And what is the discourse number?

Discourse 45. And it was the last paragraph of that discourse. "If a man is born without feet to walk or hands to write, or ears to hear or eyes to see, nostrils to smell or a mouth to speak, a tongue to taste, what would be the purpose of his being?"

Indeed, what would be the purpose of his being? Have you read the rest of that discourse? The answer is—Read the discourse from the beginning. The answer is there.

All right. [The student reads from Discourse 45.] *"Greetings, fellow students. We are discussing at this time the reasons for the delay, the procrastinations, and the seeming difficulties as we strive to find the light of truth.*

"Why is it that so many take so long to make changes in established patterns that have proven to themselves to be detrimental and not in their best interest spiritually?"

There's the answer. Go ahead.

[The student continues to read.] *"Why is it such a seeming struggle? Why is it that man speaks forth his desires to do and to be and becomes so very lazy, so to speak, in application? Then of what benefit is any teaching at any time? Think, my children. On what level do we find ourselves grounded? And if so, why do we remain there?"*

Of what benefit is it to a human soul to garner up knowledge and awareness if the soul is not willing, ready, and able to demonstrate it, to apply it? Of what benefit is it?

Yes. But it isn't the answer I got. My answer is that it is not right.

Perhaps it is for the level that you're expressing. Please express it.

Well, it seems to me to be the duty of the person to manifest the spirit within with whatever handicap that they have merited.

Absolutely! That is also an answer. Definitely and positively.

By the law of . . .

By the Law of Merit.

Right, yes.

That is also an answer. That is another level of awareness. And it all applies. Absolutely. Thank you very much.

You see, students, what does it behoove us to bother to study, to take classes, or anything else if in our study we do not make application? If you study *The Living Light*, go over and over and over it again—and it has many, many teachings, much more than what the surface of the little book seems to show—but if you do not apply it, it will be of no benefit to you.

They give an exercise in here. It's called a fountain exercise. He gives many exercises in this book. What is this fountain exercise? If we study the book, we're going to find out what it is. I look over there and I happen to see a fountain; it happens to be a little bit green and a little tan or beige. All right, now what does that mean to me? Why is it those two colors? Well, it is very simple: it just happens to be the level of awareness I happen to be on at this moment. That's what the fountain exercise really is, my good friends: it's yourself. That's where you are.

Now isn't that a great benefit, if you do something about it? But if you don't do anything about it—you know, I say here, "Well, fine, Richard, that means there's a little mental and a little soul mixed up there." Because I understand the colors that have been given. Don't you see? But what good does it do? We might as well go home and watch television if we don't apply what we're receiving. Use it every moment of every day. I try to apply it myself.

When we recognize, friends, that the first step that we have to walk through in awakening spiritually is what is known as the emotional realm—and I assure you, it's a mighty difficult step to make, because we've all got emotions. You know, we just don't say, "Whoops, I've gone through the emotional realm. It's all over now." Well, if it worked that way, I want the pill or the key, because I haven't found it that way yet.

In the course of any moment, something can trigger our emotional realm. How can you grow through something, and stay through it, that you're a part of? And we're in this thing. We're in it and we never know when it's going to get triggered. So let's face the truth about the matter. There are ways to help keep us on guard by staying aware of our thinking, by becoming aware of ourselves. Our inner being will say, "Whoops, don't walk over there because you're not strong enough yet; you'll dip right down into that level." That's the way that we can protect ourselves. There's an inner feeling. There's an inner knowing.

And when we do have an experience, let's just pause and say to ourselves, "Fascinating experience I'm having." Be objective and ask yourself, "Now what did I do to set this law into motion?" We're not going to be free until we're willing to accept the truth that nothing, but nothing, happens to us that is not caused by us. You can't be free, friends, as long as the old ego is permitted to insist that it is somebody's fault over there. You'll never be free and neither will I, until we go in and say, "OK, I set these laws into motion. This is the experience that I am having and I'm going to do something about it." Then, we're going to start on the path of freedom. Any more questions?

With the soul faculties and the sense functions, is it reasonable to think that at some point of the individual's spiritual growth that the faculties might overcome or replace or cause to dissipate or spiritualize the sense functions? Is that reasonable?

Well, in reference to your question, Is there a time in spiritual awareness or spiritual growth that the faculties overbalance the sense functions? Yes! Yes, indeed, there are those times for some people; but it is not beneficial for that to happen while yet in the physical flesh. It is not beneficial, has not proven to be beneficial.

Now as we evolve, remember this: as long as we have mind, we have form. And as long as we have individualized soul, we have form. So it is that the teaching is not to annihilate the functions. After all, we want to stay in form, so we can serve the purpose of our soul's incarnation into form. Now when we evolve out of form—it is only in form that we have self-awareness. When we go out of form, we're out of self-awareness. We're no longer aware. And so what is it that keeps us in form? It's the functions, the functions of the form. Is that understandable?

You see, what happens with these people who go off into the soul faculties or off all into the spiritual, you find them walking around like—I think they call that state catatonic—like zombies. You see, they're no longer able to function in a world of form and, consequently, that is not the teachings of the Living Light. The teachings are to bring a balance between your functions and your soul faculties. Don't annihilate them; it will not be beneficial for your soul's expression.

I wasn't thinking of annihilating them. I was thinking of spiritualizing them, so that they don't appear.

Oh, they can be spiritualized as long as they're still used. How does one spiritualize a function? I can tell you: by not being attached to the function. That's how you spiritualize it. Now let's take an example, say that a person has a function of desire known as eating. Let's face the fact: it is a function. Now when the desire to have something to eat is at its strongest and we are able to speak to the desire and not eat for maybe three hours later and have no emotional reaction whatsoever, then we have spiritualized that particular function. That is most beneficial.

You see, there's nothing wrong with desire, until desire takes control of our soul. If, for example, we have a desire and we become a nervous wreck until that desire is fulfilled, we're not able to wait five minutes or five hours or anything, then we have lost control and creation is now our master and our soul is its slave. That's the teaching of the Living Light.

This is what I was considering. Can suspicion be replaced by the force of love? There are situations in a person's life when suspicion does not appear because something else is there instead.

Remember, there's not a thing wrong with suspicion, until suspicion takes control of our soul. You see, that's where we're treading in deep water. When creation takes control of our soul, then we've lost the true purpose of our incarnation.

I'll have to think about that some more.

All right.

May I ask one more?

Certainly.

Would you please compare logic and reason?

I'll be most happy to share with you my understanding. Logic says that 2 and 2 are 4. That's logical. Reason—let me put it another way, reason has a certain element that logic cannot have. Reason has total consideration. Logic does not. Yes.

Getting back to the functions, does selfishness ever become selflessness? We have to be selfish sometimes to preserve, not the ego, but the body and the mind, because other people will simply just take over.

All right, I'll be happy to share with you our understanding. Self-preservation is the first law of form, the first law of form. Now without self-preservation, there is no continuity of the species; therefore, a person could say that everyone is selfish, as long as they're in form. Well, of course, we are.

The teaching is to balance that with selflessness, with a universality, with a broadening of our thinking, in other words, with reason, which is total consideration. And this is why the teaching is, Keep faith with reason, for she will transfigure thee. What is it that reason has that transfigures us? Why, my good friends, it has total consideration. It's all-encompassing. It leaves nothing out. Does that help with your question?

Very much. Thank you.

I never met a person that wasn't selfish. But I have met many people that are balanced with selfishness and selflessness. My goodness, if I weren't selfish myself, I wouldn't be here sitting talking to you, because that's what helps keep me in the form, that is, self-attachment. Haven't you ever seen a person having a great difficulty in getting out of the form? They're so self-attached. They're overbalanced in the self-attachment and they can't leave the piece of clay. It's a matter of balance and counter-balance. Does that help?

Very much.

Any other questions?

I've been working with the discourse that mentions the mantra. Now I could understand that your class at that time had been given a mantra of a different sort. But the way that was worded it seemed to me that a part of the teaching is to know your own aura, so I used the fountain exercise by projecting the color I thought was necessary to my aura. So I do think that could be your mantra: the color that is suitable to your aura.

If you had one word to speak, what would you speak? That's your mantra for your level at that moment. Anyone else?

I would like a little more on what was said a moment ago regarding spiritualizing the functions. I think so many people are afraid to let go of attachments, because they say, "If I let go of that, what have I got? That's all I have!"

Yes.

*And so if I let go, I haven't got anything. Well, I think that's
where the faith comes in. You're right, there won't be anything
unless you believe that there will be something. Unless you become
aware that the transition can be made, where a function is balanced with the faculties, that the function will take on a new light
when the attachment is removed.*

Absolutely and positively. Remember, as long as we shelter
anything, the longer we shelter it, the more we make it a crip-
ple. And that's why he teaches, Blessings are ever to be shared
and never to be sheltered. You see, the longer you hold to anything, that becomes your master and you become its slave, no
matter what attachment you may have, the longer you express
the attachment. This is why he teaches, When you have desire,
which is function, educate the desire, which is to spiritualize
the desire. And how do you spiritualize a desire? By keeping the
desire in the awareness that it is not master. It is a servant, a
tool to be used, not to be abused. So you see, all things in God
are good. Imbalance is all that it is. Does that help?

Thank you very much.

Yes.

*Regarding self-preservation, is it not possible, too, that as we
realize that we're going to go on—I mean, the only thing the self
is preserving is ego. And what is ego, after all? To realize that you
really don't need this big ego and you really don't need this self-
preservation, because you're going to go on and you're still the
same person, perhaps even better, hopefully. Is that possible?*

Yes, but remember that self-preservation is the Law of Form.
Now, for example, if a person in the course of a day did not
demonstrate self-preservation—I can give you an example for
myself. If I did nothing more in the course of a day than return
every phone call that I received and I spent as much time on the
phone call as the person desired me to spend, there would not be
enough hours in the day and night. Therefore, self-preservation
dictates, through reason, that I must use a limited amount of

time on returning the phone calls that I have to return. Now, you see, God doesn't come in and dictate that to me, but reason does. What is it that prompts reason? Self-preservation. Is that understandable?

Yes.

So therefore, we do have this Law of Self-Preservation. Now, for example, we could sit here this evening and say, "Fine. I find it all interesting. I'll just keep right on going." And we might not get out 'til midnight or two o'clock in the morning. However, several students, having their reason triggered by self-preservation or self-interest, you understand—some people have to get up and go to work in the morning—they would say, "I think it's time that we quit." So you see, we do not express in form without self-preservation and self-preservation serves its purpose. But when self-preservation gets out of bounds or out of balance, you understand, then we've got problems. Then we have what's known as greed and selfishness. Is that understandable?

Thank you.

You're welcome. Thank you very much for bringing that up. Yes.

In Discourse 30, a statement is made that there are so many explanations and beliefs concerning from what part of the physical anatomy the soul leaves. We are aware of the center of anatomy of air. And I would logically say that would have to do with the lungs, but I'd like to know reasonably, which part of the anatomy is it?

You want to know which part of the anatomy the soul leaves at transition? I can tell you from my personal experiences what part I see it leaving from. I have repeatedly seen the spirit leave the so-called physical body upon transition from what is known as the soft spot in the head. Now I am aware that some mediums have seen otherwise. Well, of course, that's their right. I might be seeing a little cross-eyed myself, but that's where I have repeatedly seen the soul or spirit leave the physical anatomy: through the soft spot in the head.

Could you tell us, please, in what part of the anatomy the air center is located?

The air center?

Yes.

The throat. The throat. That's also where resentment is located as a function.

That's interesting.

Yes, it is interesting. You've had class studies. Why is resentment in the air center?

Resentment is mental. Resentment is in a mental center, isn't it?

That's right!

But isn't it true that every illness we have, like a cold or whatever, has a certain reason for occurring?

Definitely and positively. What disease means is "out of ease" or "out of harmony." And therefore, the part of the anatomy that is affected is revealing to you which part is out of harmony. That's why he teaches you the parts of the anatomy. Yes. So if you have a certain condition and it's a certain part of your anatomy, through study and application you can find out the cause. And once you find the cause, you have the cure. This is why medicine is not as successful as it could be, because they're working on the effect. They're not working on the cause. They're working on the effect. Yes.

You know, it's most interesting. They say, well, what is it they call it, the Asian flu or London flu? They always call it something. And every year it goes around. Well, you know, what exists in one, exists in everyone; the potential is ever there. But I always notice, you see, it's the throats that are attacked every year. And for many years, I've asked why, and then the day came when I was given the teaching what the throat means in the air center: it means resentment. And you know it is true. You look around at this world of creation, there's sure a lot of resentment in the world to something. We either resent the Internal Revenue Service because it wants to collect money from us that we owe it anyway, or we resent something else. You know, resentment is a resentment. No wonder there's so much London flu! I don't know why they want to blame London! Any other questions?

Would reason be a key to meditation?

Absolutely and positively. It is a key to meditation.

You said that a particular ailment comes from resentment. And then you said the reason is because there's a lot of resentment in this world. But then, just looking at it that way, I could say that's the reason why I have a sore throat.

I didn't say that the reason a person has a sore throat is because there's a lot of resentment in the world and I didn't mean to imply that.

You said it was given to you. Right?

I said that the understanding of the throat and anything that affects the area of the throat is caused from resentment, yes. And it is reasonable to me, because of years of demonstration, personal demonstration. I had the flu every single year and it affected my throat for many, many years. Finally, I grew out of my resentment and I have not had an effect to my throat since.

What about other minor ailments? If you have an earache, that means something. Are you saying that the only way you can find out what an earache means is through getting it from others?

No, no. The parts of the anatomy are given in the teachings and they are demonstrable. That's one thing they are. They can be put to the test personally and they will prove themselves to the individual who studies and applies them. Absolutely. There is no teaching in *The Living Light* that is not personally demonstrable through effort, study, and application, and the wisdom of patience. Does that help with your question?

I just have to think about it.

Certainly, absolutely. Remember, friends, it is not fair to ourselves to expect to understand a lifetime of study in two or three or six or five months. It is not fair to ourselves. If we can perceive one or two things from it, through study and application, then we're doing very, very well. We must not expect to learn all about life in a given month or two. It is not just and it is not reasonable. Many people have studied the laws of communication for a lifetime and they're still working at it. You see, there is nothing in this world that we can ever get in its fullness. Nothing. We may think we can, but we don't.

Only a fool reaches his goal, because when you reach your goal, you have nothing left to look forward to but the fear of keeping it. So only a fool reaches his goal. Look at the fools that retire. Excuse me. Take a look. The moment they retire, they retire to their grave. Because you no longer have any interest, usually, and so life no longer has a purpose and life no longer has any meaning. You see, the goal is up there. You ever keep working toward it, but you never quite reach it. It's known as progression, progression of the form. Remember, it's the form that changes and progresses. It's not the formless. No. It's only the form that does that. You remember, friends, God can't grow. If God could grow, then God wouldn't be God, would it?

We think so much of form as being the form we're in now, but I think that even spirit is in form?

Absolutely.

There's always form and we go from the physical form to the spiritual form, so we're never without form?

There is always form as long as there is awareness. When you enter the Formless, there's unawareness. There is no awareness without form. It is the form that is aware, absolutely and positively. The Formless is not awareness. Awareness, my good friends, comes with duality and duality only exists in form. It doesn't exist in the Formless, in the Divine. Does that help with your question?

It's so great, I can't tell you!

Now there was another question.

I kind of lost it.

Did you lose it in the formlessness?

I think so.

[The Teacher laughs.] All right, now, it's almost time—yes, another question.

What is meant, then, by "I am spirit, formless and free"?

Absolutely! That's an excellent question and it's on all our church programs and in our newspaper ads.

I am spirit, formless and free;
Whatever I think [form], that will I be.

Thought is the keynote. And the moment you think, you guarantee creation, you guarantee duality. And this is why he teaches, Guard your thoughts, the portal to your soul. "I am spirit formless and free; Whatever I *think*, that will I be." So we are the effect of what we have thought. We will continue to be the effect of what we entertain in thought, whether we like it or not. We have brown eyes or blue eyes. My good friends, that is the effect of what you set into motion prior to this earth incarnation somewhere on the ladder of eternal progression and, consequently, your little soul is in a body with blue eyes and mine is in a body with brown eyes. Only the effect of thought.

You were saying, "Only a fool reaches his goal." If you have a goal and you reach it, can you set up another goal, starting the process all over again? Do you understand what I'm saying?

I understand wholeheartedly what you're saying. Thank you.

That is not being a fool, then, doing it that way. Is that true?

If a person has a goal and reaches their goal—tell me something, does man ever reach his goal?

I have.

You have reached your goal?

I have reached some of my goals.

You have reached some of your goals.

Yes.

When you reached the goal, did you find that it was not full, whole, and complete, and you had to start something else?

No, I reached it as something on the way to the next goal.

Then, it's a partial goal. It never ends, does it?

No, it doesn't. I'm saying one thing leads to the next. From one goal, which leads to the next goal.

If your goal is nothing more than a chain reaction, which is continuous, that, then, brings you to the Light in time. But if our goal is something that we can complete, here and now, and then we say, "There it is. I've got it!"— only a fool has that kind of goal. Because it causes stagnation, contrary to progression.

Like you were saying, if they've reached the goal and they say, "There it is! I've got it and now there's nothing more for me."

There's nothing more for them to do. Then it's a fool that reaches a goal.

Since I have this condition in my throat . . .

Oh, do you have a condition? Don't take it personally. They all have. I had it for years.

If I have a problem in finding what causes the resentment, how do I go about finding the cause? How do I go on with it?

The moment the person finds the cause, the cure is manifested. The moment the mind searches into its inner self, finding the cause of the resentment, at that moment, the cure is made manifest.

If I have an idea, if I'm not strong enough with myself—I really don't know how to work it out.

In other words, what you're trying to say is, If a person has resentment and they're aware that they have it, but they're not able to get rid of it—well, you see, you know, it's human to forgive and it's divine to forget. So one must consider working on forgiveness. And when we truly forgive the individual—do you understand?

Well, I try.

You try to understand or you try to forgive?

Well, I'll try both.

You'll try both. Very wise student, very wise. I'm sure that will disappear within the coming five to six days, maximum, because you're working on your forgiveness. Now we must not take these things personally. We must not look at a person and say, "Whoops, look at all that resentment! They've got laryngitis." Almost got it myself. *[The class laughs.]* Because then they're becoming judges, you know. Just like a person looking at somebody's car and finding out the fender's all dented in and they say, "Well, I wonder what transgression, what laws they transgressed." Well, I'd be careful with that kind of thinking, because it might just bounce right back and you might have your whole rear end smashed.

Yes, are there any other questions before we finish class?

With any illness, would you have to go on the same way, like you just explained for resentment?

To forgive is to free. When we forgive, we free from the bondage of mind and in that freedom we are relieved from these so-called discords in our own being. Forgiveness is the greatest blessing, because it is freedom. It frees us. To forgive is to free. Absolutely.

Is this not only to forgive others, but we also forgive ourselves?

We must first forgive ourselves before we can forgive another. If we don't forgive ourselves first, then we cannot forgive another human soul. It is impossible and contradictory.

What it really is, to my understanding, as soon as we have an illness . . .

A discord.

The whole thing is to learn what has affected us.

We've stayed in the level long enough to be receptive and manifest it, absolutely, somewhere along the line.

You know, I have to be careful with his teachings, because then they look at me and say they're just waiting, you know, for me to get sick. I know. I'm well aware. I can't afford to get sick.

No matter how bad I feel or how many hours I have to work, I have to stay in perfect health. You understand? I have a whole multitude of people telling me if anything happens. I had a flat tire the other night and they wanted to know what law I had transgressed. *[The class laughs loudly.]* Of course, the tires on an automobile, that's what moves it: it's the feet. And my understanding wasn't up to par or I would have listened to the Spirit two weeks ago when they said, "Get the tire changed." Well, now I've spent $28.95 and I got them both changed. You see, so you have to be—you know, it isn't easy being a teacher, because you're constantly behind the eight ball. People say, "What's the matter with him? He's going away to get sick?"

Well, friends, our time is up. Let's go have coffee. Thank you all very much.

FEBRUARY 22, 1973

CONSCIOUSNESS CLASS 8 ❦

Well, tonight, before getting to your questions and answers, I would like to speak for a few moments on what he has so often spoken about, the Law of Change or the Law of Progression. Now we all agree, of course, and know that you cannot progress—nothing can progress—without changes, internal changes. And so it is that the barometer of success is simply an effect.

Now when we speak of change or progression or success, the reason that it is so very, very difficult for most people to be successful, to change from one level to another, is because the mind is completely and wholly conditioned to failure. Now the reason that the mind is conditioned to failure is simply because the mind has accepted fear for untold centuries. So whenever we have accepted fear, we guarantee what is to follow as failure. And, therefore, it is very clear to any student on the path who is seeking success in their spiritual efforts to recognize that the struggle reveals the extent of the success or change or progression that they are making. Now the struggle we experience is simply because of the way our minds have been conditioned, conditioned to failure and conditioned by fear.

Now I am going to go to your questions and answers.

In Discourse 8, which we just read, he is speaking of the spirit of man, not of the form of man, as far as finding the missing link here on earth, which comes from another planet. Am I correct in understanding that we could find the missing link for the form of man, but not necessarily for the spirit of man?

Well, when he's speaking in Discourse 8 in reference to the missing link of man, this will not be found on your planet because from your planet it did not come. You see, he's speaking about the missing link between the so-called four-legged creature and the so-called two-legged creature. He states in Discourse 8 that the reason that missing link (that they have not yet been able to find) will not be found on your planet is because on your planet it does not exist and did not exist. That's what he stated in Discourse 8. Yes. Thank you.

I wonder if you could give us some practical exercise or suggestions for how to visualize? Some people are very good at this and others kind of think of an image but are unable to project it in front of them.

I would suggest to anyone having any difficulty with the techniques or the processes of visualization to choose something that you desire, for then it is the easiest thing in the world to visualize. For example, if a lady desires a new mink coat, she usually does not have any problem whatsoever in visualizing a mink coat, simply because the desire for it has been awakened within the mind. So the easiest thing, of course, to do would be to start with a visualization of some strong desire that you may have. You will then find that it is much easier to visualize that that you desire, because energy is already being expended into the form of your own desire. I would suggest

that the student try that in the beginning if they have difficulties with visualization.

*There's the mental, the physical, and the spiritual. Does emo-
tion come under the heading of the mental?*

Yes, that's in the mental realm.

*Could you perhaps tell me what it is when you are with a
group of spiritually oriented people and you feel yourself getting
very high? Does that come from a bad emotional level or is it a
good emotional level? A high, uplifting energy kind of thing.*

Well, that would depend, of course, on what the delayed effects are, if any. That would depend: if you get emotionally high,
then you guarantee an emotional low. But there is such a state
of having a fullness of the spirit, where you would not have the
reaction of an emotional low. There is a difference. That would
depend, of course, on your experience and would have to be
judged accordingly.

In The Living Light *the Old Man speaks about the Law of
Magnetism and in the past weeks, he had been watching the
group he was working with and saw they were being "drawn like
sponges." Does he mean the energy? Whenever I have given, I
feel I have gotten. Since I have been doing my spiritual work,
I feel my energy levels are very high.*

Yes, well, he was speaking to the students who had not chosen to give. That was not what they were doing. They were expressing on levels in such a way that they were being depleted.
For example, when man discusses things of a spiritual nature,
by the law of discussing them, he becomes attuned to a spiritual
dimension. Now how attuned he becomes to that dimension is
totally dependent upon the receptivity of the individual at the
time he is discussing spiritual matters.

When we discuss spiritual matters on a brain or mental
level, then we are taking a great chance of depleting this life-
giving force. For what we are actually doing, we are putting this
refined level of awareness into a much grosser one and we are

depleting ourselves in the process. Now the Bible puts it in a fine way when it says, "Cast not your pearls before the swine." If a person is spiritually in tune, then they are going to be replenished by the spirit in which they are in tune. If they are not spiritually in tune and they are expressing spiritual matters, then they are going to become mentally exhausted and drawn like sponges. This is why a person does not, having awakened to some extent to the power of the Spirit, they do not intellectualize it and they do not waste their energies in trying to put it under a microscope.

Now if you have shared things of the Spirit, then you have shared them in a spiritual vibration. Consequently, you would not be depleted. But if you share those spiritual things in a mental level with those who are not as awakened, then you're going to be vastly depleted. That's this "drawing" of this magnetism that he is speaking about.

Does everything have a soul? And is there a soul in everything? I know there is spirit.

Everything that has form is soul, and has a covering.

Thank you.

Yes. Soul is the essence of the form itself. It is what the form gathers itself around. Yes.

When we incarnate, could we progress from being a rock or a plant and in the next life come in and be a higher form of animal on the next planet? Have we gone through incarnations, let's say, of inanimate objects and plants on other planets?

Let me explain it this way; perhaps it will help you. The Divine Spirit, which is formless and free, has expressed and is expressing through a multitude of forms. The Divine Energy, which is presently expressing through ourselves, could have expressed through a rock or a tree or an animal or a mouse or a dog or a cat. Remember, that is not form. We are now speaking of the formless. The Divine Power is one. One. It is not a million. It is only one. So the energy, the so-called spirit, that is flowing through us this moment, is identically the same spirit that is holding the atoms and electrons and molecules together in a rock or in a blade of grass or in a tree or in a bird. It is the same Power, the same God. The only difference is its covering, which we call soul. Soul is form. Spirit is formless. That is the difference between the two.

Now if you want to say, for example, "I now have the form of a human being. Did I have the form of a blade of grass before?" The form that comes from this planet has in it all of the forms that have preceded it. So in that sense, yes, you do. Also the form, which we are now expressing in, has all of the knowledge that has been gathered by all of the forms up to this present moment. And in that sense, yes, we have. Does that help with your question?

Yes, it does. Thank you.

Yes.

Once we have incarnated into the human form, can the soul incarnate in a blade of grass or a rock?

The soul does not regress. Eternal progression is the Law of Form, whether it's the form of a blade of grass or a tree or a human being. It is eternally progressive. It propels itself, constantly evolving. That is the very Law of Form itself. You see, when people speak of the disintegration of form, they must consider that which disintegrates, integrates. When you have death, you have birth. And when you have birth, you have death.

Now he stated in these classes once that man is never born. He simply becomes aware of the dimension in which he is expressing. And so it is that we are presently aware of this dimension, for this is the dimension that we are expressing in. Some of us are aware of several other dimensions because we have awakened to those dimensions, and by awakening to those dimensions, we have become born in them. You see, we cannot be born until we awaken. And this is what the Bible prophets spoke about when they said a spiritual birth, that you may be born spiritually. You can't be born spiritually until you awaken to the spiritual. When we awaken to the spiritual, then we have spiritual birth.

Now when we awaken to the astral, we'll have astral birth. We've already awakened to the mental, because we have mental birth. We've already awakened to the physical, because we have physical birth. Don't you see? It is only a matter of awakening. That's all that it is. But, you see, if you want to awaken spiritually, if you want birth, you must be willing to accept death. You can't have birth without death, and you can't have death without birth.

So it isn't a matter of what you must garner up to awaken. It's simply a matter of what you must give up. What you give up dies. And what dies, something else is born. But, you see, that takes faith. You have to have faith in birth, in something that you're not aware of until you're born in it. So that's the great important thing that faith serves. Faith is the bridge between the dimensions. It's the bridge from the material to the mental, and from the mental to the spiritual. The only bridge you're ever going to find is known as faith. And you cannot be born until you're willing to die. Does that help with your question? Yes.

When you do the fountain exercise, I always start out seeing the fountain, but I cannot help but become the fountain. And I feel good about that. I feel that perhaps that exercise is when the prana starts moving up, it is a help to release it, which is more comfortable. They say you go through chemical changes. I think perhaps spiritually, you can, by using that exercise, control that chemical change.

Yes. The fountain exercise is designed to reveal your level of awareness at any given moment that you are meditating and visualizing and seeing the fountain. What it actually does is reveal your state of consciousness or awareness. Now as you study your colors and you study your numbers, you will become aware of what level you're on. Any time that you visualize the fountain, it will reveal that level to you.

Now people who practice, students who practice their fountain exercise, have found how quickly the fountain changes and how very difficult it is to keep the same color or the same fountain. It's almost impossible. The reason that it's almost impossible is that's the way the mind is working. It's constantly flipping up and down through the levels, second by second. This is why it is so difficult for the students to have this peace that passeth all understanding, because they haven't taken the time—the years—and the effort to concentrate and to stay on one level long enough to fully experience the level. You know, you're not born in just an instant. You don't become aware in just an instant. It's a process. You've got to hold it long enough so that it will happen.

I wondered what it meant when I saw a certain color. I had chosen three colors. I visualized a fountain at Forest Lawn because I was familiar with it. And then, all of a sudden, the color changed and another color entered and I'm very happy with the color.

Yes, now that's a change in your vibratory wave, so that's what you experience, don't you see? A student asked this evening, Is there an exercise whereby a person who has difficulty with visualization could make it easier? I tried to explain at that time, just choose something that you desire greatly and, believe me, you will visualize. It will come before your sight before you know it. Yes.

How could you visualize wisdom?

Very simple. The mind—a wise philosopher once said whatever the mind can imagine, it can and does create. I am sure that we will all agree here this evening that our mind can imagine wisdom. You see, we would have to be able to imagine wisdom in order to think wisdom, because we can't think anything we can't imagine. It's impossible. So it is that the mind has imagined wisdom and we think wisdom. Well, what does wisdom mean to us? That's the first question one should ask. What does it mean to you?

A knowing.

And what does knowing mean?

A truth.

It means truth.

A truth.

It means *a* truth. Then that means that your mind accepts more than one truth.

At the moment, yes.

Therefore, you see, this is how we get to know ourselves, by questions, by questioning the self. First off, we say that it's a knowing. And then, we say that it's a truth. Now that means that we accept the possibility of more than one truth; you will agree on that, won't you? That is what your mind accepts. Consequently, if the mind accepts *a* truth, then it must accept *many* truths. And if it accepts many truths, it must accept variety. And if it accepts variety, then it has accepted creation. And if it has accepted creation, then it has accepted duality. And if it has accepted duality, then we don't have truth. This is why I wanted to clarify that with you. Was it truth, does it mean truth to you? If it means *a* truth, then we're in creation, don't you see?

For example, there is only truth. There aren't two truths. There aren't forty truths. There aren't five hundred truths. There is just truth. Now some people might say one truth. I say there is truth. Truth is truth. If you say *a* truth, then you've got *many* truths and you're guaranteeing contradiction. You're guaranteeing duality.

I understand what you mean, but I . . .

If you say the truth wherever it may be found—because you can find truth anywhere, wherever—then that's different. That's a vast difference. Now truth expresses through everything at all times, because truth *is*. It just *is*. There is no place in all of the universes you can't find truth, because truth expresses everywhere. Truth is the Divine. Would you not agree that Truth is God?

Yes.

Because if we say that truth is not God, then we have to say that truth is created. And if we say truth is created, then we no longer have truth. So we agree that Truth is God. Are we in agreement? If we say that Truth is God, do we admit that God is everywhere, never absent or away? That's where Truth is. It's everywhere. And all we have to do is ask for it inside of ourselves. And when we ask for it inside of ourselves, by the Law of Asking, we become receptive. And by becoming receptive, we have a tendency to become aware. And becoming aware, the law says we shall experience that which we become aware of. Does that help with your question?

Thank you.

You're welcome. Yes.

Does the visualization of the color gold, which is universally known as the color of wisdom, help in visualizing wisdom?

If the color gold or golden means wisdom to the conscious and the subconscious mind of the student, then, indeed, would visualization upon it be most beneficial.

How many times does the mind have to hear truth before it can accept truth?

That depends upon the mind of the individual. For example, a person, any mind, can accept truth on Tuesday, and totally, wholeheartedly, and completely deny it on Thursday. The reason that that happens is very simple: the student or individual was on a level which was receptive to the expression of truth on Tuesday and was on a level which was not receptive to it on Thursday. In other words, desire may have taken precedence over one's search for truth.

Ofttimes this happens on the spiritual path. Many, many times a student will come in all gung-ho in seeking Truth. That's what they really want. They want the Light. They want Truth. Fine. They will study and do what they feel is great effort for a certain length of time. Then, all of a sudden, all these submerged personal desires start to come up and well up within their being. And when that happens, Truth goes down there and desire fulfillment comes up here. And so we don't see Truth. We're grounded in self.

Balance is the keynote of what the Wise One has tried to teach over these many years. You see, you have the day and you have the night. Let's not deny the truth of creation. Let us not deny that it is dual, that it has its highs and its lows, that it has its ups and has its downs. But try to reach a balance between the two. All things in their proper place will bring harmony to the soul. Yes. Now are there any other questions?

Could you elaborate a bit more on the understanding of the Living Light regarding the terms electric, magnetic, *and* odic, *which were given several classes ago? And the terms* energy, force, *and* power?

Energy, force, and *power.* We'll start with *electric, magnetic,* and *odic.* According to his teachings, he teaches that the conscious mind is the electrical mind. It is the positive. He also teaches that the subconscious is the negative or the magnetic, the great attractor. He teaches that the superconscious is the odic, the neutral, the power itself. He teaches that power, force, and energy are also another trinity, that power is in the conscious or the positive, that force is in the negative or the magnetic or subconscious, and that energy is the odic or the neutral. Does that help with your question?

Thank you.

You're welcome.

Do we attract guides while in class? And if we drop out of class, do these guides leave us? Or do they go on to another student or someone else who is interested in this by the Law of Attraction?

In reference to your question, I have never conducted a class of his teachings that there weren't those interested from the other side who were attracted to the students. Of course, we understand and accept that if one goes by the wayside, that that is the fulfillment of the Law of Merit of the individual, either in the flesh, of course, or out of the flesh. They bear that personal responsibility, through vibrations that are predominant during the class meetings. When a class is given in the physical world, there are those in other dimensions who are interested in the subject being taught. For example, in reference to these little teachings here, they came from the other dimension, and there are those in the other dimension very interested in not only how they're being received, but how they're being applied.

It is the application of the Living Light that changes one's life. And in changing one's life, their spirit, indeed, is born. But without the application of it, it has no value, except as a pretty cover. There is no other value to it, unless they are daily applied.

So many people think in unfoldment that we can sit for a certain length of time each day religiously, seven days a week, and that's going to unfold our spirituality. How far that is from the truth! And that will be demonstrable to anyone who tries it. It does not work that way.

When you are trying to unfold spiritually, you don't do it once a day in your closet and forget about it the other twenty-three and a half hours of the day. You put your spirit, your soul, into all your acts and activities. You keep the thought of the Divine foremost in your mind, whether you're typing a letter or sweeping the street. If you will do that and not forget who is first, if you will really do that each day, every moment in every way, you will unfold your spirit. And you won't be concerned about all of this mundane creation that seems to plague the mind. If you'll always remember that there's a Divine power and it's working in everything you do, whether you like it or not, and you will put that Divine power first, and stop forgetting the Divinity, you will unfold spiritually. And be willing to accept whatever job comes your way, because no matter how humble the job, it's God's work, if you are godly at the moment that you're doing it. Thank you. Now someone else had a question, please. Yes.

I wonder if you would expand a bit on the Law of Disassociation and offer some technique that we can use in everyday living to practice it?

Yes, the Law of Disassociation, as mentioned in *The Living Light*, is a very, very important law. Because in our daily activities we ofttimes find ourselves exposed to a multitude of levels, we're constantly having to be on guard. We best be on guard, or we're going to slip into levels that we don't care to visit, because we know them too well. So he has given the Law of Disassociation. The Law of Disassociation is to disassociate one's inner being, one's spirit, one's soul, from the personality form of the individual.

Now if you find yourself in levels that are not beneficial to you, the first thing is to recognize that the level is not beneficial. How do you recognize that the level is not beneficial? Simply by remembering that you were there before and no good results came out of that level. So why bother to entertain it again? It's only a waste of your time and a waste of your energy. Now if you can remember that, as you're being triggered to another level, then you can disassociate yourself. You can think of a multitude of things. He gave a specific teaching, a specific exercise, in how to become another person; to get outside of yourself, to get out of your self-related thoughts.

Man's greatest problem is his own grounding in his own universe. He's narrowed himself down to what he calls an individual. He's forgotten all about God and has become an individual. That's what the problem is: why we have so much of this upset and disturbance. He forgot how great he truly is, that he's the stars and the moon and the sun, that he's every blade of grass, that he's a part of the trees and the dogs and the cats and all people in all universes. He forgot that and became a kingpin. And when he became a kingpin, he had nothing but problems, because he had a whole kingdom to run: his own. Think of the power that runs all the kingdoms!

So we want to know something about how to disassociate ourselves from ourselves? Well, you think of many things, anything that will take you outside of yourself. If you can think of another individual who has a need, a great need, and you can find yourself in an attitude of mind to be of service for the greater good, you'll immediately get disassociated from your own personal acts and activities. And, of course, by so doing, you will be greatly benefited.

Remember that energy follows attention. So choose wisely where you place your attention, because that's where you're directing your life-giving energy. Every time you look around in this world and you feel yourself disturbed, remember, you're sending your energy to that disturbance. You're feeding it and it will increase and grow. The longer you entertain the thought, as I have often spoken, the more difficult it's going to be to get out of it. And so it is that we have these difficulties, seemingly, in making changes. As he explained in the opening of this class, the reason that change is so difficult is because we're so conditioned to failure. The mind is totally conditioned to failure because it accepts fear, which is nothing more than energy expressed in the negative.

I would like to go back to the missing link for a moment and say that many of our scientists today are starting to feel like this business about evolution has been a multimillion-dollar scientific hoax. That they're feeling now that animals can evolve, insects can evolve, but man himself has freedom of choice and a free mind, and he cannot evolve. He has to use his mind to adapt himself to environments. Could you comment on that? After that, I have one small question.

Yes. He spoke in Discourse 8 in reference to the missing link: it will not be found on your planet, because on your planet it did not exist. Without going into too much or too long a discussion in regard to the evolution of the species, it is my understanding that the human race, the human being, has evolved, but has not evolved on this particular planet on which it is now residing. Therefore, the physical form (missing link) will not be found here.

Now the student has specifically, I think, asked a question in reference to the difference that the animals, no matter how high they evolve, they do not have this free will or choice that the two-legged animals seem to have. There are nine species, basic breakdowns of life, on each and every planet. The epitome of this particular planet is known as the human race. Now animal, tree, and mineral are governed by what you might call a group intelligence. That is about the best way that I can explain it publicly. In other words, the dog will never evolve to the point of free will that man experiences. His species never will. Neither will the elephant or the tree or anything else. It has a limited choice or free will in the species that it is in; it really does. A dog has a certain limited choice. He can choose between this dish of food and that dish of food, but he is definitely limited. What was the other question?

In regard to the Living Light, I would like to have your comments on the difference between wisdom and knowledge.

Oh yes. To my understanding, wisdom is a total awareness on a spiritual level. Knowledge is a total awareness on a mental level. Yes. Does that help with your question?

What about the many, many people who are selfless, who give their lives for others and do so much good work: how can they know these lessons, so they can evolve to a higher rate of vibration or a higher level? I think of people who have gone into a leper colony and have helped people without thinking of themselves. And they say their mental level is very low.

The what level is very low?

The mental. I mean, they couldn't understand all these teachings that are given to us. These teachings are given to us. How can they—

They may not need these teachings, because they may have received them before. Man is evolving, do you understand? You see, this teaching, this is not new. It's very, very old. Its centuries cannot be counted. Teachings come in different forms at different times to different people. Now some people are born in this earth realm and they're just basically very good people and they try to help, etc., but they haven't had these teachings. And I tried to explain to you, perhaps they don't even need them. Perhaps they had them before and they are expressing, you understand. They are applying the teaching, you see. They don't need it, because they're applying it. They put it into application. So they wouldn't need to read it or study it, because they're applying it. Hopefully.

You stated a little earlier that spiritual awareness is not possible without application, without daily application of the principles; that wisdom is total spiritual awareness—

Indeed, it is.

And application is absolutely inseparable.

It is. The light can only grow through application. Application is the law through which the light shines, and without application, it does not shine. It just does not shine. Now people apply the law in many ways. No one is to tell a person how they are to apply the law, because that is their individual right. But without application, there is no light. It cannot be. The energy cannot express itself until it is applied. It lies dormant, like the Divine. You see, God is like a great slumbering wisdom, just waiting to move. But it takes man, it takes will, to make the move. And when man makes the move, the Divine keeps him going.

I feel a little different about the dog and truth situation, because I don't feel that they are limited at all. I think they reach their highest form of evolution. Because it's different from ours does not necessarily mean it's limited.

All form is limited.

Well, limited to that extent, but not for judgment.

No, there's no judgment on animals, dogs, cats, trees, or flowers. In fact, they're my greatest friends.

Can you run through that?

Oh, certainly! There's no limit to the Divine. The only limit that exists, you understand, friends, is in the form. There is no limit to the Divine. You cannot limit the Limitless, of course. Definitely.

I heard it explained one time about group thought. We're in a group thought right now. When someone who believes in reincarnation passes on, they go into that rate of vibration, because this was their level of thinking. It isn't all unlimited. They are limited because of their thinking. Well, wouldn't this be the same thing? A tree thinks, but a tree is thinking tree consciousness.

Absolutely, because that's what its soul is.

Well, that's what I get right now. I'm very inspired right now. Does a rock have a rock consciousness?

Definitely.

It thinks rock.

And that's what it thinks, so that's what it has, of course.

In other words, everything has its natural rate of vibration by this group thought. I mean, a mother is always a mother, if she's gone on a thousand years before, the sanguinary tie—

As long as she's governed by the thought.

By the thought.

And when we're no longer governed by the thought, then we're governed by something else. Because, you see, form cannot exist without being governed. It's impossible.

Is the sanguinary tie ever severed? Does a mother or father go on so far that they aren't that any longer?

In time, some do. All do in eternity. Certainly, because the only reason they're a mother—they're a mother in this particular expression of life and look how short it's been. Very short, wouldn't you agree?

Yes, but I do know that—

You have one mother.

Yes.

One earth mother. Well, you don't think that this is just the beginning of our life or the end, do you?

No.

We came from somewhere, from something, and we've got to go to somewhere, to something. Not just to Summer Land. That's only another step.

I'm trying, I'm, I'm—

Well, yes, because, you see, if you have an earth mother, you have one earth mother. You have one earth father. So we're speaking about earth. What about the rest of the solar system?

Well, in time, yes.

Yes. We are attached to the forms that we need. When we outgrow the need, the attachment disappears. As long as we need identity in this particular form, that's as long as we're going to have it. Remember that the universe is the law's meditation and man is an idea of it. As mind is ever one in substance with the idea, and the whole idea, so man and the law and the universe are one and the same. There is no difference. We are what we think. And so we think the way we are. Does that help with your question on the sanguinary tie?

Yes. I was just trying to clarify that people from the spirit world come and say, Your mother is here, or Your father is here. And I just wondered how long this thought continues.

Well, you see—

A thought is a thought.

A thought is a thought, absolutely. A thought continues as long as there's energy feeding the thought. You see?

Yes, I have a glimpse of it, yes.

As long as we think pink, we're going to see pink. If we think blue, then we're going to see blue.

Well, as long as we have need for that thought.

As long as we have a need, we will have the attachment. So the wise man starts eliminating his needs, because they're false computations caused by brain stuff. Yes.

Where do our thoughts come from?

Excellent question. Where do our thoughts come from? Anyone have an answer? Well, being thought, my friends, that's where they come from. We are thought. Consequently, when you ask the question, "Where do our thoughts come from?" they come from what we are. We are thought. And they just multiply themselves. You see, man is a thought. The tree is a thought. The stars are a thought. That's all thought. That's what it is, in truth.

Isn't there something that comes before thought?

Isn't there something that comes before thought? Absolutely and positively. The Divine. The formless and the free.

Didn't you say that the universe was the Lord's or the law's meditation?

Indeed, the universe *is* the law's meditation.

Well, that would be thought.

Absolutely. Yes.

It is often spoken of, where we are now is illusion, which is thought.

All form is illusion. All form is illusion. And the reason that we experience so much delusion is because we are illusion. Only the formless is free and only the formless is truth.

Would it be possible to see the stars if you didn't believe in the stars? If you didn't believe in its form, would you not see it? Do you understand what I'm trying to say?

Absolutely. You cannot see what you do not believe. Definitely. Now many people say, "I don't believe that, but I see it." You believe it in your mass mind and that's why you see it. You cannot see what you do not believe.

Faith! Is faith belief?

Faith is greater than believing. Faith is an absolute *knowing* of things that cannot yet be believed. It is greater than belief. Faith is spiritual and belief is mental.

But you have the thought, the thought is spiritual?

Thought is mental. Without mind, nothing exists. Mind is the great illusion. Mind: without it, there is no form.

The mind is mental, right?

Yes.

If you were able to get yourself off of the mental level and onto a spiritual level completely, would that mean you would not see people? You would not see, but yet feel?

You would be. You would *be*.

You would just be, but there would be no thing of form that would enter your mind.

You would have no mind for it to enter.

Right, because you wouldn't have a mind.

That's right. Then you're formless and free.

Is there any—there really isn't a way to do that if—

It's known as cosmic consciousness.

Yes. I just can't see how somebody could do that, though, because of everything they have to do with this world every single day that they live. They have to go out to the grocery store and they have to see the grocery store in order to get there.

It happens in moments to some people, but it's a fleeting moment.

But is it what you're striving for?

No. I didn't say I was striving for that. No, I'm still in form. We're striving to be free from the bondage of form, to find the peace that passeth all understanding. We're not striving to get out of form. We're striving to refine form with new thought, with new belief.

Like recognizing form while you're in it?

We already recognize it by the Law of Being Aware of it. By being in it, we've recognized it.

Therefore, being able to have a concept in your mind of the spiritual world afterward—therefore, it would help you all the more along, when you die. Is this what you're—

Yes, to be aware that everything is a passing illusion, that all form, in truth, is illusion, it's made of mind stuff. Absolutely, then you would not put your faith in form. You would put your faith where faith truly belongs: the formless and the free. That's faith. That's the faith that moves the mountain. Because, you see, it comes before the mountain. That's why faith moves the mountain: it precedes it.

Are there any more questions? Time's getting late.

I'm still kind of stuck on the word thought. *In other words, do you mean, Don't worry about thought because it's just illusion?*

Yes! Absolutely! Definitely! Worry is thought also. So that's thought in thought. *[The Teacher laughs.]*

In other words, thoughts really don't mean anything.

Well, they mean things to those who are living in a thought dimension. And especially to the poor souls who are attached to a thought dimension, because then they're governed by all these thoughts.

Well, then, should you just go through life saying, Who cares, it's just a thought?

Well, if that's what you've merited.

I remember reading in The Living Light *that thoughts are things; therefore, beware of what you think.*

Definitely. Can you show me anyone that's stopped thinking since you've been in class?

I hope not.

Yes.

On the difference between thought and idea, that thoughts can be good and bad, but an idea is always Divine. It can't be a bad idea.

Can't be, because it's neutral.

And so if you can take your thoughts and try to change them into an idea, you have something good to work on. Am I not right?

Well, we're speaking on another level now. Yes.

If you can't have thought, then how can you send a healing or vital force or whatever name you call it, but you're still speaking of the Light, the energy—How can you send that out in a positive form?

In order that it may reach a soul who is yet in creation, it's necessary to use the laws of creation, which would be the vehicle of thought, you see. Remember, we must use the vehicles of the dimension in which we are expressing. Consequently, like the lady has asked in reference to healing, certainly we must use the vehicle of thought, because the person that we're praying to be healed is in thought and, therefore, receptive to thought.

[End of recording]

MARCH 8, 1973

CONSCIOUSNESS CLASS 9 ✄

Now this evening, before starting our regular discussion of questions and answers, for those of you who care to take notes, I'm going to give to you the laws governing health, wealth, and happiness. So if you wish to write them down, the law governing health is harmony. The law governing wealth is rhythm. And the law governing happiness is unity. Now we'll carry on with our questions and answers.

I have a question regarding returning to Allsoul.

Yes.

As a person reaches total awareness, do they not become literally at one with that Allsoul?

That's when they return to the Allsoul.

Or lose their identity as an individual totally?

Absolutely. Definitely. They lose their identity because they become aware of the Allness, which they truly are. Yes.

Then are they at that point still a soul?

They are soul, but they are not individualized. In other words, you could term it soul essence. They remain spirit, but they do not have an individualized covering.

As something returns from this, wouldn't it be the Allsoul, or rather a group effort, as opposed to an individual effort, if the individual had lost his individual identity?

Yes, it could be. You mean in a soul that had come out anew from the Allsoul, an illumined soul? Yes, they could become what is known as part of—instead of what you would call a group soul, I would rather term it a soul principle. They could become a part of a spiritual principle, instead of the individualized soul or group soul effort. Anyone else?

I would like a little clarification on the spheres and the planes. In totality, we have eighty-one planes.

Levels of awareness.

Planes, levels of awareness. Is not each one of these a plane and at the end of nine, you're in a sphere?

That is correct.

And then you go on to a higher totality. Are there nine spheres of totality, because each one starts with one and ends with nine?

There are nine times infinity.

I agree. Could I have a little more clarification, please?

You cannot define that which is indefinable. When we have total, we are encompassing all that it is possible for us to be aware of at any given moment. For example, we have a totality of an awareness of being in this room at this moment with a group of people. We look and see that there are laws, etc. Now that is the total awareness that we have at this moment, but that is not the infinite awareness. It is only the total awareness for the level of consciousness that we are expressing on at the particular moment. Does that help with your question?

It certainly does. Thank you.

Thank you. Yes.

Is there a nine times nine level? When an individual has reached the eightieth level and he is able to move freely through that many levels, can he die? Is the eighty-first level the Infinite Soul, the Allsoul?

The Divine.

Is he free to dive into that for a vacation, if he so chooses, or does he go from that eightieth level and then go into another universe and another set of nine times nine?

Once having passed through the eightieth level, there is no longer any desire for such things termed as vacations. The eighty-one levels that are total awareness, that have been given at this present time, govern strictly what man in his present state of evolution can become aware of at this time. There is no limit to the Infinite. This is only one planetary system of many planetary systems. And intelligence exists and expresses on all universes and in all levels.

Do all universes have the same levels or do they have a different frame of reference?

Creation is not the same. No, it is not. They have a different sense of reference, yes.

I have a question about the solar plexus. In The Living Light, *you say that the solar plexus is the father aspect of the universe and I would like you to clarify that.*

Yes, it is stated in *The Living Light* that the solar plexus, the solar, the center of our anatomy is the father aspect. By father aspect, he is referring to the positive, the positive aspect. The solar plexus is the sun of our universe. We are a small universe of this mass universe that we look out at. And the planets are located in the human anatomy in certain areas. The sun is located where we term the solar plexus. This is why he teaches, Do not concentrate upon the solar plexus; it is the seat of all power in your anatomy, and if you do, it could blind you. Yes, it means the positive aspect, the sun, and that is its location in the occult anatomy. Yes.

Does the solar plexus correspond to the fourth center?

The solar plexus is the center. It is the circuit of the entire human anatomy and it is the place where most all people, if they feel any impact, they're going to feel it in the pit of the stomach or in the solar plexus. It is the center. It is the sensor in the human anatomy. The sensor or the main circuit system is located in the solar plexus. It is where all of these—you have nine bodies in one body at the present moment. Some of those bodies are fully created and some are not. They are all connected to the main circuit system, which is the solar plexus. Yes.

Almost every psychic that I've ever read said undoubtedly that their power was in the gut. And they claim, Arthur Ford among them, that everything that they received was right here.

Yes, because they had their conscious awareness in the solar plexus. As I said, that is the sensor. It is the main circuit system, the main nervous system of the human anatomy. Now if a person, for example, if they put their attention upon the main circuit center of the human body, then they cannot expand their consciousness to a universe, because they are putting their attention on the microcosm and do not have their attention on the macrocosm. Therefore, they can be extremely psychic. There is such a thing as solar plexus mediums and then there is such a thing as universal awareness mediums. This is because some mediums think that the power and everything is received in the main circuitry system and they have limited their awareness to that center and have not expanded it out into the universes. And some are very fine and excellent psychics and mediums, but it is not the best phase of mediumship to unfold.

Do I understand, then, that almost all mediums receive through the solar plexus, but those with a spiritual awareness would be on an entirely different level?

Absolutely, positively, definitely. Definitely! An overconcentration upon the solar plexus would put one very quickly in tune with the astral realms, very quickly in tune. To anyone that is in any degree at all receptive. Yes.

I really feel that when we are in meditation and we're eager to learn and these other souls join us from the other side, that that is a form or a level of Allsoul awareness. I don't mean that we go back to the Allsoul, but there is definitely a feeling of unity of purpose in that Allsoul vibration and that consequently opens the door to awareness, I think.

Absolutely. Whenever two or more minds are together in a spiritual purpose and endeavor, they cannot help but tune into a spiritual level where there is a unity expressing itself.

Now I think there is some confusion on this solar plexus, this energy psychic center, still in the atmosphere, so I would like to express a little bit more on that. You know where the solar plexus is located. Now it's halfway between the spiritual and creation. And that is another reason that you do not concentrate upon it, because the tendency to go down to creation is stronger than the one to go up. Now I hope that clears up things for people here. Yes.

Regarding Discourse 31, we have a spiritual responsibility to our spirit friends, I have been told. Is it wrong for us to give out what we have learned in class to others who are in need of help? We find in our daily life people who need help and we give this out. Well, I have been cautioned not to give out what I have learned.

The thing is, I think we'll find, students, number one: Are we aware in our giving of the spiritual responsibility that we have incurred in the giving? Are we aware what is going to happen to that individual that we are sharing this awareness with and how much of their path will we be responsible for, you see? So the keynote of the whole thing is spiritual discernment.

You see, a person can be given a light. Instead of the light leading them through the darkness or through the forest, it could be too bright for them and it could blind them. And then they would stumble and they would be worse off than before they had met us. And so it is, we, indeed, would bear a personal, spiritual responsibility for what we had done. Now that, of course, does not in any way exempt the Law of Merit. The individual having solicited, if they had solicited the help, would have merited what they had received. If they had not solicited it, they would still merit it, if they stayed and listened to it. So that does not exempt the Law of Merit. But in giving out any type of awareness, we are incurring a direct spiritual responsibility for what we have done. Now that does not mean we shouldn't give it out. And that does not mean that we should give it out. But it does mean that we should use spiritual discernment.

That would also have to do with starting a circle or a group?

Absolutely and positively, because anyone that starts any kind of group or meditation or discussion, they bear a personal, spiritual responsibility for what they have set into motion. Absolutely.

Thank you.

Definitely. I have one philosophy: No matter what you do in life, no matter who you meet, leave them as well as you found them and, hopefully, better, but never worse.

I didn't intend to leave them worse.

Yes.

In the eighty-one levels of awareness, it's human nature on our level of awareness to want to retain our personal identity. How far up this ladder of eighty-one levels do we go before we lose our personality, our own personal identity, and say I am I, and what happens at that point?

We must reach the twenty-seventh one before we grow out of this individualization.

Twenty-seven?

Twenty-seventh, yes.

Then we don't care whether we're ourselves or not?

As you grow through those levels, you will find that things are no longer as important as they used to be to you. You see, it's kind of like you outgrow a family. Sooner or later, you know, you really do, and you outgrow your various friends and acquaintances. And as you're growing on up, as you outgrow the few, you encompass the many and that's when you become more god-like. Yes, in other words, you grow out of personality and you grow into principle, and then you start losing this self, self, self-vibration. Yes.

I have a fairly bold question to ask. And I'm wondering if you're using spiritual discernment by not introducing us to teachings of the Bible as yet?

Yes, if I am using or not using spiritual discernment?

If you are using spiritual discernment.

Well, yes, that's a wonderful question. I appreciate your question very much. I appreciate your boldness and especially the challenge. I have tried for a lifetime not to judge a person's thoughts or activities, accepting the divine law, which states, That that I judge shall judge me in time. Now no one wants to be in the witness box being judged through eternity, and, of course, we do that to ourselves, you know. No one sits up there to do it. So the lady has asked if I am using spiritual discernment in not introducing—I presume you mean the Christian Bible.

Yes.

Because there are many bibles in the world—the Christian Bible in the spiritual awareness course? No, I think great spiritual discernment was used by the teachers who brought this course into being, considering that it is not a Bible course.

Now I will be more than happy, if there are a sufficient number of dedicated, spiritually interested people who want to take a course in the Christian Bible as it relates to Spiritualism, I will be more than happy to give that type of a course to anyone that is interested. However, in my thirty-two years of serving the world of spirit, I have not found, as yet, a sufficient number of people who are interested in Spiritualism and the Bible at the same time. However, of course, if we take Spiritualism out of the Bible, there is nothing left to the Bible but the cover itself. So if there are a sufficient number of people interested in the Christian Bible as Spiritualism relates to it and vice versa, I will be happy to set up a special course for those students.

How many are sufficient?

Twenty-seven.

Twenty-seven?

That's right.

Intuition made me feel that we're preparing for growth here in our little band and it made me feel that this would be a logical step along the path.

Well, I can understand your feeling. Personally, myself, I would think the logical growth step for the group would be the Bhagavad Gita, the bible of the Hindus. But, you know, I would also be happy to give a course on the Bhagavad Gita as it relates to Spiritualism, if there are a qualified number willing to sign up for the course.

It may not be important to sign up for it, but it is precisely what was going through my mind and you beat me to expressing it.

The Gita? It's a wonderful book. I highly recommend it. I recommend it as much as I do the Christian Bible.

Isn't there a Bible available for us? A Bible that explains the . . .

Spiritualistic? Absolutely. The *[Johannes]* Greber translation is sitting on the book table. I highly recommend it. It's in today's English and it's the ancient codex manuscripts from the Vatican itself. It was transcribed by Father Johannes Greber, a German Catholic priest in 1936, I believe the date is. Yes.

Getting back to the discourse, what is the purpose of the ego and why was it given to man? I know it's to grow, but where does the ego come from?

Wonderful question. Thank you very much for bringing it up. What is the purpose of the ego? Well, let us look and see what the ego does, then perhaps we'll find its purpose. Without ego, how many would bother to take a bath? Without ego, how many would bother to brush their teeth or comb their hair? Without ego, how many would have the drive to live in a better house or have a better car or produce more work? Without ego, how many would go out into the world and, through the trials and tribulations and the struggles, to bring some light to this old world? Ego definitely serves a purpose and it serves an excellent purpose when it becomes educated.

Now how do we educate the old ego? Usually, we walk around in creation and our little egos are swimming around in what we call personality. In other words, it's being expressed in a very personal way—that's what I mean by personality—a very personal way. Well, when we start to educate the ego, we use this energy and this drive, not in a personal way, but to accomplish something. We send it up into a dimension known as principle.

Let's take this little church, for example. Now no one can tell me that a church doesn't have an ego. I know better, whether it's the Serenity Church or it's the Catholic Church or anybody else's church. So a person, having to express their ego, could express it in a most beneficial way by making their church a better church, by having the things that their ego demands, taking it out of the personal and putting it into the principle. Why do you think we have cathedrals with stained glass and golden altars and everything else? Well, God doesn't need it. Neither do the so-called saints, if they're saints. It's the ego that needs it, don't you see?

So when the ego becomes educated and you use the ego and its drive in principle, then a lot of good comes into the world. But when it's not educated, you get an awful lot of problems. If you see a nice-looking church someplace, you can be rest assured somebody, or many somebodies, have a mighty potent ego, don't you see? It has to be the best, because their egos won't permit them to have anything else. So there's ego everywhere. Some of it's educated, in the sense it's working in principle. A lot of it is in personality.

Why, I heard on the radio just today on a newscast that they're having problems with the international sports here in the Olympics because of power struggles. So the United States government is thinking of taking punitive action against those athletes, and probably they'll have to have government control of it, because they walked out on the Russians. That just came over the news today. Well, if that isn't a demonstration of ego that's expressing through personality, then I don't know what it is, don't you see? Wherever you have human beings—the ego serves a good purpose the moment you educate it.

Now they have a nice big church in San Francisco, a beautiful church. Well, it took a lot of ego to get the building paid off and to get the whole thing taken care of. It took a gigantic ego. I ought to know: I was a part of that church and we had a wonderful ego for a teacher. She was just great! She worked like a dog and she had a mighty potent ego and she did a lot of good in the world. My goodness, if you don't have ego, you'll never get through the struggle; you won't get through the trials and tribulations. You see? You'll just sit down and say, "That's it! It's too much. I can't make it. I'm not going to work twenty-two and twenty-three hours a day, year after year." It takes an ego to get you through that. There it serves a good purpose.

Where does the ego come from? Does it come in with the soul?

The ego exists in the form.

In the form?

Oh, absolutely and positively. The ego exists in the form and if the form has a gigantic ego, then that's what the soul merited. What it is going to do with that giant ego, now, is something else.

It seems to me that also in that discourse that the main thing is to find your purpose in life. And so if you were to find your purpose—

Purpose in life, and use your ego . . .

Then you educate it?

Then you've educated it. Absolutely.

And then you are aware of where you're going and you get away from self.

Absolutely, definitely! And if you find your purpose, let us hope and pray that you've got a giant ego, because it'll take a lot of ego drive to keep you going, yes. You see, I do not believe in annihilating the ego. Just look at the people who suppress their ego, just look at them. They're usually an absolute emotional wreck. Use your ego wisely to accomplish some good in the world. Yes.

Would you please give us your understanding of racial differences, why some people merit coming back in a different race and at what point in the hereafter do the physiological differences fade away?

In reference to the differences of color in the species, the souls, of course, merit whatever form they are incarnated into. Now when the soul evolves into the higher spheres, there is no such thing as color, for there is no such thing as personality. They have evolved out of it.

Now the question that you have asked, the reason why some souls merit certain types of bodies and other souls merit bodies a little bit different—you understand, that's the question you're basically asking. In order to explain all of that, we would have to explain the causes of all the differences. Because if you couldn't explain the cause, then you're not going to have reason and understanding in explaining that this one, because of certain transgressions of certain laws, has merited that kind of body. Well, we have to know what caused that kind of body for them to merit it in the first place. Are you particularly interested in why you're in the particular body you're in? Is that the reason for your question?

No, I'm—[There was a break in the recording at this point.]

You're always going to have that and you're always going to have souls that are on different rungs of the ladder of eternal progression, you see? You'll always have that in creation. It is when you finally evolve out of that, that there is no longer any duality; there is only the Light, the oneness. Yes, someone else had a question? Yes.

I didn't have one on my mind, but I—

Oh, you didn't?

Well, I—I—this is a little more personal, but when one is beginning to experience phenomena, which we all will, because we are unfolding, and one begins to hear, it isn't always a voice, is it?

You mean is it always an audible voice or do you hear it inside?

I heard something and the voice was right inside of me.

Oh, definitely. Sometimes you'll hear it in the inside of your head and sometimes in any part of your being.

And it was in a foreign language, which surprised me, but I just wondered whether this voice is from within?

Definitely. That's where the spirit is. Your spirit is within. When we awaken to the spirit within, we know the spirit without. But we do not know the spirit without until we've awakened to the spirit within. My goodness, how would we recognize it? You see, spirit recognizes spirit, and mind recognizes mind, and body recognizes body. So we cannot recognize the spirit without until we've recognized the spirit within. And this is why they always teach, "O man, know thyself, and ye shall know the truth, and the truth shall set you free." Well, when you make the effort to know yourself, you're going to know your spirit. And when you know your spirit, then your spirit, you understand, being spirit, knows all other spirits.

Thank you.

Does that help with your question?

Then after that, I heard from without and then within and I was totally confused. Was it from within or without? Within was a voice and definitely saying something definite. And without, it was a sound, but it was definitely a sound.

Absolutely. It is the spirit within that registers it when it's from a spiritual dimension. Yes.

It's my understanding that we all go out of the body each night and sometimes during a dream . . .

We do. The vital body leaves the physical body for a very short period of time during sleep; that is when it goes out into the cosmos and rejuvenates. That's why—it takes about nine minutes and you can do that sitting in the chair or lying down. That's up to the individual. Now that's the only time you're being rejuvenated with energy. All the other time, you're dreaming.

But my question is, If we go out, we certainly do contact other dimensions.

When the vital body goes out, it goes out to the universal cosmos, where it is totally rejuvenated in a matter of minutes.

But it can and does have contact with other . . .

That's another body. That's known as the astral body.

What I'm confused about is the change called death. Why is it that there are so many people who are confused about whether or not they're dead? And some are unable to accept it at all.

It's most understandable, because they do not have any conscious recall of all of their travels for a lifetime. They have no conscious recall. Now it is within their being, but they are not consciously aware of it. And so when they leave this physical body, they find themselves in a body, usually the astral body, and it looks the same and everything else and they have clothes on, usually the last suit or whatever they were wearing before they passed on. And they're totally bewildered because they're walking around in the atmosphere and they see the astral duplicate of this table, you understand? That's what they see, but their hands go right through it. They talk to people and the people don't hear them. That's why they're confused. Yes, you had a question?

Well, we understand God as the Universal Law of Life. This has puzzled me for a good many years and I see it here in Discourse 10.

Yes, what does it say?

[The student reads the following from Discourse 10.]

> *Know within and unto thee all shall be.*
> *Thy will shall be done, oh God.*
> *Not my will, but thy will.*
> *This will is within thee.*
> *It is known not by the mind,*
> *But it is known within thee.*

Yes.

Well, thy will be done, if we don't have predestination—we are free now, as we ever will be. What is meant by "thy will?"

We have 10 percent free will, 90 percent cause and effect. We're constantly working out the effects of the causes we set into motion yesterday, but we have 10 percent free will to make a change. For example, what you did today is the effect, only the effect, of what you set into motion before. So when you are experiencing the effect, in experiencing the effect, you're setting into motion a new cause. Don't you understand?

I mean, I lift the book. By lifting the book, you see, that's a cause, and the effect is, it's in my hand. By experiencing that effect, I set another law into motion, a cause, and I set it down. That is the law governing form and you cannot escape it in form. So a man chooses very wisely how he experiences his effects, because in experiencing those effects, he's setting into motion new causes in that very instant. For example, someone says something to you and you have an effect, a reaction. The reaction is an action on your part and in so doing, you have established a law and set it into motion. And that goes on moment by moment by moment, every day, everywhere. But you have that 10 percent free will to be perfectly still and be not moved by all those things.

At Stanford University, they say that they have just found out that after death, there are changes in the human body that go on for three days.

Yes.

It goes back to some of the old beliefs that you shouldn't bury anybody for three days.

Seventy-two hours. They should not be touched.

Does this have some spiritual background as well?

Absolutely. It takes seventy-two hours for the astral body to be freed from the physical body after the so-called transition. It takes seventy-two hours. And the astral body experiences whatever is being done to the physical body within that seventy-two-hour period.

Is it true, then, that someone that was embalmed within that time, is it possible that they could feel pain?

They do. Or cremated within that time, they most certainly do. Because, you see, it takes that seventy-two hours for that substance, which forms your astral body—it goes out through this cord, this silver cord—for it to completely leave the physical body. And there is still some registration of feeling, because it's still connected.

The scientists found out last year that this is true.

I am very happy to hear it, because the Spiritualists have been teaching it for 125 years. Yes.

Then—

Just in time. They said it was just in time for me. I'm very happy to hear that. *[The Teacher laughs.]*

Also, that would take into consideration willing your body to the eye bank. They do it so fast.

Yes, definitely.

I know some of them who did and they did suffer pain.

Yes.

They came back in a seance and said they did.

Absolutely and positively. Definitely.

After the seventy-two hours, then, it really doesn't make too much difference whether you're cremated or you go underground.

It makes no difference whatsoever unless the individual whose body is left here on earth has some strange belief that fire is hell itself and it's the devil's work. Now if you have a soul that believes that, you understand, then, cremation would not be recommended. Myself, personally, I'm being cremated. It's the safest, the most sanitary way that I know of and it's one of the oldest methods, long before the paganism of embalming and the paganism of burials. You know, we're supposed to be in a great Christian Age of enlightenment and sometimes it is sad to see so much paganism with these burials and funerals and everything. That has nothing to do with our soul and with our spirit, and it has a great deal to do with feeding the funeral parlors and making them a nice big business. Yes.

Also, we could have a little faith for people who need it here.

Yes, we certainly could. Of course, they're building hotels or something, I hear, in Italy, where they put those bodies in to freeze, wait, and reanimate. I think I read something about it a few years ago. I think they'll be waiting a long time. Yes.

I'd like to ask, is the seventy-two hours sufficient, then, for all the other bodies, too?

Absolutely and positively. It only takes seventy-two hours for them to be completely free from the piece of clay and its effects. Seventy-two hours. Yes.

Can the soul incarnate or reincarnate at any point along the evolutionary process or must it wait until it reaches a certain level of awareness?

There is a Divine Law governing incarnation and it cannot be transgressed. It is known as the Law of Merit. For example, I just might say, "Well, now I'd like to go off there, off into the universe in my next incarnation beyond such and such a planet, because I happen to feel that would be a nice place to be." It doesn't work that way, because there are laws set into motion that we alone have set into motion. They cannot be transgressed.

Remember that—someone asked me how many laws are there. There are as many laws as there is thought or imagination. Whatever your mind can imagine, it establishes a law of that imagining and that is how man is a law unto himself and this is why they teach, As you believeth, you becometh. For each thing that you entertain in thought is a law that you and you alone set into motion. Yes.

As you believeth, you becometh, but then you also say that you only have 10 percent free choice.

That's right, because you have set that law into motion. Form has set that law into motion of mind stuff.

In other words, are you saying that people only have 10 percent chance of changing?

That's just what I'm saying, yes. There is 10 percent chance.

And that's all?

Well, I haven't found a higher percent. I've been looking for a lifetime, but I hope maybe sometime I'll find a higher percent. But I'm very grateful for 10 percent. Yes, there's 10 percent chance, yes.

I don't know how to word this. Speaking of thought, if you want to put something into motion to improve yourself, how you would be in your next level, if you were not starting to create that in thought form now . . .

Yes, but you've already been creating it, like all the rest of us. Our tomorrows, you understand, are what we're constantly setting into motion.

So if you wanted to be a better person and alleviate all the thoughts that you had in this incarnation, let's say . . .

Yes.

. . . you ought to be creating mentally what you would like to be.

What you would like to be, yes. Well, you see, that's very important, the question that you have brought up, because, you see, man is aware of his own frailties. You know, a lot of people would prefer to say they're not aware of their weaknesses and continue to demonstrate them. How ridiculous! We're all aware of our weaknesses and we all have weaknesses. We might not want to think about them and, of course, that's good in a way, not to. Because, first of all, we're aware of our own weaknesses, so we decide, "Now, all right, I want to outgrow that, that, that, that, and that." How do we outgrow something? By making a decision and, once having made that decision, completely take our thought, which is our energy, off of it.

Because as long as we entertain it in thought, we hold our vibration right to it. The key is to make the decision, you see. Then that great power, the power that holds all things in space, if we're really tuned in when we make that decision, the change takes place. We don't keep thinking about it, because then we hold it on a mental level and we guarantee the continuity of the thing we're trying to outgrow. We guarantee the continuity of it because we keep feeding it energy, so it stays alive in our universe. Is that understandable?

Somewhat. So it would be taken care of for you. You wouldn't be creating any thought form yourself as to your growth.

The moment you make the decision, that sets a law into motion of the new form. Do you understand? So you take your thought, which is your energy, off the old form. See, what happens when a person—say that a person wants to become a musician, all right? And they're not a musician, and they've tried several times to be one, but it is their weakness that they just don't seem to have the talent. But they want that. All right, fine. So they decide, "Well, I'm really going to be a musician." Well, every time they think about being a musician, this thing back here keeps reminding them that they're not one. Don't you see? They defeat their own purpose. They defeat their own purpose.

That that we entertain in thought, we become. So if we keep entertaining in thought our frailties, then we become those things. We become them even more so. This is why—that's known as negative thinking. That's what happens to us. If we keep saying, "Gosh, this world is so tough. It's just so unbearable and everything is going kaput." Well, the more we say it, the more we become it, because man, not God, is the creator. Man, not God, is the creator.

This could also tie in with analysis and going to psychiatrists, speaking out all these negative things.

That's what they do. They free themselves of one consciously, only to become another, because they keep feeding it. They keep pouring their life-giving energy onto their problems. Now, usually, the thing that helps most in psychiatric treatment is the inflation of the ego, you know. There's no greater topic, you know, someone once said, than to talk about yourself. You know, people love to hear about themselves. This is why Spiritualism should be the world's greatest.

I was just thinking that this whole thing of cause and effect is a giant chain reaction going along and with seventy billion laws of cause and effect at any moment. You can draw from that, I suppose, a net direction of where these laws, taken as a whole, are taking you.

Yes, then we must—we must be aware. Remember this: that a law set into motion is set into motion from a level of awareness. So that law set into motion on that level of awareness applies whenever you're consciously aware of that level. Then, that law governs you. But now, you may be coming up. Say that you're on level seventeen and on level seventeen, you are setting a law into motion. OK, fine. Every time you, your soul, your spirit is expressing on level seventeen, you are governed and affected by the law that you set into motion on level seventeen.

But now, two minutes later, you may dip down to level six. Now, on level six, there are other laws that you set into motion that govern level six. And this is where man has so many problems, so much confusion and difficulty. First of all, he will have to learn to become aware of what level he is expressing on. And while he's expressing on that level, then he must become aware of what laws he's setting into motion. Then, he must remember, when he goes back to that level, he must remember those laws that he set into motion on that level. Does that help?

That helps a lot. That's why change is rather difficult.

Change is extremely difficult because—for example, he teaches in his book a law that is very important: Choose wisely your associates and with whom you spend your life-giving energy. For this reason, if you don't choose your associates wisely, with whom you spend your life-giving energy, you can be triggered to levels. Say, every time you meet Mary Jane, she's usually on level four. Well, her level four triggers your level four—you understand?—if you're not really strong. So she's in a constant mess and has nothing but problems. So every time you're in her atmosphere, you start to get nothing but problems. Well, she didn't give them to you. You simply let yourself be triggered to level four, where all those problems exist, for all those laws you set into motion on level four. Do you understand?

This is why it's so important—you know, so many people sit in Spiritualism and meditate and they just open themselves wide open. Why, my God, just because the spirits have left the flesh—they still have all those levels expressing. I choose very carefully who enters into my spiritual atmosphere. I don't open up the doors to my home to everyone. You know, you ought to be very careful who comes in and test the spirit, test the spirit and find out what level they're on. Is it going to be compatible with you? Because it could be a real, real sad trip.

How do you find out? How do you test a spirit to know what level you're on?

Because, you see, you have to know yourself. You cannot test another until you're able to test yourself. I don't know of any way of testing a spirit until we've tested our own spirit, you see. And how do we test our own spirit? By knowing our spirit. You see, when we know our spirit, then we know when our spirit is expressing. And if we don't know our spirit, then we don't know whether it's our mind or our brain or our spirit. So the first thing to know is ourselves. That's where it all is. It's inside ourselves. We must learn to know our own spirit first, because if we don't, then, you see, we see these entities flitting around in the atmosphere and say, "Oh, that's a new guide of mine." Guide, hell! It might be from the mental realm! It might be from the astral realm! Or it may be the projection of somebody that's still in the flesh, you know. So you see, you want to check yourself first, really and seriously.

Now this is why some people, writing on Spiritualism, have talked about mediumship and things and they said, "Well, some mediums, they even give fictitious relatives and stuff." Well, you know, what happens with some poor mediums is you get some of these big brain intellects and they go to a poor, humble little medium there and she's doing her bit. And perhaps she doesn't know the difference between the desire world and the spirit world and the mental world and the astral world and the cosmic world and all those other worlds. And so the guy says, "And how about my Uncle Jim? How's my Uncle Jim doing?" And so the poor soul says, "Well, just fine and dandy." Well, his Uncle Jim is a figment of his imagination! Now I admit that's happened, you know, with some mediums. And it's not really very fair, because the individuals doing things like that are only deceiving themselves. You see, the poor medium is receptive and she's gotten triggered to the level of imagination. Yes, that's happened to some of our mediums. It's in our history; not often, fortunately. Usually, their spirit guides will sense that kind of stuff and have nothing to do with them, because all they want to do is play games.

Many mediums are in trance and others are not in trance. You seem to tune in and just speak naturally as you do. I mean, you're so integrated with your guide that—

I'm a firm believer in integration.

So am I. This word seems to come from this church. I've never used it before.

Because it's an integrated church.

It really is a lovely church. Anyway, the thing is that many mediums do not have to go into trance. What is the purpose of trance? Why must a person be—

I can tell you what's beneficial in trance. I can tell you its benefits. I can also tell you its detriments. Which would you like to hear?

I'll take them both. There has to be balance.

Well, let's give the Light first. Its benefits are very simple: when a person is in a phase of trance mediumship, there is less tendency of the brain for colorization. And do you know what *colorization* means?

Yes.

Coloring the messages because of the subconscious. That does not mean that they are 100 percent free from colorization, because the medium can fluctuate in the trance, do you understand? But it is more beneficial for accuracy and for the brain getting out of the way, to be in trance. Now when a medium is not in trance, they face the ever-present danger, you understand, of thoughts welling up from the subconscious or from the spirit.

Now, for example, you take anyone in any circumstance and say that they're consciously aware and they're giving a message to a person that they know something about. The tendency of this old thing back here, that records all and loses nothing, to speak or to send forth a thought, an image into the awareness, is ever a critical and present danger. It's ever there, don't you understand? So there is a great benefit to trance mediumship. That doesn't mean that everybody should go out and be a trance medium.

But in giving communication, we must all recognize and realize that there are many levels that we may be tuning in with. Now I am well aware, because I've been repeatedly told in the past two years by my Crystal and my guides and teachers, that there are some people who enter these church doors who try to play their little games of telepathy. But it seems it just doesn't work for them, because they just don't get their billets and they don't get the messages they want that way because that isn't the way the spirit works. But I always feel, when I become aware of that, and when I'm informed about it by the spirit, I always feel for any student. Because, remember, it's a potent force. Thought is force and it's a very potent force.

And so you must remember that in communication, it is very wise to give what you have to give and care less what anybody does with it. And if you just give it and you give it quick and you get out, and you give it quick again and you get out, you're going to keep yourself from being pulled down into mental levels, you see. Because it is not easy to unfold mediumship, as I'm sure you well know, and any mediums here in the class. It wasn't easy for me and of course I'm still working on it. You know, you never stop working on it. But when you're consciously aware and you're facing a group of people, then you've got to be that much more alert. Does that help with your question?

[End of recording]

MARCH 15, 1973

CONSCIOUSNESS CLASS 10 ✄

The question is asked, the triune law that was given last class of harmony, rhythm, and unity, Are they faculties? And if so, are the others functions? Yes, that is true. Happiness, my dear friend, is a function, because, you see, the Divine Spirit, formless and free, does not express happiness because it does not express sadness. The God that we are trying to teach, the Divine Power, is totally neutral. It is creation that is sad or happy and creation is function, yes. Does that help with your question?

Which group of faculties is it? The first one is duty, gratitude, and tolerance, and the second is faith, poise, and humility. And beyond that, I don't know which is what.

What will benefit you the most: to know what number faculty they are or to find the way to apply them?

That would be better, to find the way to apply them.

Then, I think that is what we should discuss.

Yes, sir.

If that is what you would like to discuss. How does one apply the Law of Harmony?

By applying peace in one's universe. Peace is harmony.

And peace is power.

Yes.

And what does harmony bring?

Health.

And what is health?

Health is harmonious action.

And so it is that health, the Law of Harmony governs health. And wealth—What governs wealth?

Rhythm. Repeating the same goals, time after time, day after day, until finally they are reached.

A cyclic pattern?

A cyclic pattern, yes, sir.

Yes.

And week after week, month after month.

Year after year.

Yes, sir.

And happiness?

Happiness is unity, is oneness, one with another, and then you have happiness yourself, as well as happiness for your brothers.

And wouldn't you agree that the Law of Unity would govern that type of an expression?

Yes.

And so it is that now we have a greater understanding of that triune faculty and that understanding leads us and opens the doors to application. Isn't that more important than knowing what number it is at this state of our growth?

Certainly.

Now as soon as we're able to apply that, then it's time to reveal what positions they are in the soul faculties.

Thank you, sir.

Thank you kindly.

You were discussing earlier about the functions and the faculties and some people are confused. I don't think I'm completely unconfused. The faculties, to me, would appear to be the attributes of the soul.

Yes.

Then the functions are just the opposite. Are they not the functions of the material?

The physical.

The physical.

Definitely. And the mental.

And the mental. Well, that's what I wondered. I just wanted to get it clear in my mind. I had heard the word attribute *in connection with the faculties.*

The soul faculties, their expression, are what create, out of the divine essence known as spirit, the spiritual body. The functions are what create the physical body and the mental body. So one is creating the higher bodies, through which to express and have awareness on higher levels, and the other is creating the more gross levels. And they both serve their purpose and that is why he teaches to balance them, so that your energy may be directed, not only down, where it usually goes, but also upward. And in so doing, you will have this great peace. Because this peace is only experienced through balance of soul faculties and sense functions.

Now the sadness is that a person starting on the spiritual path of awareness will start to pour more and more energy into the soul faculties, more interest and more energy. And then they'll reach a certain leveling-off point for them and the energy will start to go downward into the functions at the total sacrifice of the soul faculties. Then problems begin to reign, because they go totally out of balance. There is no balance, don't you see?

First of all, perhaps they've been 99 and 9/10 percent into the sense functions. Then they come to the light of awareness and they start to go 99 and 9/10 into the spiritual and into the soul faculties. When that happens, it's like a boomerang, and then they usually are just blown apart inside themselves and their wings sprout and off they go. And then the days, the months, and the years pass and they come trotting on back. It's simply a matter of imbalance. That is not the teachings. Imbalance is not the teachings of the Living Light. Balance is the teaching. Yes.

Would a good example be a man who has been very materialistic and has the teachings of, let's say, here or some other spiritual teachings, and then all of a sudden, he doesn't care for money at all and pushes that aside and thinks that he doesn't need the material—

He transgresses the divine Law of Balance.

That would be an example of imbalancing—

Absolutely.

—the faculty against the function. Because he has to apply reason.

Yes, because, you see, reason is a soul faculty. You see, the tendency of the mind when it gets a little bit of light to this great eternity that is here and now—because it has totally, almost totally, starved the spiritual dimension, its own being, spiritually—then it goes completely out of balance. You see, slow steps are sure steps and a slow growth is, in truth, the only healthy growth. Because what happens when you go out of balance like that into the spiritual, you guarantee the day that you lose value for what you are receiving. And then the day comes when you no longer receive it, and then value once again comes into your universe.

Because, you see, that that is easily attained has no value to man. How do we value the air that we breathe? The only time that man has started to value that wonderful element known as air is when it has become so polluted with smog that he starts to become irritated. Well, of course, the law is ever demonstrable: irritation wakes the soul. That's when we have value. We have value when we no longer have what we think that we need; otherwise, we have no value. We don't value the water, unless we're extremely thirsty. In fact, we waste it. We have no consideration or appreciation for it.

But whenever we entertain that type of thinking, we guarantee the loss of what we have received so freely. We guarantee inside ourselves that loss, and when we lose it, it is not easily once again attained. The first step is the most important step. It is the second step that is the most difficult step in anything. Does that help with your question?

It certainly does and thank you.

You're welcome. Any questions?

I'm curious as to why, well, I get the feeling that it's music symbology, as far as rhythm, harmony, and unity. I'm curious as to why music symbology is used. Am I mistaken?

Music symbology in regards to the laws that are being expressed through the soul faculties?

Those particular terms I see as music symbology.

And you see it as musical symbology?

Yes.

Why, certainly, if that is the level that you're receptive to, that's most understandable. But remember this: that whatever is beneficial to us, 'tis wise to entertain in thought. But that does not mean that the soul faculty is a musical faculty because we receive it in that way, do you understand? But it could be for us, because that would be our level of receptivity at the time of our receiving the understanding. But if it serves a good purpose, as St. Paul said, "Hold fast to that that is good. Let all other things go from your universe." Anyone else?

I still feel quite confused about what I was reading today in Discourse 30.

Yes.

About past lives, it states that the question was asked, Why can we not recall past lives? Well, if we could, there would be no reason to be here going to school.

That is very true. If the lesson is already learned or we already have the answer, then, of course, there would be no purpose to the soul's evolutionary incarnation.

Which I could also apply to the law of karma. Now my question is, How can you explain people who have glimpses, including myself, of so-called past lives if they're only here on this planet once around?

If the student, for example—I believe that you are referring to the soul's incarnation into a return to this particular form and this particular planet. Is that what you're referring to when you say that you have glimpses of past lives?

Yes.

Yes. When a person reaches a level of awareness where— and that could happen in a glimpse and in an instant or in a moment—where they are at oneness, then they are aware of being all things, whether those things are past, present, or future.

Now, for example—also, it could also happen in another way. If a person comes into rapport with a certain era, say the seventeenth century, you understand, he could become a person who expressed himself in that era. That's another way that that experience comes to us. Another way is, many times the spirit will enter our aura from who knows what era or age, and because our communication or awareness is not fully open, we feel and absolutely know that we have lived a certain life at a certain time because, you see, that particular spirit is impressing itself, impinging itself into our aura. We are not aware of their presence, but we are certainly aware of their history and of their life. And if we do not have awareness, then, of course, we understand, then, we have been in that particular era and age. But remember that to God, all things are possible. In truth, we are one. And being one, we are everyone and everything, in truth, this instant and this moment.

The teachings of the Living Light are evolutionary incarnation: that your soul was not born brand new out of the Allsoul just at the moment of your conception in this particular earth realm. He explains in his teachings that your soul has entered a certain form in a certain time. It has set certain laws into motion and, therefore, you have guaranteed certain experiences in your life, 90 percent guaranteed, that is. Consequently, we get a greater understanding, perhaps, that there isn't some partial God that has given to one all of the good and robbed another soul of all those things; that it is the Law of Personal Responsibility; that the soul and the soul alone, the individualized soul, has merited this lifetime, this experience, as it has merited all lifetimes and all experiences throughout eternity.

You see, the great sadness is that man thinks that the human soul has just expressed itself, maybe, for the past few million years. Well, what kind of thinking is that? That all of a sudden, God has created an Allsoul and that out of this Allsoul have come these individualized souls known as human beings? This is, you see, like if I were to sit here and say, "Well, here is the human race and this is the only place that this intelligence is expressed to this extent in form on any planet at any time." That is such a limited view of this great eternity, which we are this very instant, this very moment.

What is truly important to us? What is really important? Learning the laws that we and we alone are setting into motion and learning how to change or, let us say, to use higher laws on all of our levels and, in so doing, awaken to the great truth, awaken to the eternity that is this instant and this moment.

You see, we become attached to so many things. We become attached to this piece of clay and all of the experiences that it has. And when we become attached, in that attachment, we set a new law into motion that governs our ship into the next expression, and the next and the next and the next. This is what we have been doing. The reason, my good friends, that your soul is impressed, impulsed—I beg your pardon—into this particular form at this particular time with these particular experiences reveals to you, my good friends, what you were attached to the time before and before and before and before.

So, my God! If you do not learn about your attachments today and do something about it, you're only guaranteeing another expression in another time in another place with the same attachments and the same experiences, until in time you accept, recognize, and appreciate that you are formless and free, that you use your mind and in so using it, you attach yourself to things, experiences, and creation. So if we cannot learn to be free while in creation here and now, we're not going to learn that hereafter, because what you set into motion today is your effect in the hereafters. And there are multitudes of them.

Don't ever think, my good friends, that this is the first time you've been in a physical body or that it will be the last time. That is not, and is far from, the truth. So look at your attachments, because that's what your eternity is. See, whatever your attachments are, you can say, "Thank you, God, I see my eternal prison. Here I am." Because that's what it is. You can't be attached to anything, leave the physical body, and all of a sudden—"zap"—all your attachments are gone. The mind doesn't work that way. You see, if you've come into a body and you've had attachments while you were young and they just keep getting stronger, that only shows you, my good friends, that you were attached in your last expression and you kept on the cycle. You know, it's like a circle, goes 'round like a merry-go-round, around and around and around and around again. If you have prejudices and you entertain those things, well, my good friends, that's what you had the last time and you just keep trying to work them out. Yes.

I'm trying to divorce this from reincarnation, but it sounds like it to me. I know it isn't, because you don't teach this.

It isn't reincarnation. I do not teach reincarnation.

I know, but the thing is, the Old One is supposed to be six thousand years old.

Yes.

And has his cycle gone on? I don't mean his particular cycle, but these ancient ones who come to teach us and who have been over in spirit all these thousands of years?

Let me explain this: the divine laws are totally impartial and man is a law unto himself, and man is the divinity. That's the law. Think about it. Now there is no set time of years, you understand, that you're going to live on this earth realm. Some of you live to be twenty and some of you live to be one hundred; is that not true?

Yes.

There is a basic span of time, but there is no set number of years. But there is a basic span through which you could pass out of those dimensions any time within the span, which is under a divine ruling power, which is set into motion. It has always been; therefore, it will always be. For example, it's like going to school and you have four years to get through high school, but you could take six, and you might make it in three. Do you understand?

Yes.

But it's a much broader span. But that is the principle. Now the question is that the Old Man stated in his book [*The Living Light*] that he spent his time on earth in the year 6000 B.C. Is that not correct? I think that's what he stated. Now the question is, Does that mean that we, as individuals, will be floating around over there for six thousand years? Or will we be impulsed into being in another planet in another place in another day and in another age? How do we know that he hasn't already gone through a few experiences in a few dimensions, and under his merit system he has come back here to share his understanding with us earthlings? How do we know? He's never said. I don't even know myself. But, you see, I try to judge the tree by the fruit that it bears.

To me, it is not important whether he's six thousand years old or he's a two-year old expressing his understanding. It's not important to me. It is important that what he is teaching is demonstrable and can benefit and awaken mankind. That, to me, is important. But as far as how many years we're going to be here or there, that is not important. Because, you see, if we are concerned about years, that means that we are not spending the thought, which is our energy, on this eternity of now. This is the only moment that we have power over. There is no other moment in the illusion of time that we have power over. Only this one and this one alone can we do anything with.

Now any time you think about what has passed, you're only reviewing it in mind. You can't do anything, really, about it. It is already a past experience. But what you do with this moment starts to set into motion a law that guides your soul, your ship of destiny. You see, if we see the oneness starting with ourselves, if we see the oneness, we will know the Allness, but we cannot and we will not know the Allness until we first find the oneness which is inside of ourselves. And this is why I try to teach the students to concentrate upon peace, because you're directing this power, you understand, back home. You're getting yourself out of the way when you're at peace and God is expressing itself. Any other thought is creation. Peace is the power, because when we are truly at peace, all creation is moving in perfect harmony in here. And when that happens, you have awareness; and when you have awareness, you have Light; and when you have Light, you have Truth; and when you have Truth, you have everything. Does that help with your question? Yes.

If one has complete faith in the dogma of reincarnation and if we go into realms that can be the thoughts that we have sent out when we were on this plane, then couldn't one create a reincarnation situation for one's self, if one had that much faith in it?

Absolutely. After all, we're living in delusion and illusion right now. This is all a delusion. So if you want to create another delusion, that is your divine birthright. You see, the mass mind has created a multitude of illusions for us. Now if we want to add to the mass mind another delusion and illusion, that is our divine birthright, don't you see? Now you believe that you're here in this room, etc., and that you're having a certain experience. You believe that, don't you?

Yes.

Because you believe it, my dear friends, you are experiencing it. But we could be in this room and we could be experiencing another dimension and have absolutely no awareness whatsoever of this one. Do you understand?

Yes, I, I . . .

So as you believeth, you becometh. But you're asking about belief and you're asking about faith. Do your belief and your faith move the mountain literally? When they do that, you will be expressing the godhood within you and then whatever you think, that you will become, truly become in all dimensions. That is the power of the Divine expressing through form. Do we say to the mountain, "Move!" and the mountain moves? If not, then we're not yet receptive, fully, to the Divine Power that moves the mountain. But when we become at one, then and then alone will the mountain move. But we cannot move physical mountains until we learn to move mental mountains, which are known as obstructions, for thought moves easier by far than physical substance. Does that help with your question?

I think so.

Yes.

Thank you. I've had a couple of questions that have threaded through all of this. It was stated that the mental body is a function.

Yes.

And yet you spoke earlier on the steps of creation, that the mental was somewhere in between the soul and the form.

It is.

Exactly what is a mental being? Can it be defined? If so, could it be made more clear?

He's asking in reference to the mental being and it was stated here, earlier, that the mental being is a function, not a soul faculty. Remember that the mental being is composed—naturally, it stands to reason and it follows—of mind or mental substance. There is a power that flows through the human being that has the ability to garner up mental substance and, in so doing, create.

You will notice in the five steps of creation that midway, the mental is mentioned. Is that not correct? Because the mental or mind is the creative principle. Now the creative principle is not a soul faculty, for the soul faculties, though they garner up from the spiritual substance and create a spiritual body, they are not the creative principle of the mental or the material or physical worlds. If they were, the spiritual body could not change in the flash of an instant and have the appearance of youth, of age, or

of anything that the mind chose it to be. What it is—the mental
body or mind being—though it has this potential of creation and
is a creative principle, it is a much slower process in this physical world.

For example, a man may entertain in thought that he is going
to fly. And in entertaining that thought, he would fly, literally,
with no problem whatsoever. But because the mind, expressing through the physical creation, having its attention upon the
gross—that moves at a much slower speed than the higher levels of awareness or being—because it has lost sight of its own
divinity, it takes years ofttimes, and sometimes lifetimes, for the
mind to create what it entertains in thought. It does not hold
to one thing. If man truly held to the thought that he is flying,
then man would levitate the physical body, because the power,
you understand, which sustains the laws of gravity, is greater
than the laws of gravity. Remember, that that sustains a thing
is greater than the thing, because the father is greater than the
son, his own creation. Does that help with your question?

Very much. And may I ask another one?

Yes.

The term planet, *as used in* The Living Light, *does this refer
to a physical thing, such as the planet Earth or the planet Mars or
the planet Venus? Or does it rather refer to a spherical relationship of relative infinity?*

It refers to both, for the planets are nothing more than the
effect of the other.

Thank you.

You're more than welcome. Any other questions?

*What is the purpose of aging? Why can't one live a youthful
life until their time is up and then disappear or exit?*

Man has accepted that wisdom comes with age and in accepting that, he seeks wisdom, and in seeking it, he ages. This is a
law set into motion untold eons and eons ago. Man, not God,
set that law into motion and so man ages. Now I know that

the brain says, "There's a physical deterioration, etc., etc., etc." The body is constantly being renewed, instant by instant. Constantly. What happens is that some people, they're not as receptive to that renewing power and so they start to age. Certainly, the mind is what sets that law into motion. Definitely. Do you believe that wisdom comes with age? If you do and you seek wisdom, you guarantee age. Think about it.

Well, there are many people who are much younger than I am who have more wisdom than I do.

That's beautiful. Then perhaps you will stay young. It's all a mental process. The mind affects the body, for the mind is greater than the body. But how many people stop to think, and think more deeply? The mind is too entertained with the children of creation. It's too entertained with how much stuff it can add up, not how much stuff it can get rid of. Stop and think. The mind's nature is like a sponge: it keeps absorbing water. But then the day comes that the water drowns the sponge. Don't you see? "Dreamer, dream a life of beauty before your dream starts dreaming you." That's what happens.

You see, when the cup is full, it runneth over and so few people know how to empty the cup. Their minds have decided, "Well, I can serve in this way, which empties my cup, or I can serve in that way." And they limit themselves because they've decided what God's work is. They don't let the Divine Power awaken their minds to what God's work is. They tell the Divine what God's work is and then they act accordingly. And then they say, "Well, no, that mundane job, I don't want to be bothered with that," simply because their faculty of humility is usually closed and locked with the key of error, known as ignorance. Did that help with your question?

Yes, sir.

Yes.

You've given each one of us a handle, like unity or perseverance.

You mean a word, yes. I wouldn't give you a handle or tag. I wouldn't be so unkind.

It would become one if we don't learn how to—

If we don't apply it.

How does one really think about a spiritual thing? I mean, really deeply. Do the answers come in thinking or do they come after the thinking, as an insight?

They come after, as an insight. They do not come during the processes of thinking. No matter what the mind thinks, that is not when it comes. When he says, Think, my children, and think more deeply—when you have thought enough and you are totally exhausted, you will pause to rest. That means your brain will be still and while your brain is still and is no longer whirling, a light will come on, perhaps only for an instant, but it will come on and then you will know. The light comes after the thought process, not during it. However, a person thinks, "Well, I'm thinking real hard and I'm thinking and I'm thinking and I'm thinking, whoops, and the light came." Well, the light came the instant they stopped thinking. See, the mind got still for an instant, the ego came down off its helicopter, and the spirit spoke in its still, small voice and in its humbleness. Yes, it comes after.

And so many people, you know, they do their concentration and their meditation, you know, and they say, "Ugh, I'm not getting anything. Not a thing. Nothing!" Well, isn't it wonderful that they're not getting anything? Because if they did, on the level that they were on, it would be all mental garbage. I always say, "Well, that's wonderful. You're not getting a thing. I mean, that's just beautiful. Considering the level that you were on at the time of your sitting, God was truly working with you, you know." Besides, God's greatest work is done in silence, yes.

We're not supposed to be on a merry-go-round and viewing a TV set during our meditation. But, you know, sometimes things come through. But if nothing comes through, be very, very grateful that you had no thought and you had no vision and you heard no voice, because you got a break for a few minutes a day: your mind was still. That's real growth. Real growth. Yes.

Well, I was thinking about what you said about building a spiritual body and so many people think that they go from this world into a spiritual body. How does one gather spiritual substance? I know that good deeds help, but they aren't the whole thing. How do we go about building from this earth a spiritual body, and do many people go into that spiritual body?

Very, very few. In reference to your last question, very, very, very few. Service is spirit. But you must remember, in expressing service, what was the motive that prompted you to do it? Because the motive will reveal your level of awareness and whatever level you are expressing your service on will determine how much good will be accomplished. There are very few people, very, very few people that—outside of the little children—that leave this dimension and enter a spiritual world. They enter an astral dimension, an ethereal dimension, not always on the darker levels of it, fairly high and light levels. We call them spirits, because the world isn't yet ready for us to say, "You know, Aunt Tilley is still on the astral realm." The egos aren't ready for that yet, my good friends. But there are higher astral realms, too, you know.

But let's open our eyes and be realistic. Let's be realistic. Are we saints or are we potential ones? Do we think for an instant that if we zip out of this body this minute, we're going to go up to a beautiful, nice spiritual world where there's lots of light? Well, how much light do we have now? Ha! We're only going to have that much to take with us. How much have we really got in here and how much of it have we actually applied? That's the key. Are we doing our part through service to the spirit in expressing the soul faculties, that we may be garnering up spiritual substance, and have a spiritual body, that our soul may express itself?

How much time in the course of a day, of twenty-four hours, are we truly setting aside to serve the Light? How much time? I think we ought to ask ourselves that question. There are seven days to a week. If we cannot give one hour out of twenty-four hours to the Divine in service, which means seven hours a week, then we're in pretty sad shape; at least, that's my understanding. And I don't mind sharing it with the world. We're in pretty sad shape. If we can't give one hour a day to total selfless service to the Divine Light, known as God, then I wouldn't even entertain that maybe in fifty centuries I would have a spiritual body to express through. I wouldn't even entertain it in thought, because I'd say I'm just being absolutely stupid and foolish. Just think logically and reasonably. My goodness sake, there's no Divine Power that's going to say, "Oh, you're a pretty nice guy. Here, you can have a spiritual body." Well, that's stupidity and superstition and paganism, that's what that is.

And if we think we can believe in some great prophet, some poor medium who's gone on, that billions of people are crying to help them, you know—because they've created their cross, and everybody's got their cross—and if we think we can say, "Oh, God, now save me. Save me," while we're not doing a damn thing about it, except when we get to the bottom of the barrel, well, isn't it ridiculous! Why, that's transgressing every single commonsense teaching that the Living Light has brought to the world. It doesn't work that way. That's only delusion and illusion. It doesn't work that way, my good friends. If we can't take—what is one out of twenty-four? One-twenty-fourth? Sure, it's one-twenty-fourth. Why, my God, if we can't give one-twenty-fourth of a day to the Divine, we're in very sad, sad, sad shape.

Now a person might say, "Well, I can't spare an hour a day." Well, if they can't spare an hour a day, how do they think that anybody in any intelligent realm of Light is going to spend ten minutes with them? I know I wouldn't. That's total stupidity. How can we expect the angels from the realms of Light to help us through our trials and tribulations when we're not willing to help them with the work they have to do? That doesn't make good sense. Yes.

I think that probably everybody does want to be spiritual. I think this is the soul's—

It's the soul's aspiration, but you must realize that the sense desires are pretty potent, you know, especially if they're not often entertained.

What I wanted to say is that I think that most people don't know how to serve. They haven't—

Have they asked the question? I'm not here judging. I'm only sharing with you my understanding. Have they asked themselves the question? Have they really? You see, the power of the mind to question presupposes and guarantees, no less, its power to answer. Have we asked ourselves, "God, how may I serve you best today?" It's been a long time, but I never forget when I open my eyes to ask that question. Because, by so doing, we become receptive, at least we make the attempt to become receptive to a divine Power and we will be inspired. Yes.

The Living Light teaches us that God is neutral, which is probably the most revolutionary teaching that I have ever heard, and it answers most of the questions that the organized religions cannot answer.

Absolutely.

Some people think that if you ask God for a nice car, why, he'll give it to you.

Yes.

Also, if you get into trouble, why, all you have to do is seriously ask God and he'll take care of you. If God is neutral, of course, he isn't going to.

That's right.

Since that opens up the Pandora's box of God being neutral, there's lots of other questions, such as what kind of wheels can we put into motion to get help on this world. If we need a medical doctor, we know we pick up the telephone and we phone a doctor.

Definitely.

Since God is neutral and gave us freedom of will, which is why he is neutral, of course—otherwise the whole thing would be a farce—he must have had other preparations so that we could put certain wheels into motion and get some help when we need it.

Absolutely.

Can you comment on that?

Definitely. And I'm very happy that you brought that up. When the mind, going through its struggle, entertains the thought that it needs help and it is not able to see help in itself, within its own powers, simply because it does not see the light, and the light is reason, a soul faculty, then it asks God or it asks spirit or it asks something or someone to help it through those trials and tribulations. When we entertain that question in mind, we become receptive, through the law that like attracts like and becomes the Law of Attachment, to those who have passed through those experiences, who, guided by compassion, enter our universe and try to reveal to us the causes of why we are where we are. They do that and try to inspire us: that it is because we are transgressing certain natural laws. We can express new laws, and we will not have these trials and tribulations.

Now it has been stated in the Bible that God answers a prayer through his ministering angels. But what are these divine, ministering angels through which God answers prayer? Well, man has created a belief in what you call God, a great power that will help him through his struggles. Because man, the mind, has created this, through its belief, you have these souls who have evolved, who come to us according to the laws of like attracts like and according to the laws of compassion. And so it is that greater and greater light is brought to the world.

Now that does not mean that we are teaching that prayer is of no benefit. Why, prayer is as much benefit as you demonstrate through your own faith. Now you could have a little rabbit's foot, if you wanted, and you could say to the little foot, "I have great faith in you, rabbit's foot, and I'm really praying to you to bring me a house of my own, etc." And if you really believe that, of course it's going to work, because then the rabbit's foot is your god, because you have given power to it.

The potential danger of the inner teachings of the Living Light is very obvious to me: that man, through this understanding, will go from liberty—because it is an understanding that frees the soul—into license to do who he wants, when he wants, do what he wants the way he wants to do it, and believe that it's all fine and dandy, and he's totally free. One mind is not stronger than millions and it is millions of minds that have created the laws of cause and effect. It is billions of mind-power over untold centuries in many universes that have created this divine justice. And so it is that man is his own best friend and man is his own worst enemy. And don't think for a moment, friends, that we have reached such illumination that we can say, "That's it. I can do whatever I want, whenever I want, and because I know the laws, it will have no effects."

When you truly reach the Light, you will have great consideration and value for it, knowing that it is totally impartial and that, in truth, "Vengeance is mine, said the Lord." It means that the law will extract every iota. That it is very vengeful in the sense that the law—as the Bible says, the Lord—is totally impartial. It is not concerned whether you have five kids to support or twenty-five. The law works impartially because that is the way that it is. Black is black and white is white and shades of gray are illusion. We have time for just a couple of more questions and then we'll go on.

If man's incarnation is a result of his having set a law into motion, would you please explain how and by whom the law is set into motion for animals to incarnate?

Yes, that is a most interesting question, and I will be happy to share with you my understanding. It is the teachings of the

Wise One that the soul is on an evolutionary journey; that it incarnates into form, the forms that it has merited. He also teaches that there is nothing without soul or soul essence. And so it is if a law is universal, then it is universally applicable. And so a law that governs form, whether we call it a two-legged form or we call it a four-legged form, is the same, the one and the same law. And so it is that some of us are in light bodies and some of us are in dark bodies, and some of us are here and some of us are there. And so it is that some animals merit a good home. And so it is that some animals merit a home where it's totally a real suffering experience. And so it is that some dogs have giant uneducated egos and some are very humble little dogs. It is because that is what that soul has merited, according to laws that it has set into motion.

Let us not forget, my good friends, that ignorance of the law is no escape from its fulfillment. Just drive down the street and go through the red light, thinking that it is green, because you've got too much on your mind. Do you think you're not going to get a ticket? Well, of course, you're going to get a ticket. The law is totally impartial. That's the law and that's the way that it is. And so it is with animals and all other things. Remember, we must learn to separate truth from creation or we're not going to be free.

Truth is one; creation is dual or two. Remember that God, the Divine, is one in essence and three in manifestation; that when you split the atom, you experience power. And so it is this divinity that lies within us, there it lies sleeping. The moment you awaken it, you split it and the power is expressed into creation, because it becomes creation. And that is why, until you decide to return to the oneness that is within you, you won't find the Light or the Divinity.

Think about your day. How much of your day is entertained with thoughts of creation? Stop and do yourself a great favor. Keep a little chart and find out how many times a day you think about wholeness and oneness and the Divinity and trying to help some poor soul up the ladder and think about how many hours you spend in your own little merry-go-round. You'll be doing yourself a great favor, because you'll be looking in a mirror and you'll see right where you are and no one will have to tell you. See how many times you get upset because you can't tolerate a certain level inside yourself, and you say it's that person over there. See how many times it happens to you.

How many eternal centuries are we going to continue to sleep and to lie in lethargy? How much of time, eons and eons and eons and eons, are we going to continue to dream and not awaken to the great truth that frees us? If we come into this world and we're such and such years old and we're still dreaming, and we're still going through all of our trips, well, my good friends, it's a very good indication that you had a pretty rough time the last time, somewhere in some universe someplace, and you weren't man enough or woman enough or strong enough to say, "That's it! I have a right to divine freedom and I'm willing to pay the price."

Remember this, friends: there's a price to awareness and you never know how big the price is. Because that price tag is what you have set into motion inside yourself. And it's known as giving up. So you might have to give up twenty things, you might have to give up two, but you can be rest assured, you're going to have to give up something to gain awareness. Because if you didn't have to give up something to gain awareness, then you'd already have awareness. But you have to give up something and if you're willing to give that up, believe me, it's worth it. If you're not willing to give it up, then stay on the circle of eternal experience and bondage.

Thank you, friends, and good night.

MARCH 22, 1973

CONSCIOUSNESS CLASS 11 ✺

Good evening, students. I'd like to give a few words before we start our class tonight. I know that many of you have been to the three courses that we have already conducted and, therefore, are familiar with the procedures of the Living Light awareness classes. However, I see that there are quite a number of new faces this evening, so I would like to briefly review our procedures.

Our classes start at 8:00 p.m. sharp. After tonight, the door will be locked at 8:00 o'clock. The requirement of the class is that you are here on time, that is, 8:00 p.m., and registered in. The classes last for approximately one hour to one and a half hours. After that time, we go to the restaurant to have a social hour and discussion. We will have a short meditation at each class. Was everyone given the "Total Consideration" affirmation when they came in the door? Everyone should have that. Would you kindly take it out at this time? We will be reading the affirmation at each class, followed by a reading from *The Living Light* by students in the different groups. After the reading of the discourses, we will have a short meditation time, followed by your questions.

Now at the question time, whereas the class is only an hour to an hour and a half, I do know that many students are still with us who have been here from the very beginning and are anxious to share their understanding of the course. This is the reason that we have this social hour after the classes. Kindly reserve your understanding for that time. During the classes we will have questions from the students and answers from the Spirit Teacher.

Now a little discussion of meditation, when we come to that time. We teach a type of meditation in these classes of concentration upon peace. Now the reason that we have chosen the word *peace* is simply because peace is the power. When you are able to tune yourself into the vibratory waves of peace, you will become aware that you have always been, and having always been, you will always be. And so it is that when we come to our meditation, you simply sit with your feet flat on the floor, your hands uncrossed, and concentrate upon the word *peace*.

Now the first thing that usually happens to the student when they're concentrating, they will reach a level of their subconscious known as the level of association. When they think of the word *peace*, they may see the Liberty Bell, they may see a peaceful scene or a lake. That is not the level of your soul. That is the level of your subconscious, where, through the laws of association, you will see these different scenes.

These classes are designed to help you to help yourself to think and to think more deeply. They are not dogmatic. They do not have a definite, positive way of you finding the Light that is within yourself. They do, however, share with you an understanding that, when put into application, will free you while yet encased in form, in the flesh.

So we will begin this evening's class with a speaking forth into the atmosphere of our affirmation entitled "Total Consideration":

I am the manifestation of Divine Intelligence. Formless and free. Whole and complete. Peace, Poise, and Power are my birthright.

The Law of Harmony is my thought and guarantees Unity in all my acts and activities, expressing perfect Rhythm and limitless flow throughout my entire being.

Without beginning or ending, eternity is my true awareness and sees the tides of creation, as a captain sees his ship.

As the Light of Truth is sustained by the faculty of
Reason, I pause to think and claim my Divine right.

Right Thought.   Right Action.   Total Consideration.
Amen.   Amen.   Amen.

*[At this point in the class, Discourse 1 is read aloud by a
student.]*

We'll go into our meditation. Remember that we are concentrating upon peace, and when you concentrate upon peace, let yourself relax, that you may feel that vibratory wave.

Now many people state that they seem to have problems in concentration. Well, we understand, of course, friends, the only problem is in our thought. Sometimes we try too hard to concentrate. Concentration is not a forcing of the mind: it is a state of total relaxation. It is a drifting into the dimension of your choice. And if you choose peace, you will become peace, and becoming peace, you will know peace. So let us relax and drift off into this dimension of peace through the powers of concentration.

[After a short period of meditation, the Teacher continues.]

Remember that the spirit is the spirit of spontaneity. It doesn't take an hour or two to get into a receptive vibration or meditation, and this is one of the reasons that we have these short meditation periods: in order that you may tune in at your choice and at your decision without having to go through an hour or two of paraphernalia and different types of mantras and all the other things involved. Because either the Divine Power is ever present, never absent or away, or it's something that we have to travel a thousand miles to get to.

Feel free to ask what questions you have concerning the teachings that are offered, concerning anything of a spiritual nature.

Yes, thank you. I have a question about each time we go to a different stage and we come once again from the Allsoul.

The question is in reference to each time the soul is incarnated, does it come anew from the Allsoul?

Well, then, what is the overall purpose of this . . .

Soul's incarnation? Is that the question?

Well, yes, and the many trips and the restarting, in my understanding, of these continuous repetitions?

Yes. Now that's a very interesting question. In other words, the question, I believe, from what you're stating is, What is the purpose of the soul's continuous incarnation into form? Is that correct?

Yes. When you go up to higher levels and then you just continue to . . .

Do you continue to go into other bodies and other forms? Is that the question? Thank you very much. In reference to your question, What is the purpose of the soul's incarnation continuously expressing through form? First of all, for the benefit of our new students, I would like to give the expression that he has given to us in his understanding, that soul is not Spirit; that spirit of God is formless, free, whole, and complete; that soul is the covering. It is the vehicle through which the Divine Spark, known as God, Infinite Intelligence, or Spirit, expresses itself. Therefore, soul, as it is taught and understood in this understanding, is the covering of Spirit. Now, that that is a covering is form. That that is form has beginning and it has ending. Therefore, the only part of us that has no beginning and has no ending is the Divine Spirit.

For example, we all have name tags at this time. We were born on this particular planet. Now we were not born on this planet by chance. We were impulsed into being in the form that we are in according to the divine law known as merit. In other words, we merited being John Doe, etc. We merited the soul's incarnation into certain circumstances and conditions, according to choices that we have made along the evolutionary path of soul incarnation.

This is not the beginning of life and it is not the ending of life. It is merely one of its multitudes of expression. As the soul continues to evolve, you might liken it to a grade of school. This particular earth planet offers many things for the soul's unfold- ment, and man is never left without choice. In other words, if we were born in wealth or born in poverty, born in health or born in its opposite, that is what we have merited along the evolution- ary path of the soul's incarnation.

According to his teachings, the soul, after leaving the physi- cal body, expresses through whatever body it has created. Now we all have a mental body created; we all have a mind. Now our mental body is composed of mental substance. Many of us, upon leaving this physical body, will express through a mental body or an astral body, which is the duplicate of the physical form. There are some who will express through a spiritual body, but a spiritual body is made up of spiritual substance. Therefore, the teaching is that through directing the energy in expression through the soul faculties, we are garnering up spiritual sub- stance with which to build a spiritual body. If we have done that while yet encased in flesh, in this physical body, then when we leave this dimension, we will express in a spiritual realm. If we have not, then we will not express in a spiritual dimension. We will express in a body that we have already organized and composed, an astral body or a mental body.

Now the question arises, as it has in each class, Then, what about the children? My dear friends, we are born in this dimen- sion and we have a spiritual body. What happens to that spiri- tual body is that simply through directing of the energy through the functions and becoming unbalanced in the material dimen- sion, the spiritual body is not sustained. Consequently, as we grow up and we receive our so-called education, we no longer have spiritual bodies to express in spiritual dimensions. When a child leaves this physical world, they do go into a world of spirit because they do have a spiritual body. When the soul returns to the Allsoul, it impulses out into the universe once again.

The purpose of the soul's journey is the evolution of the forms in which it expresses itself. And so it is that eternity is the moment of which we are consciously aware. If we are not consciously aware of this eternity, this moment, that's quite indicative we're not going to find this eternity in the next moment, because we are in a constant ladder of progression. We're stepping ever upward. Whether we believe it or not is immaterial. There is the drive of the spirit to express itself and that drive is never, never outside ourselves: it is eternally within us. Because the true us, the true being, is the Divine Spirit. It is everywhere. And when we become aware of it, we will unfold the first faculty of being, known as duty, gratitude, and tolerance. Anyone else?

What happens if a person is working toward rebuilding their spiritual body and there is an accident and they pass over before they've had enough years to finish?

Yes, that's a very good question. And the question is, if all the students didn't hear it, If a person is working and expressing their soul faculties, which garners up spiritual substance for a spiritual body, and there is an accident, what happens to that person? That depends, my good friends, entirely on how much of a body they have composed. Now many mediums and clairvoyants, looking into the atmosphere, have seen a part of a body, a foot, an arm, a half-body, and they wonder why they see those things. That simply means that that particular individual has that much of a spiritual body garnered up from spiritual substance. Now if an individual has an accident while they're in the process of garnering up this spiritual body from spiritual substance, that, my good friends, is simply that particular individual's merit system. Those are the laws they have set into motion.

I sincerely hope, in these classes, if I have but one student who is able to apply the teachings of the Living Light, only one teaching, then I will indeed feel that my duties as a teacher have been fulfilled for these classes. And that one teaching is very simple: whatever, in all the universes, that happens to us is caused by us. When we apply that great truth, we will indeed become free. We will no longer give power to people, to places, to things. And, my good friends, when you apply that one teaching, of all the teachings I have ever heard, that one teaching will free your soul as nothing else could possibly do. Because you will go back inside yourself and you will recognize that you and you alone are the master of your ship, that you and you alone are the captain of your destiny. Remember, whatever happens to us is caused by us. If you will only apply, in your day-to-day activities and in your thinking, that one simple teaching, you will indeed free your soul.

Stop and think. In the course of an hour, how much of your divine right do you give to people, to places, to things? Anything that disturbs us, my good students, controls us. So if you feel disturbed, remember, in that moment of disturbance you have sold your soul that moment. Yes, anyone else?

In Discourse 1, it states, "All things that are to be, or have ever been, to thy soul are known. For thy soul is part of Allsoul." Is everything contained within our aura, so-to-speak, or do we tune into something that is outside of ourselves, like a reservoir?

Yes, that's a very good question. And in reference to All things to our soul are known, all things that have been, that are, that are to be, the soul of man is likened unto a drop of water from a great ocean. It is inseparable from the Allsoul. When man becomes receptive to his own soul, he, in that process, becomes receptive to Allsoul. And in so doing, all things that have ever been, all things that are, all things yet to be, to the soul will be known. It is not a matter that it is a separate reservoir, because we are an indispensable part of Allsoul. Does that help with your question? Thank you. Anyone else?

Could you clarify the terms plane *and* sphere? *Exactly what is* sphere *and exactly what is* plane?

We understand, in this understanding, that there are nine spheres; that there are nine planes to each sphere; that there are eighty-one levels of awareness or eighty-one states of consciousness. Now the question is, What is the difference, if any, between a sphere and a plane? A plane is a graduation in a particular sphere. For example, a soul may be expressing on the second plane of the fifth sphere. It is a state of consciousness. And the difference between the sphere and the plane is as different, for example, as an entire course in college or one semester of it. Does that help with your question? Any other questions?

Is the population stable or fixed on this planet or other planets, or are there new souls coming into existence so-to-speak?

Thank you. The question is, Is the population fixed on this planet and on other planets?

There is a law known as the Law of Expansion and the Law of Contraction. In reference to the question of whether or not the population of the planets is fixed, they are, in a sense, fixed to this extent: they are constantly expanding. When they expand to a certain point, they will start to contract or lessen. And so it is not only with the population of planets, including the earth planet, but so it is in all of nature. Wherever you have form, you have the expansion and contraction principle. Does that help with your question?

Are the terms Allsoul *and* Spirit *synonymous?*

The question is asked, "Are the terms *Allsoul* and *Spirit* synonymous?" I couldn't say that they are exactly synonymous, because when we say *Allsoul*, the moment we say *all*, we are, in truth, declaring limitation or limit, because the word *all* implies total and the word *total* implies a boundary. Therefore, in that sense, I could not say that the word *Spirit* and the word *Allsoul* are synonymous.

*Could you discuss for a moment the interaction or the whole-
ness of sound and sight and the tangibility of form? I've heard
that music and color and vibration are interrelated.*

Thank you very much. In reference to your question, there
is no difference, in truth, between sound and color. They are, in
truth, one and the same thing. They're all mathematical; they're
all number. Now, we have a different receptivity or awareness:
we say that that is sound and that is color. Each color is a sound;
each sound is a color. Therefore, there is, in truth, no difference
between the two. They are all vibration. One we seem to receive
by our physical sight; the other we seem to receive by our physical ears. The truth of the matter is that it is all vibration, like
a tuning fork, and we receive them as a vibration. We believe
that we see one thing and we believe that we hear the other.
The truth is, they're merely vibration. Does that help with your
question? Anyone else? Yes.

*I was wondering in the evolutionary processes of incarna-
tions, why do we come in with our weaknesses? And also, what
is the determining factor when we are a human and not a flower
or something else?*

A very good question and thank you very much. In reference
to your question, Do we come into this particular incarnation
with our weaknesses? a similar question to that, I believe, was
discussed during our last class.

The trials and tribulations that we, seemingly, are born
into in this incarnation merely reveal to us that we flunked
those tests in our last incarnation. That is the reason that we
have them now to work through. For example, if a person is
born with a great temper and a lack of patience and a total
lack of tolerance, that means that they have flunked those
particular lessons along the evolutionary path and again are
having the blessed opportunity of growing through them here
and now.

Also, in your question was the statement—or question, Why is our soul in a human form? Why is it not expressing through a flower, a blade of grass, a tree, or something else? The reason that our soul is expressing in what we call a human form on this particular planet at this particular time is because this is the grade of school that we have finally graduated to.

Remember, my good friends, that there is no difference, in truth, in the Energy or Divine Spirit that expresses through the blade of grass or that expresses through the human being, the dog, the cat, or the tree. It is one and the same energy. Its seeming difference is the limitation imposed by the form through which the Divine Power is expressing. For example, a dog doesn't speak English or any other so-called human language, but a dog does speak. Now the power that causes the dog to bark, to communicate with other forms of his kind (or her kind) is the same power that is causing me to speak at this very moment. There is no difference in any way, shape, or form. The power is one and the same. Any other questions?

Thank you. Do the planets themselves set into motion laws of merit? For example, certain things happen to our planet, like an earthquake or pollution. Is this something that we have set into motion or is this the law that the planet itself has set into motion?

It's a combination of both. Everything is governed by what is known as the Law of Merit. It doesn't make any difference whether it's the planet, the stars, the universes, the human being, or the animals. According to what has been set into motion, all form is governed by the Law of Cause and Effect or the merit system. For example, as humans, we merited this expression at this time on this particular planet. And the planet, in the question you are asking, merited having us be here. How sad, but true. Any other questions?

When you were speaking of nine levels, couldn't that, too, be related to vibratory colors and sounds?

It is.

That was one thing I wanted to clarify. And then there was the question about an accident while genuinely working toward the spiritual body. It seems to me there are no accidents in divine . . .

There is only the merit system. Are there any questions?

Does there ever come a time when the spirit does not have to be incarnated into, let's say . . .

Thank you very much. In reference to the evolution of the soul, remember, friends, if we have evolved to the so-called human race, there is no retrogression. We continue to evolve ever onward and ever upward throughout eternity.

Now, you wanted to know—What was that last question?

I wanted to know if there would ever be a time when it didn't have—

Oh, I see. Thank you very much. Remember, my good friends, the Divine Power, known as Infinite Intelligence or God, the Divine Spirit, its only awareness is in form. In other words, it is like a sleeping substance. The moment it moves, it has motion—and that is caused by its impulse into form—it has what is known as awareness. It does not have awareness outside of form. In other words, we see God in form. You say, "Well, I look at the sky and I see God." Is the sky form or isn't it? It is to the viewer. You look at a person, you see God. Unless the power is expressing through form, it has no awareness. Think about it.

Does that mean it's always going to come out to form, always?

It is the nature of the power itself to express itself and its expression is in form.

After the body dies, is there a certain time period before each separate soul can be incarnated again?

Yes, we discussed that at the last course. In reference to how long or how many years or is there a time period for the soul's incarnation, for example, you can go to college and it's basically a four-year course, but you may take six, do you understand? Some people live on this earth planet for twenty years, some for seventy, some for ninety or a hundred. Do you understand? But there is a span of time in which a person can live on this planet. Some of them go after only two or three years, but there is a basic span of time. Yes.

Now the Old Man, will there be a time when he will be in form again?

He's already in form, not in a physical dimension.

Will he stay there forever?

I never asked him the question and I certainly doubt it. That's not progression. That's not evolution. If he stays where he is forever, he's not evolving and that's contrary to his very teaching. No.

But I was wondering about the form that I'm in, also. Is it for always?

Now the nature of form, friends, is constant change and evolution. For example, this very instant, in a split second, the body, which is form, is going through changes. It constantly is. The Law of Creation, the Law of Form, is the Law of Change. The Divine Spirit, and the Divine Spirit alone, is the only thing that does not change. And the reason that God, the Divine Intelligence, does not change is because the Divine Intelligence is not form. It expresses through form, but it, of itself, is not form. Wherever there is form, there is change. This is why he teaches, Hold not to form, for form shall pass. A wise man does not attach himself to that which is form. Because in so doing, he guarantees his own destruction because form cannot, by its very nature, and does not last. It is not eternal. There never was a form, there never will be a form, that is eternal. Does that help with your question?

I think I understand . . .

Thank you very much. Anyone else?

In the evolution in the twentieth century, we seem to have experienced more technological benefits than we have had for thousands of years and it seems to accelerate. We've just had the moon shots, for instance. With this constant acceleration of forms or knowledge, where does it go? How much more can we, as finite beings, absorb of this technological accumulation? Where does it go and what is the net result?

Thank you very much and that's a very, very good question. I'm sure that most of us are aware of the technological advances of these past years, especially these past fifty years. Now remember, my good friends, there was a time on this planet when there was technological advancement far beyond our fondest dreams of this moment. That's the Law of Creation: evolution and devolution. It only rises to fall, to rise again, to fall again. That is the way form is; that is creation.

Where is this technological advancement leading us? Yes, this is not the time when I usually give forecasts; however, I'm happy to tell you, in one sense—and sad in another—that the technological advancement is leading us to inhabit certain planets in the solar system. The centuries will pass and in turn man will take his wars and his disturbances throughout this so-called solar system. But remember, out of war comes peace, and out of peace comes war, because man's peace is peace of the mind, not peace of the soul. This is why there is such a great need in using the power of the word of *peace*, peace of the soul. When we use that kind of peace, we'll no longer have these great disturbances in the atmosphere.

But out of this technological advancement will come a great awareness of man's true purpose, of the real reason why he is encased in form, and that will be a good purpose. And it will help mankind to a greater understanding that we are all one; that separation is an illusion and a delusion that is created by the thought process. It's created by the mind.

You see, my friends, we have attached ourselves to form. We've attached ourselves to our names, to our families, and to all the things that we care to possess. Remember that that we possess, in truth, possesses us. We are the slave of all our possessions. The reason that we are the slave is because we sold our soul to things. And when we stop doing that, we're going to be free. But fear not from the technological advancement, because creation itself and her very laws bring balance, though at certain periods of history it does not seem to be so. Thank you very much. Any other questions?

I would like to learn something about the Law of Application. How does one best spiritualize one's thinking?

It's a very good question. And the question is, How does one best spiritualize their thinking? And I can only say to you the best way that I have found of spiritualizing thinking is to become aware of thought. You see, my friends, so many, they think they're thinking. Unfortunately, they're not thinking at all. How many people are consciously aware of the thoughts their minds are entertaining in ten short minutes? They're not aware. The race has become a robotical race. And by robotical, I mean that we have permitted ourselves, by selling our divine right to creation, we have permitted ourselves to be influenced by whatever thoughts are swimming in the atmosphere. Most of the thoughts that we're controlled by, they didn't even originate within our being. We just became receptive to that particular level of awareness and we acted accordingly. We have sold our right to the material world.

And so the best way I know of spiritualizing one's thinking is to make the moment-by-moment application of awareness of what your thoughts are. If I took a census here at this moment and I asked each student, "Give me a list of your thoughts during the past nine minutes," I seriously question that there would be 1 percent capable of doing so. Now I do not mean to imply that you do not have awareness. I just mean to say that you have not practiced or applied the Law of Conscious Awareness of what you're thinking. My friends, whatever we're thinking, we're living. Because it's a thinking world and all of our experiences, they are not caused by anything outside of us. That's the illusion. They're caused by the thoughts that we entertain in the course of a day and in the course of a night. Does that help with your question?

It does.

Yes.

Do we build our spiritual body, which is our ultimate goal, by our thinking? I know we do by our—or do we do it by our acts or by the good that we think we do, which may not be good at all?

All acts are preceded by a thought. Now just because we have become habituated to certain thoughts and we just act, does not in any way declare there was no thought to precede it. The body cannot act without a thought. I move my hand. My conscious mind says, "I didn't tell my hand to move." No, because I have moved it for a lifetime. But the thought registered in a level of my awareness: otherwise, I could not move my hand. So all acts are preceded by thought.

And when you become aware of that, you will open up new dimensions and you will begin to see how the mind really works. You will awaken to different levels of awareness and you will see, as you go out in your day-to-day activities, that you are simply moving according to the law that you have set into motion, as man is a law unto himself; that all the experiences on your job, and wherever you go and whatever you do, you could not escape those experiences for the simple reason that you did not make conscious choice in your thinking. And that is why you are reaping those experiences that you dislike. Any other questions? Yes.

I would like to ask about predestination. Some people might say I get to that level of awareness regardless . . . while some struggle and struggle and never get there. So what is . . .

In reference to your question concerning predestination, let me say this: Our destiny of today is merely the effect of yesterday's choice. The moment we choose anything, we set a law into motion. The law we set into motion becomes our destiny, but we are never left without choice. And so it is that man chooses one thing on Tuesday and changes his mind on Wednesday and chooses just the opposite. This is the reason that man is not successful in his desires, because his desires are contradicting each other. In other words, the power is being dissipated because he forgets so easily what yesterday's desire was. Or he has a desire today, and a few months pass, that desire is no longer entertaining his mind: he has a new desire. But that desire is still back here. And so what happens, those desires keep going to war. They neutralize the life-giving power and man is not successful, unless you can call failure success. And failure, of course, is success in a negative, absolutely. Does that help you?

Some time ago we were talking about the form and that man was the ultimate form of evolution—

Excuse me, please. I do not believe that it was stated that man was the ultimate form. Thank you very much.

Well, that was my question. I wanted to ask if there are greater forms than man that will appear later. Will it be, perhaps, a civilization of ants that will take over as the superior form?

Do you believe in the teaching of evolution that the soul is ever evolving upward to greater and greater perfection?

Yes.

Then, that very teaching would imply that the soul would not regress into the form of an ant, wouldn't it?

Yes.

However, of course, to the Divine Power, all things are possible. And there is no question whatsoever in my mind that there are intelligences in forms that don't particularly resemble the so-called human race on different planets and in different times. Remember, my good friends, that the forms of the planet are composed of the elements of the planet. And therefore, man should not expect in his journeys ever outward and onward into space to find forms with intelligence that have brown eyes and black hair necessarily. Because they might be two feet tall instead of six, etc. But there is constant evolution. Yes.

Could be little green men from Mars, for instance, that would be more intelligent than we are.

That is within the realms of possibility. That is not the teaching of the Living Light, but it is within the realms of possibility.

It seems that so many of us find what we thought were values, say, family values or society values, but we find so much questioning today and so much change. In fact, it almost seems as though we face more challenges today than ever before.

Yes, I'll be more than happy to speak in reference to the seeming challenges of today in comparison to twenty, thirty, or forty years ago. Each particular age has certain challenges and those challenges are ever different. They are ever varied, as time herself, the great delusion, reveals to us that this moment is not the moment that it was yesterday. But remember this: the challenges of yesterday were ever as potent to those who were challenged as the challenges are here today. The only difference is that as we look at today and we look back at yesterday, it seems that life was a bit simpler. It seems that things were not as complicated as they are today. It seems as though our educational system was more down-to-earth in common sense. We went to school and learned the ABCs and 2 and 2 is 4. Today, we have all this advanced technology and all these different things, and there seems to be a greater challenge.

The truth is that the challenge to the youth of today is equal to the challenge of the youth of yesterday. But because we are no longer a youth, we see the challenge as much greater than we saw the challenge in our days of youth. The reason that we see it that way—most of humanity—is because we are no longer the thirsty youth. We have certain patterns established as we become older. The mind finds false security in the patterns of mind with which it is most familiar. And so it is that the real challenge of today to the adults who have had their challenge of youth in yesterday, the real challenge is the threat to their security, beneath the conscious level. Remember that many of us adults consider ourselves very progressive and, consciously, we are. But we are also—our subconscious security patterns are constantly being threatened by the seeming new challenges of the youth today.

In Discourse 1 it states, "When of thy mind thou seekest to know the truth, on the wheel of delusion thou shalt traverse." Does that mean the intellect will never find truth?

The intellect, in and of itself, is incapable of perceiving truth because the intellect, the mind, can only conceive: it does not perceive.

How do we perceive truth?

Through the soul faculties. It is the soul that knows truth, that is truth. It is not the mind: it is not the intellect. The mind and the intellect serve a very good purpose. But its very nature is to conceive; so it's constantly conceiving new things, constantly adding and subtracting. And in this constant exchange that takes place in the intellect, we have this delusion.

So we seek truth with our heart, because that's where our soul is. My good friends, truth is not something you read in a book. It is not something that your ears hear. It is not something that your eyes see. It is not something that your hands feel. It is something that your soul knows. And this is why these classes are designed to help you to help yourself to think, to think more deeply. You have the divine right to truth because there is a part of you—of all things—that *is* truth. It doesn't have to be told. We're not telling you how to think in awareness classes and we're not telling you what to think. We are sharing with you a certain path, which, if you apply, demonstration has proven the student will find truth. When we find truth, we respect the rights of all individuals, of all expression, because that is what truth does. Remember, truth is everywhere. It wears many garments and deceives the wisest minds of men. Any other questions?

If the Wise One is not in a physical form, what form is he in?

A spiritual form.

It was stated, "We have waited so patiently for we know that all is given to those who give." Why does the Wise One say that?

I would say in reference to your question, Why is it stated in *The Living Light*, "We have waited so patiently for we know that all is given to those who give"? the teachings are that like attracts like and becomes the Law of Attachment. To the giver, all is given because they are the giver. They are in the vibratory wave of giving. Consequently, you cannot be in rapport with a vibratory wave, a level of awareness, a state of consciousness, without becoming affected by it. For example, man can only be affected by that with which he is in rapport. So if man is in the giving vibration, then unto man shall be given. If man holds and is in the holding vibration, through lack of awareness, through error of ignorance, which is nothing more than fear, then from him all shall be taken.

Because, you see, the divine law is everywhere present. It is constantly demonstrating itself to us wherever we go. When the sun shines, it shines on all creation. It does not choose the apple tree and deny the oak. But it shines on both trees. It shines on all creation. And so it is when we hold, from lack of understanding, the only one we're holding from is ourselves. We are denying our own divinity. In other words, my friends, our faith is in lack and in limitation; our faith is not in the divine, infinite abundance, that nature herself is constantly demonstrating. My good friends, take a look around. Is there any spot that you can find on this globe, known as earth, where the Divine Intelligence has withheld the element air? Is there? No! And so it is to the giver, all is given. Yes.

Why does he say that he waited so patiently? What is meant by that?

He stated that he had waited so patiently. Tell me something, my good friends, when you wait for something, are you patient? The one sentence is revealing to mankind the wisdom of how to wait for anything. He states, "We have waited so patiently." If you do not wait in the vibratory wave of patience, you set different laws into motion and you might not wait until the victory comes. But if you are patient, you will know. Remember that wisdom, and wisdom alone, lives in patience. No patience, my friends, no wisdom.

But he combines the patience with knowing that all is given to those who give.

That is correct. He combines it because wisdom lives in patience. Wisdom is that that knows and doesn't have to be told. So he states, "We have waited so patiently knowing that all is given to those who give." Absolutely. That's why he waited so patiently. He knows the law. He knew it would come to be, it would come to pass. That's wisdom. Anyone else?

Going back to truth that we spoke of a moment ago, did I understand correctly that truth is not the same to all of us?

Truth is individually perceived. According to our view, we get a portion of it. For example, take a round sphere and take a look at it. Depending on where you're looking at it, you will have a different view. Is that correct? And so it is with truth itself.

Does that apply according to your level of where you are?

Definitely! Now the teaching does not teach that truth is individual. It is individually perceived. Truth is one and truth is everything, but it is individually perceived. This is why we have so many philosophies in the world and so many different religions and so much different understanding. Because those are all different levels of awareness looking at the same globe of truth. They all see it, but they see it from a different view.

Thank you.

You're welcome.

I'm having trouble with the word Light. *Would you define what is meant by the word* Light, *as in "the Light within"?*

Now when he uses the word *Light,* he is referring to "truth" and if I attempted to define *truth*, I would lose truth in the attempt to define it. So it is not possible for me to define the word *Light* in the use that he uses the word. He uses the word of *Light* as "truth itself." And he says, "Love all life and know the Light." Love all life and know the truth. Anyone else? We just have a few moments left before we go for our coffee break.

I just want to understand something and perhaps you can reiterate. Does the soul perceive truth?

It is our understanding and teaching that the soul perceives truth, not the mind. The mind conceives facts and many there are, but it is only the soul that perceives truth. You see, the nature of mind is change. Now, if the nature of mind is change, how can it possibly perceive truth that is changeless? It is not possible! It is not possible for this thing, this intellect, to perceive that that is changeless and eternal. It can only conceive. It can have thoughts about it, etc., but it cannot perceive, because its very nature of mind stuff is constant change.

Is the soul conscious?

Is the soul conscious? Our soul is consciousness. Yes, consciousness.

But not conscious?

We can be consciously aware of our soul. Yes, we can be. We can be consciously aware of our soul. The awareness comes in what is known as a clairsentience. In other words, you cannot, with the mind and the intellect, define my soul as such and such, etc. You can feel it, you understand. There will be a feeling in the mind and a knowing, of course, in the soul itself.

Is the original sense of touch clairsentience?

That is the original sense, the original sense of touch. You do not need to physically touch an object to feel an object. That depends upon your receptivity to the vibratory waves that the object is emanating at any given moment. All objects, all things emanate a vibratory wave. You do have the power within yourself to turn to that particular channel, to that particular conscious awareness level and feel it.

Our conscience, then, would be, if something you were going to do wasn't right, you would feel consciously aware that this is not right. Your clairsentience—

That's right. You would feel it. That is our conscience, which is the spiritual sensibility, with a dual capacity, knows right from wrong, does not have to be told, and that is expressed through our sense of feeling. For example, a person knows they are not supposed to be doing that. They *feel*: they get an inner feeling. That's their conscience. That is their true clairsentience.

The soul perceives; the mind conceives. The spirit knows, for the spirit is. The spirit knows only by being encased in form. It has no awareness until it is impulsed into form, which we call *soul,* the covering of Spirit. Now remember, friends, we are using a different understanding between *spirit* and *spiritual body.* They are not one and the same.

Thank you very much, students. It's now time to close up the class. We'll all go to have refreshments.

MAY 3, 1973

CONSCIOUSNESS CLASS 12 ✒

Before reading from *The Living Light* this evening, we'll speak forth this affirmation entitled "Total Consideration."

[The class speaks forth the "Total Consideration" affirmation.]

We'll go into our meditation this evening for a few moments. Remember, friends, that the type of meditation that we teach is a meditation of peace, for peace is the Divine and peace is the power. Remember also that simplicity is the path to truth. The mind ever seeks to complicate the divine, simple truth in order to entertain itself. Let us be at peace and accept the divine flow.

[For a few minutes, the class meditates in silence.]

Now this evening we will start with our questions and answers.

In Discourse 2, what is meant when the Wise One says, "You are making the world and the world is making you." Well, I understand the first part, about making the world, but the second part, "and the world is making you," is not clear to me.

Yes, the statement is made—the question is, What is meant by, "You are making the world," which seems to be understandable to the student, but the statement that is given in Discourse 2, "and the world is making you," is not understandable to the student.

Whatever we become in rapport with, we are affected by. So that that we are making is, in truth, making us. It is the Law of Cause and Effect. For example, you cannot become in rapport with anything without being affected by the very thing. So if you are making the world, which is an understandable statement, then that world that you are making is also making you. It's an interaction. Whatever goes out, comes back. And that is why he teaches, my friends, look at life, look at her experiences. It is only the mirror reflecting where you are at any given moment. Anyone else?

On page 7 [Discourse 2], it mentions going to the astral world or the mental world. Is it known whether that is according to where you are in your spiritual evolution? Or is it that you first go to the mental and then the astral or vice versa?

Yes, thank you very much. In reference to the question of going to the astral world or mental world or the spiritual world, we are in those dimensions here and now while yet encased in the physical form. We're all in the mental world, expressing through what is known as mind. We are also in the astral world here and now. Few of us have experiences of that dimension, simply because we have not awakened our conscious awareness to those dimensions. There are a few who have a spiritual body completed while yet in physical form and, therefore, they go to the spiritual world.

Now in reference to transition, when we leave this physical body, it does not mean that we're all going to land in a mental and an astral dimension. If we have a spiritual body created, then we're going to go to a spiritual world. But those dimensions, friends, we're going in here and now as we unfold within our own being. Does that help you with your question?

Yes. Thank you.

Yes.

I don't quite understand the meaning of this: "My children, when of naught desire is, in vain doth sorrow speak [Discourse 2]*."*

Yes, thank you very much. The statement is made in *The Living Light*, When of naught, or nothing, desire is, when there is no desire, then there is no sorrow. For desire is a function, and our sorrows, our sadnesses, are ever equal and in harmony with our desires. Consciously aware of them or unconsciously, desire is desire. It is a directed energy. And when we have no desire, we cannot experience any sadness or any sorrow. For example, say that a lady desires to get married, to marry a certain person. Well, if it doesn't work out the way that she desires it, then she experiences sadness. Would you not agree? Or say that a person gets married and it is not in accord or in fulfillment of her desire; therefore she experiences the opposite. And that's why he states in his book, When there is no desire, there is no sorrow.

Along that vein, then, what do you think of people lowering their expectations of another?

In reference to your statement of people lowering their expectations of another, if one expects nothing, then they have no experience to encounter. If you don't expect from people, then you will never be disappointed by people. If you expect from the Divine, you will not be disappointed if you are expressing your divinity. But if you expect from the Divine and do not express your divine right or your divinity, then you'll be disappointed. A wise man chooses what he expects anything from and in choosing it wisely, he learns the laws governing receptivity to its fulfillment. Thank you very much. Anyone else?

Will you explain to us the Law of Attraction and the Law of Attachment and how we move from attachment to attraction? If we attract—do we attract the wrong things and attach ourselves to them, or do we attach ourselves to the right things? So many people have said they were afraid to attach themselves to a certain condition and I think of how many people attach themselves to the right conditions, and I'm rather confused.

In reference to your question on the Law of Attachment and the Law of Attraction, if we will stop to think, we will realize that the Law of Attraction is nothing more than an expression in this dimension of the Law of Desire. Whatever we desire, known or hidden, is attracted to us, according to the magnetic laws governing creation. And so it is that man attracts unto himself what he desires, whether or not he is consciously aware of those so-called hidden desires.

Having attracted something to him, he has a choice, as we're never left without choice. We may choose to be adverse to the very thing that we have attracted and in the adversity become controlled by it. Or we may choose to remain in rapport with that that we have attracted and become attached to it. There are two ways of attachment. Or we may choose to remain neutral, accept it as something we have set into motion, and rise our level, our conscious awareness, to a higher level, and it will dissipate, according to the law that has been set into motion. Does that help with your question?

On page 6 [Discourse 2], *I wonder if you would explain why "we who are wise, or try to be, tarry not in spheres of beauty."*

Yes. The statement is made that we who are wise tarry or linger not in spheres of beauty. It is my understanding from those words that a wise man recognizes and realizes that life's fulfillment is indeed dual. Therefore, in order to remain in balance, one does not remain in one particular expression, whether you call that expression *beauty* or you call that expression its opposite. We recognize the duality of expression and, therefore, do not keep ourselves out of balance by remaining in one particular expression.

It also says, I believe, something about, we work: we tarry not in the spheres of beauty, but we work. Does this mean we do become guides and teachers or we help others on the earth plane?

It means, to my understanding, that the very nature and purpose of the soul's incarnation into form is to express. It is not to bask in the sun like a toad throughout eternity. Therefore, I am in accord with your understanding that we're here to serve, whether they call the word *work* or they call it something else. The purpose of the soul's incarnation is motion: to move, to act, to be.

This reminds me of a rough stone being polished and polished and polished, rounding off the rough edges.

Exactly. That is how form is refined or evolved or spiritualized. Any other questions?

I have two questions. One is about the Law of Attachment and that is, Can you become attached to divine wisdom?

The question is asked by the lady, in reference to the Law of Attachment, "Can you become attached to divine wisdom?" Whereas divine wisdom is not, in and of itself, form, it is not possible to attach to it. For example, if you feel that you are

attached to what is known as divine wisdom, then divine wisdom is yet to be found. Attachment deals with a mental body
and does not deal with a formless Divine Spirit. Remember, it is
our spirit, and our spirit alone, that recognizes divine wisdom.
Does that help with your question?

It does. The other question was about the line that confuses
me: "The climb, my children, is never higher than the fall [Dis-
course 3]*." Somehow, I think it should be, The fall is never lower*
than the climb.

Yes. The question is of the statement from *The Living Light*
that the climb is never higher than the fall. We obviously can see
from that one statement that expression of duality is involved.
In other words, the higher we go, the lower we fall. Now one
might say, then, why bother to climb anyplace, if, in the climbing, you're only going to fall? It's very clear, my friends, the
higher the climb, the lower the fall. In other words, he's speaking of the rising of the spirit through the eighty-one levels of
awareness. When your spirit, your consciousness, rises up to
higher levels, these other levels have fallen from your conscious
awareness. And they are ever in proportion to your climb. If
you're on level twelve, for example, and you climb up to forty,
well that's the extent that level twelve has fallen from you, from
your conscious awareness. Does that help with your question?
Thank you. Any other questions?

Does self-pity inevitably have attachments? I think it does.

Yes. The lady is asking in reference to self-pity, Does it have
anything to do with attachments? It is not possible to experience what is known as pity of the self, it is not *possible* to experience pity of self unless self is attached to something or someone or someplace. The only way that we can experience pity of
self is through the Law of Attachment. Think about self-pity.
What are you thinking about? Are you thinking about the way
things are going? Or the way things haven't gone? Or this par-

ticular situation that you're in? Those are all your attachments. That's the only time you can experience the pity of self.

Thank you. In reading the first and second discourse, it seems that it is a lesson mainly on the difference between aspiration and desire. And I'm thinking in connection with laws that we've put into motion. If one were working with their affirmations and putting laws into motion that were directly related to laws of wisdom, rather than self or desire, then one would not be subject to laws of motion, but only to God's law, because they would no longer be attached to self or self-desire.

Without motion, there is no awareness.

No, putting the laws of God into motion, rather than laws of attachment or desire. I'm trying to understand the laws of motion better. And when someone starts talking sometimes about how to put the law of motion into action, and it doesn't sound like anything that's coming from divine wisdom, to me, I'm trying to think of how you balance that and bring it back into God's creation.

The thing is that all things, all things are an expression of divine wisdom. The expression, of course, varies with the forms through which the divine wisdom is expressing itself. There is no expression in any universe at any time that is not the expression of divine wisdom. Now I know that may seem difficult for some to understand; however, when you take pure energy and you use it to illumine the room—the same pure energy can and is used to electrocute and to kill. That energy is divine wisdom. Because man, on the evolutionary path of his soul, has experienced and continues to experience what is known as free will or choice, man decides to use or to abuse what is divine wisdom. Divine wisdom, being divine, is not partial. It does not decide how you're going to use it. It simply expresses itself through all forms at all times. Man makes the decision.

And illuminates . . .

It illuminates. Man makes—

What I'm trying to do is break these down for my own understanding.

Yes.

When I relate desire, thoughts that come from the realms of desire, I become caught in attachment. But when I start thinking of laws of aspiration that are more from the soul level, I then see more the Law of Attraction and I'm trying to think what that is.

Yes. Like attracts like on all dimensions, on all levels. Identically, it's the same law. The law that expresses in a spiritual dimension expresses in a material dimension, expresses in a desire world. It is one and the same law. There are different experiences by the individual of the expression of that law, but it is the same law. The Law of Attraction is identically the same in spiritual matters as it is in mental or material matters. It is the same law. Anyone else?

I have a question about laws that we set into motion in respect to debt. Let's say we set a law into motion regarding another human being. If we do not work out the fulfillment of the law that we have set into motion when we're, let's say, on this planet in this plane, will the debt continue when we've both passed on to another plane? Will we work it out then?

Yes, that's a very fine question. And in reference to that, we most certainly will. We have what is known as the memory par excellence, which records all things, loses nothing. There is no escape. The reason that there is no escape is because man is a spiritual being and has a conscience. The conscience is that spiritual sensibility with a dual capacity, knows right from wrong, does not have to be told. Man also has what is known as the memory par excellence. It goes with him into the other dimensions. Whatever his conscience has recorded as a debt goes with him and is fulfilled, as man is a law unto himself. Yes. In other words, my friends, if you think you're going to escape anything, it is only a delusion created by your mind, because there is no escape. All of our experiences we've brought into action into our lives, and all of them shall we disintegrate through the laws of fulfillment. Does that help with your question?

Yes, it does.

Thank you kindly.

What determines how we balance our life and is everybody in their balance?

Yes, a fine question. What determines what balances our life and are we all in balance? If we are all expressing a divine neutrality, if our minds are not disturbed at any time, at any moment, then it is evident that we are in balance. From my particular view, I have yet to find a man that is in balance. I have never yet seen a person expressing perfect divine neutrality. Not even Jesus the Nazarene expressed that perfect divine neutrality: otherwise, he wouldn't have thrown the money changers out of the temple.

Now what is it that determines balance? Remember that there are eighty-one levels of awareness. What determines balance on one level does not determine balance on another level. And so it is that each individual, through a harmonious communication with their conscience, knows what is their balance for any given moment. Therefore, it is the conscience that knows what is balance for us at any time. Does that help you with your question?

In thinking about how to set a law in motion, I really don't feel that I understand, in everyday terminology, how this is done and how a law is transgressed. And I wonder if you would talk about that. Also, can a law be set into motion both by the mind and the soul? I thought in the last class that you said that the soul sets a law into motion in determining its birth date when it incarnates. It's through the Law of Merit that a person incarnates into either a rich or poor family, but for how long must a person stay in the circumstances of his birth? Is it only until he can set different laws into motion to change his situation or is

there kind of a time? And does he set a law into motion before he
incarnates as to how long he's going to live here?

Yes, thank you very much. I have fifteen questions in which
to discuss. They're very deep questions, my good friends. So let's
begin with one of them in reference to the soul and the laws that
it sets into motion.

Now we have discussed before that the soul has entered form
according to laws that it and it alone has set into motion, in
reference to your question about the wealthy and the poor and
vice versa, etc. Now, for example, if a soul enters form in this
physical earth in this dimension, it has set laws into motion to
enter a certain body at a certain time into a certain family in a
certain country in a certain place. Now it does not haphazardly
choose the parents. The parents are merely an effect of laws
set into motion. For example, the parents in their evolutionary
soul incarnations have merited this particular soul to be born.
All right? And that particular soul has merited those particular
parents. Now how long will the soul remain on earth is also
a law—a combination of laws, that is, that have been set into
motion through prior expression.

Now can the person neutralize laws that they set into motion?
Yes, indeed, they can. But remember, if it takes 90 percent of
one's life energy to set a law into motion, it's going to take 90
percent of their life energy to neutralize it. And so it is ever in
harmony: the divine law is ever eternally balanced and just, and
the laws are set into motion by us each and every moment.

Now don't misunderstand that a soul enters form and their
entire pattern is set. Their basic pattern is set. A soul enters
form with basic talents, not just one; some have several talents.
Now some souls have merited never finding their natural soul
talents, and consequently, they do not find them during this
earth expression. Does that help with one of your questions?

Yes, thank you.

Now, what is your other question? We'll take them one at a time.

What I would really like to know—going back to the first part— is, could you give us some examples of how a person actually sets a law into motion and how he transgresses it and what happens, the mechanics of it?

All right, I will be more than happy to. The transgressing of the Law of Commitment is one of the greatest transgressions known to man. That is why he teaches that hell is paved with good intentions and broken promises. Because a good intention is a commitment on a certain level. A broken promise is a broken commitment on another level. When man says he is going to do this or that, when man says he intends to do this or that, he sets a law into motion. If he does not fulfill that law, that commitment, it comes back into his universe. The sadness is that man does not recognize his effects as transgressions of the Law of Commitment. But that is indeed exactly what it is, and it is demonstrable to he who chooses to make the effort to awaken his vision and see more clearly. The Law of Commitment, the transgression of it, breaks the back of man. Sooner or later, he will awaken and recognize and realize that his grief and sorrow is because of his good intentions and of his broken promises.

Now, when man says, "I'm going to do this," and he does not do it, he is only breaking the commitment to himself. What happens? Something else comes along and he changes his mind. You see? Man has this free will. He forgets that he set this law into motion. And I'm very happy that you brought this up, because I want to give a little homework exercise to the class, something that you can do daily at home. When man becomes aware of his feelings, when he speaks the word, he will awaken his consciousness, which is sleeping in most of us.

Now we find in this world, you know, we speak and then we just speak right on it at quite a fairly rapid speed. How many of us speak one sentence, and when we speak the sentence we become aware of the feelings that we're having? For example, when a person says the word *drive*, there are all types of feelings taking place within his emotional body. Through the Law of Association, these are being expressed within himself. And so man goes out into the world, he listens to a million words, he has all kinds of feelings, and he doesn't even know why. Therefore, we have given an exercise for you to do at home each day. Speak just a few words. Learn to speak much slower. When you say a sentence—"Learn to speak,"—say it slowly. Say the word *learn*. What happens to your mind when you say the word *learn?* What happens to the mind? What are your feelings? You must have some view taking place. That word operates through the laws of association. You might be thinking of school a long time ago. You might be thinking of your children. The Law of Association, it brings all of these feelings, all these emotions into your mind. But because we're speaking so rapidly, we have gone to sleep and we have lost the power of the spoken word. Any other questions?

I believe that you talked about how the mind sets a law into motion. Would you discuss how a soul can be—

The mind is an effect of the soul's expression, as the body is an effect of the mind's expression. They're interrelated and inseparable while in expression. Does that help with your questions?

We're told in Discourse 24 that love is the creative principle and that love is the Allsoul. But we're also told that individualization takes place before other steps. We know that man has free will and, therefore, may, in and of himself, complete those four other steps and manifest or express through creation. What, then, of the lower kingdoms? It is stated that the planet was already here when man entered onto it. How were the steps of creation then completed, or, more specifically, what provided the impetus to set the physical universe into motion before . . .

Fine, thank you very much. We'll take your questions one by one. So instead of—I appreciate the form in which you have presented them; however, we would like to break them down, beginning with the last question that you gave. What provided the impetus for what?

It was actually only one question. What provided the impetus to set the physical universe into motion before the entrance of man?

Yes, and the question is, What provided the impetus to set the physical world into motion before the existence of man in the physical dimension? Is that the question?

Yes.

I wasn't going to get into these types of questions this early in an awareness class. Some of you, I know, are aware of the gods and goddesses of creation. However—and I'm sure that some of you are aware of what is known as nature spirits, etc. Remember this: that the teaching is the Divine Intelligence sustains all of this creation. It, in and of itself, does not create it. Now if you are asking from whence cometh the gods and goddesses of nature, then what you are asking for is the cause of creation herself, because that that is in form is only an effect and is not, in and of itself, a cause.

So we're going to go to this Divine Intelligence and we're going to go to the first chapter of Genesis and it says, In the beginning was the word and was created the day, the light, and was created the lesser light or the night. So what we're saying, in truth, is that there is no difference between the light and the night except a different degree of expression. And so it is in reference to the cause of creation herself. Man cannot perceive with the mind. We can only conceive with the mind. And so we can conceive that there was a cause prior to expression. But because we are conceiving and using the intellect in order to do so, we're going to remain in the duality of expression or form and not go to the cause itself. It is impossible for the mind to perceive the divine impetus of expression. That can only be perceived by the Divine within us, which is our spirit, our soul. We cannot express in words what God is, without creating God. Therefore, the question has been asked to define or explain the cause of causes. That is impossible to do with the human mind, because it is an instrument of cause and it is dual. Does that help with your question?

Some.

The rest will come from your own divinity and your own spirit, because our spirit is one; our minds are two. Therefore, your question is a question of oneness and cannot be expressed through the form known as mind. Thank you.

Thank you. Could I ask another question?

Certainly.

It is spoken in Discourse 2, regarding the various realms and, for instance, the astral and the mental, as to what degree people go to. Could someone expressing from a higher realm, such as the spirit teacher has spoken about, go to be spirit teachers? How can they express in an intellectual way without being a mental being? And how could they express through the gap to the physical world without being an astral being? And, if we do go to a spiritual realm, must we then necessarily cast off these dimensions of being an astral being and being a mental being?

In reference to your several questions contained in one, I would like to say this: If a channel has awakened and is expressing a degree of spirituality known as the spiritual being, then a spiritual being, discarnate, may express through that being without using their so-called astral body, which has been shed. Number one. Number two, in reference to the rest of your question, How can we express or do we express through the astral body and the mental body, or is it necessary? Is that your basic question?

The basic question was to go to a higher realm, are these necessarily shed?

Yes, they are. But that that has once been may be again. For example, a person may have a thought of peace. Once having had the thought, it is ever in memory par excellence and may once again be used. Remember, whatever the spirit has expressed through at any time throughout eternity, it may once again, through the powers of recall, use once again. It is stated in *The Living Light* that our soul can and does all things create, for the creative principle is on the soul level. Therefore, whatever is recorded in memory par excellence may once again be created to serve the purpose that we choose it to serve. Does that help with your question?

Thank you.

You're more than welcome.

My question seems so simple compared to all these rather deep questions, I'm almost ashamed to ask. I would like a little more explanation on the spheres and the planes.

You would like some explanation on the spheres and planes? We've covered that—pardon?

There are three of them. Does each one have a relation to the next one? How do we know where we stand in relation—

There are nine spheres and nine planes to each sphere. Yes. And we are expressing through different planes and different spheres here and now at this very moment. Your question is, How do you become aware of them?

Yes.

I'm more than happy to share with you my understanding. If you will use the exercise of homework that was given to you this evening, a few moments ago, you will become aware of your plane of consciousness and your sphere of action. Thank you very much.

Now a student had a question from last class in reference to soul mates.

Yes.

Yes. At that time you had not read thoroughly *The Living Light*, had you?

No, I had not.

No. I know if you had, you would have found in Discourse 49 a discussion of the so-called soul mates. Now the Law of Division is the Law of Creation or the Law of Form. And so it is when the so-called soul is impulsed into being, it splits. A portion of it, or half of it, is expressing through this form. The other half of it is expressing through the spiritual form. Now that spiritual form has been called many names. It has been called by some a guardian angel. It has been called by others our soul mate. And so it is the teachings of *The Living Light* in Discourse 49 on page 133—and there was a typographical error by the printer, it should have been "or" instead of "of"—the soul mate is ever with us. We communicate with our soul mate, our better half, when our conscience is speaking to us. That's the spiritual side. That is our soul mate.

When we return to the Allsoul, there will be an amalgamation between these two halves and we will be whole and complete. Does that help with your question?

Yes, thank you.

You're more than welcome. Anyone else?

I apologize for having such an uneducated ego, but I'd like to take advantage of the classes. If God is neutral, what is the most effective way to pray?

The question is asked by the lady, "If God is neutral, what is the most effective way to pray?" The most effective way of prayer that I have found is to declare truth. For when we speak into the atmosphere and we're speaking from the level, the soul level, where all things are known—you see, when we recognize truth, we recognize that we are formless and free, whole and complete; that need is a delusion created by our mind. That's all that it is. And if we come out of the delusion of our ego, we will pray in the sense of gratitude that all things the lower self desires have already been made manifest in our universes. Consequently, that declares truth. Know the truth and the truth shall set you free. And the truth is that there is no need. It is merely a delusion created by our big, uneducated ego. That's the best form of prayer that I know.

Thank you kindly.

You're more than welcome. When you express gratitude— gratitude is a recognition. When you recognize that you have a delusion, which is computing in your brain *need*, when you recognize that all things you are, have always been, will always be, when you recognize that, you accept it. And you come out of the delusion of the brain and express your divine right. Thank you.

The Old Man says in Discourse 2, "Have I wandered so long to find so little? And yea, I not have the energy to climb so far down to get it."

Yes?

"And in my despair I fell asleep and in my sleep I heard a voice so beautiful sing to me. It was the first voice that I had heard in many, many a year. And the voice sang unto me:

> *No one can carry your burden,*
> *No one can lift your load;*
> *But Angels of Light wait patiently*
> *To tell you their stories of old."*

Yes.

Would you explain the last four lines?

The last four lines: "No one can carry your burden, / No one can lift your load; / But Angels of Light wait patiently / To tell you their stories of old." Absolutely no one here, hereafter, or anywhere can fulfill the law of your own personal responsibilities. There may be many who will share with you their understanding and tell you of their experiences, but it is contrary to divine, natural law for any man, anywhere, to take on the responsibilities that another human soul has incurred. Remember, friends, we get ourselves into our experiences and it's our responsibility to get ourselves back out.

Now we may, on this evolutionary merit system, merit talking to someone. After all, we have lawyers in the universe, we have doctors in the universe, and we have mediums in the universe. So according to our merit system, we may merit a few words of advice from an attorney or from a doctor or from a medium. But it is contrary to the natural, divine law that some other human soul in the flesh or in the spirit world can lift all of your responsibilities or any of your responsibilities from you. They can, however, counsel you and, in so counseling you, reveal unto you the causes that you have been setting into motion. And, through a change in your thinking and through a sincere effort not to have any more of those experiences, you will set new laws into motion and your so-called experiences will improve ever in accord with your own merit system. Does that help with your question?

Yes.

Thank you very much. Are there any other questions?

I have two questions. The first is that we tend to think of spirits helping. We constantly talk about them helping people here on earth. Is it conceivable that they are helping forms on other planets or in other universes at the same time?

That depends on the evolution of the spirit, whether they are still captured in the earth atmosphere or they are in universal atmosphere.

Is that dependent upon the merit system?

That is dependent upon the merit system, what they've gravitated to.

And secondly, on page 6 [Discourse 2] *the Wise One says, "I am so honored and grateful to be with you because of the time I have waited. Like waiting for anything, does it not fill the heart with joy?" Is he, in this sense—could joy be synonymous with gratitude? Or is joy—*

Joy is fulfillment. When man is fulfilled, man is joyous. And when he is not, he is its opposite. Any other question?

Well, he talks about having a memory of his earth plane life in other parts of The Living Light. *But we have no memory of where we came from before coming to this plane. Would it not give us some strength in carrying on and in believing in what's happening from here on if we had some memory of having lived before?*

Definitely and positively. It's a matter of awareness. But how does man become aware? If man cannot be aware of what his day-to-day thoughts and words are doing to him, if man cannot become aware of that, and make the effort to demonstrate it, then it's most indicative that we're not going to become aware of the incarnation prior to this one. You see, my good friends, if we cannot consciously recall the things that we were doing yesterday or we cannot even recall the thoughts we had ten minutes ago or two minutes ago, then it only stands to reason that we're not going to recall what happened when we were four years old, what happened when we were two, let alone what happened prior to this incarnation here and now.

Therefore, anyone who seeks to become aware of their evolutionary path through incarnations must first become aware of their thoughts, of the here and of the now. And as they become aware of those, they will open up a door of awareness and they will become aware of yesterday, the day before, the year before. And so the mind will start to expand and it will see greater things. And then they'll become aware of all the causes that they're setting into motion. That's when man becomes aware of his prior expression. Does that help with your question?

Yes, it does.

So first things first. Become aware of this moment. When you have an experience, become aware. "Interesting experience. It's an effect of what I set into motion three years ago and here I am. Thank you very much." That's awareness. Start practicing that daily, moment by moment, and you will have your awareness of your soul's incarnations, why you are here, what you have to learn because you flunked the last time, and what you should do with it to help you on through this grade of school. You know, why stay, repeatedly, in the fifth grade when you can gravitate to the sixth one?

Well, of course, a person says, you know, "Well, I could become aware after I leave this realm. I'll take care of this one first." Well, that's the reason we're in such messes! Because we had that kind of thinking before. Don't you see? That was the lesson that we had to learn. We flunked that lesson before and that's why we're having the experience today. That's why. All of our experiences, you understand, these are the lessons we've been flunking. Any other questions?

Edgar Cayce, in his readings, talked of many cases of previous incarnations on this planet. According to what I'm learning here, we have had no previous incarnations on this planet.

The teachings of the Living Light are evolutionary incarnation: a constant evolving through the universes. That is the teaching of the Living Light, yes. Not all teachers agree, you know, because they're not all from the same dimension. They have not all had the same experiences. Yes.

I wondered why, when he was receiving as a medium and a guide, he would see previous incarnations of a person on this planet.

Well, that's most understandable. Remember, that depends on what they're receptive to. Not all mediums agree in this century, because they never agreed before. If you read the Christian Bible, the first three hundred years, you know—Saint Paul was writing to the various Corinthians and the Galatians and the different ones, and warning them against the diverse teachings that those mediums were expressing in the early formation of the Christian religion.

And so it is today, you know, investigate the Spiritualist movement. I know many don't agree with me. But, you see, if I disagree with them, I respect the divine right to disagreement. And so it is with all prophets and all teachers and all mediums. Some things, there may be a harmony on and many things, there is a division. That's creation, isn't it? You'll find your light, for your light is within, waiting for you to view it. And so it is with the teachings of these classes.

Now many people, you know, would like to change the classes around. But then again, you see, they didn't have that divine right or the responsibility of founding them. You know, that's like, say, for example, you have a few children, right? And somebody doesn't like the way you dress them, so they come and say, "I don't like the way you're dressing these kids." Well, then, give them the kids and let them bring them up. You know what I mean?

But, you see, while we're here, let's share our understanding the best we can and in so doing, we're all evolving here and now. I mean, after all, I look across the room and I know beyond a shadow of any doubt that more people here as students are discussing spiritual things today, more than they did yesterday. And remember, the spoken word is life-giving energy. That that you put your attention on, you have a tendency to become. So if you start discussing spiritual matters, you're directing energy to your spirit and in so doing, you're going to start to experience it. Man talks of peace because he thinks of peace. And then he finds peace. Same thing with the Spirit.

It just occurred to me that if we leave this life and we go to whichever world we merit—mental world, astral world, or spirit world—in order to progress in the evolutionary incarnation, do we have to progress out of the astral into the mental and eventually get to the spirit?

We're doing that here and now, some of us.

But if we aren't, what happens?

Then we go into the lower astral realms, whatever realm we're on here and now, you understand. And it's much more difficult there than it is here. We don't have this dense physical brain to buffer the experiences, you know. So this is why we teach that man is strongest while he's here in the flesh. Learn the lessons here and demonstrate the law.

So that you really could not progress in evolutionary incarnation until you eventually do get into the spiritual world.

We're all in the process of progression, but remember, what takes ten years to learn here and now of a spiritual nature takes one thousand years in the astral realms. That's an average. That is an average. And so a wise man doesn't mind spending ten short years to study some of the spiritual things, considering how long it takes.

When you view the astral realms, you'll have great compassion for the struggles that multitudes of souls have trying to evolve themselves through it. For example, you know, when you have a thought of pity here, it might last with you an hour, it might last a year. Usually, it doesn't, however. But you have that same thought in the astral realms, the impact is phenomenal. You will find instead of that thought of self-pity disappearing in a few hours, days, months, or a year, it sometimes takes twenty or thirty. It locks you into the vibratory wave and you're in an astral body, you don't have a physical buffer. So the influences of all people in that vibration of pity just bombards and consumes you. That's why it takes so long in the astral to grow through the astral realms.

If you have a relative or someone who has passed on and is in, say, the astral world, can you help them by, like, with our healing prayer, shorten their term?

You can help them. No, there's no good thought that ever goes in vain. Remember that untold multitudes come from the astral realm and the summer lands to serve down here on the earth realm. They're working their way up, believe me. But don't misunderstand. Don't, just because you get a fine guide to help you and a teacher and a helper, don't say, "Well, he merited that." Because you're going to find that that particular one will disappear and you'll get one equal to your own vibration, you understand? So don't look at it the wrong way and say, "Well, now these spirits around me, they have to work. They're lucky that I'm here." Because you'll lose them and you'll pick up some of those other dudes. Yes, you can help these spirit and these astral souls. Certainly you can.

Now, remember, there are many levels of the astral worlds, you know. They're not all dark and dense. These souls are trying to evolve themselves. And they're trying to serve. Now you can understand what it's like if you've had a multitude of experiences. So you can understand, friends, when you're helping anyone what you're doing, in truth, is helping yourself, for that's the truth of the whole matter. Don't you see? And when you're not helping people, then you're not helping yourself. You're deluding yourself is what you're doing.

You know, there's a statement that God helps those who help themselves. Well, my friends, you don't help yourself unless you help God and God's work. Now there are a variety of ways of expressing it. And it's ever up to yourself. You see, stop and think. Psychologically, if the thoughts you're entertaining in your petty little universe, you know, are about this big and all you can think about is your house, your car, and everything that is self-related, well, sooner or later, you're going to get very disgusted with the way things go. You know, you're going to get just totally bored. Expand your horizon. Broaden it. Encompass God's world, you see. And then you will find this great peace. Get out into the universe. Because when you're helping people, there's a wonderful thing that takes place. They remind you how fortunate you are not to be where they are. Thank you very much.

Total consideration.

Yes, total consideration.

Yes, that's total consideration of God, right?
What's God? Is there anyplace that God isn't?
No.
Is there any expression that God is not the cause of?
No.
If there is, then we believe in a devil and that is not the teachings of the Living Light. Therefore, all things in God are good. Therefore, all things are good. Now depending on our level of awareness, we say they're terrible. We say they're bad. But to those on that level, they are good. And if we want the right of expression for ourselves, then we must express the tolerance for the right of other individuals, according to their levels. Yes.

You know, man is freed from this emotional—if man wants to enjoy the world and enjoy life and the full purpose of his being here, he looks around at God's variety and he says, "I don't like that. That poor soul. Look at that fool over there. The way they're acting, it's just terrible." But, you know, if he learns the levels of awareness, he can say, "Let's see, oh, number twenty-two today. Fascinating. Thank you, God. I'm not there and help keep me out of there, whatever you do! Because I know right where it leads." So you see, friends, it depends on opening up the faculty known as duty, gratitude, and tolerance. Then you can look at people, you can look at the world, and you can say number so-and-so and be very grateful and respect their right. You know where that level's going to lead. After all, you experienced it yourself somewhere along the line.

Of course, the old ego has a great way of suppressing those things, pushing them way back there so you're not consciously aware. So that when someone else is expressing the level that you expressed in a different age in a different time, you have no tolerance at all. My friends, it's the ego that has no tolerance. And when you're expressing through the ego, and it's not educated, you have no tolerance at all. Your soul has all the tolerance to encompass all the universes. It is your brain and my brain and everybody's brain that has no tolerance. It's only our brains that deceive us. If you are expressing your soul's expression, then you have the tolerance for everything because you know that everything is one, in truth.

Now when a person disagrees with us, what does it do to us? What part of our anatomy does it affect? Why, my good friends, it affects our king brain. They're not agreeing with us. That's our ego that's upset. Don't you see? It is not our soul, but it is our ego.

Now you may ask your questions. Yes, go ahead, please.

In The Living Light, *in the discourses we read, and all through the book, they refer to think, think, think. And occasionally I get very confused, because I'm thinking too much or I think I'm thinking too much.*

The moment that we think we're thinking too much, that reveals to us the level that we're thinking on is beginning to bore us. So the only thing I could suggest in reference to that is to become aware of different levels of awareness. Now the moment the mind says, "I'm thinking too much," that simply means that that particular level is getting bored with the thoughts we're thinking. Do you understand? What are you thinking about, that you're thinking too much?

Trying to work everything out in my head, figuring out what things, what levels to stay away from, what ones I should try—

Does the Living Light teach you to analyze yourself mentally? Or does it teach you to think, my children, and think more deeply. Which does it say?

Think more deeply.

Think, my children, and think more deeply. It does not teach to analyze, "How am I going to stay out of this? And how did I get into that?" Is that not correct?

It's what I'm doing.

Try the other way and I'm sure you will never again feel that you are thinking too much. Now we have just a few moments left for some of the independent questions. Yes.

Saint Paul says, "Now I see through a glass darkly, then I shall see face-to-face." Does that mean that sometime we'll be able to know what is impossible for a king brain to realize right now?

What is impossible to the mind is possible to the spirit. When we're expressing the spirit, there are no impossibilities. Impossibility is a mental conception. It is not a spiritual perception.

I think this relates, too, to the question: Can spirit, when in the spiritual world, use the astral body to project to the medium here? For instance, a mother, a father has gone on into the spiritual realms. Are they too spiritualized to come through in that condition through the medium? When we say your mother is here or your father is here, can they use the astral shell or the astral body that they have discarded?

They can use a mental body. Yes. And then there are times when some will use an astral body, composed of astral substance. Now remember, friends, that mental shell or astral shell doesn't lie there waiting for you to decide someday to use it again. It is composed of astral substance and goes into the astral dimension. When a spirit chooses to use an astral body, it once again cloaks itself. Because it has the image of that body, it cloaks itself out of astral substance and appears in that dimension, you see.

Now remember, a person has a spiritual body. A person in an astral body that has not yet created a spiritual body through the soul faculties cannot image a spiritual body and appear in it. That's a delusion. Yes.

Thank you very much.

You're more than welcome.

You mentioned "memory par excellence." I'm not used to that term. I don't know what you mean by that.

Why, by "memory par excellence," I mean that there is within the soul what is known as memory par excellence. That means that it records all things and loses nothing. Ever since the soul was individualized, there has been that awareness. There, all things are recorded.

It's not a function of the physical brain?

It is not a function of the mind or the brain. No. Absolutely and positively not. It is a soul faculty, known as memory par excellence. Yes.

What is meant by nothing is ever written on the soul?

Is that from the Living Light? I'm not familiar with it.

I don't know where—

I'm sure you will not find that statement within the contents of the teachings of the Living Light, whether it's in discourses, lectures, or *The Living Light* itself. We have never taught that nothing is ever written on the soul. If you mean by that statement—"Nothing is ever written on the soul"—if you mean by that, that the soul does not record all experience, I totally, fully, and wholeheartedly disagree. That is not the teachings of the Living Light.

I don't know where I read it.

Yes, I know you did not get it in the Serenity Association in its official presentation of this understanding. Thank you very much.

Going back to the spoken word, am I putting the same law into motion if I think I cannot understand something as when I actually speak the words and say, "I cannot understand this?"

Yes, you're setting a law into motion when you think or speak the words, "I cannot understand something." There is a better way. When a person thinks they do not understand something, they change that thinking to "I am in the process of understanding." They set a new law into motion. It is much better to set a law into motion that leads to freedom than to set a law into motion that leads to limitation. And so when you think that you don't quite understand, you entertain the thought, "I'm in the process of understanding." And by entertaining that type of thinking, you will understand, because you will be governed by a higher law, a law that leads to freedom.

So that would apply to anything you're thinking.

Anything and everything! Remember, it's the ego that enjoys saying, "I don't understand. That's it! The door is closed. I don't understand." Our soul is ever willing to strive to understand. It's the brain that closes the door and doesn't understand. It's not your soul.

Does that apply, then, to saying, "I think I have a headache," the same as thinking it out loud?

Applies to all things. Yes. We have time for just one more question.

Thank you. I'm really kind of changing the thought pattern here. Would you please comment on the phenomenon of senility, which affects large proportions of our aged population? And if someone could work therapeutically with patients at the outset of senility, could these symptoms be reversed through some spiritual avenues?

So-called senility is not a natural process of the form, but man has accepted it as a natural process because he sees so much of it. The direct cause of senility is those people, which are the majority, who entertain thoughts of self. And the degree of senility is a direct revelation of the extent of the thoughts they have had concerning themselves. That is the only cause of so-called senility and it is not a natural process of creation herself. It is a transgression and an interference of what we term the uneducated ego. There are people who age most graciously and there is no senility expressed whatsoever.

Thank you, friends. Our time has passed.

MAY 10, 1973

CONSCIOUSNESS CLASS 13 ✻

Good evening, students. Many questions have been asked concerning meditation. And remember, friends, that meditation is, in truth, attunement: tuning oneself into the Divine Universal Principle. We happen to use, in this understanding, the word *peace* in order to attune ourselves. And so it is when you think of peace, let that vibratory wave encompass your entire being; then you will experience what true meditation really is.

I was curious why you were receiving with so much difficulty throughout the first few discourses.

Thank you. I won't say I'll be happy to answer that, but I will answer it. During the early days of this phase of mediumship, of trance control, it was very difficult for me because I have quite an analytical mind and I wanted to be absolutely positive and sure, that is, to the satisfaction of my brain, what was being said, of whether or not I would approve of it. Because you must realize that in those early sittings I had a group of students, and I didn't want to have something coming through that was not in rapport with my understanding at the time. Of course, I did not have the understanding at that time (in 1964) that I could not attract anything into my universe that I was not already in rapport with. That understanding, you realize, came at a later date. And so that was one of the basic difficulties in going into the unconscious trance, because the mind was so active and questioning about what was going to take place and what was going to be said and whether or not it would please my brain. Does that help with your question?

Thank you so much.

That was the reason. Anyone else?

He just mentions patience as pain. Why should patience have pain?

That's a very good question, a good statement. Patience is pain, the pain of patience. The reason, the basic reason that man experiences pain when he has to be patient with his desires is simply because desire has no light. It has no reason. It cannot see that its fulfillment is already on its way, according to laws that man is setting into motion. And because desire has no light and no reason, it is painful for desire to wait for its own fulfillment. Does that help with your question?

Yes.

If man, having desire, would pause and start to think and think deeply, then he could see the necessary steps to the fulfillment of his desire, whatever his desire may be. He could also see the payment for its attainment and then he may change his mind about the desire that he's entertaining in thought.

In this little parable, I guess it is,

Be ever ready and willing to give
That which you hold most dear,
Then, my child,
You shall not know of fear.

Do I interpret correctly when I think that this means the giving up, finally, of the body and not being afraid of this going on to a higher dimension?

It means the giving up of everything, moment by moment. The only thing that causes us to experience fear is our attachments. Fear is an expression of energy; the same expression of energy that goes into the faith, only it is the negative expression. Man experiences fear when his attachments, consciously known or unknown, are threatened; then, man experiences fear.

Is this not true with money? For instance, I mean, would it be intelligent to have a certain amount in a bank account, let's say, which would pay for your physical comfort, your rent, your taxes, whatever you have to pay for?

Then you've set a law into motion and you have limited the Divine. In other words, you've set aside so much money and that represents, to your conscious mind and your subconscious, your security. Therefore, if anything happens to X amount of dollars, you experience this insecure feeling. It comes out in all types of emotions. It comes out in irritation. It comes out in anger. There are many different ways that it expresses through the emotional body, but, you see, that is simply man's own transgression. In setting aside X amount of dollars, man has denied, you understand, his own divinity. You see, man has decided what is his security and he has set a law into motion that represents to him his security. Consequently, when that X amount of dollars disappears, or whatever may happen to them from bad investment, etc., then man's security is threatened, his false security. See, that's a created security—that's not an eternal security—that's a created security that man has done. Does that help with your question?

Is it an extension of the ego to—for instance, someone doesn't have it and they buy a big car and they don't even have the money for gas? I mean, where does intelligence or where does thinking come into this thought? I mean, people do. You see them all over the street with tremendous cars. And I'm in the business where the next day they're in the junk lot or they're being refinanced.

Well, I would say that is the person's individual desire. I mean, some people buy big cars and some people buy big houses and some people buy yachts and all these different things. However, you see, each individual, all of us, have been programmed different ways. Now this programming has been going on not just since we became aware in this particular earth realm, but we've set these laws into motion. And so, like little robots, we have entered this pattern that we have established. Now if the pattern is for us to have silk suits and whatever goes with them, then those are the patterns we've established.

But as far as intelligence, now, we cannot judge intelligence by one simple experience. Or say that a person—some ladies like fur coats. And if they don't have a fur coat and it's wintertime, you know, that really attacks their security. Some ladies like diamond rings; they're programmed to that, you know. A young girl, if she doesn't get a diamond ring, well, she's just out in the cold; something's radically wrong with her. You see, this is a type of programming that we have received and, consequently, we cannot, in all honesty, decide whether or not intelligence is expressing itself. First of all, a big car, somebody had to have some intelligence to create it; second of all, it must take some degree of intelligence for an individual to get a hold of it. Now I admit it probably takes a great deal more intelligence to keep it, but, you see, that's up to the individual. Anyone else?

How does one use reason to adjust oneself to living in this world with material needs in relation to the question just asked about financial security and the needs of living must be adjusted to reason?

The degree and extent of man's expression of reason is equal and proportional with his awakening of knowing himself. After all, friends, you can't reason something that you're not aware of. So we cannot reason inside of ourselves in areas that are affecting our lives that we're not even aware of. It's not possible. You can't reason something that you're not aware of.

Now as far as the material dimension is concerned, as long as you entertain the thought that you need this and you need that and you're on the need cycle—you know, it's kind of like being at the merry-go-round at the carnival. And as long as you want to entertain that need program, you're going to go around and around and around and you're going to find a multitude of needs, because you keep creating them. For example, man decides he's going to buy himself a radio because he likes to hear the music. Well, sooner or later he decides they're not playing the programs that he wants to listen to; so he decides to get himself a tape recorder and tape his own programs. Well, that may last for a while. Then he decides that he has to have a TV.

Maybe he can only afford a black-and-white one. Well, that lasts for a little while, and then he decides that he has to have a color TV. Don't you see? It's the ego drive that has to have something bigger and something better.

I mean, after all, the ego serves a very good purpose, because it's that drive that drives us on to the perfection and to the refinement of form. But unless we hold the reins on it, we're going to find ourselves in the biggest houses, the biggest cars, the biggest suits, and the biggest of everything because that is the demand of the uneducated ego. You see, it has to be bigger and better. This is why they've lined the churches and the cathedrals with gold and all these precious jewels, because the congregation and the people that have participated and members thereof have to have something bigger and better. The ego demands it. You know, after all, the Divine Spirit doesn't need diamond-studded idols in the cathedrals in order for us to worship the Divine. But if that's what the people need to get themselves closer to God, then, of course, we could see that it serves a good purpose.

And so it is with your question. It depends on what you, as an individual, care to entertain in thought as your needs. Now if you have friends that have X amount of things in their life, etc., and you associate with that type of people, well, then, you have to have that, too, because if you don't have it, you don't feel at home with them. You understand what I mean?

Yes, I do.

Now if they wear $300 custom-made shoes and you wear shoes that only cost $10 or $20, then you're going to feel uncomfortable, don't you see? Your understanding is not going to feel at home.

I've been thinking about this: "God bless you in accordance to the Law [Discourse 4]." Accordance to what you put into your universe? God bless you according to what you put into your universe?

That is correct. Absolutely and positively! That's the Law of Balance. Receive what goes out. If you give freely, you receive freely. If you give stingily, then that's how you receive. That's why he teaches in his study book be ever "ready and willing to give that which you hold most dear *[Discourse 4]*." When you give that that you really hold dear, you understand—that's your real attachment—when you give that, you're going to receive something, yea, even greater. Because it will be greater to you, because you're not truly aware of how attached you are to the thing you hold so dear. Do you understand?

I do. Thank you.

So, as we say each Sunday morning, we give the congregation the opportunity to demonstrate their faith in the divine Law of Abundant Supply. When they give, whatever they give and how they give and what feeling they give with, is their living demonstration, do you understand? There is no one here or hereafter to judge them. We don't need anyone to judge us. We're judging ourselves all the time, you see? We judge ourselves repeatedly. That's why we get into so many messes. Anyone else?

There was something about what they were talking about this evening—gold and diamonds. You said it would take intelligence, first of all, to create the gold.

I would say so.

So it made me think that people needed gold and diamonds in order to make themselves feel closer to God. They needed a way of expressing their love that would make them feel—

Why, certainly. Absolutely and positively. That's their way of expression and, of course, their right to it. It's the same thing with a man or a woman with a big car: that is their way of expressing their love, which is their right. Certainly, absolutely!

I was thinking about . . .

But remember, balance is love all life and know the Light. Love all life and know the Light.

It says in The Living Light, *"You cannot serve to and serve spiritually. You serve through humanity serving the one and only God." I haven't been able to understand the meaning of this.*

If you're serving "to," you're serving form.

You're serving form.

And form is dual.

And if you serve through humanity . . .

Then you're serving the Divine Spirit that flows through all form.

He mentions [Discourse 4]—*here let me read it:*

> "We have listened to many visitors who claim they know all about that and we have listened to them and have thought for some time. For we surely would like to know where we came from, meaning the expression of life, if any, prior to the earth life. Because we feel that if we can know of that, we can know yet more of this life eternal."

Now I was under the impression that when we went to spirit that we would be able to recall our earth life. Maybe we can't recall our earth life. Perhaps you can set me straight. But I thought maybe we would be able to recall what happened before. Because you say, when you're a spirit, you have to work on your mind to get up to higher and higher levels. Right?

Yes, that is true.

I just don't understand, really, why you can't remember what happened before your earth life. Can you talk a little bit about that?

Well, it would be the same thing as you trying at this moment to remember what you did on July 12 in your fifth year. Do you understand? You see, you don't recall the past years of your present incarnation.

But there's no form, though. Doesn't form bind you to memory in any way?

There is a soul faculty known as memory par excellence. And when that is awakened within us, then we will have a greater understanding, a broader horizon to look at. We will be able to see the causes of things. And when we see the causes of things, the effects are known. You see, the causes reveal all of the effects. It isn't a matter, as he stated in *The Living Light*—and they were discussing theory. Of course, they're discussing theory. They're discussing theory until such a time as they awaken through the memory par excellence and are able to view the eternal journey.

Now remember this: it is not the mind that views eternity, because the mind is not eternal. It is not the mind. It is the spirit that sees eternity, because the spirit is eternal. The mind sees its own duality because the mind is dual. The spirit sees and knows its eternity because it is eternal. And this is why man cannot define truth, because in the very definition of the word, we have lost it. Do you understand? We're trying to use a vehicle of expression to express a level that that vehicle is not capable of expressing because it is not composed of those elements. This is why you have so many religions and philosophies in the world. They may have gone to the finest point of the mind, but every single one will differ because the mind is not eternal.

Then, getting off the mind for a moment, going back to the spirit, you just said spirit is eternal and then you talked about the memory something or other.

The memory par excellence. The spirit is eternal: it knows all things, seeming past, present, or future. The spirit knows.

But they just can't remember because they aren't in tune yet.

They have not awakened that much.

You said that spirit is eternal, but the mind isn't. Now when you pass on to the other side, you said, what did you learn on this side while in form? Now what bothered me is, Do we have a mind on the other side?

Yes.

Oh.

We do.

Because otherwise it would be sad, because we couldn't think. So how do you explain, then, that if the mind is not eternal—you almost need a mind to continue to grow. Otherwise, I mean, the spirit doesn't have to grow because the spirit knows it already.

The mind, in and of itself, is not eternal. The mind comes, the mind goes. For example, your mind, at this particular moment, at this particular time, recalls many things, but it does not recall all things. It is your spirit expressing through the soul faculty known as memory par excellence that recalls all things. It is not the mind. In fact, the mind has great difficulty even recalling what it did yesterday, with most people—not everyone, fortunately. And it has even greater difficulty recalling what it did on a particular date two years ago. Do you understand?

Yes, I do.

However, that experience is recorded in the memory par excellence. It records all and loses nothing. Now that is a soul faculty. Yes.

About this memory par excellence, may I ask, is that one and the same as referred to as the akashic records?

Yes, it is.

What is meant by the term race mind?

Yes. Now that's a very good question. There's the mass mind; then, there's the race mind. Well, we're all aware that there are a number of races in this world. A different race—you're from one race, somebody else is from another race. You understand that, don't you? We all agree on that. There is a race mind that has been created over a period of many, many, many centuries and people of that particular race have a tendency to think in a particular pattern, a certain way. Do you follow me? That is known as the race mind.

Then, we have what we call the mass mind. You have a mass of people and they're basically thinking on a certain level or in a certain way: that's the mass mind. Now if we are expressing through the level known as the mass mind, we're going to be governed by that particular level of the mass's thinking. Now we have a great responsibility to all creation in our thinking, because we indeed are building this world and the other ones, and they, in turn, are building us.

When you entertain a thought, you release from your cranium, from your brain, as he has repeatedly said, electromagnetic energy. Each thought you have creates a form, an actual form in another dimension. When you speak, you give that form created in this mental atmosphere, you give it energy. And this is why he teaches that the spoken word is life-giving energy.

Now a person may say the word *joy*. What form do they create? Now the form that they create depends on what level, what plane of consciousness, what sphere of action they're thinking the word *joy*. They, in turn, in thinking that word, will release from their subconscious this electromagnetic energy. And there's the form out there. When they speak it, that strengthens that form. Therefore, a wise man chooses what words he speaks, and he thinks before he speaks. Those forms, in turn, become our children. Whereas we have been their creators, we are now responsible for them. And those are the things that are in our auras. Does that help with your question?

Yes.

Thank you.

Suppose someone asks you how you are and you're not feeling so hot and you say, "Fine, I feel just great." Wouldn't that be lying?

Now that depends, of course, on the individual. What's a lie to one, another takes as a truth. Now, "What is the wisest way of expression?" is the question you have asked, isn't it?

Yes.

If you think you're not feeling well, that simply means you are entertaining that level of awareness. Is that not true?

Yes.

If you have control, if you have some strength to your fiber, your character, and someone asks how you're feeling, you can say, "I'm feeling better," because in that moment of thought, you'll rise to another level and you will feel better. Isn't that a better way?

Are there levels of mind in each sphere and plane? We're talking about the mind now. Going back to the mind, that mind is not eternal, but spirit is. Spirit speaks to spirit. But to be able to think on each of these eighty-one levels of awareness: does the mind follow each time, of course, changing its thought to each level as it climbs, but it's still mind that we think through on all of these different levels of awareness?

Yes, there are—

Changing constantly?

It's constantly changing. It's changing right here and now. There have been a multitude of levels already expressed here this evening. And, yes, it changes constantly.

These thought forms you're talking about, these thought forms become the elementals that we have to deal with?

That's exactly right, my friends. And if you'll really stop and think—you see, man entertains a multitude of thoughts in one given day. He entertains an untold number of desires in the same day. What happens is, you entertain these thoughts, these feelings, these desires, you're creating these elementals, these children, which are yours. And they are there, looking at you to be fed; you have created them. Now you decide that you want this or that done—you've gotten yourself all mixed up and you want help. The reason that man ofttimes is incapable of helping himself is because of his creations. Don't you see? He can't see his way clear. He has all of these different forms that he has created and is responsible to.

The first thing that a teacher does is go to work on the creations of the student he or she is trying to help. Those, first, must be disintegrated, because they are literally sapping the life-giving energy of their creator. That's what is actually happening. So it is that I teach the students to concentrate upon peace, to entertain thoughts of beauty, and to stop speaking and entertaining those thoughts and speaking those words that are detrimental to them. See, there's no power outside us that causes us all of these disturbances.

Look, when a person is going on a very important appointment or something, if they'll pause and think and be at peace, then they will take a brighter vibration, electromagnetic vibration, with them. Do you understand? And consequently, things will have a way of working out. Look, man all of a sudden says, "I don't like this. I have to make a change." All these different things, these are all his children, his creations, you see, and there are eighty-one levels of awareness. Think how many kids you have running around you! Yes.

I'm familiar with another teaching and I'm trying to synthesize at this time many teachings. Could I parallel these elementals that you just spoke about with the low self?

Yes, that's where they're created. That's where they're created.

Are these also known as nature elementals?

Nature spirits are not the elementals.

Nature spirits. They're not nature elementals?

No. No. Now we're getting pretty deep here.

Is it possible to select some of the elementals and nourish them, and refrain from nourishing the others and thus select the path you want to go? Is that—

Absolutely and positively! Entertain thoughts of beauty. Express your soul faculties. You'll have no problems.

Elementals, then, are not all bad. If you select good ones . . .

I wouldn't consider all functions bad. I'm drinking some water right now and that's a function.

As we become closer to God, we become closer to nature. What is there in nature that brings us closer to God?

God.

Could you be more specific? [The Teacher and the class laugh.]

Well, do you want me to say what kind of trees to meditate under? Nature is nature.

Are trees and flowers more conducive to being closer to God?

Than the sky and the ocean?

No, than, let's say, electric lights and concrete.

It is more conducive, yes. It's a living thing.

The difference is living, as opposed to nonliving?

Natural, yes, yes. Has to deal with its magnetic fields.

Does a living thing have a larger magnetic field, is that it?

Purer.

I'm confused by the difference between the elementals and the nature spirits.

The elementals are created by man and the nature spirits are the workers of nature: the trees and the flowers and all of the elements of nature.

The elementals, then, they are not spirits at all?

No, they're not.

Are they physical things?

They're very physical to those who experience them.

I still don't have a clear picture of what they are.

Well, have you ever had a trip that wasn't what you would call an upper?

Sure.

That's the elementals. A little experience of them. You understand?

Ah.

You still don't. You know, when a thought gets into the mind and you can't get rid of it and it's not a beneficial thought.

Yes.

You know what that experience is like? It's the elementals. In other words, they take control of your soul and you just can't stop it, you remember?

They do?

Certainly. You've created it.

Oh, OK. Well, it's your own creation.

That's true, but that certainly doesn't help you when you're having the experience. It doesn't help you to have the knowledge that it's your own creation if you can't get rid of it. Isn't that true? See, knowledge without application has no value. You know, it's like telling a person when they're feeling really lousy and you say, "Well, you merited it." Well, that doesn't make them feel any better. You know, I mean really! It's the same thing.

Could you explain this sentence, "So many things we seek without, when truly they have to be within in order to be without [Discourse 4]."

Yes, I'd be more than happy to. Anytime the mind seeks anything without, it has to be within in order for them to even seek. You see, the recognition of it is first within. Whatever you're seeking, you understand, is already in here. Otherwise, you could not have the recognition of it. Now a person might say, "Well, let's see, I want to go to New York, but New York isn't inside me." My dear friend, the thought of wanting to go to New York is in our own head. Do you understand? It's in here first. That's where it is. Then, because of the illusion created by the mind, we have to physically move to the thing that we seek. You understand? You follow me? It is truly inside.

Now this is why man believes if he wants a vacation that he must move the physical body to enjoy a vacation. Well, I've talked about a vacation for eleven years. Of course, in the meantime, I've been experiencing a few without moving out of my house. If I hadn't, I probably wouldn't have made it. But what I'm saying is that everything, everything exists inside us and that's the place to go looking for it. It's the illusion of the brain that keeps driving us out there to find it. It's in here. When you find it inside, you will know it outside.

You see, the moment you find it inside—the thing you're seeking—you set a law into motion: it's known as the Law of Magnetism. You use this electrical vibration to find it, but once you find it, you understand, you're finding its magnetic field. Now the moment you have found it, you get in, your consciousness goes into that magnetic field and you experience it out there. That's how it works. So in all your seeking, seek inside, because that's where it really is.

Now you got married and you have a family. Haven't you? Where did you seek it first? In your head, in your thought, didn't you? Is that not true?

Yes.

Did you not possibly entertain in thought that you would like to marry a dark-haired man with dark eyes? Did you?

Yes.

Well, there he is. That's a demonstration of the law. My friends, that's how it works. It works through these energy fields. It's going on all the time. Stop deluding yourselves. It's in here first. You've got a job? How did you get the job? You got it in here first. Then, this magnetic power propelled you, and it, and you met. And it happens with everything. There's no exception to the divine laws. Does that help with your question?

How is it possible, the question is asked, that spirits, on occasion, can prophesy the sex of a child? By what laws does prophecy work? Why, my good friends, the individuals have set certain laws into motion. And if it's going to be a girl, then it's going to be a girl. They've set certain laws into motion. That's the power that lies hidden in man. There's no power out there that says, "Now, let's see, you're going to have a girl or you're going to have a boy," etc. We set these laws into motion on levels that we have blinded ourselves to, because we've gone to sleep.

You see, our minds are so entertained with this physical dimension that we're not even aware that this other dimension exists and it's everywhere and we're controlled by it all the time. We're controlled by it because we're not awake consciously to it and therefore are not setting into motion laws that would be beneficial to us. Repeatedly, he has said in his book [*The Living Light*], what you entertain in thought, you experience in life. Life herself is only a mirror reflecting back to you what you are entertaining in thought. Now if that is true—and I know it's true because, to me, it's demonstrable—when you want something, go to work inside. Get into the magnetic field of its existence, express the power of your spirit through that magnetic field, and you will experience it. Any other questions?

I am very interested in understanding a little more thoroughly about how your own spirit doctor is able to work through you, say, for an example of self-healing. On this growth path, does the attraction of one's spirit doctor—Is this the same doctor that I will continue through life with, as I understand life here now in the physical flesh? Or is it due to the lack of my complete understanding yet that I'm able to say, "Look, pick me up here" or, "Look, can you help me?" See what I mean?

Yes, I can understand. You must realize that a person, and with all of us, we don't awaken overnight, considering we didn't go to sleep overnight. You see, it's ever equal in proportion. We don't awaken in a moment because it isn't in a moment that we went to sleep. We've been sleeping, most of us, for this whole earth life and many of us for many before that. Now I believe from your question, you're asking in reference to receiving a healing from sources outside of yourself, is that not correct?

Yes.

Well, remember that God works through man, not to man, this Divine Power. Now if a person has not established within themselves, through experience, sufficient faith through which a discarnate doctor may work and heal them personally, you understand, from lack of experience—you follow me? However, a person has seen another discarnate doctor accomplish certain things. What that simply means is where the individual's faith is placed. You hear me? I'm sure the answer is—you'll perceive it. In fact, I know you will. Give yourself a little chance to have more demonstration and experience. I mean, after all, you know, though I hate to admit it, I am going on my thirty-third year.

I can't quite differentiate between neutrality, which the teacher talks about, and my own concept of neutrality and indifference.

The lady has asked a question in reference to what is the difference, if any, between neutrality and indifference. Is that your question?

Yes, sir.

Yes. Indifference, in its very expression, recognizes and accepts the possibility of difference; neutrality does not. Do you understand? Indifference, in its expression, recognizes and accepts the possibility of difference; neutrality does not accept or recognize the possibility of difference.

Well, isn't that what indifference *means: "being not different"?*

Exactly. And that's why indifference, in its expression, recognizes difference. Because if it didn't recognize difference, it couldn't be indifferent. Neutrality does not. Will you think about that? Neutrality is balance; indifference is not balance.

Right.

All right. Thank you.

Would you explain the difference between magnetic and soul or spirit healing? Is one more beneficial than the other? And why is magnetic healing in some animals? How exactly do our spirit doctors work through us as channels?

Very good question. We'll take the last one first. How do our spirit doctors work through us as channels?

Man cannot work through anything that he has not established a rapport with, principle number one. Number two: To the degree and extent that we, as individuals, are willing and able

to demonstrate a stillness of the mind, a bowing of the will to
humility, to accept the possibility that there is a power expressing through all of us, that some people are a little bit more open
to it and, therefore, can accomplish things that perhaps we have
not yet grown to, we can become in rapport with intelligences
outside ourselves who are able to work through our true spirit
of humility and accomplish a spiritual healing. That faculty, by
the way, is faith, poise, and humility.

Now in reference to your question concerning magnetic healing, every human being, every animal, every plant, every form,
including the rock and the pebble, is electromagnetic. We can,
through certain exercises, release an ever-increasing abundance
of magnetic energy from our aura. Now it is stated in *The Living Light* that love is the great magnet that holds all things in
space *[Discourse 55]*.

And so it is that science within the coming ten years will
definitely and positively prove beyond a shadow of any doubt
that love is the great attractor; that what we secretly love, we
experience. And so it is through the power known as love that
magnetic healing is accomplished. If you are able to express
a great feeling of love to a person or an animal or a plant,
the more love you are able to express—that's magnetic energy.
You may direct this energy in the form and a certain type of
magnetic healing is accomplished. Does that help with your
questions?

Yes, very much. Thank you.

You're welcome.

*There was something asked about this, but I'd like to ask a
little deeper. What is service and does it know limitation? Then,
it goes on to say we must serve through humanity rather than
serve to humanity. Two questions growing out of that: One about
the phrase "through humanity." Does this imply that humanity
or physical man is the greatest expression or the greatest potential form of expression at this moment?*

On this planet, yes.

On this planet, but not in all universes.

No.

OK. The other question is, Does it know limitation? It is inclined, so far as I can see, serving through humanity without limitation and yet the form is limitation.

That's why you don't serve to man; you serve through man. That that you serve to, you limit, because form is limit. All form is limit. It is only the formless that is limitless.

Euthanasia is practiced in some countries to shorten someone's life when the doctor feels that they have a hopeless illness. In this country, animals are frequently put away when they are considered hopelessly ill or for other reasons. We also practice artificially prolonging life and I wonder if there's ever any justification for either taking or prolonging life artificially?

When man prolongs life, he interferes with the natural expression of the particular individual. In other words, they've transgressed so many particular laws of harmony, they're reaping that harvest. However, they have now merited to have their life prolonged. If we prolong life, we interfere; if we shorten life, we interfere. However, if we are interfered with, then that's what we have merited. And so it is, my good friends, with whether or not we decide. If we have a mother-in-law and we want her life shortened, not prolonged, we must realize that that's the mother-in-law's merit system, and it's our merit system if we're placed in a responsible position to make that choice. And, of course, my good friends, it's also our own conscience that we're going to have to live with.

There is, to the best of my awareness, no set rule of thumb or law governing the decision whether the world should accept, which it already has—unfortunately in many cases—the prolonging of life or the shortening of life. That, my good friends, is society's merit system. And in certain countries, society has merited the shortening of life, as you know; and in other societies, especially here in the United States, society has merited the prolonging of life: that many people live like vegetables in many of these rest homes, etc. But there is no divine law that dictates either way.

Could you expand a bit on the Law of Identity?

The Law of Identity. Thank you. The Law of Identity is mentioned in *The Living Light*. Let me speak forth in this way concerning the Law of Identity. The moment the soul identified, it became aware of this dimension, known as the earth realm. The moment that you identify with anything, truly identify with it, you experience it. And so it is that whatever we, in our minds, identify with, we become. Now a person can say, "Well, I identify with a million dollars and I don't have a million dollars and I've identified for years." You haven't really identified. You know, it's the most interesting thing concerning the Law of Identity: the moment that it's demonstrated in our lives, in that very moment, we usually don't want it. And this is taking place all the time. Now I know that you want a deep discussion concerning this Law of Identity; however, you have just asked the simple question on expansion of the understanding. But I am sure that you are interested in the Law of Identity in reference to perhaps the creative principle or appearance. Is that not correct?

Yes.

Well, the Law of Appearance follows the Law of Identity. And if you will study the creative principles, of which there are five that are given in *The Living Light*, you will find that the soul moves from identity to appearance to creation. Does that help with your question?

Thank you.

You're welcome. Now we must move on, because we have so few minutes left. Yes.

I was wondering about when you were talking about awareness with another student, who asked, Can you gravitate to a level of awareness of the earth realm after you lose your clay body? Well, at least the way I understood it, you could, at least at a certain time, gravitate to that level. At a certain time, you could, like when the Old Man was referring to the time of chariot and going on and on—

Well, certainly, yes, you can become aware of those times, yes.

It takes opening up awareness.

Awareness, yes. Remember, friends, that man's awareness is in proportion with his selfless thoughts. The more self-related our thoughts are, the more unaware we become. You know, that only follows and it's truly demonstrable. Just try it for an hour. Entertain thoughts of yourself; see how unaware you become. You know, some people say, "I can't remember anything. I'm so forgetful, I misplace things, etc." Well, that just reveals how self-related their thoughts are, yes. See, this is how we became asleep. You see, we overidentified and when we overidentified, we lost the light, awareness. Anyone else?

I should like to know what happens to the individuals, for example, if we are working on creating a spiritual body on the other side.

On this side except, yes, we're just not yet aware. Because the spirit, remember, friends, is here. You see, we're waving our hands right through it and it's in here. Everywhere.

Now if we should backslide in life and get into a very mental level, what happens to . . .

The substance that's been created? It disintegrates and returns to the source from whence it was drawn. It has to be sustained. Does that help with your question?

Can we become aware on earth of what we had before coming to earth, if we reach that level of awareness on earth?

Yes, man can become aware, but remember the importance of educating the mind, the brain, that it does not continue to entertain self-related thoughts. The reason that we cannot, most of us, remember ten years or twenty years ago or five years ago is because we are overidentified with our so-called present situation. And as we are overidentified, we cannot become aware.

When we are in a depressed mood and we put something or say something—

Or you express something and you set a law into motion, yes.

Is there a way to . . .

Can it be neutralized?

Yes.

It most certainly can. The amount of energy that you poured in when you were in those bummer levels, the same amount of energy must go into neutralizing it. Remember that expression is dual, so you must find the opposite of any given expression and pour your energy into its opposite and that neutralizes it.

I'm sorry, students, but we're out of time. Thank you very much.

MAY 17, 1973

CONSCIOUSNESS CLASS 14

Let us speak forth our affirmation into the atmosphere and let us declare the truth and we will not entertain these illusions of limitations and lack. So let us unite in thought as we speak forth the affirmation of Total Consideration.

[The class speaks forth the "Total Consideration" affirmation. See Consciousness Class 11.]

This evening, we'll carry on with our class work. I believe we're up to Discourse 5.

[Discourse 5 is read aloud by a student.]

This evening, instead of going group by group, we will answer your questions at random; that is, whoever has a question will kindly raise their hand and they will be taken accordingly.

I'd like to have clarified the hereditary laws. How much of this plays a part of what is destined for us to be, to act, or to see? For example, a person might think, "Well, what do I care what I do now? I'm destined to do this or this will happen and so what do I care? I might as well sit down and wait for it to happen."

Thank you very much. And in reference to your question, before answering, I wanted to state that this evening, as an aid in helping the students to awaken to their own soul and their own inner light, the level from which all questions are to be asked at this class will be revealed by its color. And so it is my responsibility, in keeping with what was established before this class started this evening, to reveal the color, the predominant color, emanated in the particular question that you have asked, that color being orange.

In reference to your question concerning so-called predestination, your first question, we must consider and realize that whatever man sets into motion, man is governed and controlled by. For example, man set into motion various laws in prior incarnation; therefore, his soul is destined into a particular body and a particular family, etc., which we have discussed before. Now what percent of the laws set into motion yesterday govern today's experiences? That is your basic question, is it not?

Yes.

Man is governed and controlled in all of his acts and activities by 90 percent of what was set into motion yesterday or the years past. He does, at any given moment, have 10 percent free will to change any condition or circumstance that he is experiencing.

Now I do not mean to say that laws set into motion prior to your soul's incarnation dictated that you would marry a certain person by a certain name and etc. It's not exactly that way. It did, according to the laws set into motion, dictate that you would have certain lessons and experiences in order that the soul may evolve. The difficulties of today simply reveal what we flunked out of yesterday. So if we will look at the struggle that we seem to be entertaining at any given moment, we will find that at other times we try to take a so-called shortcut to escape those experiences, those effects. Consequently, as our soul goes on in the eternal journey of the Light, we find, as we try to grow or to become more spiritualized or awakened, the struggle ever increases.

Now the reason that the struggle gets greater—it doesn't get easier, friends. Perhaps in any other study you can say it gets easier, but not in awakening of the soul. The reason that it doesn't get easier—it gets harder or more difficult—is because we have spent so much time and so much energy being controlled by the patterns of our functions. Remember that the function known as self-preservation is the first function of form; therefore, it is the strongest function that we have to express through.

Now when we are expressing in this function of self-preservation, we are governed by what is known as fear: the fear to preserve what we and we alone have established. The animal, the lower kingdoms are governed by fear. You all know what fear is. Fear is nothing more than the direction of energy into the negative. You use the same energy, you direct it into the positive, and you have what is known as faith. If a student is having difficulty in human relations with his own kind—because, after all, we're all a part of this so-called human race—that simply means that the function of self-preservation is expressing itself to a greater extent than the soul faculty of reason.

Now the soul faculty of reason, of course, is total consideration. The sense function of self-preservation is a total expression of self. It does not recognize that it is a part of the whole. Consequently, by making a greater effort to express total consideration and reason inside oneself—because we cannot express to another what we cannot express to ourselves; it doesn't even stand to reason or logic. So the only thing I could suggest in reference to that is to make a moment-by-moment effort to recognize, to realize, that there are eighty-one levels of expression in the universe; that we are a part of those eighty-one levels of expression; that we are, at any moment, capable of expressing the levels that we cannot tolerate in others. In fact, that that we cannot tolerate in another we have not educated in ourselves, and through that law we will guarantee to be attracted to it. That's known as, "Our adversities become our attachments."

If we have an adversity to people because we cannot tolerate the various levels that they're expressing, we're channeling energy. And that energy is electromagnetic; it will go out into the universe and it'll pull all these people to us that we can't tolerate, until we have become educated. And, consequently, when we have become educated, we will be freed from attracting the things that we cannot tolerate.

Well, this is not true confessions, but my back's OK now. It really is. And I'm really grateful that it is, but I can remember when it wasn't. It got to where I couldn't even stand up.

Yes.

I don't mind telling you that I expressed a few words; it wasn't too desirable.

All people are capable of that. Of course, not all may do it, but all are capable.

I can remember when I would have probably laughed it off and said, "Well, that's just the breaks." But I find myself at this point where I don't want to take it.

Well, that's most understandable, because, you see, once having learned the law and accepted that whatever happens to us is caused by us, no one, believe me, appreciates accepting some difficult struggle they may have to go through, because—don't you see?—that awakens our conscience. Our conscience, being a spiritual sensibility with a dual capacity, knowing right from wrong, does not have to be told, does not appreciate facing that we're flat in bed in great pain and we did it to ourselves. But, in time, we will grow through that level. All of us. Remember, that color of your expression is orange. Yes.

On gravitating to a mind of logic and reason, I wondered if logic and reason could be different things to different people? But if we are confronted with some questions or with some confrontation of intolerance, if we gravitate to silence for a moment or two, would that mind right itself into logic and reason?

Thank you. The color is light green, in reference to your question concerning the words "logic" and "reason," and are logic and reason individual. In other words, what is logical and reasonable to one may not be logical and reasonable to another. Logic is individualistic and individually expressed. Logic deals with the awakening mind. Reason, however, is total consideration. And what is reasonable or reason to one is reason to all, because true reason is total consideration. Logic is not total consideration: that's why the teaching is that reason is greater than knowledge, for reason knows better.

Now the question on whether or not a person, by going into an attitude of mind or a level of peace, may adjust or balance themselves, is true and yet not true. It is true that a person out of balance in what they call logic, what they call reason, going into a silent, peaceful attitude of mind, would, in that experience, have a peace and a perfect balance, because that's what peace is. However, coming out from that attitude of mind, they would once again express through the imbalance that they expressed prior to going into a meditative or peace vibration, the reason being that they had not corrected the cause which reaped them the effect of the imbalance in the first place.

You see, my friends, meditation on peace and meditation on anything is not a cop-out or an escape from our responsibilities. Consequently, we come out of our meditation and, you be rest assured, we're going to go and we're going to express back through the level that we have locked ourselves into in that particular case: the imbalance of logic and reason. Does that help with your question?

Thank you very much.

Yes, keep faith with reason. Remember that that question deals with the conscience. Thank you very much. Yes.

Recently, I've had a cold or the flu and Sunday's billet said to release it to God. And I worked very hard, I thought, trying to release it to God. And I feel I still have a little bit of it and I just wondered, could you explain how exactly—

Well, my good friends, in reference to your question, the color is brown. And in reference to that, you perhaps won't like me and I don't know whether you'll decide to take another class or not, but when we find difficulty in releasing anything, it reveals the degree and the extent that we habitually hold to things. You see, this is why the teaching is, "The joy of living is the art of giving." Now if we cannot learn the art of giving, when we have colds, they'll stay with us because habitually we hold onto things, to thoughts, perhaps even to people or form, you see. And so it is when things come to us, according to the magnetic laws of attraction, that are distasteful, we go through quite an experience trying to get rid of them. That means that we, you understand, are not habituated or trained to the Law of Giving. So be grateful for the experience. If you catch a cold and it takes you two months to get rid of it, say, "Thank you, Divine. I see that's how much I hold onto things." You see?

Now sometimes, you see, if you receive a little word, release it to the Divine, release it to God. This is a wonderful experience for anyone to see how long they hold onto things, how hard it is to give, you see? I don't think there's anyone within the sound of my voice that wants to hold onto everything, because not everything is pleasing to the old ego. And so let's learn the true art of giving, so that we may experience the joy of living.

A state of confusion is the reason that we hold onto things. We are confused, we cannot see clearly, and we find false security in things. And that's why we have these experiences and we hold onto them.

It seems not only in The Living Light, *but in most great teachings of this type, they use parables. What is the purpose of using them?*

Thank you very much. The color is purple in reference to your question, What is the purpose of using parables in *The Living Light*? The basic purpose of putting the higher teachings in allegorical form or in parables is simply a method that has proven itself useful over untold centuries to protect various teachings from what is known as contamination. Now the question arises in the minds, "Why is it necessary to protect a teaching of truth?" My friends, we all know that truth needs no defense. Remember this, truth needs no defense; its expression needs protection.

Many people think, for example, that they're working for freedom. That's fine. We all want to be free and we're all striving in our ways to attain the level of awareness where freedom flows. But freedom, my friends, is perfect control: control of the things that are not free. Without control, there is no true expression of freedom. There is, however, license. But there is not freedom. And so it is that higher teachings throughout untold centuries are protected in their expression, given in allegorical and symbolical form and in parables. Then those people who, through their efforts, have knocked and, through their efforts, have sought shall see the Light that the teaching contains.

Remember, there is the divine Law of Merit. "If the Light is too bright, it is best that we see it not now" simply means, if our awareness of the Light exceeds our ability to apply and to demonstrate it, then it is best that we see it not, for the knowledge without understanding, my friends, is of no benefit to the human soul. Thank you very much.

Your definition of the word conscience *is beautiful. Is the definition contained in* The Living Light? *If it is, I'll search for it.*

By the way, that's light blue. The question is, Is the statement on conscience in *The Living Light*? To my present recollection, I don't think the words are exactly there. The conscience is a spiritual sensibility with a dual capacity, knowing right from wrong, does not have to be told. No, but you may have it after the class if you like.

Thank you.

Thank you very much.

This is in relation to both the Law of Merit and to self-preservation. I would like to hear your comments on suicide in relation to both those things.

Yes, in reference to your question, the color is red. The lady would like to hear comments on those who take their lives or attempt to do so. That's your basic question, is it, in reference to self-preservation and—what was the other part of your question?

And the Law of Merit.

Self-preservation and the Law of Merit. Number one, the Law of Merit is demonstrating itself, if that's what a person does. If, for example, we do not face our spiritual responsibility to take care of the vehicle that our soul is expressing through, if our awakening to our spiritual responsibility does not balance or exceed the function of personal desire, then the possibility of so-called suicide is ever present. Now the question may rise, then, What is this self-preservation and this Law of Merit and how are they balanced in the case of suicide? It is simply an expression of the imbalance between the sense function and the soul faculty. If self-preservation is not expressed in equal balance with the soul faculty of reason, the potential of suicide is ever entertained in the mind. Does that help with your question?

Well, in other words, if a person makes this kind of decision, should it be acknowledged as part of what he or she is putting into motion?

Absolutely and positively! If a person commits suicide, that's the laws that they set into motion and it is their divine right, if that's what they decide to do.

Well, last year we had, in Serenity Church, a suicide prevention service.

Yes, indeed, we did.

Well, should they be preventing suicide, or should they be allowing these people to flow with their laws?

Thank you very much. In reference to your statement, last year we had a special service for the benefit and the funding of the Marin Suicide Prevention Center, for those of you who were not present. That was set into motion by the Spirit Council, which operates and runs this association, because the doors of that particular organization were about to close and it was the request of those from other dimensions for us to help them. And by setting that law into motion and offering that service they did receive a sizable grant shortly after.

Now whether or not the Suicide Prevention Society of Marin County or any county should be trying to prevent suicides or not prevent suicides does not involve the Serenity Spiritualist Association. For example, it is, one could say, compassion that drives a person to prevent another individual from committing suicide. Now we could say that. It's rarely ever true, but we could say that. Usually, it deals with our own functions that we do not want someone, especially someone we know, to commit suicide. First of all, there is no such thing as death, because there's no such thing as birth. But as long as society and people are in the level where they believe in death, where they believe in birth, then society, of course, has its right to do what they feel is best for society. Serenity Spiritualism and the National Spiritualist Association of Churches has no comment on suicides. The Living Light philosophy and the teachings here have this to say: they have set that law into motion. If you have set a law into motion to prevent them from doing that, that is your divine right.

When you have thoughts or impressions, how can you tell if they're for real or if they're really from spirit?

Very good question. In reference to your question, the color is yellow. When you have impressions and thoughts, how can you tell whether or not they're from your own mind or they're from spirits? Is that the question? Discarnate entities from other dimensions?

Well, I've always tried to explain a very simple thing: to judge the tree by the fruit that it bears. We cannot be sure whether an impression that we receive is from our brain or from the world of spirit unless we have awakened the spirit that is within us. Now the question arises, How do we know whether our spirit is awake or asleep?

So we move to step two, which is, of course, creation and duality. When our spirit awakens, that is, I mean to say, when our mind awakens to our awakened spirit (for our spirit is always awake)—it is the mind that sleeps, you understand? You see, the mind is the vehicle through which the spirit is expressing itself. Now when our mind awakens from its sleep, then, we will know what is spirit and we will know what is mental. Right now, most of us, I'm sure, know the difference or think we do. What is physical: my hands are touching it. And what is mental: my mind is seeing it. You do know that difference, don't you?

Yes.

Fine. The next step is that inner awakening, that inner knowing. There are times when you know something, but you don't know how you know it, is that not true?

Yes.

There are a few times when you know something beyond a shadow of any doubt and you have a strange, but wonderful, feeling in that knowing, in that instant. Is that not correct?

Yes.

That's the spirit.

Is our intuition always right?

Our intuition is never wrong. But let us make sure that we know the difference between intuition—you hear?—and suppressed desire. Does that help with your question?

Yes.

Thank you.

When she was talking about suicide, I was thinking, "Well, isn't the function of this church to help people that want to be helped?"

The function of this church is to help those who are willing, ready, and able to help themselves, who solicit the help from the church. It is not the function or the expression of the Serenity Spiritualist Church and Association to go out into the world and interfere with the divine individual rights of the people passing by. If a person enters the doors of this church, calls this church, and solicits help, it is the purpose and function of the church to give help accordingly. I deal with suicides seven days a week. I never try to convince a suicide. My phone rings two, three, four o'clock in the morning. I have yet to try to convince a suicide not to take his life. I simply state my understanding of the divine natural laws, and I have yet to have a person call me who's attempting suicide to actually complete the act.

So then, you do have the right to express your understanding?

If it is solicited. If it is asked, yes. You see, unsolicited help is never to any avail. Say, for example, that you have a great feeling for your religion, your understanding, and you have a friend, etc. You try to share that with your friend, right? Can you not see from personal demonstration that it is of no avail? Only if they ask; otherwise, you're casting your pearls before the swine. If it is asked, then the door is open. Why is it that unsolicited help is ever to no avail, that it is only solicited help that contains the possibility of being successful? My good friends, when it is solicited, there is an opening in the door of understanding. And when it is not solicited, there is no door open to understanding. That's why one is successful and the other is not.

Last week, I think, you gave an answer that love is power and this power becomes magnetic, in a way, to heal. On the other hand, if you are indiscriminately healing, so to speak, sometimes you are adding power to something that maybe you don't want to add power to, because this power should be placed where it should be, rather than just scattered.

Absolutely. If we do not use discrimination in our efforts—physical, mental, or spiritual—then we will just scatter this energy and it will do no benefit to that that we're scattering it to and will be of no benefit to ourselves. When you have a feeling to help someone, go to your faculty of reason, where all things are balanced. After you have gone to your faculty of reason, be guided according to your intuition. Then, discernment, discrimination will prevail and you will not be casting your pearls before the swine.

You know, truly, friends, it's such a simple thing. If you want to learn to be a baseball player, you associate with baseball players and you go to the baseball park. Now if you want to awaken your soul, you think, "What is it that helps me awaken my mind to my soul that it may have a greater expression and bring balance into my life?" Ask yourself those questions. If going to the movies every night does it for you, fine. If going to church now and then does it for you, fine. If studying each day does it for you, fine. If going out into the world making money does it for you, that's fine, too. But at least become aware. At least give yourself some credit and find out what helps you to spiritualize yourself. Don't you see?

Now once you find out what it is that you need to help you to become a more spiritual person—you know, just going to church doesn't make anybody spiritual: it only makes them spiritual if that's what they put into it. But, you know, if they just go to take, well, they're not getting a bit spiritual. In fact, they're going farther down. You know, they say, of course, some of it can't help but rub off, but, I mean, how long does this stay with you if you don't sustain it? But let's at least become aware of what it is that's helping us to awaken; then, logically, naturally, you want to take care and cherish that that is helping you wake up. That's only good common sense. Thank you very much.

And by the way, the color of that was violet. Thank you.

I'm interested in spirits in relation to the art world: in music and art. Is there a spirit of art or of music and if so, how do we communicate with that spirit?

Yes, thank you very much for your question, and the color is deep green.

In reference to your question, Is there a spirit of the arts— that's what your question is, isn't it?

Yes.

If you can call the multitude of dedicated people, dedicated to the arts, who have passed from this dimension, who are now in higher levels of light and realms of awareness, if you can call those multitude of spirits that are so dedicated to the art, the spirit of art, then, yes, there is a spirit of art.

Now how can we come in tune with this spirit of art is the question you've asked, isn't it?

Yes.

Number one, if I wanted to become in tune with something, I would first learn its vibratory wave of broadcasting, so that I may tune myself in. Otherwise, I couldn't hear it. You understand that, don't you?

Yes.

So the question arises, well, How does one learn the vibratory wave that is broadcasting from the spirit of art? Isn't that a good question that follows?

Yes.

Quite simple: we first learn what art is, so we can know what its vibration is, because we can't know its vibration until we know what it is. Do you understand that?

I don't know what it is.

That's just exactly what I'm saying. I'm trying to help you with your receptivity to the spirit of art. First, my dear, learn what it is. Make that effort, you understand? When you learn what it is, you will recognize it as it is broadcasting. Will you remember that? You cannot learn what something is unless you make the effort. You cannot become aware of it unless you know what it is. You see, we face truth moment by moment, but we don't recognize it, because we're not familiar with it. That's why we don't recognize it.

May I ask one more question?

Yes.

Is there a universal art that is good?

All art is good, if it is art. Think about it, my dear.

When these guides and teachers come to us from the spirit world, if we do not apply the teachings, do we keep them in bondage? Can they not grow unless we grow?

Thank you very much, and in reference to your question, the color is brick red. And I would like to give an expression on that question. That is a teaching that you have received, that when a spirit guide comes to you and if you do not make the effort to do what they inspire or tell you to do that they would be, so to speak, put into prison. Is that what you're talking about?

Well, I meant on a higher spiritual level than that. I mean, if we do things to degrade ourselves or we continue to lie or be in delusion. I meant in character.

You see, now everyone—this is what few people realize—everyone has guides and teachers. Everyone. There's no human being without them. Now from what level they're expressing, that remains to be seen, of course. Our conscience knows what level they're expressing from, because our conscience knows our own level.

If a guide is attracted from, say, level eighteen to someone here on the earth realm, they're attracted through the law that like attracts like and becomes the Law of Attachment. Now the person becomes attracted to the one here in the physical form and the one in the physical form rarely ever expresses level eighteen; however, this is what the discarnate entity has set into motion, has merited, and this is what the one that's still in the flesh has merited. Now I've heard many people say, "Well, why didn't my guides warn me?" or "Why didn't my guides tell me about this disaster? Why didn't they talk to me and let me know?" Well, it's very simple, my good friends: when you were about your business of setting these causes into motion on level two, your guide on level eighteen didn't even see you. There's no connection. There's no communication. So you see, whenever we stop and we think, "Well, my guide should have let me know about this and my guide should have let me know about that," well, my good friends, your guide couldn't even communicate with you because you're on such a low level. You see, there was no rapport.

Now, sometimes, I admit, when people are on those low levels, you know, they say, "Well, my guide, I kept seeing my guide." My dear friends, that wasn't the guide from that higher level that you had originally attracted. That was just the illusion, created by the old gray matter.

Now it is true that if you have attracted a helper or a guide and a teacher from high realms of light and you do not sustain those levels—say that you decide to entertain all the functions and forget about your soul and your spirit—it is true that the day will come when they will no longer enter your universe because there's no door open. And you will have those guides and so-called teachers from the lower realms that you've been entertaining, you understand? And they will pose or become the impostors in your universe, because that impostor, you understand, is illusion. But then again, we did it to ourselves. We made the choice of wallowing down in the realms of illusion. Does that help with your question?

It does. I'd like to know what brick red means. I know what red means.

Confused action.

Confused action?

Yes.

Would you explain, line by line, this parable: "As the frog croaked / And the wolf howled, / The ears of Ego heard not / For the door was locked / By the key of fear [Discourse 5]*?"*

Turquoise. Now what does that parable mean to you? It has entertained your thought to the point that you would ask a question concerning it. What does it mean to you? As the frog croaked, is that the natural thing a frog does?

Yes. Well, the frog croaked and the wolf howled, these are things that happen in the evening, at night.

With both animals?

Yes.

Is it natural for them? Is it the normal thing?

Yes.

Yes. Read the next line.

"The ears of Ego heard not."

What are the ears? Why do you think the line says, "The ears of Ego?" Let me give you a key: the ears represent perception.

Well, it's not very possible to perceive or see if the ego is in the way.

Yes.

"For the door was locked / By the key of fear." Of course, fear would lock the door. But what does fear have to do with the other three lines?

Did it say "fear" or did it say, "The key of fear?"

"The key of fear."

Now let's stop with that line. Why would it say, "The key of fear" instead of the word "fear"? What does a key represent?

A key is something that you can use to open or lock.

A door?

A door. The door was locked by fear.

No, "the key of fear." If you do not have the answer to your satisfaction from your own light and your own spirit by next class, we'll be happy to discuss it further.

And what is turquoise?

What color makes turquoise?

Blue and green.

Blue and green. And what does green represent? Human intellect.

Is all green human intellect?

No. But that that's combined to make turquoise is.

Going back to the spirits who are working with art, are spirits still in the act of creation? Do they still create music and create paintings and the like up in the spirit realm? Well, you said that all artwork is spiritual. And is it possible to make some artwork more spiritual than others?

Thank you very much. That's your basic question?

Well, basically, is there an exercise that would really open you up as a channel in this respect?

Thank you very much. In reference to your question, silver. There are multitudes of dedicated spirits carrying on with the so-called creation of art; yes, there are. There are also multitudes who are trying to express their art through channels here on the earth realm through people that are still here. How can one become more open or a better channel for the influx and flow of the spirit of art, is that right?

Yes.

Through recognition. Recognition that you are not the doer: you are only the instrument through which it is done, if you wish to open up a wider channel to the spirit of art. In reference to artwork, if it is art, it is art. Beauty, as often has been said, is ever in the eyes of the beholder; therefore, there is no such thing as bad art, in truth. Thank you very much.

I was wondering, if we love all life, will we overcome our adversities without having to educate that adversity?

Thank you very much. The color is golden. And in reference to your question, if you love all life—is that what you asked?

Yes.

But you forgot part of it, didn't you? Love all life and know the Light, not just love all life. Many people love all life. But it's love all life and know the Light. When you truly love all life, you will know the Light. There is no possibility of adversity, because what could you be adverse to if you loved all life and knew the Light? Does that help with your question? Thank you very much.

I'd like to ask you, if you would, please, to expand on the understanding of awakening the mind to the spirit. You just said to recognize that you are not the doer, but that the spirit is. Could you give us an exercise that we could use to awaken our minds?

Yes, thank you very much. The color is pink. And in reference to your question on an exercise that would help us to awaken our minds to the Divine Spirit that flows through us, I think the best possible exercise that any student could use would be anything that they found that would help them to educate what is known as the ego. Now the end justifies the means when the end is an eternal thing, such as the spirit, and the piece of clay is coming and going.

Our greatest obstruction, the biggest stumbling block in our path to awakening is what is known as the ego. We do not teach an annihilation of it, but we do teach an education of it. You see, we spend so much energy while we wake and while we sleep on telling ourselves how great we are. We don't necessarily use those particular words, but we use a multitude of expressions to kind of fatten us up and make us look better or make us at least think that we are better.

Now any exercise that comes to your mind that would help you to educate this three-letter wall that we all have would be of great benefit in awakening the mind and permitting your soul and your spirit to express itself. However, I know you would like something specific—that's the way the mind works—and so if you would consider, before you express, to ask yourself in all honesty, "From what level cometh my thoughts?" Before you express. And you'll start to look objectively. Ask yourself, "Why am I thinking this and why am I doing this? Is it something that I want or is it something that my inner being knows would be for the best for all concerned?" That's a simple exercise that I've used for a number of years. It cannot help but benefit, because that that benefits one has the potential of benefiting everyone. Thank you.

In reference to that passage, if the door is locked by the key of fear, can we not open that door with the key of faith?

In reference to the question that was asked, If the door was locked by the key of fear, can it not be opened by the key of faith? the color of your question is silver.

We know that faith and fear are one and the same thing, in truth, that it is all an expression of the divine neutral energy. That that we have faith in, we fear; that that we fear, we have faith in. We have discussed that before. And so this key of fear is also the key of faith. You see, it is not the key itself: it is how you use it. Does that help with your question? It helps the lady that originated the question, I can assure you of that.

What does the color silver represent?

Sterling character.

Is that good or bad?

Quite good.

That could be bad, too, couldn't it?

Not silver couldn't, no.

Oh, I see. What would be bad, then?

That that illumines is only good and silver is quite illuminating.

In healing, I experience many spirit lights and recently, I have been experiencing symbols. My question is, Should I convey to the person the symbol?

No. Thank you very much. Does that finish your question?

I have one more.

You have one more, fine. Remember, friends, there's one basic teaching of the Living Light philosophy. We are all seeking the so-called secrets of the universe. We all want to awaken and a secret is only that that is not known that lies waiting to be discovered. And we all know that the secrets of the universe are never given to the blabbermouths. And so in reference to your question, if I wanted to awaken my soul and my spirit, I see a multitude of things, but unless they are asked for, unless the student knocks, the door does not open. Because if we give unsolicited help or advice, we're only going to deprive ourselves of greater understanding of a greater light that is waiting to be discovered.

I understand. Thank you.

You're welcome.

Now one more question. What does cosmic consciousness mean? Does it contain a light?

In reference to your question on cosmic consciousness, light blue. Cosmic consciousness, in my understanding, is a conscious awareness. It is the consciousness of the cosmos. Not this little cosmos, but the cosmos. That is my understanding of cosmic consciousness.

What do you mean by cosmos?

That vast universe that is everything and everywhere. Awareness.

What if one was to receive three?

Three what?

Cosmos, cosmic . . .

Cosmic consciousness *is*. It cannot be divided into three or thirty. It cannot be multiplied. It cannot be added to. It cannot be subtracted from. It is it.

I'm not sure I know what you mean.

You cannot add to, subtract, divide, or multiply truth. It is not possible.

In a discourse in The Living Light, *it makes reference to not going into personal messages, but it seems this whole session so far, everyone's been talking about personal things. I just wanted to make a comment.*

My dear friend, that's beautiful. That is green. But remember this, all questions are personal to the questioner. All questions are personal to the one who asks them. They may also be harmonious with our interest of the given moment and they may not. If they are not harmonious with what we are interested in, then, of course, we do not see them as a universal question. If they are harmonious with us, then we see them in that light. But remember that all questions are personal. Now many times, a person, in expressing their question, not being well-versed in the art of questioning, has a tendency sometimes to give a statement, meaning, in truth, to give a question. Does that help with your statement?

In the beginning of the discourse, it says—I have to find it now.

I think that you will find that the answers given forth are on principle and not personality. Thank you.

OK. I didn't understand what you just said.

I think you will find, upon checking the tape, that all answers given are from the level of principle, though they may seem to have been asked from the level of person. Thank you.

Thank you. OK, here it says, "Oh, so difficult and heavy is the work of those from the realms of light. For indeed, my children, we witness untold numbers of entities which are drawn close to the earth planet at this time." And then he states, "However, my children, it works through one of the many of God's natural laws and I do not wish to dwell upon the cloudy side of things at this time [Discourse 5]." *Why did he call it the cloudy side of things?*

Because in the minds of the students, it appeared not to be the most tasteful thing. You understand he was talking to a group of students at that time. If the word "cloudy" is a word that is understood by the student and justly represents their feeling, then the word "cloudy" is justly used.

I'll work on that. I had my question a second ago. I'll ask it again when I remember. I think maybe I'm supposed to think about the first question before I ask a second one.

Thank you very much.

I noticed a date on this lecture. Was this the Easter time?

Yes.

When all these entities were coming down with this other philosophy of the Crucifixion and the sadness, and he didn't want to discuss the cloudy side and bring this negativity into the group?

Absolutely.

The discourse goes on to say, "God bless you with his love and from those angels from above you, who are so close beside you." Are the angels above us or are they around us?

Now in reference to your question, Are the angels above us or are they beside us? (and by the way, that color is light green), if we understand by the word "angel", a person who is illumined—is this our understanding of the word "angel"?

Yes.

Yes, one who is illumined, applies and demonstrates the illumination, would that be harmonious with your understanding of the word "angel"?

Yes.

Yes. Would you not agree, in accordance with the law that like attracts like and becomes the Law of Attachment, that these angels would usually be above us, because it is not often that we are demonstrating this illumination and applying it? Would you agree?

I agree.

Therefore, when they speak of these angels above, they are simply stating a fact of the positioning, mentally and spiritually, of these guides who come from the higher realms of light. Now when they are beside us, that is when we have become receptive to their degree of spiritual expression; then, we find them by our side. They are able to stay by our side as long as we are able to express that degree of spiritual awakening. Does that help with that question?

It certainly does. Thank you.

You're welcome.

Is that an example of the magnetic nature of the mass mind? If so, is there a like example with the electrical nature or is there an electrical nature to the mass mind? Is that the vehicle through which things such as the parting of the Red Sea in the Bible and that sort of thing are accomplished?

In reference to your question, tangerine. In reference to your question, do you mean to say that the question is concerning the mass mind, is it electrical or is it magnetic? Is that your question?

It's kind of a two-part question. One is, Is it electrical or is it magnetic? The second part would be, If it is magnetic and that is an example of it being magnetic, then what would an example of it being electrical, if it's also electrical?

Thank you very much. The individual mind is a part of the mass mind. And so it is that we go to the individual expression to find the whole expression. The mass mind or the individual mind is electric and magnetic. Thought expressed outward is electric; thought expressed inward is magnetic. Once a thought expressing outward leaves the aura of the individual—the moment it leaves that field, that magnetic field known as the aura, it becomes magnetic. When it returns, it is electric. Electric and magnetic are two ends of the same pole. Depending upon our view of them at the moment, depends on whether or not they are electric or they are magnetic. Does that help with your question?

Somewhat, yes. In reference to so many souls who are drawn to the earth at this time, I assume that is in regard to attachment to the vicarious atonement by the individuals who have passed on.

That is the magnetic vibration.

Is there also an example of an electric nature to the mass mind?

Well, they are attracted to the earth realm at that time of year by the expression of thought leaving the aura, that is electric and becomes magnetic the moment that it leaves. Do you understand? When the thought leaves the aura, it becomes electric; its expression, then, is guaranteed to be magnetic.

For example, if you think it's a beautiful day, you send that thought out into the universe. You see, very few people realize what they do with thought. Not all thought leaves the aura of the individual. Some thoughts go inside; some thoughts go outside. This is why people have such a difficult time in what they call positive thinking. They sit around and they think positive, positive, positive, positive, positive and nothing happens. Thoughts that go inside have feelings; thoughts that go outside do not. The inward ones are magnetic; the outward ones are electric. Does that help with your question?

Very much. Thank you.

But remember, when an electrical thought going out into the atmosphere comes back, it becomes magnetic, yes. You see, it's very simple (these atoms, electrons, and molecules), it's very simple what man is doing to man, to himself. If he has a thought, he feels that thought; that attracts. If he has a thought without the feeling, that's the electrical thought. One goes into the depths of the subconscious, where it pulls from the atmosphere the very thing entertained; the other goes out into the atmosphere to boom around with experiences of another kind.

All dreams—perhaps this will help you—all dreams during the so-called sleep state are magnetic. All dreams in the so-called conscious waking state are electric. Think about it. The answer is waiting at your fingertips.

Now, friends, we've gone five minutes over. So let's adjourn.

MAY 24, 1973

CONSCIOUSNESS CLASS 15 ✤

Before getting into our questions this evening, because of the ever increasing interest in a part of the studies dealing with the human anatomy and what it represents—and some of you already have been given some of those; don't ask me for more than I am privileged to give to you—but this evening, I would like you to know that the part of the anatomy known as the kidney is controlled by the faculty of giving. And when it is obstructed, we have problems. So you have been given the faculty of giving and where it is represented in the human anatomy, which is the kidney. Now you may raise your hands for any questions of a spiritual nature and I do once again want to remind all students that questions are of a principle nature. Try to refrain from any personal experience questions, because our time is limited, of course, to one hour. Thank you very much.

I am very, very grateful for the affirmation "Total Consideration" and I wonder if we are privileged to know if peace, poise, and power is a soul faculty?

It is a soul faculty. Also patience, perseverance, and promise are a soul faculty. Does that help with your question?

Yes, thank you.

You're welcome.

Could you elaborate on disassociation?

Yes, the question is, Can you elaborate on disassociation? Until man learns to practice, to demonstrate, and to disassociate from the various levels that he expresses inside of oneself, he will not be in a position to disassociate from experiences that are outside of oneself. Now the nature of the mind, its magnetic field, is to hold whatever is attracted to it. This is the nature of the subconscious mind, which is the magnetic field. Consequently, many of us find great difficulty in disassociating. Now the reason that we find such difficulty is because our emotional body is not in balance. If it were in balance with the faculty, the faculty of reason, then there would be an electromagnetic balance in our aura or in our so-called electromagnetic fields. Consequently, we would rise to what is known as the odic vibratory wave, which is the neutral wave, and we would be able, at that point, to disassociate from anything that we chose to disassociate from.

You were given this evening the part of the anatomy that deals with giving. I'm sure that most of you are aware that one of the first things that a doctor recommends to a patient is that they drink a certain number of glasses of water to flush the kidneys. Well, the reason that is recommended is because unless there is a flowing through that part of the anatomy, an unobstructed flowing, the poisons, you understand—there's a filtering system there—these poisons build up in the body and we have these so-called physical diseases.

Now if you want to practice and demonstrate disassociation, then make a great effort in working on your emotional field, your magnetic field. For example, you know, it is the emotions that get us—why do the people say it is the emotions that get us into so much hot water, into so much trouble? Well, because the emotions, the magnetic field, it's the attracting field. And that's why the first thing we do in spiritual awakening is to work on our emotional body. And if you do that, then you will bring it into balance with the faculty of reason and you will be transfigured, in perfect balance.

Last week, a question was asked about the electromagnetic properties of thought and about these entities coming to us from

the other side, the other spheres. As we think electrically of love,
beauty, our affirmations, and our class work, are these electrical
thoughts that go out and magnetize those guides and those teach-
ers and whatever good that comes back to us?

Thoughts within are magnetic. They leave the aura electrically. When they go out into the atmosphere they become
and return magnetically. And this is why electric and magnetic
are inseparable. They are two ends of the same pole, the pole
itself being the odic. When the electric and magnetic vibratory
waves are in perfect balance, when they're in balance—you do
not annihilate the emotions. You do not annihilate the ego: you
simply educate it, and educate means to balance. When that is
in balance, you, as an individual, are expressing from the odic
vibratory waves or the balance, the perfect balance, between the
electric and the magnetic. Being at that position in your state
of consciousness, there is nothing that is impossible. For you,
yourself, become in harmony, a part of the universal laws of life,
an inseparable part of the One. Being an inseparable part of the
One, you are, in truth, everyone.

How long can you stay in that precarious place?

It is only precarious to what is known as the self. You can
stay in it momentarily. I couldn't say how many seconds, but you
can momentarily reach that point of that perfect balance. But
it cannot be sustained while yet in form, if that helps with your
question.

As dreams, quite often, in my understanding, are of desire, may
I ask also are dreams to more or less rewind the subconscious?

Well, in reference to your question, I think that it was already
discussed that dreams are magnetic. They operate through the
magnetic field. And instead of to wind up the subconscious,
the truth of the matter is that they unwind the subconscious.
There's all of this suppression of desire. If the form did not
dream, you understand, it would be impossible for it to keep

any degree of balance in order to stay in form itself. This is why all forms dream. It's not just the human being that dreams. The dog dreams, the cat dreams, the tree dreams, and the rock dreams. All forms dream in order that they may release this magnetic energy that is going so far out of balance. You see, man suppresses so many thoughts and educates so few. Does that help with your question?

It states in Discourse 7, regarding the visitors from other universes, "They all have soul and the ones who have conversed with us through the magnetic and vibratory waves, for we do not and cannot communicate with the so-called spoken word." Is there a difference between magnetic and vibratory waves? Could you expand upon that?

Yes, in reference to your question, "Is there a difference between magnetic and vibratory waves?" the only difference between what is stated there as magnetic and vibratory waves is the difference in their expression. Now it is true that some vibrations are more polarized in the magnetic than they are in the electric, and in that sense of the word only would there be a difference between magnetic and vibratory waves.

Referring to Discourse 6, I wonder if you would be good enough to elaborate on the exercise that was given to visualize a cloud.

Yes, I'll be more than happy to. In reference to the exercise that was given to visualize a cloud in order to experience some of these different dimensions that are floating right here through this room and through our own brain, it has been said that beauty lies in the eye of the beholder and, indeed, that is where it does lie. And so it is that man sees the dimensions that he himself entertains within. I'm glad you brought that up, because one of the things that happens in unfoldment, unless one is extremely careful, is to view objectively what is known as reflections from within. We must learn to accept the truth that every thought entertained by the gray matter of the brain is, in truth, a form in another dimension, that we may at any moment touch that dimension and see that form, having forgotten that we, and we alone, were the originators of it.

So the only way that we can truly perceive is to first educate the self to become aware of how the mind truly functions and then we will be aware here, while yet in the flesh. For example, a person may say, "Well, if it's all in the mind, then I will create heaven." Fine. But what happens when a person thinks that way? They say, "If it's all in my mind, OK. I will see beautiful things and I will create beautiful things and that will be my heaven. I don't have to do this and I don't have to do that in order to attain it." It doesn't work that way, but it does place us into the realms of illusion and delusion.

The reason that it doesn't work that way is because the mass mind has been programmed over untold eons of time. Such and such, and such and such, and such and such lead us to a certain state of consciousness known as heaven or hell. Now we are programmed that way. Some people are programmed that unless they believe, for example, some particular book or the Bible literally and accept it that way, that they're not going to enter heaven, which is their state of consciousness. You understand? Fine. Now, programmed that way, they cannot reach heaven until they fulfill the particular laws that they, as an individualized soul, have set into motion. So it doesn't work by just thinking, "Well, I'm going to think of heaven and then I'll be in heaven." It doesn't work that way, because you have all these patterns that have been established. Your particular soul, in its evolutionary path, has merited a body that has certain programmed patterns on the hereditary lineage and the environmental lineage. Do you understand?

And so it is when you become aware of these different dimensions, that the mind operates according to the patterns that the conscious mind is no longer aware of. And this is why he says, Visualize a cloud. It's so easy to visualize a cloud. Then, see what happens to the cloud. What happens to the cloud is what's happening to your mind. What's happening to your mind is in accord and in harmony with the patterns established by the mind on levels much deeper than the conscious level of awareness.

According to what you have just given about the levels of the mind, is there a norm in the spirit world that would point out that we are in the spirit world?

Absolutely.

There is a norm?

Norm is neutrality and we reach neutrality through balance.

When we gravitate after so-called death to the first, second, third, whatever spheres we may go to and the loved ones are there, will we recognize territory? Will we recognize lawns and houses and places that we see sometimes in our dreams?

Definitely. Because we have given them control over us, we will therefore recognize them. Man recognizes whatever he has given power to. So if man gives power to the good, he recognizes the good; if he gives power to its opposite, he recognizes its opposite. Do you understand?

I'm trying to. Thank you.

Remember that the Divine is a Divine Neutrality, an Infinite Supreme Power, everywhere present, never absent or away, known by most people as Love, Divine Love. And so it is that man has the choice to do with that great magnetic power what he chooses to do, according to what he has already established, not in his short years in this physical body, but in his eternal journey of his own soul. That doesn't mean that we can't change things. We're constantly doing that. Every moment that we breathe we're constantly setting into motion new laws, according to basic patterns that we have already established. Remember, we discussed before, I believe, that we have 10 percent free will, and this moment, and this moment alone, is the only moment that you can truly change.

So become consciously aware of your eternal now. By becoming consciously aware of your eternal now, you will then be in a position to use that power more wisely. Yesterday has gone. Only a fool entertains it in thought, because one who entertains in thought what has passed in yesterday, simply dissipates the life-giving power of the Divine. It's like going to the movies and watching a movie. You can do nothing about yesterday; you can do a great deal about this moment. How you feel this moment— not how you were five moments ago—but this moment, and this moment only, is the only true moment that you have power over. Does that help with your question?

I'd like a little bit of an explanation on the difference between the conscious mind and the subconscious mind, and also the collective mind.

Yes, you would like discussion on the conscious mind, the subconscious mind, and the mass mind. Is that correct?

Yes.

The reason we don't call it the collective mind is because the mass mind does not collect; therefore, it is not termed a collective mind in these particular teachings. The conscious mind is an instrument of electrical impulses; the subconscious mind is an instrument of magnetic impulses. The mass mind is a fluctuating combination of electromagnetic impulses. The soul faculties reach the conscious mind direct; however, the subconscious mind expresses them. Communication with the world of spirit or with the spiritual energies is through the conscious mind and the subconscious is what expresses. Now I know a lot of people who will say, "How's that possible? When people go off into trance, they're no longer consciously aware." The truth of the matter is they're consciously aware, but not on the dimension of which the masses are consciously aware. Do you understand?

That I understand. What I don't understand is how the subconscious expresses.

It is the reactor. It is the reactor. The conscious mind is the mind that thinks. The conscious mind is the only mind that has the ability to express what is known as choice or free will. The subconscious mind is the reactor of what is fed into it. The subconscious mind is the patterned mind: it has no choice; it has no free will. It simply reacts to what is fed in with the electrical impulses of the conscious mind.

So it's like a receptacle?

Yes, it could be termed that. It's like a vast computer, you see, and it simply reacts. Now there have been many, many teachings and many different ways tried to reprogram the so-called magnetic field of the individual or the subconscious mind. The subconscious mind, which is magnetic, reacts to feelings. You could sit down throughout eternity and tell yourself positive, positive thoughts; the subconscious could continually reject them. Because you have to learn to put feeling into the subconscious because feeling is what it reacts to. It's the child. The conscious mind you can educate: the subconscious mind you cannot. You can only repattern or reprogram it; you cannot educate the subconscious mind.

In other words, dreams are a reaction to what has been fed into the computer?

Dreams are merely a reaction of suppression of what you have pushed down in there with your feelings. For example, a person goes out and they have an experience with another individual and they really want to tell them off, but they don't do it. Well, that feeling doesn't disappear; it doesn't dissipate. It disappears from the conscious mind, the conscious awareness, perhaps. Sometimes it stays a while here. But it's got to go someplace. It wasn't expressed. So it goes into the computer with all of those feelings and then the old subconscious pattern expresses itself.

Now if you're fortunate, if you have made the effort, then when you're dreaming, you may become aware of your dreaming while you're dreaming. In other words, it is possible to bridge the gap between the electro and magnetic fields by sending your own soul, your conscience, to the odic or neutral field. Then, while you are sleeping, you may sit as an objective viewer in a movie house and you may watch your subconscious, your magnetic field, express itself and you may reason out those things at that time.

This is why so-called dreams analysis and all of this foolishness is such a waste of time. Who's going to analyze your individuality? There's no growth, there's no awakening in that type of a programming, my good friends. Don't you see? If you, as an individual, cannot objectively sit back and watch your patterns express themselves, then you're not going to help yourself. You're not going to be in a position to do it. And besides, I've seen all kinds of dream books and everything else on the market and who is to say that a toad means supply, etc., unless it's demonstrable.

Remember, a lot of that stuff in the subconscious, those are patterns, and that's programmed. You have done that and you have to get into rapport. And there's no book that you can publish or put together that's going to give every single symbol that the subconscious mind expresses. It's not possible, because you'd have to have the akashic record itself, you see, because of all of these different programs.

So if you care to make the effort, you can program your subconscious as you're going off to sleep to let it go ahead and dream its dream while you lie there, consciously awake, and watch it go through its many experiences. It is not only educational, it is, indeed, soul awakening. And then you'll be able to take corrective measures in yourself and have a greater degree of freedom. Does that help with your question? Yes, certainly.

Well, how do you go about programming yourself?

Well, you go about programming yourself—say, for example, you start with a very simple program. You start with a program and one of the easiest things to do is to establish, as you're going off to sleep at night, that you will awaken at a definite time. You see, that's a little open door and a good, practical one. You know, I believe in being practical. To me, Spiritualism is a religion of practicality, common sense, down-to-earth, and reason, here and now. We're not just interested in all those eternal hereafters: we're interested in what we can do this moment. So once you have become successful, over a period of at least nine or ten weeks of repeatedly awakening yourself at a set time—and vary the timing—then that means you've got a little open door to the magnetic field. Then, the next step is you start programming certain feelings, like you're going to awaken in the morning, you're going to feel a certain way, and then you awaken in the morning and you do feel a certain way.

All right, that's the next step. You're beginning to open the doors to your other self. Then, you start on a programming of talking to the other person. You see, friends, it just seems so difficult to get through the cement to get the world to recognize and to accept the truth that we are not one person: we are three people. Whether we like that or not, the truth of the matter is that's what we are. So why ignore the very person inside of us that's bringing to us all of these experiences that we consider consciously (electrically) so distasteful to us? So you start making the effort to talk to the other person. Don't worry, you'll get some answers back and they usually will not agree with you.

Now that's a very sane, normal, natural thing to do, because that other you is running so much of your life, just like everybody else's life. And therefore, when you start using reason and you start talking to that other person inside of you, it'll get all emotional, because emotion is its nature. It is the magnetic attracting field. And it will not agree on many things that are reasonable in your conscious mind. But if you treat it as you would treat a little three- or five-year-old child, then you've got a good chance of getting it reprogrammed. If you try ordering it

around, that other you, then you're going to get some very serious reactions from it and experiences, you see.

Now, whenever you have a thought, "I don't like the way that
person's doing that," and you don't express that thought, that triggers the magnetic field inside the subconscious and you start
sending energy down there. Do you understand? Fortunately,
the Divine Wisdom, in its infinite intelligence, has caused us to
have what is known as the state of sleep, so that we can dream
and release those hostilities that we keep putting down there,
don't you see?

But if you will learn to recognize that you are a conscious
being, that you are a subconscious being, and that you are
this divine neutrality, this superconscious being, then you will
bring the poles of opposites into balance and you will express
through the trinity of truth, and you will know your freedom.
And you will no longer be bound and enslaved by the dishar-
mony, the discord, and the imbalance between the conscious
and the subconscious being, which we truly are.

*I have a problem with imagination and spiritual awareness
or spiritual growth. Could programmed patterns be equated to
imagination? In other words, we all imagine at a different level.
Some people are more creative in their imagination. So where is
the thin gray line here as . . .*

Which is reality?

*Well, not which is reality, but—or the difference between imag-
ination and people that just have spontaneous visions, let's say.*

Spontaneous vision doesn't come until we have expressed
through the level of imagination. This is why we teach that
imagination is the doorway to the world of spirit, but it is not
the world of spirit itself. It is the doorway through which we,
as individuals, must pass and this is why he gives certain techniques, such as a fountain exercise and different things, in *The
Living Light*. That is to get you into the creative principle. And
once starting to express through that on finer dimensions, or

vibratory waves, then you will pass through that door to a spiritual dimension, which, of course, is within us and without, you understand. So we must raise our conscious awareness, through varying techniques, to stimulate this creative principle that flows through us, you see, to become aware of it. Do you understand?

Now in the spiritual awakening and unfoldment, one of the great difficulties is to get the student past the door of imagination, to get them to enter the Light itself. Because, you see, the reason that it is difficult to get past the door of imagination is because people have great difficulty with imagining, unless you use a technique of their personal desire. Now no one has a problem imagining something that is very desirable to them, that they really want. Do you understand? Say, for example, if you wanted a strawberry shortcake and you really love strawberry shortcake, you see, you really love it, so you've got that much magnetic attractive field operating from your subconscious, then you can feel or sense or see a strawberry shortcake. Do you understand? All right. Because man has almost lost the creative art of imagery, unless it is his personal desire, there is a great difficulty in getting the student past the doorway of imagination, because the only way he's found to imagine is through his own personal desires. Now if you can get a student to say, "I see three trees in front of me" and *pow!* the student sees three trees, then the creative principle is flowing more unobstructed, you see. If you can say a word and instantaneously the mind creates it, you've got a very, very good chance. But that takes technique and that takes time. So a person having difficulty with imaging should start on things that they desire, but should ever strive to broaden it to become more universal in the creations.

Can you explain how we can find out which is the right or the wrong or the good or the bad in the subconscious, since everything is there, good and bad things that might have happened to us? If you want to pull something out of your subconscious for your own benefit or use it or bring it to the conscious or even to the superconscious mind, how can we know that it is good or bad to bring something up?

Very simple exercise: Whenever you have an experience, simply ask yourself a question, "Why this? Why now?" Now if you are patient with that, in time—maybe not tomorrow, maybe in a month, maybe in a year, maybe ten—in time, you will trigger this doorway in between the two dimensions there and you will see why this experience and why now. Why not yesterday, why not tomorrow, why not next year, why this, and why now. But you've got to keep knocking, see. Knock and the door shall open, seek and ye shall find.

So that's why he teaches the wisdom of patience. Wisdom only lives in patience. Did you ever see an impatient person that expressed much wisdom? I never have, but we can keep looking. Maybe we'll find one.

As all things are a reflection or mirror within, is it, in truth, or an essence of truth that there is no such thing as form, only what we have programmed or mirrored it to be? Also . . .

Yes?

Also, to my understanding, we could pass through certain areas or realms. How far could we reach through all eighty-one? I really have those two questions. They're really kind of important to me.

All form is effect: it is not cause. It is the effect of image. You image a tea kettle, and the form of a tea kettle appears. Now if a person truly demonstrated the laws of concentration, the tea kettle that appears in a mental dimension would appear in the physical dimension, because through the magnetic powers, it would attract the atoms, electrons, and molecules necessary to create the physical form. The reason that man is not able to do that yet—although I have seen some people create varying things—the reason that he isn't, is because man thinks of concentration with this electrical mind. He doesn't feel it. When you concentrate on peace and you feel peace, then you are using both the electric and the magnetic fields. When you use the electric and magnetic field in perfect balance, through what is known as the power of concentration, then this mass is gathered. Therefore, all form everywhere—always has been, always will be—is an effect of image or imagery.

Now how does one go through the various levels? Well, stop and think how many images one has in their universe and they've got to get through those to get to any particular level or state of consciousness or awareness. These are the obstructions that we have created; no one else, of course, has done it for us. But these are the images that we hold in mind, you see.

And we must learn to free them from the bondage of our own aura, because they've built up such a mass in front of us that we cannot see clearly. You see, the mind is constantly building, building, building. We must learn to let go. I think we discussed once before the art of giving: to learn to give. See, he's not just talking about form. The greatest gift that anyone could ever give is the gift of self. When we give the gift of self, we express in totality our divinity. Because the gift of self is the gift of the image, the image we love so much. And when we give that gift, the Divine moves unobstructed. Does that help with your question?

Yes. And one more question, if I may. I know I've heard you say it many times and I've forgotten. Why is it always 10 percent? In observing things, I say, "Thank God we don't have any more than 10 percent. I think we would be dangerous if we did."

Very true.

Why is it 10 percent?

To my understanding, as we've expressed this before, man has this 10 percent free will. There are forty functions and forty faculties. There are eighty-one levels of awareness. This 10 percent that he speaks about simply means when we are in the odic vibration, which is the neutral vibration, at that point of balance between the other, at that point alone, do we truly express what is known as free will. You do not express free will when you are either in the electric or the magnetic vibratory fields. The only time that free will is truly expressed is when you are in this divine neutrality, this perfect balance. Otherwise, your so-called—what you think is—free will is controlled by your magnetic, your subconscious or your conscious mind.

Why do we remember our dreams sometimes and not other times?

The reason that we remember our dreams sometimes and not other times is sometimes our dreams, you understand, have made such an impression—the thought that caused the dream in the first place, the conscious thought I'm talking about now—has made such an impression upon the conscious mind, fed into the computer with sufficient energy, that it bounces back to the conscious mind and we remember that particular dream. Now many times we can program ourselves so that we not only have recall, but we have conscious awareness during all dreaming, you see. We're dreaming now and we're consciously aware. Well, we're dreaming when we're sleeping and we can also be consciously aware, yes.

In our affirmation, we talk about right thought and right action, and this intimates doing something. It is expressing. And then we go into a meditation on peace, which almost means lack of action. Does one contradict the other?

Not at all. All action is reaction and all reaction is action. That's all electric-magnetic. Inaction, without any action, is simply the point of the triangle: it is that perfect balance. Now, for example, I have, over the years, had people ask me, "Do you, when you contact the world of spirit, become negative or receptive to contact them?" Of course, but you must first become positive before you become negative. In other words, you, as an individualized soul, must set a positive law into motion, an electrical vibration. Once having established that, you must make a complete reverse and become magnetic. Now that is not possible without the power of concentration. See, concentration is not only a sending, it is a sending and a receiving simultaneously. See, most people think that concentration is, "I'm thinking of a pink vase over there. I'm sending my thoughts out and I'm creating that." Well, my good friends, you couldn't be aware of the pink vase if you weren't receiving it. So what you're truly doing is, you are sending and you are receiving and it's the same way with your question.

Thank you.

It is one and the same.

With regard to disease, we are taught that whatever happens to us is caused by us. We're also taught a subdivision of that law, or, at least, that is my understanding, that it is something with which we have become in rapport. With regard to disease, would different methods of healing be implied, dependent upon the degree to which that law has been manifested?

Absolutely and positively! That's why some particular types of healing work for some, and some don't work for others.

Is there a particular type which is more successful with the one, while a particular type is more successful with the other?

With the masses of people?

Yes.

Mental healing is the most successful, because that's where the masses are. Now I'm not talking about people who seek out spiritual healing, because those who seek a thing had first entertained it in thought and, having entertained it in thought, have a degree of receptivity. Do you understand? But most all healing done by the medical association is mental healing. It works through the conviction of the masses in what they have been programmed is possible. Now, for example, the cancer cure has been prophesied for a number of years here in this Association, for at least nine, and here in this year of '73, '74, and especially '75, many types of cancer will be cured without operations or all this other stuff. It's a matter of changing levels of awareness, is what it really is. Yes.

Could I ask one more question? And it comes out of just what you said. It mentions in Discourse 6, why isn't more demonstration given. Is this because it says we can only give to you what we can draw from you? Well, I take it that there is really no lacking of mediums in the world.

There isn't.

Is that meant to imply that the reason that more demonstration from higher spiritual realms has not been given is because the individuals have not merited that?

Yes, the individuals are not emanating (sending out electrically) on a sufficiently high frequency from which they may receive greater demonstration.

From those particular ones.

From those particular ones, absolutely.

Thank you.

You see, it has to deal with the energy laws. And there's no one that transgresses or can transgress divine natural law.

Would you say that Jesus gave the gift of himself of self?

In reference to your question, Would I say, Did Jesus give the gift of himself? I do not feel in a position to decide whether he did or he didn't. I'll be happy to share with you my feelings from having read the so-called history of his life. Through his demonstration of so-called sacrifice on the Cross, that would imply to me that he was willing to give the gift of self; that would imply that, yes. Now I am not in a position to say whether he did or he didn't and I think it would take a phenomenal presumption to decide that he did or to decide that he didn't, you know. And I don't want to put myself in that position. Thank you very much.

With reference to that, what is the church's or your contact's understanding of the sacrifice or the passions of Jesus, of his death or so-called death?

Well, that is the recorded history of, according to history, a very illumined person. However, I'm sure you realize, being a member of this church and a student, that we do look upon any great spiritually illumined person—there was more than one or two or three or four. My personal feelings are, I am not partial to any particular name or any particular time of recorded history, knowing that God, the so-called Divine, this Infinite Power, this Love expresses through everyone. Therefore, we do not pick any particular personage, either ancient or modern, as the example that we particularly choose to follow. This is the individual right of every Spiritualist, whether they want to choose Jesus the Nazarene or they want to choose Buddha or they want to choose Mohammed or they want to choose any of the leaders of recorded history. And that is a very individualistic thing and it depends upon the individual for their own expression. This church, this Association, does not pick any particular individual as that one person to follow.

I understand that. What I was wondering was if there was any significance given to his death at all by . . .

You mean by this particular church?

No, by your understanding or by . . .

By my understanding? Absolutely. I am happy to share my understanding. Obviously, according to history, the man did a great deal of good. There is no question he was one of the world's greatest mediums, if not the greatest, according to the very book that was written about his life, because he demonstrated all of the various phases of mediumship, of telepathy, of clairvoyance, of clairaudience, etc. There's no question about it. And as far as my thoughts are concerned, if the Spiritualist movement decided to take the Nazarene as their leader, the movement of Spiritualism within twenty-five years would become one of the largest religious movements that the world has ever known. There's no question in my mind at all about that.

His so-called sacrifice and passions on the Cross, then, have no significance?

No more than his sacrifice to his belief and to the Divine: it's the only meaning it has to me. I see many people, even in this day and age, sacrificing, but, you see, their sacrifices are not so obvious to the world or to the people. Everyone sacrifices something in life; some sacrifice more than others.

Would you consider his death a suicide?

You're speaking in reference to his knowledge that his death was impending if he didn't make certain decisions. I understand that's what you're implying?

Yes.

Well, if you prefer to call a person or an act of an individual who chooses to stick and to be dedicated to his particular belief and to his knowledge that there is no death and there are no dead—as he stated, "I shall be with you this day in paradise"— if you prefer calling that suicide, that would be a very individual thing. That would be your choice to do so. In my own belief, if a person is working for what they believe is right and they have the knowledge that by working for that belief and that understanding, they are putting their life in danger, that, to me, does not constitute suicide. For example, that would be like saying, "I'm not going to cross the street ever again because there are cars passing by and there's a possibility that I will be killed." Don't you see?

Well, in other words, we all are committing a little bit of suicide.

Well, we're committing suicide all the time. Look at the air we're breathing. Thank you very much.

What is sacrifice? And is there such a thing as sacrifice? Whenever we give up something, doesn't something else enter in? And if life is eternal, can we say that we're giving up our lives? Or are we giving up an expression, an experience of the moment to go on to other expressions?

Sacrifice is simply a conscious awareness of giving up something that we did not choose to give up.

I should like to get back to the—

That we did not—excuse me—*consciously* choose to give up.

Thank you.

You're welcome.

I believe that you stated that the balancing point for the electric and the magnetic is the odic and that's the completely neutral point. For if someone were ill, to heal them would be to bring them back into this neutral position. Is that correct?

When the electric and magnetic are in perfect balance, that is the odic. Yes.

Is that the purpose of acupuncture?

It releases energy. And in releasing the energy, there is a realignment or a balancing of the electromagnetic field of the recipient. Yes, that is what actually takes place in acupuncture. Yes.

Is it because of the spiritual implications or the unknown implications, is this why a Western physician has great difficulty in believing the concept of acupuncture?

Yes. Well, it is simply the Western physicians are not educated to this energy and exactly how it works. There are a few, fortunately—and they are increasing in number—who recognize these electromagnetic fields. But remember, it is only of recent date that the medical profession has become interested and is learning about these energies. However, this will increase, this awareness, in the Western world. And within the coming fifteen years, I believe, is what has been prophesied, acupuncture will be used in various hospitals throughout the United States.

And has there been any prophecy as far as healing or spiritual healing?

Yes, that also has been prophesied and it is a longer-term process, simply because the so-called enlightened Americans, meaning ourselves, are more superstitious than many other races. You know, we think here in this civilized Western world that we're more educated; we're not as superstitious as some of these other races in the other parts of the world. But, my friends, if you take a survey in this United States, you will find that Americans by far are one of the most superstitious people that there are in the world today. We're extremely superstitious. If you go to other countries, you don't have to worry about room 13 or the thirteenth floor. Of course, I admit many of them don't even have a thirteenth floor, but they do have rooms numbered 13. We are extremely superstitious here in the United States.

You know, we're constantly believing in disaster and depression and limitation and all of these things, simply because, perhaps, you know, we've got indigestion of all the things that we've become exposed to and we've forgotten our birthright that God takes care of the smallest sparrow and the lilies of the field.

And so we've become so superstitious that we're kind of controlled and we live by so much fear. Look how much fear we express when the stock market drops, you know, or with this or that dealing with business. Well, that doesn't happen to a lot of the other races in this old earth planet, but it sure happens in this Western world because, you see, we're so superstitious. We're superstitious about that mineral known as gold and we're superstitious about green pieces of paper. And we're superstitious about every disaster that is going to befall us any minute, you know. And we're superstitious about all kinds of earthquakes and tornadoes and hurricanes and all of this other paraphernalia. Well, it's obvious where we've put our attention.

Now if we had put our attention on looking out at nature and seeing how beautifully balanced she is, then we wouldn't have all of these hang-ups. I mean, after all, it is a known fact the United States of America has more psychiatrists, what they call headshrinkers I believe, than any other country in the world. Now it's also a known fact that we're not exporting them to Europe or to Asia to take care of the people over there. So what are we doing with all of those psychiatrists that we're bringing through our universities and our academies? They have to make a living, so they've got to be working on somebody. So consequently it must mean that the people here have several hang-ups in order to keep them all in business. Now let's go onward and upward and what was the next question, please?

How come there is no concept of time on the other side?

And the question is, Why isn't there any concept of time on the other side? There is a concept of time for those who are in time dimensions. There is no concept of time for those in the higher realms. And the reason there is no concept of time is because the Spirit is timeless, formless, and free. And they are expressing their Spirit and, therefore, no longer have time consciousness. Does that help with your question? Remember, Spirit is formless and free. It can only be formless and free by being timeless. If it weren't timeless, then it wouldn't be formless and it wouldn't be free. We have time for one more question.

Thank you. In Discourse 6, we were discussing a Law of Eternity and it was stated, "It is the soul and only the soul that knows. For what the mind may know today, the heart shall close and know not tomorrow." I would like to ask, What is meant by "the heart shall close"? And how does that work?

In reference to your question, what the mind shall know today, the heart shall close and know not tomorrow, the heart is the part of the anatomy through which divine love flows. The mind gathers up many things. There is a memory par excellence, where all things are recorded and nothing is ever lost; it is a soul faculty. However, the heart, which is the instrument through which this divine love is expressed, is not governed by the multitudes of changes that are created by the mind. And therefore, it does not know—you understand?—today or may not know tomorrow. Divine love has no partiality. Partiality only exists in the mind because the mind is the dual vehicle through which the soul expresses. But divine love is not a dual—it is not dual: it is one. That is why that it loves for the sake of love, for that is its own expression. It doesn't choose: it doesn't have the ability to choose, you see. It just is. The mind knows one thing today; it forgets it tomorrow. It constantly changes. It's constantly going through a process of new values.

Now, as a person's soul starts to rise to the light within themselves, the things that were important to them yesterday are no longer important and soon they are forgotten. When a person becomes aware that they have always been and will always be, they start to readjust their thinking. They stop and they say to themselves, "Well, if I have always been and I will always be and I am controlled by the Law of Merit that I set into motion myself and I have merited this earth and all of these experiences, I'm going to start putting a little attention upon my eternity, because I don't want to keep repeating these things that are so distasteful to me."

Form comes and form goes, but Spirit lasts forever, because it is forever. It's the only thing worth your energy and time. Now, I often hear from students, "Well, you've got to live in a material world." Well, I live in a material world, too. But if this material world, this passing panorama, has greater priority, if that has greater priority than your eternal soul journey, then life is going to be most difficult. At least, bring them into balance. At least, give 50 percent chance to your soul that has been struggling along for who knows how many eons and eons and eons of time, just to get to this grade of school. I don't think this grade's about the highest. I'm sure of that.

Thank you, friends. Our time is up. Let's go have some coffee. Thank you all very much.

MAY 31, 1973

CONSCIOUSNESS CLASS 16 ✤

Good evening, class. Before going into our regular reading of the discourses this evening and our question-and-answer period, I would like to share with you the levels. And tonight I'm going to give to you the levels of soul, mind, and body. Soul level: through patience, peace, individuality, principle. Mind level: through perseverance, poise, personality, detachment. Body level: through promise, power, materiality, acceptance.

Now remember, friends, that all faculties and all functions are triune in expression; that each faculty, being triune, is triune itself. For example, at one point of the triangle, you have neutrality, positive, and negative. Each one of those points are in and of themselves triune. Now the Law of Division is the Law of Expression and the Law of Expression is the Law of Creation. And so it is that mathematics is the key to the universes within and without. There is never division without multiplication and there is never subtraction without addition.

Now we will go on with our class. *[Discourses 8 and 9 are read aloud. Prior to the meditation period, students were instructed to direct their energies, their conscious awareness, to their ears.]* I know that some of you were aware of quite a difference in your concentration by directing the energy to your perception. It is not recommended that that be done daily, but periodically it can be done. Now we will continue on this evening with our class and your questions and answers at random, if you'd be so kind as to raise your hands.

When we pass from the earth planet and we drop these heavy physical bodies, how do the people on the other side recognize us since we're not carrying this, you know, this vehicle with blonde hair and green eyes?

You carry the vehicle of the astral body, of which the physical body is a duplicate.

Thank you. And in respect to animals, when an animal passes on from this plane, does the soul—let's say it's a cat—does it remain feline on whatever level that it's on or will it change and go into another form, perhaps?

All forms change, but they change according to the Law of the Progression and the ability of the particular form in which the soul or soul essence is encased. Therefore, that varies according to the attachments that the form has to its own form.

So it could be possible, let's say, for an animal to work its way upward, out of the animal form?

And return to the Allsoul, yes, in that sense, it would be and it is.

But it wouldn't change from, let's say, a cat form or cat soul into some other animal?

Not in that sense, because it does not have the potential of which to express through an intelligent human being. It would have to absorb much more from the Allsoul in that sense.

My last question is, Is there such a thing as divine grace?
Yes.

Can you explain how that works into the Law . . .
Divine—Into the law of what?

Cause and Effect.

There is such a thing as divine grace. In some teachings, it is called the spiritual bank account. You make deposits, if you want to call it that, if you want to put it into that type of an understanding, into this bank through various thoughts and acts that you do. Now whenever you do something that is not directly motivated by an expectation of gain for self, you deposit in this spiritual bank account a spiritual substance. When you have a great need and you are experiencing the effect of certain causes that have been set into motion by yourself, you may draw upon this so-called spiritual bank account, which we term in this understanding as divine grace, and it will neutralize the effect of what you've set into motion. However, there comes a time, unless repeated deposits are made, that the bank account is empty, and there is nothing to draw upon. In that sense, there is such a thing as divine grace.

Thank you.
Does that help with your question?
Yes, it does.

Yes.

I've been trying to figure out where my last incarnation was and I have a few questions related to that. Did souls on this earth come from any planet? Is there an order of planets? If we're more progressed, do we go to a planet which is more progressed?

As life itself is perfect system and order, so it is in the sense that you are asking a question, it is progressive order. Yes, it is.

Now this moment alone has often been spoken of as the only moment over which you have power. You have no power over those many centuries and days of yesterday. And so we try to teach the student to become aware of the eternal moment of the now. We do discuss the future and the past, only in the sense that it will help us to make necessary changes in the present to free our soul while here this moment. Now we have discussed—I believe you missed that particular class—that man is, his soul is incarnated into this school under certain seeming hazards or difficulties. Well, those difficulties are nothing more than the lessons that we have to learn and they are indicative of the ones that we flunked at another time. Thank you.

A parable in Discourse 7 reads, "For as the moon sets, / The sun can never shine / Until the stars doth shine." I wondered if that meant that each star is a sun and they shine in conformity or they are all light or the sun isn't the only light. I really do need help on that. I just couldn't get anywhere with it.

It does seem that you did get somewhere on it: otherwise, the question could not, of course, have been asked. Now in your particular understanding and the question that you're asking at this time—the lesser light always precedes the greater light. And I think if you will ponder upon it, you will find the answer that is meant for you at this time.

In today's lesson, it was stated, "I know that I always have been and I will always be. My children, I speak of 'I,' I do not speak of 'me,' as you perhaps conceived in your mind [Discourse 9]." How does he mean "himself"?

When he is speaking of "I," and he is speaking of "me," we mean to imply the "I" as the eternal Spirit; the "me" is the form. It is only the form that changes, as many times it has been spoken. But the "I" is the Intelligence that has always been and, therefore, will always be. The individualization of soul is not an eternal expression, for that that is individualized, you understand, returns to the source from whence it was given birth or individualization. And the "I" is the "I" of the eternal Spirit, formless and free. Does that help with your question?

Yes, sir. Thank you.

Yes.

I still have problems with the parable back in Discourse 5, which says, "As the frog croaked, / And the wolf howled, / The ears of Ego heard not / For the door was locked / By the key of fear." In this particular meditation, I saw myself with huge ears. So this probably has a great deal to do with my personal feelings about fear. I worked on it a great deal today. And if there is anything that you can say, that can help with the key of fear—and how does one perceive ideas which are the cause of fears? Also, how does one build the faculty of faith and how does one really practice faith?

Very good question in reference to the parable and especially to the ears, which represent perception and which also represent ego, and in reference to your question concerning especially fear. We have often discussed that there is one divine, infinite, intelligent, neutral Energy, which is an odic power; that man, through his own choice, directs this energy in a constructive way and we call that faith. He directs it in a so-called destructive way and we call that fear. The question is, then, How does man direct this energy so that he may experience faith and greater faith?

We have to go to the inner mind or the so-called subconscious mind and be objective with it, for it is another part of ourselves. And we must learn to talk to it as you talk to a little child, for this inner person that we all are is very childlike. It has very sensitive, strong feelings. It responds to love and to consideration. It cannot be coerced into anything and it can only be guided through a feeling of indirection. Otherwise, this child that is inside of us, known as the inner mind, will retaliate and will revolt against any suggestions that do not fit into its own programming. So when we experience fear, what we are really experiencing is a multitude of experiences that are in this inner mind from very early childhood. These experiences well up within us because we did not have the understanding of what was happening to our minds when we were little children. We did not have the conscious understanding. And so if a person will make the effort to sit down with themselves, to use their faculty of reason under any and all circumstances, then they will be able to demonstrate the faith that moves the mountain.

Whenever we express fear, we are giving our divine birthright to the thing that we fear. For example, if we fear that there is going to be a financial depression in the United States, if we entertain that thought, we start to experience an ever increasing amount of what is known as fear. We have in that very thought denied our divinity and we have given this life-giving power to a so-called thought of lack or depression. You see, we're doing that all the time, friends. That's what fear does to us. We stated once that which troubles us controls us; and so it is that we are controlled by the things that we fear.

It is a very simple thing—and perhaps it's too simple for most minds to accept—to take the time each day and talk to the other self. Whenever you start to experience inside of yourself this feeling that you recognize as fear, stop that moment as quickly as you possibly can and declare the truth: "Whatever I give thought to, I give power to." So if you give thought to, perhaps, your car isn't functioning properly, you give power, your power, your peace, to that object. Therefore, it controls you: it robs you of the peace that passeth all understanding in the sense that you gave it away. You gave away your peace of mind. And that's what we're trying to get an understanding of to the students of what is happening all of the time. You're giving away your joy, you're giving away your freedom, you're giving away your peace and your power to so many things that the day, sooner or later, comes that you wonder why it's worth being here or why make the effort. It is definitely and positively in the thought, but the thought can be controlled by the will and that takes concentration. Does that help with your question?

Yes. Greatly. Thank you.

Thank you.

I have concentrated on the first line of the "Total Consideration" affirmation: "I am the . . . " Oh, I'm not concentrating right now, but . . .

Manifestation of Divine Intelligence.

Just those lines alone in several situations have brought me back to my thinking. I haven't tried to go through the whole thing, but I do want to understand it. It's so powerful in me and I feel that when I'm getting negative, I can pull myself back with just that one line and I'm grateful for that.

If the statement is true, and I believe and know that beyond a shadow of any doubt that "I am the manifestation of Divine Intelligence. Formless and free. Whole and complete. Peace, Poise and Power are my birthright," in the one statement of the "Total Consideration" affirmation, the truth is declared. If a person truly accepts that truth, there is nothing outside of him that has power over him, because he is no longer giving power to it.

In your answer to an earlier question, you said that fear controls us. If fear is part of the opposite pole of faith, can it not be so that faith can control us as well?

Faith and fear, in truth, is one and the same thing: it's a matter of direction.

In other words, you're saying that fear is simply a strong belief, a conviction, and faith is also a strong belief and a conviction?

And a conviction. It's the direction of the one Intelligence. Yes, absolutely and positively. You see, as we stated earlier, that division is the Law of Expression and expression is the Law of Creation. Whenever you divide something, you multiply it. For example, take a little, small pool of oil. Take some out of it and put it over there and there and there and there. Now the whole batch, they're individuals: you have divided them. But each one of those little pools attracts unto itself its own kind. Therefore, you have multiplied them. So whenever you have thoughts, and these thoughts are all diversified, that means they're all divided, you multiply them. This is why when a person has one thought of confusion, they guarantee a hundred thoughts of confusion, because they keep multiplying, don't you see?

And this is why I teach the students to concentrate upon peace. You concentrate upon peace, then you multiply that vibratory wave, to be expressed through your life. You know, they say in business that nothing succeeds like success. Well, of course not! It's the same Law of Division and Multiplication. And so it is with spirituality. You see, the more you put into a thing, the more you get out of a thing. You see, you cannot, you cannot give without gaining, because you cannot subtract without adding.

Now, you see, I admit that many people may feel that they do a lot of giving and they're having no gaining. That's not true at all. You see, the thing is that they don't recognize the level on which they are gaining. You know, a person may give, give, give, give, give materially and then they say, "I don't get anything back." But that's not true: they're gaining on other levels. But because they cannot see that gain, does not mean that that gain is not there. That's a law of the universe: that's the Law of Creation. You cannot give without gaining and you cannot gain without giving. You know, many people feel that they can just gain, gain, gain, gain, gain spiritually without giving. Well, my good friends, the day comes when something's taken from them and they wonder what happened. Well, that's only the balance of the Law of Creation, you see. So the more that you give, the more you gain. The more that you give of yourself, the freer you become from self. So when you help another, the truth of the matter is you're helping yourself. But, you see, the sadness is, when you try helping yourself, that's when all the problems start. You see, you help yourself by helping another. You help yourself by getting outside yourself. That's what really helps the self. Thank you.

I don't mean to be impertinent, but as you know, I work in a very large office in the city. And there's a gal who gives, gives, gives and another gal who takes, takes, takes. She thinks it's her right to take from the gal who gives.

Then the gal that gives has merited that and so has the gal that takes. But, you see, the truth of the matter is there is an interchange going on. Now, sooner or later, one of them will wake up. Probably the one that's computed she's doing all the giving. But, you see, in her giving, perhaps she needs a sounding board and that's her taking, do you understand?

Yes.

Someone else had a question.

There's one particular sentence in Discourse 8 which I've found a little bit puzzling, because I recall a discussion which seemed to go exactly the opposite to what seems to be said here. So I'll ask if you may elaborate upon, "Before, we have mentioned the necessity for those who are on the paths of Light to protect themselves from this idle thought and chatter. I again speak to you of this for you are holding the progress of another from con-tinuing to permit the magnetic powers to be drawn and depleted." Could you elaborate on this?

Yes, absolutely and positively. There are times when a person will find themselves in a position—we do not deny that they have merited the position that they have found themselves in. But, without conscious choice, they are being magnetically drawn of their life-giving energies, do you understand? Without conscious choice. Consequently, he is stating in that particular sentence that he made in Discourse 8, to help the students to become more aware consciously of what they, in truth, are doing to themselves.

Now a person, of course, is never left without choice, if a person chooses to exercise choice. But it is not a frequent thing that a person chooses to exercise choice. Very few people, in truth, make a choice. Their seeming choice is dictated and controlled by patterns of long standing in the inner mind. It is a rare occasion when a person makes what is known as a free choice. Because of the patterns established—that is what governs and controls the choice that is going to be made by the conscious mind. Now I am not saying that the conscious mind does not think that it is freely choosing, because it, in truth, really does think that it is making a free choice for itself. Man makes free choice when man becomes aware of the patterns of the three beings that he is in truth. Then he makes a limited choice. And so it is with the statement in Discourse 8: there is no contradiction between the tape that you heard and the particular line in Discourse 8. Does that help with your question?

This, then, is referring to holding back the progress of another individual by imposing your will upon them simply because they are not aware of it?

Exactly.

Thank you.

Because they are not aware of it.

Thank you very much.

They are not *consciously* aware. Now remember, friends, that the faculty of reason flows through the conscious mind, not the subconscious. Do you understand that? And so when a person is not consciously aware, you understand, then the faculty of reason is not expressing.

I would have to ask this at that point. The faculty of reason in expression, what is its expression?

The faculty of reason is the expression of a balanced being. That means—

Does the expression have a label?

We will discuss it at a future time. Does someone else have a question? Yes, you can give it a name tag. We will discuss that at a later date.

I'm not sure whether I should ask this one either. I'm trying to clarify the levels of soul, mind, and body, which you gave us in the beginning. If you put these on a diagram, the soul level would be at the apex and the mind level would be to the left and the body would be to the right?

No, the mind would be to the right and the body would be to the left.

Would the superconscious, then, flow through the soul level or does the soul level flow through the superconscious?

No. The superconscious flows through the soul level.

And then the conscious mind would be the mind level?

That is correct.

Getting back to the topic of reason, when you have to put something into balance, like a problem that is right here and now, to make a decision on, what do you do? Do you stop and let the mind become still? How do you put this into balance? How do you get into balance?

By becoming aware of oneself. You see, my friends, one cannot balance what one is not aware of. So the first thing is to become aware of the minds that we are and the patterns that we have established. Then, we become in a position to balance them out. Now we may attempt to balance, but until we become aware of what and who we truly are—and that is within the realm not only of possibility, but it is within the realm of probability, here and now. You don't have to wait years to become aware. This is what these awareness classes are all about: to help you to become aware. Now that doesn't mean that every student in the class is agreeing about what the teachings are all

about, because not every student is on the same level of awareness. Now there are moments when some students are on the
same level. Sometimes it lasts almost for a full sentence of communication and gradually it begins to last a little bit longer. But,
you see, they have a rapport because they're on the same level at
that particular time and, therefore, they're able to communicate
in a clear and intelligent way.

*Relative to the idea of awareness, what is the Wise Man's po-
sition on mind stimulants and drugs?*

Yes. First, I would like to know the purpose of your question. Is this for a personal reason or is this for some other reason? What is the motivation of your question?

*It's personal. Some drugs lead a person to another realm of
consciousness.*

Yes, and there is no control of it. There is no control because,
you see, it is not done by the conscious will. There's no control.
That does not mean that you cannot experience different dimensions through various stimulants because that, of course, we all
know is possible. However, during the experience, there is no control. There is no *conscious* control. In other words, you cannot will
yourself to another experience in another dimension of mind.

*A friend of mine had an experience where he was able to do
that.*

You did not have the experience, did you?

No.

Truth is individually perceived. I'm sure if you will ponder
upon that, you will have your answer waiting at your fingertips.

*In going back to last week, you told us that there are forty
faculties and forty functions.*

All triune in expression.

Will we be given these again in this class?

You will be given sufficient unto the need. Yes, before this
class ends. You will.

Is there such a thing as fate?

Would you mind sharing your understanding of that word with the class, in order that we may answer it, please?

Are our lives prejudged? Are we set on a certain path?

In other words, we do not have any control of changing them. That's what you mean, is it? No, we have established certain patterns, and they're 90 percent predictable, but there is that 10 percent choice that we all have. We did discuss that before. So in that sense, we would not say that there is such a thing as an absolute fate or predestination. No, there is not. For example, if you go to school to be a doctor, then you become a doctor. And so it is in the evolutionary incarnation, that we've gone through varying schools for varying purposes and here we are today. Of course, some went to school to be a jack-of-all-trades, you know, and so we have jacks-of-all-trades. Yes.

Do all souls have a soul talent that travels with them through their incarnations?

All souls have soul talent, yes. All souls.

Does that talent travel with them and stay constant or does it change with the incarnations?

Now that's a very good question. Does the soul talent that a person is incarnated into, in this particular earth plane, at this particular time, does the soul's talent stay with them? That depends upon the use thereof. Lack of use is abuse, and therefore, it does not stay with them. Does that help with your question?

That 10 percent free choice that you were speaking of, is that what you call will?

Oh no, no, no, no, no, no! People will many things, but the willing of them is not necessarily, in and of itself, choice. They will them according to patterns established, according to being triggered into certain levels, etc. No, that's not will, not in our understanding.

How does choice come in, then? I mean, what is . . . I don't—

For example, you chose to come to class this evening.

Yes.

Was that a full, free choice? Or was that a pattern established?

No, it was not a pattern established. It was a choice, a definite choice.

It was a definite choice.

A definite choice.

You're sure of that?

I'm positive.

It is not because you were here last week and the week before and the week before and you had certain desires?

No.

It was a full choice. Then, that means, if a person is aware that they have made a complete, wholly full, free choice, then they are completely aware of their subconscious and its patterns and can never experience fear in their life. That's what it means. Because, don't you see, if we have a full, complete awareness of our, what we call a free choice, that means that we are aware on all levels and all levels include our subconscious—because there are patterns and programs that are there. Now a person may say, "I have made a complete, free choice and I came to class this evening." Now when they make the statement, don't you see, are they aware of all of the levels of mind that control their life? But on the conscious level, yes.

All right. I have to admit something, then—Is this free choice? I didn't feel like coming to class tonight. But I felt that since I didn't, I understood there were some problems within that were causing this conflict. So therefore, I decided, no, the place for me to be is in this class. Is that free choice?

I would call that definite choice. Of course, it is choice, but that simply means that one level is stronger than the level that didn't want to come. Now we may call the level on which you made that choice, a level that is reasonable and logical to you, you see. However, is it not questionable, that due to experience, when perhaps you felt badly, you found you felt better by going to class or better by exposing yourself to friends of a spiritual, up vibration? Now that question we must ask ourselves in order to get a clear picture of what truly controlled the choice that was made. What controlled the choice?

That's what controlled it.

So you see, we have choice, friends. Now I'm glad that we cleared that up, because I'm sure that that's going to help all of us. We have choice and we say, "Well, I made a free choice," but that's not true. It is not true until we are aware of the eighty-one levels that control our life. Then, becoming aware of all the interrelating patterns, etc., we can say, "All right, I looked them all over and I made this decision." Otherwise, my friends, it's known as controlled choice. You understand now, don't you? Thank you very much. Not that it wasn't most beneficial to you.

Oh, it was extremely beneficial.

But, you see, that's my controlled choice, to see it that way. Thank you.

Could you help me, please, with the understanding of will, as related to the creative principle?

Would you like to speak forth into the atmosphere the steps of the creative principle, considering you have asked the question?

Love, belief, desire, will, and creation.

Will in action.

Will in action.

Is that not correct? Are there any questions in the class on the creative principle? Now you want to know what part will plays in creation? It's the motivator. It's the thing that moves it. Without will, there's no motivation.

I'm sorry, but I still don't quite understand what will is and how it works.

When you stood up, you willed your body to move. Do you understand that?

Yes.

Now because you have done that willing so many times, it's become habitual and you are no longer consciously aware of the exercise of what is known as will, as far as getting up and down from a chair. Would you not agree?

Yes.

Now will is this motivating force in the universe. When you will something into manifestation, what you do is direct your energies into the oneness of the particular thing, the particular object, or the particular motion. That's what really takes place inside the mind. And some people, you know, they get into these positive types of thinking, studies, etc., and they're going to *will* themselves a new car and they're going to *will* themselves a new house, etc. Well, that is fine and dandy, but in that willing, you hear me, they are breaking down certain patterns within themselves and, therefore, ofttimes it is psychologically very detrimental to the individual. And ofttimes, it does not come to pass, what they have willed into motion. And the reason that it does not come to pass, they're just using will in the creative principle and they're not using the full five steps. You understand? They're taking out one part of it. It doesn't work that way.

Would you give a little more on entreating for material things, as some of these other organizations do, when they entreat for houses, for money, for this and that. Do they delay the building of their spiritual body? Is that correct?

Well, any time man uses his energy more for material building than a balance between the mental and spiritual building, he cannot help but experience a loss in the dimension in which he is not expressing the energy. In that sense, that is wholeheartedly, 100 percent true, yes.

You see, we try to teach a balance between the three dimensions, because it is the three dimensions that we are expressing through at this time. Now if we use all of our energies into the physical and the material, you understand—and we're not using proportionately equal energy into the mental and into the spiritual—well, then, of course, when we're no longer aware of the material, and we're now here in the mental and then in the spiritual, we look, and there is nothing there. Well, it's most understandable, friends, because we never put anything there, you see. We didn't put anything there; so there couldn't be anything there. Now that's like the man spending all his time in the mental and spiritual and he looks over there and there isn't anything in the material. Do you see what I mean?

Yes, I do.

You see, most people, I have found, have what they call money problems because they spend so much of their thought and so much of their time in fear of what the government's going to do and what the government's not going to do, and what somebody else is going to do and what somebody else is not going to do, and what the stock market's going to do and what it isn't going to do. So you see, they're giving all of their power, this God power within us, to all of those people and all those kinds of things. Consequently, what happens is, they come under the control and the influence of those people and things. So when the stock market goes down, they go down, business goes down. When this politician does this or does that and, according to what thinking they put out into the atmosphere, they're affected. Do you see what I mean? Constantly, all of the time. And it's a sad thing, but, of course, like everything, we do it to ourselves. It is nothing more than an error of ignorance. As long as you spend your time, friends, in thought—thought, remember, is expression of the greatest power that holds all things in the universes. It is the vehicle through which this great power expresses itself: thought. So when you spend your thoughts in those ways, you become controlled by those things. Does that help with your question?

Very much. Thank you.

You're welcome.

May I ask a question about the first soul faculty of duty, grati-tude, and tolerance?

Yes.

Is duty operating at the body level, tolerance at the mind level, and gratitude at the soul level?

Yes, it is.

Thank you. Can we assume that the functions also flow through these three levels?

All functions and all faculties are triune in nature and, of course, they do flow through all levels, yes.

I enjoyed the Wise One's reference to the planets, but when he first said, "universes," exactly what did he mean? If he did mean our universe and our galaxy—I recalled the saying, Look beyond the furthermost star and what shall you see? More galaxies.

Absolutely and positively. There is no ending, in that sense. You cannot find the end of the universes. The reason you can't find the end of them, my friends, is because you can't find the beginning of them. Look at a circle and tell me where it started. That's what it is. Yes.

Aren't we universes within ourselves?

Yes, indeed we are. We are the miniature universe of the universe that we experience around and about us and, of course, this outer space. We are indeed.

Well, it's so important to know this while we're here. When we say will, we impulse the will, which is the motivating power to do and to think properly, when we go from a negative to a positive thought or impulsive will power. What about the prayer that says God's will, "Thy will be done"?

That depends on what "thy will" means to the human beings. Sometimes people compute that "thy will", which they refer to the Divine or God, is to do what they want to do and that depends on the level from which they're receiving the thought. That does not necessarily guarantee when a person says, "Well, O Lord, thy will be done." Well, what does the inner mind understand as "thy will"? Now, you know, some people may understand as "thy will", their parents' will, even though they're adults and grown up and the parents are a long time gone. That depends on what they themselves have computed in their own life experience.

That's why this is so confusing, because I wonder what the positive meaning of it is.

There is such a thing as divine order and there is such a thing as divine grace. And there is such a thing as divine time. And there is such a thing as divine wisdom. Now when man releases to that level, within himself, whatever his problems may appear or seem to be, whatever his seeming request—because remember that desire is nothing more than a denial of what we already have. So we desire on levels that don't have light. Because if desire had light, then we'd know we already had it. Do you understand? Therefore, whenever we desire, we're in the darkness. So when we desire, if we release that desire to the divine wisdom, etc., and it's gone, you understand, then there is a higher intelligence inside of ourselves that looks down at the little children of desire and it says, "Well, OK this one is fulfilled." That's, of course, according to patterns of our own inner mind, you understand, and according to priorities that we alone have established in lifetimes, you hear.

But why stay down in the basement with all kinds of desires, beating yourself around, hitting yourself against the wall, when you can come up out of that basement and look down and say, "Fine and dandy," and let it work according to the priority system of the Intelligence that you are capable of being receptive to. Isn't that a better way?

What is divine timing?

Divine time. Divine time—now remember this, that time is an illusion created by mind. There is no time and space, in truth. So when we speak of divine time, what we are doing is releasing it, in truth, to what is known as divine priority. But it is a much better statement to say "divine time," because all minds are computed to time in their illusions and our illusions and delusions. But divine time would be the fulfillment according to the priority that you, and you alone, have established inside of your own inner mind. Do you understand?

Slightly.

Well, for example, say that you've got seventeen priorities and you have a desire and it's sixteen on the list, you hear? And you release desire number sixteen to divine time under divine guidance under divine wisdom and divine grace. OK, after fifteen of your priorities, that you've already forgot about, are fulfilled, then this number sixteen priority is manifest, because that's the law that you've established unto yourself. But, you see, you're no longer frustrated with the waiting for the fulfillment of the desire that you have set into mind. So it's according to our own priorities. Don't you see? If you stop and think, in the course of a week how many different desires one human soul has—I mean the being, the mind. Constant, constant desire. All right. Well, they're all going in the computer for their fulfillment and so you've got quite a priority list there, you know what I mean.

Now if you want to say to the desire, say, "OK, I desire this. Now I'm trying to get this through my brain that it is a number one priority and knock off all other priorities." Well, that's not a very wise thing to do, because you may have priorities back there that you have long ago forgotten about, that have not yet been fulfilled. That's why we release it to this Divine Intelligence.

But that's how it is, you know. So many of our desires are waiting according to the priority system that we ourselves, and we alone, have established according to our own patterns of mind. And you know, it's like a man, well, first, he wants a Ford. And then he wants a Chevy. And then he wants a Cadillac. And then he wants something else. And I mean it's a constant, constant panorama going on in the mind. If they ever developed a television set that truly expressed what the mind goes through

in one short hour, I'm afraid we'd have to have a 100 percent increase in the psychiatrists to take care of the watchers and the
viewers, because that's what the mind is doing. Now we have
time for just one more question.

Would you comment on people being vegetarian?

Well, my dear, what is the comment in the sense that some
people choose to be vegetarians and some people choose not to
be. Now if a person who chooses to be a vegetarian—and I question whether they made a free choice; they usually have a friend
who turned onto it or some other friend and then it spreads
on, you know, kind of like cancer. But if that's what the person
chooses and if that person believes that that is going to help
them spiritually to awaken, do you understand, then it cannot
help but do so. But it is true, according to my understanding, I
do not partake of meat that is not well done, but that's my particular program choosing.

*Well, do you feel that the law, some law, is working when food
is eaten that has been prepared through some kind of violence?*

All food is prepared through violence. Whether—

Well—I'm sorry for interrupting.

Whether it is the carrot that's growing out of the ground
or it is the seed that drops from the head of the sunflower, all
so-called food comes to us through what the mind computes as
violence. For example, it is a violent shock to the carrot to be
pulled up from the ground. It is a great shock to the celery to
be cut off at its head. Whenever a nail is set into a tree, there
is a violent shock to the tree. Because man has not awakened
to the truth that God is everything, in everything, expressing
through all, that all things have feeling, including the rock, does
not mean that the head of lettuce, the carrot, and the apple do
not experience emotional shock. Fortunately, in this day and
age, science has gotten to the point where they are able to register certain emotional impulses in the tomato plant when people
are picking tomatoes. It is able to register certain impulses and

shocks to the average plant when a person comes within two feet with a pair of scissors or a knife. Think of the intelligence that expresses itself, that the plant is already aware that the guillotine is about to drop on its head.

Thank you very much, friends. Please give it some consideration. Let us go have refreshments.

JUNE 7, 1973

CONSCIOUSNESS CLASS 17 ✄

Good evening, students. This evening, after reading the discourse and going into our meditation, each student will be asked what is the most important thing that that they have gotten from this awareness course at this point or to this date. So I'm giving you a little time to ponder upon it before asking the question. Now let us begin. Let us all turn to Discourse 10.

[Discourse 10 is read aloud by a student. The class then says the "Total Consideration" affirmation, which is followed by the meditation period.]

This evening, before going into your questions and answers, as I mentioned earlier, each student will be asked what they consider to be the most important thing they have gained from these classes thus far. And so we will begin.

Well, there's so much I've gained. So many things that I feel that—the very most important thing, I think, is, well, it's like a beginning almost, beginning to learn what giving is all about.

Thank you very much.

I would have to say that it has given me far more depth of feeling for the spiritual world and the laws that govern it. Also, the question-and-answer periods have been most informative about many questions that were formerly very perplexing to me.

Thank you kindly.

I believe that I have gained an awareness of the self and what motivates it. And . . .

Thank you very much.

It has given me a better understanding of the Living Light.

Thank you.

Well, I have been very much aware of my responsibility to Spirit after being in these classes and the responsibility to my teachers to unfold as much as I can; to aspire to neutrality, if I can, as much as it is within me at this time; and to keep an even mind, to be tranquil, try to be tranquil. I haven't always had this. And it's putting it into action. I think I've learned more about impulsing the will into action in these classes than I have—of course, I've gained so many other things that I couldn't begin to say them. But I do feel a great responsibility of spreading the gospel of Spiritualism.

Thank you very much.

I have learned something about my own levels of awareness and how to, within the limits that I have allowed myself, to get off a bummer level and get onto something higher. That's been very important to me, because I used to get so down. And there were downers all the time and I've learned to be able to cast them off.

Thank you very much.

I came to the study of Spiritualism quite some years ago and I had a wonderful teacher for some years. And if I can explain it, it's like having gone through kindergarten and elementary school and so on and having graduated and then put these teachings on a shelf, so to speak. And it's very gratifying to find another teacher again and feel that one can step out and maybe learn something new.

Thank you very much.

Mainly in increased awareness of what I'm doing and why I do it. And, also, consideration.

Thank you.

It's helped me gain an awareness and an understanding of how I relate to the universe and myself and what is happening around me, not only in the immediate vicinity of myself, but the interaction of the entire universe and how it is a oneness.

Thank you very much.

I think it's helped me with my thinking: to think more deeply and on a deeper level, and to understand more.

Thank you very much.

With having a few short years of this guidance, it's more gratifying for me to see the expressions of togetherness, the peace, and the serenity that establishes itself among us. I feel that this is possibly the beginning of what it's all about.

Thank you.

I've received a better understanding of Spiritualism and the things that it does. And it's helped me to understand myself better and other people better.

Thank you.

I think the single most important teaching has been how to find peace.

Thank you.

I would have to say that I am finally beginning to learn to think. And it is a great comfort to me to find that at least I am beginning to learn to think. And that I have gone so long without knowing how to think. And through that learning, I am beginning to know the meaning of the words Love *and* Light. *And the expressions within this class mean a great deal to me and I'm certain mean a great deal to all the students.*

Thank you.

To be very succinct, there are three things that it has brought me. I didn't know anything about the "ism" in Spiritualism when I first began coming here. Secondly, it has enabled me to find peace within myself, which was something I desperately needed. And thirdly, I found my little niche in the universe, so to speak. It's kind of presumptuous, but I feel that way.

Thank you.

I feel the most important thing at this time that I've learned is that whatever happens to us is caused by us. And I'd like to say my feeling is that these classes, to me, feel like a point of stability in our growth as we're trying to climb up through the levels. Thank you.

Thank you.

I've gained knowledge on how life truly is, instead of the way it appeared before coming to class.

Thank you very much.

I believe the most important thing that I've learned is what true faith is. That if one has true faith, then there's nothing without that is really needed; that all is within. Thank you.

Thank you very much.

Like the other student, my choice was what happens to us is caused by us. And the other thing was, Spiritualism has helped me find faith in myself and God and the universe. And I'm very grateful for that.

Thank you.

I found that it has helped me to shed light inside myself onto a lot of the dark corners and it has helped broaden a narrow understanding.

Thank you very much.

It has not only helped me reach a deeper depth of my spiritual faculties of clairvoyance, clairaudience, and clairsentience, but it has also helped me reach into the deeper depth of the world of spirit.

Thank you very much. Thank you, class.

One of the seeming, ofttimes called strange, phenomena of these classes is that people are changing for the better inside of themselves. And the greatest of all things, I think, is that they are aware that this process is taking place.

Now the question arises in the mind, What is it that causes these changes inside of ourselves? What is the particular thing, if anything, that is making this change from level to level on the upward climb happen inside of our being? Because a person, one person, does a great deal of studying and another one doesn't do as much studying; one feels this way in reference to the teachings and, of course, one feels another way. We all know that truth is individually perceived and we all know that truth is one. And so it is that we, as students of the Light, are viewing it from different directions. We're all looking at the same Light, and when we recognize that great truth that there is only one Light, one Life, which is the eternal moment, then we come to a greater awareness and understanding of everyone in all the universes that's looking at the very same Light.

We then know and appreciate and understand that man, no matter what his path may be, is, in truth, climbing the eternal Mountain of Aspiration. The great danger of climbing a mountain is that we will reach the top of it, for the top, you see, belongs to the Divine itself. Whenever man, on his eternal progress through the universes, comes to the top of the mountain and decides that he has it, that moment is the moment that he loses it. For, you see, it is not within the divine nature for the form to capture the formless. It is within the divine nature for the formless to ever sustain the form, but it is not the nature of the form to ever capture that Eternal Light and call it its own, for that is something that does not belong to the form. And so it is we find in our day-to-day activities, as long as we remember that we are ever striving and never, in truth, have it all, no matter what the subject, no matter what the effort, then, my good friends, we will always experience that freedom and that peace that passeth all understanding.

The world is filled with a multitude of philosophies and religions; they are all teaching about the Light. The moment they start teaching that the Light is everything and everywhere and all people's path, then they will shine with the Light.

And so it is that we must first gain understanding in order that we may have tolerance to those levels inside of us that think we have it all. And when that happens, when we gain that understanding, this great phenomenon, this divine love will ever sustain us, and that is what actually takes place in the Living Light classes. It is known as the phenomenon of divine love, because each person is seeking that which they believe will grant them the peace that passeth all understanding. We are all seeking that, where we can feel this great freedom and this great joy of the Divine itself. And in the very seeking of it, it manifests and expresses through us and to us. And that is the greatest help that anyone could ever receive.

Now, my friends, you're free to ask the questions that you have. If you will kindly just raise your hands, I will answer them to the best of my ability.

In the discourse we read tonight, it mentioned the plane of ozone, and in several of the discourses up to this time in this particular semester there has been mention of life prior to the earth form. And if there is some indication that this is a plane prior to the earth form, could you elaborate a bit on the plane of ozone?

Yes, I will be happy to share what I am able to at this time in reference to the plane of ozone. Speaking of what the material scientists may call the plane of ozone, they are speaking of a particular belt of gaseous substance that encompasses the so-called earth realm. This plane of ozone is a plane of expression prior to the soul's incarnation into the physical form. Each planet where life is expressed has a belt or plane surrounding it through which the soul must pass before entering the physical body of that particular planet. When the soul expresses through this particular belt or plane, which is an etheric plane, at that time, it sees all of the experiences which are to take place on that planet and through the particular form in which it is being encased; and this is how certain people have an inner knowing and an inner drive to do certain things at certain times. This has already been reviewed by the soul prior to its incarnation into the form of that particular planet.

Now when man makes the effort to still the mind and to go through the levels of awareness deeper inside of himself, then man will have glimpses and become aware of certain things that he will experience in this particular earth realm. But of course, my friends, that is a very individual thing, because that is dependent upon the effort that the individual makes to become aware. Does that help with your question?

Did I perceive correctly that when you were speaking on divine love that divine love actually is cooperation?

Thank you very much. In reference to your speaking on cooperation and divine love, and it could be stated that divine love is cooperation; however, I would prefer to state that divine love is the expression of Infinite Intelligence in harmonious action. Now we can cooperate with many levels of awareness and through cooperation become controlled. However, we can harmonize with all levels of awareness, which is the vehicle through which the divine love is expressing itself, and be with all things and not be controlled by all things. So there is a difference between cooperation and harmony or the expression of divine love. Now a person, for example, could share their understanding with someone who has a different understanding and not be controlled or affected by the expression that the other one is giving of their understanding. However, if they cooperated with their understanding and the other person's understanding, then that would not necessarily result in harmony, but would definitely result in some degree and extent of control. Thank you very much.

Does thought begin as a feeling first of all? Does it begin as a feeling and then does it become like an impulse and a mental picture and then a thought is formed?

In reference to your question, Does thought first begin as a feeling? That, of course, is dependent upon from whence cometh the thought. For example, man is a receiving-sending mechanism and man also is a feeling being. But man is not always, and usually is not, aware of his own feelings. Now the reason that man is not usually aware of his feelings is simply because his thoughts and attention have been for a lifetime entertained with objects and things outside of himself. And because of that type of brainwashing that man has put himself into, man is not usually aware of his own inner, deep feelings. Consequently, all thoughts, though stimulated by feeling, are not recognized as such in most people's minds. For example, a person says, "Yesterday was a nice day," and they have no feeling about yesterday. Well, the reason that they don't is because when they experienced yesterday as a nice day, they did not let this experience fulfill itself within their being, you understand? The mind has constantly been going outward and it has not been truly associated with its own thoughts because the mind has lost control. And it lost control because we gave it the power to do so.

We can demonstrate that to ourselves by choosing nine minutes and saying to ourselves, "I will not permit my mind to entertain any thought but the thought which I choose it to have." I seriously question that any of us present can keep the mind still to one thought and one thought alone for nine minutes without having some other experiences take place within ourselves. That reveals to us, my friends, how much we have sold our own divinity. When we are enabled to keep this vehicle on one thing for at least a few minutes, that will show us that we are gaining control of the vehicle that we're driving.

I mean, think what it would be like, my good friends, if you went into the car and you started it and it moved anywhere that it felt like moving according to the patterns of the roads that it had traveled upon. Well, this is what's happening to us. You see, our minds and our bodies, our emotions and our feelings, they're moving along the ruts that we, of course, have created. Now it isn't easy for any of us, you see, to dig ourselves up out of those ruts that we put our minds into. But let us just stop and be honest with ourselves and let us see how Pavlovian we truly are. You know, let us awaken and see how conditioned we have made ourselves. Let us see how we react in certain ways under certain circumstances.

You know, all we have to do, my friends, is to have our bank accounts wiped out and you be rest assured you will see an absolute predictable reaction. You see, now the reason that it's predictable is because all of the masses, like sheep, move in the same direction the moment their bank account is wiped out. Now you take any other mass computation and you can tell that the sheep are all going to move in that direction, and that's just the way that we as individuals react.

Now we've spoken before, that that troubles us controls us. So all we have to do, if we want to free our soul, is to watch the things that trouble us. Take a look around and see what irritates us. Take a look around and see what hurts our feelings. Take a look around and see when we feel happy and when we feel sad. Those are the things that, inside of ourselves, are habituated patterns that have and are controlling our soul. So it's really quite simple, students: if we want to know where we are, all we have to do is stop and think what we are, and then that will reveal to us who we are. And then, we may be rest assured, we will make greater and greater and greater effort to free ourselves from these chains that we alone have created and continue to do so.

Now, your question was in reference to thought. We first feel, then we think, according to the feeling that stimulates the gray matter of the brain. Of course, the sadness is that most of us are not aware of that feeling. We are aware of the thought. Now, for example, you could be with someone and you have nice thoughts and you just feel so great. Well, you feel great and then you have nice thoughts because, you see, the feeling precedes the thought. Now because we are not self-aware as much as we would like to be, we think that the thought precedes the feeling, but that is because we are not aware of those inner levels where the feelings are registering. Does that help you with your question?

Yes, it does.

This is a question that has been on my mind for a while. Why, when different souls pass on, is there this seeming awakening much sooner in some than in others? For example, this question was asked me: What do you feel is the most important: the hereditary factor or the environmental factor? Well, at that time I had to give it some thought, and then I said the hereditary factor was more important. And I was wondering in relation to the question if that acts as a time clock to this soul awakening to a prior incarnation?

Well, in reference to your question, the soul awakening is just like the awakening we're going through each moment in each day. Now some people awaken very quickly, according to what they, as individualized souls, have set into motion. For example, you can have a discussion of spiritual values and some students will grasp it that quickly; that means they awakened to it that quickly. Some it will take days, weeks, months, ofttimes even years. That is dependent upon the soul's individualized merit system. Some people learn rapidly. Some children—you have two children—I know that you know, some, they learn quickly certain things and some things they do not learn as quickly. And so it is the same with a soul's awakening.

I'm trying to understand what you said, and it helped. But I might have to use two people as an example, if you please. One is what we consider the Old Man, who went for centuries possibly, to my understanding, before some awakening. Now take my father, who just passed away this summer and now is in school. It doesn't seem like my dad should be in school—don't misunderstand me, but I'm trying to understand this—when someone like your Teacher took so long. I don't understand it.

Well, I'm sure that you will understand that we get out of a thing what we put into the thing and if we put centuries into a study and application, then we're going to get more out of it. You see, few of us realize the purpose of the struggles that we're going through. In fact, the first thing that happens to the mind, it resents and tries to reject its own struggle of awakening. Also, try to remember that different souls awaken on different planes of consciousness and, therefore, we could not and it would not be just or fair to compare the awakening on plane six with the awakening on plane twenty-six. And I think that will help you. Thank you very much.

I feel confusion in my mind about the soul. I've been taught for ages that the soul is whole, complete, and absolute and it is part of God.

May I ask you one thing? Were you taught that the soul was the covering of Spirit?

Yes.

Do you agree that that covers must be form? Is there such a thing as a covering that is formless?

No.

Therefore, if that that covers the Spirit is form, and if form is governed and controlled by the laws of creation known as the Law of Duality, therefore, it could not, in and of itself, be absolute, complete, or whole or perfect, could it? You may go on with your question.

I think that's it. I was going to ask, Can it awaken? Is it the soul that awakens or is it the Spirit that awakens?

The Spirit cannot awaken, because the Spirit cannot sleep. You understand, the Spirit—Spirit, Divine, Infinite Intelligence— is not dual: it is one. All ones are capable of dual expression and that gives us what is known as manifestation, of course, or creation. The Spirit—Infinite Intelligence—does not sleep; it does not wake. It *is*. You see, truth—you cannot say that truth is this and truth is that, because then you no longer have truth. Truth *is*. Spirit, God *is*. The soul is the individualization or the covering of the Divine Intelligence. It is the soul expressing through the grosser forms that awakens.

Now the soul garners up greater and greater understanding through greater and greater expression through the forms. Therefore, the Divine Spirit, as I spoke earlier—formless and free, whole and complete—nothing can be added to it, for nothing can be subtracted from it. The only god that changes is the god of creation and the god of creation is equal to our understanding at any given moment. That is why a man does not put God, the formless, into a mental image, but experiences the Divine Intelligence or God in all of its expression, and that's known as good or God in all things. Thank you.

Discourse 10 says, "Intuition is expressed through reason. There is no other expression of it no matter what seems to be. God is a God of law and order, a God which is Love." I don't know why, I was listening to you there and I . . .

Yes?

I turned to that. It all ties together someplace, but I can't grab the . . .

May I ask one question? Perhaps a sharing of your understanding for the class of the word *intuition*.

I understand intuition to be an impressing upon the mind of a glimpse of reality, as it were, more a feeling than an actual perception through the normal senses.

Thank you very much. Would you agree that man cannot have realization without reason?

Yes.

Therefore, intuition flows through the faculty of reason.

Thank you.

Thank you very much.

Is intuition both sense and feeling?

Intuition may be experienced as a feeling, as a sensing. The original sense is the sense of feeling. And from that original sensing of feeling has come the sense of sight, the sense of hearing, and all of the other senses. And this is why the sense of feeling precedes the thought of mind, for it is the first thing that happens in the form.

Thank you.

You're more than welcome.

It is my understanding that life, as we know it, is only an illusion of the mind. If that is true, I was wondering if you could help us with a definition of what reality is.

For me to define reality is for you to lose it, for I am receptive through my intuition and faculty of reason to a realization of reality, which is my reality. To impose that upon you, an individualized soul, would move you from one delusion to another delusion, and I am sure that is not what you are seeking. However, you do, as all of us, have the divine birthright to experience, through your efforts of peace, the greatest realization or reality of all. And I know, as I know for myself, that as each student makes the effort daily in their contemplation and they come within themselves to that great peace—and already it has been given the steps to its attainment: the soul faculties of duty, gratitude, and tolerance. I would say that tolerance is one of the most important faculties of all the soul faculties. For without tolerance, there is no understanding; and without understanding, there is no true peace; and without true peace, there is no fullness or true awareness of one's own divinity. Does that help with your question?

Thank you.

You're welcome.

Could we go back to the fountain exercise and the meditation?

Yes, certainly.

I believe that we were to visualize the colors of green, red, and blue. And am I correct in thinking that this is from the mental into action into spiritual? Do we see these colors all at once or do we see the fountain with the green first? I've been working on this and trying to do it and it is a little difficult for me to visualize a fountain, because I always see the one in Rome in my mind. I've seen so many pictures of it. Do the colors change from the mental into action—red for action—and then into spirituality?

In reference to the visualizing of the color green, I would recommend that you choose the shade of light green, which is the vibratory wave and the color of conscience. Going under the vibratory wave of conscience, the inner being knows right from wrong and does not have to be told, because it is a spiritual sensibility with a dual capacity. Therefore, choosing that particular shade of green, which is the vibration of conscience, one will be guided into right thought and right action in the so-called other dimensions. Because these other dimensions, that are all around and about us and of which we are expressing through—though most of us are not aware of it, you see—are like a vast jungle. And there are many new courses for our soul to chart out here in these great dimensions that we're swimming in and that we have become captured in.

And so it is that it takes thought before leaping off into these other dimensions. It takes more conscious awareness that we're not just dealing with this small, little dimension known as the physical world. You see, when we speak forth a word, that is energy released from our being. When we do that, we create on more than one dimension. When we express our feelings, we must realize, my friends, that thoughts are more than forms: they are the causes of forms. So when you speak your word out into the atmosphere, be more choosy with the life-giving energy that you are expressing, because you are the mother, the father, the creator of little forms that are in your auras. You're feeding them. And then people who are tuned into those vibratory waves, into those dimensions, you see, they can see literally thousands of these forms. Because every time you express a feeling from your being, every time you speak a word, every time you have a thought, that is energy released. That energy does not go to naught: it feeds the forms of our own emotions. And that is known as the thought forms.

Now, like in this little church, when you're having a service or you're having a class, you must realize, students, that there are a multitude of forms. This little Association was wisely named from the realms of Light, The Serenity Association, that the energy directed to that word *serenity*, which happens to be a soul faculty, that it would permeate the atmosphere. Therefore, when people enter these doors they feel the spirit of love, of joy, of friendliness. But it will not sustain itself. It has to be fed. Thought has to be directed to serenity. Energy has to be expressed and that feeling must be sustained: otherwise, it dies on the vine. And so it is, there, in creation we see a multitude of things that are distasteful to us. For example, we always have those experiences here in creation. Stop and think, and say to yourself, "I in truth am formless and free. Nothing disturbs me that I do not disturb." Don't you see? And so it is that we either give away this great serenity that's in our soul or we cherish it and we protect it through expression. Thank you.

In tonight's discourse, there's a short line here, "We know that music is color." I was wondering if that meant the inner expressions that we express out, which emanates color . . .

It does.

. . . is music.

It does. All things are vibrating in a certain vibration and that is the symphony of the spheres. Every blade of grass, every human being, every animal, every bird is vibrating. And when you tune into that vibration, you hear, like a great orchestration, out in the sky—the symphony of the spheres is all of the expression of creation itself. And so it is that one has to consciously work and stand guardian at the portal of their own thoughts. You see, friends, it's not someone else's thoughts that disturb us.

It's not someone else's words that disturb us. It is not someone else's actions that disturb us. It is our own inability to control our own mind. That is the only thing that truly disturbs us.

Now because we have, from lack of use, lost control of our own mind and our own expression, because we have lost that control, our brain, the "me" part of us, says that it's out there and it's everyone else. The reason that the brain does that is because, from lack of opening the soul faculty of humility, we cannot face ourselves. And that is the demonstrable truth of why we think and believe that other things outside of us disturb us. It is our frailties that bother us. It is our own inability to self-control. That is what disturbs us. Now one says, "I'm working on my self-control and it is very difficult expressing in a world where everyone is running rampant and not expressing any self-control for themselves." Well, of course, friends, as long as we see the weakness in another, we will not be able to face the weakness in ourselves. Thank you.

I've been working very, very hard on right thought through these classes. I feel that within me I have, like, a retaliating child that I have to speak to consistently all day and I feel that it takes tremendous will on my part to—I don't know if I should get rid of this kid or get along with it or what to do with it.

That that disturbs us controls us. And remember that by working through the vibratory waves of harmony, we are freed from the things that disturb us.

Thank you, friends. Let's go have refreshments.

JUNE 14, 1973

CONSCIOUSNESS CLASS 18 ✍

We have a few minutes before we start, so I would like to share with you an understanding of what is commonly referred to as jealousy, envy, and greed. Jealousy, envy, and greed is a recognition of the unfulfilled desires within oneself and an acceptance of the frailties and weaknesses in the fiber of one's own character. And when we look at it in that light, and we consciously remember that, whenever we have those types of feelings—because, after all, it's only a level of awareness. And so those types of feelings, their potential, exists in all human forms. So whenever we have that feeling, which is an expression on that level, in anything, and if we will pause to think and we will think about what it really is, we will be able to grow through that level and in time will never again have those types of experiences. So that's what it is. I expect you all got that. Did you?

Could you repeat it?

Jealousy, envy, and greed is a recognition of the unfulfilled desires within oneself and an acceptance of the weaknesses and frailties in the fiber of one's character.

Sir, with all due respect, might one differ?

Absolutely, definitely, and positively, one might differ, but in the differing, might there be another explanation of it?

Well, I don't know, but, you see, from my own personal experience, I've been a single person for many years. I've had to work and run a household and I see people who have marvelous husbands, marvelous houses, but, you know, as time progresses, you know what, I see something about these people: they have, maybe, some congenital disease. Maybe they have some problem that in my situation I would not have, but I found out that I would not change places with them for anything in the world.

No, in reference to the teaching, that doesn't necessarily mean that we would want to be someone else. To be jealous or envious or greedy does not necessarily, in and of itself, mean that we want to wear another's shoes or have the full experience that the person is having. Do you understand?

I am understanding.

Yes. But it does mean that, for example, a person looks and they see something that they would like to have, you understand?

And they get a feeling connected with that. Now that feeling, unless it is educated in oneself, goes right along the track within one's being and it stimulates what we understand to be a tinge of jealousy or envy.

Now some of us, fortunately, have been able to recognize what is happening at those times. But, of course, I am one of the first to admit that I'm sure that many of us have experiences where we desire what someone else has and in that desiring we do not use reason and logic. For example, we don't seem to be able to understand that the law, which is so clear, "Whatever happens to us is caused by us," that whatever we have or have not is within the lines of the divine merit system, through which we are expressing.

So it just goes to show us that if we will, in that moment of those feelings, speak to ourselves that it is a level of an unfulfilled desire—see, there is no jealousy possible or envy or greed without the recognition within one's being of an unfulfilled desire. You see, we cannot be jealous of someone that lives in a townhouse and has many things that we feel that we would like to have, we cannot be jealous of them unless we recognize that as an unfulfilled desire in our being. A lady isn't jealous of another lady who has a mink coat unless she thinks that her mink coat is not as valuable as the lady's mink coat that she's looking at.

So you see, the truth of the whole matter is that it's always inside of ourselves. It doesn't exist anyplace else. The reason the teaching is given forth to the student is to help them so they will not dissipate their energy in those types of levels. Because, you see, whereas it is an unfulfilled desire within one's being that causes jealousy and envy and greed, and if a student dissipates that energy into those levels, then the student is not going to fulfill the desire within themselves because, you see, they give it away (the very energy necessary to bring it into their own life). This is what we're trying to bring forth to the students' understanding.

Yes, we have a minute to speak with one more student and then we'll get into our class work.

About this envy, greed, and jealousy. You are sometimes—I'm sure everybody has had this experience—on the phone or talking in person about someone who has made it, for instance, like your great mediumship or somebody else's—

Oh, I wouldn't say that. I keep working every day on it.

I know, but I say it. I'm saying it. Or it would be somebody else's talent or somebody else's thing and you want to cut it off. They're very negative and they are the ones that are jealous and greedy and envious. How do you cut it off?

How do you cut it off? Remember, friends, that you cannot be a sounding board to that that you do not desire to entertain. It is impossible. Now I know this seems like a very cruel and hard thing, but let us analyze it just for a moment. If somebody is saying something to someone and they are expressing a level, it is the divine right of the listening ear not to hear it. It is the divine right of the listening ear to change the subject. Now it is more difficult to close the hearing, for most people, than to change the subject.

Now what is it within us that hesitates in changing the subject when someone is expressing jealousy or envy or levels of understanding that we do not care to hear? So we must say to ourselves, "Somebody's talking to me about something that I find distasteful." So I have to say to myself, "I'm going to stop hearing the person or I'm going to change the subject." Usually I change the subject, because it's easier to change the subject than to close the hearing. Do you understand? Now if I hesitate in changing the subject, that is indicative that I have fear. There is a fear operating within my being that I do not wish to offend the individual. Because if I hesitate in changing the subject, then fear is controlling and my reason is not flowing. So we must ask ourselves, whenever we have the experience, "What is it that I fear, for I find such difficulty in changing the subject?" Do you understand?

I do.

Because, you see, it is fear and fear alone that gives power to things outside of ourselves. So now, we may like the person; we may like them as a friend, but we do not appreciate certain levels that they are expressing. Well, if we appreciate them as a friend, then we will be the first ones to change the subject when they start on those levels. Then, what will happen, they'll do one of two things: they will no longer be our friend, because they weren't our friend in the first place, or they'll start to disagree, an argument. Do you understand? See, they will have to defend their position, because the ego demands that their position be defended. Because, you see, envy, jealousy, and greed is a function. It is not a soul faculty. Therefore, all functions, you understand, demand. You hear?

Yes.

They demand their expression. So we just simply have to recognize that it is the function that is expressing itself and, you see, functions have to be defended. Now the reason that functions have to be defended is very simple: functions are not truth.

Thank you.

Did that help with your question?

Yes, it does, because I ran into that this week. I couldn't stop.

Remember that truth needs no defense. And if we feel that we must defend something, then it's not truth that we are expressing. Now a person may say, "Well, this is being expressed and that is a falsehood to my beliefs and to my understanding." You don't defend it. You express your truth, but you do not defend. Truth needs no defense. For example, two rights never made a wrong.

You know, it's just like your little discussion on these newspaper letters to the editor, etc., in the *I.J.* [*Marin Independent Journal*]. Fine. When the people who are true believers in the science, philosophy, and religion of Spiritualism, when they are impressed from within their own spirit to state the truth, they will state the truth. They don't need to battle any other philosophy. They don't need to downgrade it. All they simply need to do is express their truth, you see. Now if you go to defend something, if you go to defend your own beliefs, what you really do is support another's. And this is why a wise man does not defend his beliefs, because in the defending, he supports the opposite. Think about it, class. Remember that truth needs no defense. If it is truth, you need never concern yourselves with defending it. You may consider sharing or expressing your truth whenever it is solicited.

Getting into our meditations this evening, remember, friends, repeatedly, again and again, the Spirit has requested that you learn to concentrate upon peace. Now I know that there are many understandings of peace, but the understanding that is your peace you will find, if you keep knocking at the door long enough, with sufficient faith.

Before getting into the readings of the discourses this evening, as part of your homework, so to speak, each student is to choose a word a day for each day. Now you have been given the soul faculties, a number of them, and there are many words in *The Living Light* and many words in the universe that you may choose. However, in choosing a word for the day, the word should be chosen upon awakening in the morning and it should be the first word that comes into the mind; then, that will be the word that's meant for you.

Now when you go to sleep at night—and you should start this exercise this evening when you go to bed—as you're going off to sleep, you ask yourself what is your word. Remember that your word is your affirmation. You ask yourself for your word and your word will be given to you by your spirit immediately upon awakening in the morning. Whatever that word is, use it for that day. When I say use it—for example, you may, your spirit may choose to use the word *appreciation*. Well, in all of your thoughts and acts and activities and experiences for that day, use the true meaning of the word, for that word will help you to awaken. And it will also guarantee whatever experiences necessary for you to gain understanding. So from now on, those of you who choose to—it is highly recommended—choose your daily word immediately upon awakening. Some of you may get the same word each morning for three, four, five days. If that's what you get, don't reject it: that means something very important to you.

[Discourse 11 is read aloud by a student.]

Now before we get to your questions, friends, several students have spoken to me in reference to the seeming difficulties they seem to be having in getting through to their so-called subconscious mind. And I know that you all know that when we entertain a thought, we direct the life-giving power, the energy to it. So if we entertain the thought of difficulty, we guarantee to increase the difficulty. And that is why we try to teach in these classes to direct your thought, which is the vehicle of your divine energy that's expressing to you, on what you want to become. Keep your attention off of the obstruction, because by permitting the mind to entertain the thoughts of the obstruction, the obstruction increases in size and density and, sooner or later, the mountain will fall on top of us.

So when you have an experience that your brain insists upon computing as difficult, change the thought immediately; and in changing the thought, you will change the experience. All experience, as we have spoken again, again, and again, is nothing more and nothing less than the effect of directed energy through the vehicle of thought.

Now, if there is something that you desire to accomplish, then see the accomplishment in its fulfillment and do not tell it how it's to take place, when it's to take place, and all things involved in its fulfillment. Now that takes faith, friends, because if there's something that you want to do or to have, the mind insists that it knows the way. The Intelligence that brings it into being works by very natural, normal law and when we become receptive to the law through which it works, we will not have to be concerned with when it's to come or how it's to come. But that takes faith and that faith is something that we unfold inside of ourselves. It is not something that we garner up. So if a person is willing to release their desires and their fulfillments to the Infinite Intelligence, that moves and holds all things in space, if they're really willing to do that, and they do it, then it shall come to pass. Otherwise, they will go through the other processes.

For example, if a man wants a new house, he says, "Well, it's going to cost about $40,000, maybe $30,000." And maybe he only has about $1,000, if he has that. So the mind says, "This is what's necessary to attain it." But the Divine Intelligence doesn't say that. It's only the brain, the ego that says that. So it's simply a matter of working through another level of awareness. And it takes a little bit of faith to believe and to know inside that whatever you want, you already have and that you, in point of time, are moving toward it. Now the reason that it takes varying times for varying people to have their fulfillment and their accomplishment is according to whatever patterns they have set into motion inside of themselves. But there is an Intelligence and an Energy that's greater than all patterns. That's the Intelligence to touch. And the only way I know of touching it is through an effort of becoming at peace. Because when man is truly at peace, all things are in harmonious motion in the two minds that are the usual obstacle to its accomplishment.

Now you're free to ask whatever questions that you have.

Yes, sir. I have about two or three questions. According to our lesson today, it says, in many words, well, I seem to be impressed that this allows the Methodists to have their own Methodist heaven in the spirit world and the Baptists to have their own, and even the Reincarnationists to have theirs.

Absolutely. They have it here, don't they?

Yes, they do. So then, reincarnation does exist, if you want it to.

It exists in that sense, yes.

If you're so attached to the earth that you can't get away from it, then you can come back to it.

You can hover over the earth realm, if that's what you want, yes.

It says here that it's very, very rare for highly illumined spirits to come back.

That's what it says.

Yes. That would mean that . . .

Now, my good friends, I do hope you all understand that each page of *The Living Light* and each answer and question therein is for the level of the reader. You see, the teachings of the Living Light are not something that are set down in a dogmatic and absolute way, because the moment that man takes the formless, free truth and he puts it into what he calls fact, he loses truth. You cannot confine truth. Truth is a continuum: it's an ever flowing. It is like a river: it continuously flows.

And so it is that the reasons man has lost what is real truth is because he gets to a certain point in time, a certain level of his awareness, and he says, "That's it! I've got it!" Well, my friends, the moment you've got it is the very moment that you have lost it. Truth, don't you see, flows. And if you don't flow with it, then you don't have truth, you see. For example, you have a river and you're the log that's flowing along the river. Now the moment you stop that log, it starts a process of disintegration: you no longer have it. And so it is with these teachings. They are designed to expand the consciousness of the recipient and so, from level to level, as the student studies and applies, their horizons are broadened, and the truth that they knew yesterday is broader tomorrow.

And this is why, my friends, we have so many religions and so many philosophies in the world. It is because they got to a point in the river and they stopped. Now there's truth in their teachings, but because they have stopped, it is not the fullness of truth, do you understand? It's only the passing of it, because they are not moving with it. And so it is if your sincere aspiration is freedom, illumination, awareness, and truth, then you must learn to flow with the teachings which are truth, and they ever flow to the source from whence they came. All teachings are to be used as guide posts for the individual to find the Eternal Light that lies waiting within themselves. Does that help with your question?

Yes, sir.

If you read to page 54 and you stop and you say, "I have the truth," my good friends, you haven't yet begun. But if you read through *The Living Light* and you say, "I'm moving on in a broader understanding," and you keep right on going, then you will have your truth. Remember, friends, truth flows: it is not stagnant and it is not something that you can hold. It is only something that you can express. And when you stop expressing it, here and here, then you lose it. Remember that truth is not security. Security is not truth. Truth is freedom and freedom is everlasting and eternal. Your next question, please.

Well, I found the part here upon which I based my former question: "There are so many schools of thought, my children, on both sides of the veil [Discourse 11]*." Because there are many schools over there, there are many schools here. Is that correct?*

There are many schools everywhere.

All right, that answers my question. Thank you. And I have something to ask upon our class work before. If envy, jealousy, and greed are functions, what are the faculties corresponding?

In your understanding, what is the meaning of the word *jealousy* to you?

Well, to be covetous of what someone else has.

Which is a denial of what you have yourself.

Yes.

Is that not true?

Yes, sir. I understand that.

So what would be the opposite of it?

Well, contentment, being content with what you have.

Would you consider perhaps being grateful for what you have?

Grateful. Yes, sir.

Then you have your answer. Thank you.

Well, if truth flows like a river and has no beginning or ending, is perception, then, changing constantly? Perception is a faculty, is it not?

Perception is a soul faculty.

Is perception, then, changing as we expand our consciousness?

It is expanding and to some, from certain views, they could call it changing. But it's not changing: it's just broadening and expanding.

When we perceive what you have given us in this class, that is our perception for this point in time?

And unless it continues to expand—you see, for example, a person may read *The Living Light* once. They perceive certain things. If they read it twice, they'll perceive more. If they read it thrice, they'll perceive even more and their understanding will change as they change from level to level to level. All that is necessary for the mind's awakening to the eternal truth of the soul's eternal expression is contained within the teaching, but the teaching, in and of itself, is a continuous flow. Though it is on a printed page, the reader of it will constantly expand their consciousness, if they desire to do so; and therefore, their truth will free them. Now when they go to express their understanding, they will express it according to their level of awareness, which is in a constant state of change. Does that help with your question?

Thank you.

I would like a little more clarification and understanding on the rebirth of the soul entity in form, let's say, dealing with the merit system of parents, for example, if you would be so kind.

Yes, certainly. In reference to your question, perhaps if you will consider the truth that the soul is not personality. The soul is not where the personality exists or expresses. Personality is expressed through the mental body, not through the soul, which is the covering of the formless Divine Spirit. Consequently, if you will consider viewing it from that angle, so to speak, you will have your answer. Personality is in the mind. It has a beginning of its form and it has an ending of its form; therefore, you do not have personality in the soul's expression. You have individuality, but not personality. There is a difference.

Thank you.

You think about the understanding of the word *individuality* and the understanding of the word *personality* and you will have your understanding.

Two questions. First one is in the direction of thought. What is the best possible way to harness the power of one's feelings, of my feelings?

In the direction of thought the question is asked, What is the best way to harness one's feelings? The best way is not to attempt to harness them. You see, that that we try to harness, we hold in our aura and in our magnetic field. Now many people think that denial or harnessing will free them from a particular feeling. It is a releasing of the feeling to the Divine that frees us, not a harnessing or a limiting of it. Because the moment you try to harness a feeling or to limit its expression, what you do, in truth, is bind it to the self. You push it into the inner depths of the mind and it comes back another time with more energy and more demand for expression.

Now I know that many philosophies have taught that when you have certain thoughts or expression that, you see, you annihilate them. Well, you don't annihilate them: you release them, because they are energy. See, man's greatest problem is because he hasn't learned the joy of living. The joy of living is clearly stated: it is the art of giving. So if you have a feeling that you don't enjoy, then give it to God, don't you see? All things come from one source: therefore, all things should be released back to the source from whence they came. We have no devil in the teachings of the Living Light understanding, but we do have a divine neutral energy, known as God or Divine Love or whatever you care to call it.

So if we say that a feeling is distasteful to us and we compute that it's from the devil and then we try to annihilate it or harness it or stop it from its expression, what we're doing, you see, we're building a dam. And that energy keeps hitting this dam. And the more we build our dam, the more energy keeps hitting it. So you see, you don't do that with a feeling or with a thought. You release it to God. And in your releasing, then you start to evolve to higher thoughts and to feelings that are more to your liking. Is that understandable?

How do you go about releasing it?

I would say that giving is one of the most difficult things for the mental body to express. And the reason that it is such a difficult thing is because the mind, ever seeking to absorb, like a sponge, finds false security in the things that it holds to and that it becomes familiar with. And, you see, it is the holding of things that causes all our grief: it is not the releasing of them. If we truly believe in God, the Divine Power, if we truly believe in it, then we find no need to ever attempt to hold anything. Because what we're doing, we're making our God a miserly little god. You see, if we hold onto thoughts or anything, then what we're truly doing and what we're demonstrating is that that god we believe in, "He may or may not let me have what I need or what I think I need."

So, don't you see, we're destroying ourselves because we hold on. We hold onto our opinions. We hold onto our thoughts. We hold onto our substance. We are denying our own divinity and that's the great problem with the world today: it is not receptive, sufficiently, to the divine flow. You see, here we are a vehicle.

And the energy comes through according to what we open up to and it passes. And as it passes through us, you understand, it makes us bigger and bigger and bigger and more and more and more receptive. You see, this is why I try to teach the students that gratitude is the soul faculty that opens the door to supply. If it is supply that you are seeking, then express your gratitude, because to the extent of your gratitude, will you experience the supply.

Now to what shall we direct this gratitude? Well, if we're wise, we will direct this gratitude to the Source that does not know limitation. And the only Source that I know that doesn't know limitation is God, the Divine. And so it is that we do not experience as much joy as we would like because we have not learned, yet, the art of giving. And the reason that we have not learned the art of giving is because of our fear, which finds false security in what it can hold onto. And that's why we can't open up more, so that we can receive more. You see, our minds have done this to us through the illusion of so-called form, which is limitation.

You see, philosophers for untold centuries have taught as a man believeth in his heart, so shall he experience. Well, if you believe in the limitless Divine, then you will experience the limitless Divine. But, you see, our attention, which is our energy, must be directed to the one and only true Source and not to its multitude of effects. So anything that you do not want, give it freely to the Source from whence all things come; and anything you do want, be receptive to its influx. But man is as receptive to the influx of the Divine as he is in expressing it. This is why, as you express more, you receive more: it's ever in equal proportion, if you stay in some degree of balance. Does that help with your question?

Thank you.

Yes, sir. You said a few moments ago that, with regarding one of the minds—how many minds do we have?

Nine. You have been given three and as soon as you're able to break through the barrier to the number two mind, I will be

more than happy to share with you the other six. Does that help
with your question? Thank you.

*I think my question has to do with the number two mind, if
that's the subconscious.*

Yes, it's commonly referred to as the subconscious.

*Well, I'm very grateful for the discussion we've had and for
the other students' questions. I still am trying to get more specific
about the function of the subconscious. And when one reaches a
point where one is trying to recompute or reprogram what is in
the subconscious and it tends to protest very loudly, can you give
us some very specific examples of how we handle this? I know
you've said in the past to treat it like a child, but some of us may
not really know how to treat a child very well.*

Yes, I'll be more than happy to share my understanding. Yes?

*And what would be the role of the conscious mind in doing
this? And how does the Law of Association become involved?*

Yes, there is one word that will answer all of your questions in reference to how to help guide the subconscious mind to
change, and that one word is *kindness.* Through an expression
of kindness to the number two mind, that inner computer, you
may guide it into any pattern of your conscious choosing. But
kindness is the only way I know that it will respond.

*Thank you. Could I ask, without the subconscious coming
into harmonious relationship or balance with the conscious and
the superconscious, many problems are created for the medium.*

That is correct.

And I wonder if you could touch on those.

Yes. Well, now, first of all, the only minds to bring into
balance are the conscious and the subconscious, because when
they're brought into balance, the superconscious flows through
the three bodies of which we are presently aware. Now in reference to the multitude of complications in that computer that
is within all of us, if the person, the student that is sincerely
trying to find the truth that lies waiting within themselves

to be expressed and that Light and freedom, if they make the day-to-day conscious effort through kindness to talk with this other person—you see, it seems to take students so long just to entertain the thought and the possibility that they're being controlled by another individual. Now the truth of the matter is we're all controlled by this other individual that is within us. Now different religions and different philosophies teach different things. They say it's the animal nature. They say it's this, they say it's that, and etc. The simple truth of the whole matter is this: spend some time each day in talking with it, because it is there. It is the magnetic field that attracts things into our lives and if we are not pleased with the things that we are attracting in our lives, then we must work with the magnetic field.

Now the faculty in which kindness is expressed is the bridge between the electric and the magnetic fields. And therefore, by using what is kindness—you may use whatever words that you choose—as long as you use firmness and kindness, because if man uses what he calls kindness, it may come from his emotional realm. You want the kindness of reason, and the kindness of reason is a firm kindness. And I'm sure, through that application, that you will have a freedom from the patterns that you are seeking to be free from.

That's beautiful. Thank you. Do all three minds create thought forms?

"Do all three minds create thought forms?" Two minds create thought forms in the three minds of which we're discussing. The superconscious does not create forms. It is merely the channel through which the energy flows.

Thank you. May I ask a final question?

Yes, certainly.

Is the brain merely a physical receiving set for the three minds, which actually are a part of the astral, mental, and physical bodies?

Yes, the brain is simply like an automobile which we drive. It is simply the vehicle through which the minds are expressing in this particular earth realm. The brain, of course, as you all know, does not go on with us. It goes back to the elements from whence it came. Does that help with your question?

Yes. Thank you very much.

Well, I wonder if you could elaborate a little bit on something that sometimes doesn't always seem quite apparent, because it says here, "what has been given forth to you before is in accordance to the Law of What Can Be Borne [Discourse 11]." And obviously, sometimes people feel they just can't bear some things.

Absolutely. You see, the statement is made in *The Living Light* that what is given to you is ever in accord with the Law of What Can Be Borne. If a teaching is too bright for the recipient, it is mistaken for the night. And being mistaken for the night, it does not serve the purpose for which it has been designed. And so it is in the teachings in these classes and in the written page, that it has been so designed that the light will not be too bright for the recipient. Now I am sure that we are all in accord that each student present is on varying levels of awareness. The IQs of the students vary tremendously, and yet each student reading *The Living Light* will garner from it, because it is seemingly cloaked in so many different ways. They will garner the light that they can bear, and they will not garner any greater light until they open more and expand their consciousness more, and then they will gather unto them even a greater light. And this is why questions are answered ever in accord with the level or the light from which they have been inspired. Does that help with your question?

Thank you.

You're more than welcome.

In reference to what you just said in regard to the kindness towards this other person, your subconscious, this also relates, does it not—I'm asking a question—to dealing with individu-

als, say, your children or clients or neighbors, etc., as well as in your own private consultation in that area and also on a much broader scope outwardly as well. Am I to assume that?

Absolutely and positively. After all, you're dealing with the subconscious of the people whom you are in contact with. Remember, reaction is from the subconscious and therefore, if you express through the soul faculty of kindness, you will have better reactions in your life, you know.

I'm going to ask a question that I'm inspired to ask. How does one apply the faculty of simplicity?

The question is asked, "How does one apply the faculty of simplicity?" When one expresses through the level that is known as heart, *h-e-a-r-t*, heart, one is expressing through the level of simplicity. When one's thought rises into more intellectual levels, then one loses in expression simplicity. Remember, friends, in simplicity lies truth; however, in complexity lies achievement. Because, don't you see, one is a function and the other is a faculty. The intellect is a function, not a soul faculty. Intelligence is a soul faculty; intellect is not. Intellect is the effect of intelligence, but not intelligence itself. Remember that the effect is the function; the source is the faculty.

Yes, sir. I realize that we're supposed to keep questions off a personal nature. However, there is a thing which we have discussed at some length already this evening and which I have experienced and I'm sure many other people have experienced. It seems as though when, as was said earlier, you say, "I've got it!" at that instant, you don't have it. The mind, however, doesn't know that. The mind identifies that it really does have it. And because you don't have it anymore, you're not aware that you don't have it.

If you are expressing through the mind or mental body.

Yes. Consequently, we find ourselves in kind of a false floating along, saying, "I've got it! I've got it! I've got it!" We may, after a time, realize that the rest of the world is going by while we're

sitting with our—or the rest of the river is going by while we're
sitting with our "got it!" How can we best break the log loose and
get back into the stream?

Through a simple aspiration to serve the purpose of the
Divine. When we truly aspire as vehicles (for the mental body
is a vehicle) when we entertain in thought a sincere desire—
because the body desires; the soul aspires. So we're dealing with
the mind and we're dealing with the mind that entertains the
thought that it has it. So therefore, we must deal with desire in
order to break out of the mental bondage. So while we're in the
mind body, then, let us desire to be clear instruments through
which the Divine Intelligence may express itself, that we may
be unobstructed vehicles for its limitless flow. In that desire,
we will start to break out of the bondage of the mental realm.
And in breaking out of the bondage, we will find an inner need
to serve, for that is the first thing that happens in breaking
out of the bondage of the mental prison. And in that feeling to
serve, we will be guided by our own spirit and we will not decide
whether or not the service is too great or too small. Because if
we make a decision that that's the way we want to serve and
that's the way we don't want to serve, then we're closing the
gates once again to the prison cell of the mental body. But if we
will flow with whatever comes into our universe, by our own
Divine Spirit, into service, then we will be freed into the spiritual realm and we will continue on the stream of the limitless
flow back to the Source from whence we came, and we will do it
here and now. That's the best way that I know of getting out of
the prison house.

In the discourse that we had last week, there was a statement
that overactivity of the mental body creates a very strong pres-
sure. Is this what we know as a headache?

It could be experienced as a headache. It could also be experienced as exhaustion. It could be experienced in many different ways. Because overactivity of the mental body, that would

depend in what area the overactivity is being expressed and, therefore, it would come out in the part of the anatomy which is in harmony with the pattern that's being expressed. So it could come out as a headache or it could come out as a toothache. For example, if we're using our determination, then we're going to have that problem, yes.

Are there manifestations of this sort with overactivity of the spiritual, or can that be done?

It is not possible for such a thing as overactivity of the spiritual body to occur in the sense that the spiritual body, which is composed of a universal substance, that is in a constant, constant flux and flow. Remember, it is the mental body that holds. The spiritual body releases and it is in a constant state of flux and flow or change or motion. It is the mental body that tries to absorb everything, like a balloon. You see, the mental body may be likened unto a balloon: it keeps getting bigger and bigger and bigger and bigger and bigger. Now there is a point at which the balloon will not stretch anymore and if we try to stretch it, it explodes; it breaks, you understand. Now what happens in the mental body, then the person experiences what is known as a mental breakdown, because, you see, the balloon got bigger than what it was. It got more air into it than it was capable of containing, do you see. And so it is through service that we are freed. Does that help with your question?

Thank you.

Then gratitude really boils down to selfless service. I mean, if you're really truly grateful to the Divine, you serve selflessly.

If a person is truly grateful to the divine Source of which they are, in truth, a part and which is the only lasting part of their being, if they are, according to their gratitude, they will be impressed by their own spirit in which way to serve, but they will serve, you see. But it isn't something that someone else can decide: what they should be serving. You see what I mean? That's something that is within one's own being. Now the more that we serve in whatever we're impressed from within to serve, the more that we serve, the more that we expand ourselves spiritually. And then the balloon of the mental body, you understand, starts to shrink to the proportion that it's supposed to be for the harmony and balance of our three bodies.

If you have mental problems, friends, and you have troubles in that area, you can free yourself very easily through service. No one needs to tell you what the service is to be. If you will be at peace in yourself, you will know. And you may be rest assured, you will ever have the opportunity to serve. Now the thing is this, it is the mind that likes to say that that's not the service it wants to do and it's not when it wants to do it. Now that's a very simple thing: that's known as God at my convenience. But, you know, when we have God at our convenience, there comes a time when it's no longer convenient to God and that's when we need the help the most. Isn't it lovely? But it does teach us something. Does that help with your question?

It certainly does.

May we go into a more specific discussion of clairsentience? Yes?

I'm trying to understand whether clairsentience emanates from the superconscious, which then expresses through the conscious level in the faculty of intuition or is it an attunement with the soul mate, which has picked up certain vibratory waves, or what is it? My question, I guess, is really how are the vibratory waves picked up and through what form or forms do they express?

We're speaking now of clairsentience. Without clairsentience, there's no testing of the spirit, because it is through the clairsentience—you see, when we awaken to the clairsentience of the soul, it is a soul expression. Clairsentience is a soul expression that's felt in the part of the anatomy known as the heart. Now when we see a vision and we do not have this feeling, which is our clairsentience, then it is not from a spiritual realm. There is no other way that I know of testing the spirit.

Now many people in their unfoldment, they see various visions. And they will see people in other people's universe, you know, but they don't know how to test the spirit to see whether or not that is a spirit. Ofttimes it's a mental image. Ofttimes it's an image of the subconscious. Ofttimes it's from the desire world and from a multitude of different dimensions. And so it is that the students in this Association are first taught to awaken to their clairsentience.

All right. Now how does one know what their clairsentience is? That's the question. I am sure that you have in your life experience looked at, perhaps, a stray dog and had a deep feeling. I am sure in all of your experiences you have had a feeling when the phone rang and you picked it up and your feeling was accurate. It is that feeling, that clairsentience, that we must awaken ourselves to. Now you can't say that it flows through the faculty of intuition or that it flows through a soul mate. It is experienced in the heart. It is where the feeling actually is experienced. Now we're aware of it in the mind, but there is literally a feeling in the anatomy in the area of the heart. And when you have that feeling, that is an expression of your clairsentience. And when you have visions and things and you don't have that feeling with it, then you are not experiencing a spiritual level or a soul level. Does that help with your question?

That does clarify.

See, there is so much that is brought into the world, you know, with what they call the psychic realm. Remember, and I've spoken it before, the psychic realm is nothing more or less than a thin vibratory wave between the astral and mental realms. That's all the psychic realm is. A medium is psychic, but a psychic is not a medium. And a medium is ever subject to psychic experience. However, they jumble the whole thing together and they call all the communications psychic. Well, this Association—and I'm grateful to Isa Goodwin—has changed the name of communication to interdimensional communication, because it is a more accurate statement and it covers the wide spectrum of which the mediums are experiencing. Because for any person to stand up and state the only levels they touch or they express as a medium is the world of spirit is nothing more than a delusion caused by one's own ego. And so we have changed communications to include a wider spectrum of interdimensional communication, because we don't like to have the world think that we're so credulous. Does that help with your question?

That does. May I ask another that touches on this?

Certainly.

When we are impressed by our guides and teachers, are you really talking about a telepathic kind of communication that is received by the subconscious and how do we know that this comes from the spirit and it's not . . .

If it comes from the spirit, you feel it in your heart. If you do not have that feeling, a literal feeling in the heart, it is not from the spiritual realms. It could be from the astral and it could be from the mental realms. It could be from the desire realms. It could be from the mass thinking. There's a multitude of dimensions it could be from. The reason that the science of communication in Spiritualism is not more widely accepted and is not better understood is because in the evolution of the Spiritualist movement, they lumped it all together. They used to call it spirit greetings. Serenity Association was the first one to grow out of *spirit greetings* to *spiritual communication*. And it was the first one to move forward with the times into interdimensional communication. And I'm sure that it will catch on in the movement. After all, the words changed from *giving readings* to *counseling* and many other things. So we must move forward with a broader understanding. Remember, when a word, through usage over a number of years, through usage and abuse, no longer serves the true purpose, then it's time to change the word. I guess they call it semantics. Thank you.

About the heart, simplicity, this reaching out into the vibra-tory waves when we're standing on the platform to give, we feel the person that we're going to—may I be personal? There are times—

If it will serve a purpose of principle.

If it doesn't, I know you will stop me. When we stand to give a message, some of us new mediums, and we have a pulling toward that, is that the heart, that simplicity?

It could or couldn't be. It could be a strong desire on the part of the recipient for a message. It could also be one's clairsen-tience. Now if it is truly one's clairsentience, the feeling that is experienced in the area of the heart, in the heart itself, will not forcefully pull us to any individual. It won't do that, you see, because the feeling in the heart of the clairsentience is all-encompassing and it is all-knowing. It will not literally, mag-netically pull us.

However, the demands of the subconscious will magneti-cally pull us. This is the thing in unfoldment that we constantly must watch. Now a person may sit in the congregation, don't you see—I watch them every Sunday here before I go off to do whatever work I have to do and there are some that have such a phenomenally great need they will magnetically pull a receiving set to them.

Now the danger of this is very simple: that they may pull us into a desire realm and we may be receiving from that level. This is why, in the giving of communications, if a person is at peace, truly at peace, they're inspired by their spirit and their spirit helpers, they will give and not linger. The danger, the *danger* in communication is to linger, because when we linger, we lose, we drop to another level. Do you see what I mean? Now this is something that's very important in this science. Your spirit—you understand, if you permit the recipient to start ask-ing questions and etc., you get yourself pulled into another level

of communication. It's really very, very simple. And so it is that
your spirit and your spirit helpers, they will guide you. Remember, the spirit of spontaneity is to go here and there and there
and there and there.

And then you'll get a feeling, that's the time to quit. It doesn't
matter whether you've worked ten minutes or an hour and ten
minutes. When that feeling comes over the communicant—which
is another term that's going to be used in this Association very
soon—when that feeling comes over you, whatever you do, do
yourself a favor, whoever you are, and sit down. Because if you
go on from that point, you're all in the mental. That is why I
would rather see a lecture that lasts nine minutes in this church
than one that lasts twenty minutes if eleven minutes of it are
out of the brain. It is better to speak one word from the Light
itself than to speak a thousand words from the brain. So you
see, we must not be concerned whether or not we're working
three minutes or we're working thirty minutes.

We must not be concerned whether we've done a good job or
we did a lousy job. Now remember this, friends, if we are concerned with what kind of a job we did, it's not our soul, it's not
our spirit, and should it be our spirit guides, we'd better get rid of
them. Because the only concern, if there is to be any concern, is to
serve God. We're not concerned with whether the recipient thinks
it great or thinks it crummy, because if we're concerned with that
stuff, we're in the wrong business. We should go on to something
else. So give what you have to give, care less what they do with it,
because you are not serving man. Hopefully, we're serving God.
And in serving God, God is not concerned, and are we, with our
little egos, to be greater than God? Now if God is not concerned
and we are concerned, then we've got to work on this balloon they
call the brain. Do you know what I mean?

Yes.

So you see, just give what you have to give. And if it's simple, it's simple. If it's complicated, it's complicated. And just go

on. See, my good friends, do not be governed by the illusion of time. Go by your feeling. That inner feeling will not fail you. And if you do that—you see, again and again, I've spoken to the students: those who seek the gifts of the Spirit are distorting themselves and shall destroy themselves. But those who seek the Spirit for the sake of the Spirit, the gifts that are necessary for their soul unfoldment shall be added to them. Do not seek the psychic. Do not seek the phenomena because, my friends, you seek it at the cost of the awakening to your divine rights. This is why many philosophies have taught not to tamper with the psychic, because it is not only dangerous but extremely detrimental to the spiritual unfoldment of one's own being. If the primary purpose or motivation for seeking Spiritualism and its understanding, if the primary motive is communication and its science, then the person shall not find the Divine Light that lies waiting within himself.

The truth of the matter is that everyone is a medium or a communicant to something. And so what is the difference whether some of us are in level twelve or twenty or thirty or whatever it is, if we are willingly doing and serving to the best of our ability. Remember, he who seeks the praise of man loses sight of God's true plan.

Thank you, friends. Let us go have refreshments.

JUNE 21, 1973

CONSCIOUSNESS CLASS 19 ✢

Good evening, students. Now for those of you who have not been in our courses before, you will find, as time progresses, that there is a certain process that takes place: that some students are unable to continue on. What is the most interesting thing, that all students should be aware of, is that this is a growth level inside of ourselves. Now it doesn't mean just this particular church or this particular class: it means wherever we face and whenever we face ourselves. It is not easy for anyone, depending on the level of consciousness that we have arisen to. And so it is these classes were properly named when they first started: Spiritual Awareness classes. It helps us to become aware of our own inner being, of our own levels of consciousness.

One of the first things that happens in the awakening of our own soul is the resentment to the necessary changes to free ourselves. And the psychological reaction of that is to find disturbance outside of ourselves, when the only disturbance that exists, in truth, and the only mixed vibrations that we can experience, remember, friends and students, are always within. The only place that experience really happens is inside of ourselves.

And so it is, this is your ninth class: there are three more classes to go. There are always a few in these classes who are able to complete the twelve-week course. But, as was said by many a philosopher and many a spiritual leader throughout the ages, many are called and few are chosen. Now the reason that few are chosen is really quite simple: few choose to make the necessary changes to be the chosen ones, if that's what you want to call "Many are called and few are chosen."

So let us remember and let us consider that these things that are happening around and about us in our little universes are ever reflections of the states of consciousness that our soul is expressing through at any given moment. The easiest thing (and the thing that usually happens with all of us) is the delusion that has been caused by what is known as the brain or the ego, the house of the senses, that puts the cause out on everything that is around and about us.

It is very difficult to unfold the first triune soul faculty, which is duty, gratitude, and tolerance. It is very difficult. Now what happens is, we like to see things go the way that we are in harmony with. Each one views the world a certain way. And naturally, when we view the world the way that we think is best, we accept that that is the right and the best way. But in that type of viewing, which is level number one, we must realize that the feelings that we have about viewing the world, we must also grant to someone else. And there comes a time in our life, now and then, when we will find someone who agrees with us and then we will feel better. But it is very difficult to view a world and not find someone that agrees with us, because if we don't, the first thing that happens is we get discouraged, you see. Because there's nothing there to help encourage us to tell us that we are seeing the world the right way and that encouragement is necessary to all of us. A wise man gets his encouragement through the faculty of faith. You see, faith is that soul faculty through which we can be constantly encouraged to go on and keep doing what we feel is right.

And so it is, my friends, that you look out over the world, you can look in your daily job, you can look in your activities and we're always going to find something that's distasteful to us and that we don't like. Now we had the reporter here in this church these past few Sundays. And one of the remarks that she made was that this church seemed to emphasize only the positive; that everything in the church service was in a positive vein. And she couldn't understand that we would not recognize its so-called opposite or the negative. Well, I explained to her that we were aware that such a thing as the poles of opposites exist in all creation, but that what man puts his attention on, he becomes. So why choose to become negative when it's so destructive to oneself?

You see, it's not a matter of being out of balance: it's just a matter of being sensible. You can have all kinds of experiences in the course of a day and all of us do, but in those experiences we can choose to see the good in all of those experiences. Now if we choose to see the good in every experience that we encounter, like the magnet of the universe, we will pull the good from that experience into our lives. If we choose to see the opposite, then we will continue to experience that disturbance that robs us from all of our peace of mind and our tranquility and our serenity. So which is the wisest thing to do?

Obviously, after you've spent a lifetime choosing all of those things that you dislike and seeing the disturbance and being affected by it, there comes a time when you sit back and you pause and you say, "I've had it. I do not appreciate the way things are going in my life." And when you reach that point, you will make the necessary changes in your thinking, and you will start seeing the beauty and the good that exists in all experiences and in all things. And when you do that, that's the only thing that you will continue to experience, because man cannot see or be affected by anything that he does not direct his attention to.

Remember that Divine Love is energy; that it is the soul's absolute need to express this Divine Love or this energy. You have the divine right of choice in all things and in all situations to direct this energy, through whatever vehicle of thought, through whatever thought you care to entertain in mind. "He who sees the good becomes the good" is just not a platitude: it's an absolute truth. Now in this church and in this Association, we stress making great effort in seeing the good in all things and pulling the Divine, that Neutrality, that beautiful, so-called Divine Love, that it may express itself.

Sometimes a student will say, "Well, it's very difficult for me." As long as we entertain in thought that anything is difficult, it becomes more difficult. Now that's just the way that it is. It's all in our thinking: that's the only place it exists. And if we think in the negative, we experience the negative. It does not exist, my good friends, outside of our own thought. This is why some of us experience poor health, because we're entertaining in thought—not poor health—we're entertaining in thought disturbing vibrations. You see, if a person says, "Well, I felt fine until I met so-and-so. I felt fine until so-and-so called me," well, for goodness sake, is so-and-so our god and our master? Because if we felt fine until we met a certain person or if we felt fine until we had a certain experience, that simply means—what we, in truth, are saying—is that we have given this Divine Power, we have sold our soul to that person, to those places, and to those things. Well, which is the best way of living?

I'm taking this little time to share some of these things with you that you may make a more conscious effort at freeing yourself through the vehicle of thought. You know, if you read the newspaper and you decide, "Oh, that Watergate experience is just terrible" and you feel accordingly, well, you have given this Divine Power to that particular expression. That is no one's fault but our own. Now if we find that we don't like the job that we have and we're very disturbed in it and we say to ourselves, "Well, here I am, stuck with this job. I have to eat and I have to make money. I have to have a roof over my head," well, as long as we entertain that kind of thinking, naturally, we're going to find ourselves in that job because, you see, we keep grounding ourselves in the particular vibration and the experience that is distasteful to us.

However, it serves a good purpose in one sense, and maybe in more than one. If by working on a job we can express how difficult it is for us and what a bummer experience we have in it and, yet, we have to have a job in order to survive, if that serves to gain attention for us, then, don't you see, friends, it is serving a good purpose. If we can gain sympathy from another because of our seeming poor health, if we can gain sympathy because we don't have the things that we feel that we should have, if we can gain sympathy because of our struggle in life, well, you see, what we are, in truth, gaining, we are gaining energy. Because we'll always find a listening ear. Because we can always find someone that's a good sounding board and says, "Oh, you poor soul. What a struggle you're having in life."

So you see, my friends, what we are really seeking is this Divine Love. But if that's the way that we have found of getting it and we can't awaken to a higher level of consciousness, then we will continue to get that Divine Love in that way. Because, you see, friends, there is no experience and there is no expression in life that Divine Love is not flowing through, because Divine Love is the energy that sustains all things in all places at all times.

So let us stop and say to ourselves, "What kind of thoughts do I entertain in the course of a day? In what way am I gaining the energy or Divine Love that I think that I need?" Just ask yourself that question. Ask yourself the question of how you get attention, do you understand? Ask yourself that question and then look very clearly at the way that you are gaining this attention, you see.

You know, the mind does all kinds of things to get its attention, to get this energy. Look at the animal, look what the animal does to gain attention. It does all kinds of things. Some children, you know, will repeatedly do what they're not supposed to do just to get a beating because they're experiencing this energy, even though they don't appreciate it. Look at how many times children are disciplined and they repeatedly do the same thing again. We have to awaken to the fact and to the truth that everything in creation needs this experience of Divine Love. How it gets it is so varied and so complex, it's almost unbelievable for the mind to accept. But that, my friends, is truly what happens in this world, you see.

Now some students, of course, they've left. They got to a certain point. Some of them have talked to me and they feel, some do—they have different reasons—they feel that they have gained as much as they possibly can gain from these awareness classes. Well, I can understand that. As long as a person feels that they have gained all of the understanding that any school has to offer, then there will be nothing more for them to gain because, you see, they're no longer receptive to the divine flow. You see, you all know, you who are in this class, that there are no prepared texts, outside of the simple reading of the discourses.

And you all know that if you prepare something, you limit it. You limit it to your preparation. And this is why when there's anything you want in life, stop telling God the way it's to come. Don't tell the Divine that. The intelligence of the Divine is far superior to the intelligence of the brain and anyone who pauses long enough to think is well aware of that. Either the Divine is a limitless flow that has no obstruction, outside of the receiver in receiving it, or it is not. And so if we want to truly awaken inside of ourselves, be open and be receptive to new thought, to new ideas. And don't stunt your own growth by saying to yourself, "I have arrived. There is nothing left." Because in that type of thinking, for us, there will be nothing left.

[A student reads Discourse 12. This is followed by a short period of meditation.]

Now we'll continue on with our class. As before, those who have questions concerning the studies, you may feel free at this time to raise your hands.

My question deals with the ladder of progression and the Law of What Can Be Borne. Are they one and the same? Are they built on an idea, and these eighty-one levels, are they eighty-one individual ideas? Is the Law of What Can Be Borne and the ladder of progression one and the same? And are they built on ideas that are caused from the product of thinking and are these eighty-one individual pattern growths?

In reference to your question, the Law of What Can Be Borne and the ladder of progression are, in principle, one and the same, number one. In reference to your question, Are the eighty-one levels of awareness, are they eighty-one ideas in combinations thereof? I would not say that they are necessarily that. They are levels of awareness within one's form, on which the soul within us, it expresses at different times on different levels. Now how a person rises, so to speak, to the higher states of consciousness is through the direction of the will to the Divine: that is known as the divine lifeline.

Now it has been spoken in many philosophies to love God greater or more than all things at all times. Well, what they mean, in our understanding, by this "God" is to go back home. And love is the greatest magnet known in all of the universes. So when man expresses a great deal of love, what he, in truth, is doing is utilizing a greater magnet and, consequently, will experience more of what he desires to experience. For, you see, that is why we consider in this expression of energy, or this love, to direct it to the formless and to the free or to what is known as God. Otherwise, we will become bound and enslaved if we express more of this energy or love to any particular form. For example, two people, they say they fall in love. They get married and what happens? The next experience on that ladder of expression is usually termed *possession*. That is, the level of awareness desires to possess what it cherishes or what it loves. The same thing ofttimes happens with a parent and their children. It also happens with a human and their pets. What it is, is that this Divine Love, this energy, is being limited by the vehicle of thought and when we limit the Divine Love, which is God, when we limit it in its expression, we enslave our soul to the very thing that we limit it to. Does that help with your question?

Yes.

What is the ultimate goal of the reprogramming of the subconscious? Is it only to recall or support the positive thoughts and deeds or to remain still during meditation and spiritual counseling? In other words, how should the subconscious ideally function in order to help us truly grow spiritually?

In reference to your question, What is the goal of the reprogramming of the inner mind or the so-called subconscious? The process of reprogramming is not the annihilation or the erasing of other patterns of mind. It is not possible in the human form to annihilate or to erase any level of awareness or any program that has been programmed into the computer of the gray cells of the brain. What happens and takes place is that by entertaining new thoughts on new levels of awareness, we make a new programming. This new programming helps us in what can be borne on the ladder of eternal progression by freeing our soul, that it is not bound by the programming of levels that we no longer desire to entertain and to experience. This is possible through a conscious, daily effort, not just at meditation times.

I have ofttimes spoken to the students in the speaking forth of the affirmations that have been given to help them, not to say the affirmation once or twice and expect that level of awareness, that state of consciousness, to be with you through the rest of the day. It is a matter of expressing on that level more often with more energy, so that you may find yourself expressing for a longer course of time on a higher level of awareness. It is the subconscious mind with its programming and its limitations that binds our soul to creation. Does that help with your question?

Yes, that does. Thank you. Is there a specific affirmation that we might use in trying to release some of the negative thoughts that pop up?

Absolutely and positively. That affirmation has been given to the students. It is entitled "Total Consideration." *[See Consciousness Class 11.]* He who considers all shall be freed by all, and he who does not consider all shall be bound by the things that he does not consider. Without consideration, there is no expression of the soul faculty of reason. Without the expression through the soul faculty of reason, there is not, in truth, an expression of freedom.

That's beautiful, thank you. If the subconscious does not have the capacity to analyze or think logically, does it think at all?

The subconscious, the computer of the subconscious, does not think in the sense that the reasoning faculty is able to analyze and to weigh out various experiences. The subconscious simply is a reactor, a programmed reactor. According to whatever level of awareness of the subconscious is triggered, then it will react automatically and that is its true function.

Even people with some difficulty in visualizing will, at times,
see vague scenes of places, masklike faces of people which they
know or they don't know and these are apparently subconscious
images that float up. It's been described almost as a screen around
some people onto which these images are projected. Now would
you explain how these are produced and if the aid of the subcon-
scious can be elicited in visualizing objects composed of etheric
substance?

Yes. First of all, in reference to your statement about the
seeing of visions and etc., which are expressions of the subconscious or inner mind, it has been stated in *The Living Light*
they're termed as reflections from within.

Now the first step in freeing the mind from the bondage of
the programmed patterns of a lifetime is to become aware, number one, of its true function, number two, through daily experience, through proper meditation and contemplation, concentration, to become consciously aware of the levels that are within
the inner mind. When the student becomes aware of the levels
within, then the student will know beyond a shadow of any doubt
whether or not the experiences they are having, such as visions
and seeming psychic experiences, they will know whether or
not that is a level of the subconscious or whether that is truly
an astral experience through their astral body or whether it is
a spiritual experience through their spiritual soul faculties. I
know of no other way than the sincere effort of the student to
seek the kingdom within, known as God, first.

If the seeking is not the Divine or God, if that is not the
primary, motivating factor, then a full awareness, an illumination of the levels of the mind, is not possible. This is why if we
will truly seek to serve the Divine or God, and that is our ever
conscious motivation, then we will awaken to what levels exist
in the depths of our own mind, what lies there waiting. And in
so knowing that, we will be freed from their control and we will

have the spiritual experiences that we do not have to seek for. I hope that helps you with your question.

If, at transition, one goes to the mental realm, does one shed the astral body with its subconscious mind?

There are several bodies encased in the flesh in which we are. When one goes to the mental realms, you understand, the astral body, which expresses on the astral realm, is not the function or vehicle that the soul is expressing through. So in that sense, one could say that the body is shed. I would, however, like to clarify that whenever the soul, that spark of Divinity expressing through what is known as soul, which, in turn, expresses through other bodies, whenever the soul leaves the body, the body, if it is composed of the physical elements of the earth planet, immediately starts the disintegration process and returns to the elements of which it has been composed. Therefore, when the astral body is shed, if you prefer to use that term, the astral body immediately starts its disintegrating process and returns to the astral substance of which it is composed. There is no such thing as communicating with an astral shell in which a soul is not expressing itself, because the shell disintegrates the moment that the soul leaves it. Does that help with your question?

Yes, thank you. If one goes, at transition, to a spiritual realm, then one would have neither a conscious nor subconscious mind, is that correct?

They have a memory par excellence. The memory par excellence is a soul faculty that expresses through what is known as the soul body, yes.

So would they be free, then, from the subconscious record?

They would, yes, they would be free from the control of that vehicle because they would no longer be expressing through that vehicle. However, the memory par excellence, which is a soul faculty, goes on with the soul throughout its journey through eternity.

Loyalty and attachment. Loyalty, I know, is a faculty. I've been taught that. And when we're loyal to a group, a teacher, a class, or a spirit teacher—I won't say God, because I know better than that—does the Law of Attachment come into this? I mean, so many people are leery of this word attachment. *They think they are attaching themselves to something negative. Can we not attach ourselves to the positive and the beautiful and the good by this law, by this faculty of loyalty?*

Thank you very much for your question in reference to the soul faculty of loyalty and the function of attachment. Remember, friends, the soul faculties are not what attaches: it is our functions that attach to anything. Now we're all in a body that has functions, that is function, and therefore its tendency is to attach. What happens in the awakening of our consciousness, as this consciousness moves up into higher levels of awareness, is simply this: we find that our attachments begin to change. We may have been attached to certain material things and the fulfillment of the desires of the functions at one state of our consciousness and then we find ourselves moving up the eternal ladder of progression and we start attaching to the faculties of the soul's expression. Now this is a progressive step up the eternal ladder of progression and, in time, as we awaken our consciousness and expand it even more, we start to attach to what is known as the absolute, the formless, and the free. By "attachment," I mean to say the experience derived from such an expression, the mind entertains as an attachment.

Now it is the tendency of the mind to attach to whatever makes the mind feel better. If you go someplace and you feel loved and you feel joy and you feel happiness and you feel those things that the inner being, of course, desires, then it is only logical that the tendency for attaching to them will ever become stronger. Now the danger in attachment is simply this: when we attach, we go through many experiences when the mind, in its pattern of attachment, no longer sees things going the way that they were when we first became attached. Consequently, it doesn't mean that attachment is a bad thing or a bad word. We make it that way through our lack of understanding.

Now, as I explained, we go someplace and we have such a wonderful feeling. It's like going to a restaurant and having an excellent dinner. And we go there over a period of months, possibly even years. And each time we go, it just seems so fantastic that it's such a wonderful dinner and we feel so great. Well, the day comes that we find ourselves attached and the dinners that we used to feel were so great are no longer so great anymore. Because when we become attached to a thing, the next step that the mind comes up with, it must care for the thing that it is attached to. It is the natural instinct within the human being to care for or to protect its attachments. Do we understand, students? Now when that happens, the next step of progression is known as possession. So we find ourselves, not intentionally, but we find ourselves, through protection, possessing.

Now remember, it is the sense functions that are protection; the soul faculties are expression. And so we must weigh this out in our mind and say to ourselves, "God is everywhere present, never absent or away. I may have this joy, this peace that passeth all understanding, this love and all of these things that I feel that I need, walking down the street." It just means, my friends, that if you find God one place, you have a very good potential within you to find God all places.

So let us consider expanding our consciousness in what is known as attachment. Let us have the feeling of joy, of peace, of tranquility, of serenity, wherever we are. Let us feel the same in our little shelters at home as we feel when we attend church. Now I know that probably isn't the best promotion for Serenity, but let's face the truth: its love expands into the universe and, like the great magnet, it always calls from the universe the right ones.

But unless we can grow within ourselves, through expanding of consciousness, to have this wonderful feeling and this love and this joy wherever we are, with whomever we may be, in whatever we are doing, then we are limiting the divine expression of God itself. And if we will work on that, if we will finish our job in the course of a day, we will go home and we will prepare our meal or whatever it is we care to do and we will take a moment and we will sit down and through the power of thought, we may experience any joy and any sadness—that is the Divine Power that exists in potential within the human soul. That is why the teaching is, Whatever you need is right where you are.

My dear friends, it exists in one place only: it exists in your thought. As long as your thought insists upon telling you that it's someplace else, then, for you, it will ever be someplace else. It does not exist, my dear students, outside of your own thought. All of your joy, all of your sadness, all of your supply, all of your fulfillment exists in your thought, which awakens your own state of consciousness. It does not exist anyplace else. The mind has deluded us through what is known as the intellect. It looks out into the universe and it says, "If I had that, and it's over there, I would be so happy." My dear friends, it's in your thinking. It is no place else. I cannot impress upon your minds too strongly that everything you need is in your vehicle of thought. It does not exist anyplace else. Does that help with your question?

It certainly does.

I have two questions, please. One is, I would like to know what the chin represents. And, number two, in the very early stages of evolution, where the male and the female were as one, centered in one body, and had self-creation—I was wondering if you could kindly clarify that self-creation.

I don't believe that that has been brought up in this class.

Not in this class, no.

That is correct. And we haven't yet gotten to that discourse, have we?

No, sir.

I think that we will discuss that at a later time. Now what was the purpose for, and the motivation, for your question concerning the meaning of the chin? What motivated you to the question? Would you mind sharing that with the class?

What made me think of it?

What is your purpose for desiring to know what it represents? Will it help, will it help you in finding more joy and more love in this universe and more fulfillment of your soul's expression? Do you feel that it will at this time?

I mean, one can ask that of any question.

Yes, that's why I'm asking the question of you.

The reason why I asked was—when I looked at one of the students in this section, I could not see his chin. I felt that was highly unusual. His chin is recognizable, and I thought, "I wonder what the chin represents." That's what made me lead up to this question.

Yes, this is what we wanted to bring to the conscious awareness in order that we may find what is the true motive of our questioning. Do you understand? Because when the motive of our questioning, students, is revealed unto our conscious mind, unto ourselves, then we will become aware of the level of awareness on which we are expressing. And the purpose, you understand, students, of these awareness classes is for you, individually and collectively, to become aware of your own states of consciousness. I honestly feel, in reference to your questions, if you will give them more thought and more consideration that perhaps we can discuss them at a later time. You see, students, our questions, when they are motivated from within ourselves— now, for example, I am sure that in your driving you see the sunrise and sunset. Is that not correct? At times?

At times.

You look out into the universe and you see the light seemingly disappear and darkness come and the stars come out and the moon, don't you?

Yes.

All right. Now what I'm trying to bring up to you students in this awareness is: the question has not been asked what the moon represents and you have seen the moon and the stars more often and more frequently than you have seen the disappearance of someone's chin. Is that not correct?

I'd have to go along with that, yes.

Yes. Now I want to bring up an awareness within ourselves, students. Why is it that we ask certain questions? Is it because this is the first experience we have had of looking at an individual and not being able to see their chin? Is that the reason for our question? Do you understand? If it is, we're going to have a multitude of experiences, students, and we want to pause and to think.

Now the things that the mind becomes familiar with, it no longer questions. I haven't had any students asking me about the meaning of the stars, which they see all the time. And I haven't had any students asking me about the meaning of the element air, which they use constantly. And I haven't had anyone asking me about the meaning of the sun and these different things in nature. So the point I want to bring up to all students—and I'm so grateful that you brought up these questions—is that the mind, its normal tendency is to question only that with which it has not become familiar. When the wise man stops and he says, "I'm familiar with this pattern. I have expressed it for a lifetime. I am going to start to question it," that's when we grow. Thank you very much.

You've said tonight to expand our consciousness. The other student asked what I thought were very interesting questions regarding the conscious and subconscious minds. It has also been stated in these classes that man has 10 percent free will, due to the laws which he has already set into motion. Is the balancing of one's being the balancing between the so-called conscious mind and the subconscious mind? If we are to balance, would 50 percent free will be that balance point?

The balance point—in reference to your question, there is 45 percent control of the so-called subconscious and 45 percent control of the conscious. There is a 10 percent free will, which is the expression through what is known as the superconscious.

That would be the balance point?

That is the balance point. The superconscious is the balance point. Now this is also—in reference to your question, you have opened another door—this is also the reason for teaching the students to concentrate upon peace. You see, peace has often been stated as being the power. Peace, my friends, is the neutrality and the expression of the superconscious, through which the Divine Intelligence itself flows unobstructed. The obstruction to the divine influx and the Infinite Intelligence exists in the 45 percent of the subconscious and the 45 percent of the conscious minds. When they are brought into balance, through peace, that is when we are truly receptive to the Divine Intelligence: when we are at that point of true peace. This is why man first seeks peace, the kingdom of God. The kingdom of God, my friends, is the garden of peace and that is the first thing to seek; then, you may experience all these other things. But that must be the number one motivation within the human being. That is how we build what is known as a spiritual foundation. And unless we rise in consciousness to a state of awareness where we recognize that peace is the only thing worthy of entertaining our mind in thought, then we will continue on the cycle of so-called cause and effect. Did that help with your question?

Very much. Yes.

If indeed the faculties are 45 percent or the conscious is 45 percent, the subconscious is 45 percent, and the superconscious is 10 percent, by expanding our consciousness, does this give better control or how does this react with the subconscious? By expanding it, I think in terms of not only the conscious itself, but also numerically somehow.

In the expanding of the consciousness, the subconscious, what happens is we rise to new patterns and in the expanding of the consciousness, the subconscious is programmed on new levels of awareness; and it recognizes and accepts that there is no need, that all of its desires are fulfilled within its own self, that it no longer has this function and this expression as need.

You see, it is man's acceptance of what he calls need that causes his greatest problems. Because, you see, when we entertain in thought that we need anything, in that moment, we entertain in thought that it's outside of us. You see, man cannot possibly entertain in thought that he needs something that he already has. So it is through an expanding of the consciousness that we rise to new levels of awareness and there's new programming in the subconscious mind on higher levels. And therefore, you no longer have the feeling that you need anything, because you're on new programs and you see and you know and the subconscious accepts that you have everything and therefore cannot experience need anymore. He who experiences need experiences limitation and constant unfulfilled desire. Does that help with your question?

Very much.

Is that the idea behind the Law of Harmony?

It is the sustenance through which the Law of Harmony is sustained. Yes, indeed it is.

Spiritually, how can one strengthen their weaker personality traits or inherited traits?

Yes, how can one strengthen the traits that they are not particularly fond of entertaining any longer? Number one: by directing the energy through the vehicle of thought to the type of traits or expressions that you care to experience. Through a constant direction of the divine energy to that which you wish to experience to become, that will manifest in your life through the Law of Faith. Does that help with your question?

Yes.

Remember, friends, don't place your attention on the things that you dislike. Don't see disturbance. Because in seeing disturbance, you experience disturbance. You can't experience, my dear children, something that you can't see, that you can't hear, and that you can't feel. So when you go anyplace, see serenity, see harmony, see the divine good. Keep your mind seeing those things and those are the only kinds of things you will be able to experience. That is an expanding and an awakening of our consciousness.

It is stated in The Living Light *that discussion on the higher level of thought does seem most beneficial to ourselves and to those who are so privileged to hear it. Many times, in my experience, people have been in class and after class they want to discuss their class work. Does that not get into the intellect, with the debating mind? Is the time after class a time to be quiet and think of what these classes meant or is it well for us to discuss?*

Thank you very much. And, of course, my dear friends, that depends entirely upon your state of consciousness. If your soul is expressing through a state of consciousness that is computed as social and you care to discuss things of a spiritual nature, they don't blend or mix too well. Now the reason that they don't blend or mix too well is because the old subconscious has computed that social means an expression and an entertainment of the senses. So you see, it's quite difficult to mix the senses with the spirit, because they're different levels of awareness or states of consciousness. However, my dear children, it is the divine right of each student to express according to their own inner being. It is also the divine right of each student whether or not to become in rapport with those levels of expression.

Now if a person, after having class work, sits quietly and is absorbing the different teachings and etc., and that is what helps them, then that is the logical, sensible, and reasonable thing that that student should do. Now if that student, any student, has had experience that by discussing things of a spiritual nature in a social function robs them of an absorption of the true meaning of the class and therefore they no longer do that, because they have had the experience, then that student may sit quietly and ask please not to be disturbed with all the chatter, because it is robbing them of the absorption of the spiritual substance of the class. And in so doing, recognize that this other student here, here, here, and here has not yet had that experience and let them go ahead and stumble in the dark, because, sooner or later, they're going to wake up, don't you see? That is known as granting unto another the divine right to grow, to find God in their way.

This is why I try to practice a noninterference policy with my students. There are many times that I see many things: that they're heading on different paths that are pitfalls. The reason that I recognize and know that is because I went that way myself. But having gone that way, I do try to remember my right of my expression at a particular time and I try to grant that to another. For unsolicited help is ever to no avail. It's a total waste of energy, which could be used for one's own fulfillment.

However, if a student asks me in reference to the path they are treading and I explain to them my understanding and they continue, through their own desires, to stumble on the path, I pull my energies back. Wisdom dictates that I don't continue to waste this life-giving energy when there are so many other students that are seeking and waiting to be served. And so it is, my good friends, we all stumble along the path. But when we ask and we receive and we do not accept or demonstrate what we receive, why, the day comes, as man is a law unto himself, that he no longer receives. That's a very simple law and it's easily demonstrable.

Fine, friends, let's go have our refreshments. Thank you all very much.

JUNE 28, 1973

CONSCIOUSNESS CLASS 20 &

Good evening, class. Does anyone have any questions on the discourse that was read this evening *[Discourse 15]*?

I've had a problem with intellect. Intellect has been very dominant in my life, I feel. How does one coordinate intellect, feeling, and will?

The question is, "How does one coordinate intellect, feeling, and will?" That's a very good question. But before going to giving the answer for that particular question, I would like to know—we will get to your answer—I would like to know if there are any other questions concerning that discourse.

Yes, sir. In Discourse 15, he says, "I must not leave until I have spoken a bit on vibration." Also, in the earlier portion of the discourse, it mentions the conscious, the superconscious, and the subconscious minds. What are the minds' relationships to vibration? Because he says we will speak on vibration and then goes on to attachment, which we understand, at least I have, as a property of the magnetic mind.

Thank you. We'll get to that question. I'm looking for a particular question concerning that discourse. I'm sure it will come up.

The discourse says thought is the first cause and feeling is the second. Does that mean that feeling is a cause and not an effect?

Thank you very much. I knew if we waited patiently that the question would come up. As you will recall, students, in one of our classes, about three classes ago, we discussed feeling, the original sense; that feeling preceded thought, if you will recall. Now we notice in Discourse 15 that it states that thought is the first cause and feeling is the second. So I want the class to do some thinking, because I'd like to have you ask yourself why in Discourse 15 it states that thought is the first cause and feeling is the second, when three classes ago, if my memory serves me correctly (perhaps four) feeling is the original sense and thought, the secondary. Now there is not a contradiction in the two statements, but I would like to have you think about it, to see if you can find the reason. What is truly thought and what is truly feeling? Then, we can get to the other questions that were asked this evening. Is feeling the effect of thought or is thought the effect of feeling?

I feel that feeling is still the original sense and thought follows, even though it's put in another way. I feel, therefore I am. I think, therefore I do. But we feel and then thought follows. I mean, somebody or something comes into our consciousness and we feel with it or we don't, and our thought follows that. I think that there is no contradiction in saying that feeling is first. I still think it's first. I think that compassion dictates that the lesson be learned in another way, and that this has been given to us to ponder. But my own feeling at the moment is that feeling comes first and it is the cause for thought, because you could be in a darkened room and not see and have a feeling.

Thank you very much. Some of the other students would like to answer.

I think the two are interchangeable, that there are instances where thought is first and feeling follows and vice versa. But there is no contradiction, because it really is each other.

Thank you. Another student has an expression on that line.

Is it possible that one is thought with unconscious feeling and the other is thought with conscious feeling?

Thank you. Someone else has an expression on that discussion.

I think, so many times, thoughts are not feelings, that a feeling should come first and quite often thoughts just are thoughts. Unless they go with a dynamic feeling, then it's not a true, pure thought.

Thank you. Does someone else have an expression on the discussion?

All of a sudden, it flashed into my mind that picture of that Chinese symbol of the yang and the yin. You can't have one without the other. And where one is at a loss, the other comes in and fills in and where one recedes, the other pushes forward.

Thank you. Students, in reference to the particular statement in the book and the statement made in this class a few weeks ago, feeling in one dimension is thought in another dimension. And so it is that both statements, in truth, are correct. So you give some thought to that. Remember that we're more than one person. So when we have a thought, it was a feeling in another dimension and the thought expresses in the following dimension.

Now before going anymore into our questions—and we have two questions waiting to be answered. We're going to have—I hope you all have notebooks or at least pieces of paper and pencil—we're going to make a choice this evening. Now remember, in this choice that you're going to make, which is very individual, the choice must be spontaneous. And by spontaneous, it does not mean that you stop to think about the choice before making the choice. And this is why I'm not going to tell you about it until we're all ready. Now remember, in making this choice, write down immediately the first thing that enters your mind.

Now this is what we are to choose. Choose a word. Please write it down. A color. Please write it down. A number. Please write it down. Now, under—this should be in three separate columns—under the word that you have chosen, write down all things that enter your mind connecting with that word. Please write it down now. Anything that enters your mind concerning that word. A feeling, a thought, a memory, an experience. These are very personal and you don't necessarily have to tell anyone about them, so please feel free to write down what enters your feelings and your mind. Now under the heading of color, the color you have chosen, kindly write down anything that comes into your mind or your feelings. Please be spontaneous. If nothing appears, write nothing. Under the heading of number, kindly write down anything that comes into your mind as you think of that number. Please be spontaneous. Is everyone finished?

Now under the first heading of word, whatever word you wrote, kindly write *subconscious mind*. Under the number, kindly write *conscious mind*. And under the color, kindly write *spirit* or *superconscious*. Now we have done this, friends, so that you may see for yourselves how the mind (conscious, subconscious, and superconscious) works through the laws of association. Whenever you think of a word, there is a mathematical connection inside your own being with the word of which you think. There is also a spiritual relationship to it. So when you stop and truly think, you find that you've thought of, perhaps, one simple word. Look at all of the different things and experiences that are related with the one simple word that you have written down.

Now these classes have been designed to help us to become aware within ourselves. And, of course, we all know that without spiritual discipline, there is no awareness. One of the first indications of the difficulty of growth is continuity. And it is indeed one of the most difficult things for any individual to accomplish. It is very difficult to train the mind to stick with one thing long enough, until the individual may awaken to themselves.

If anyone in the class would like to share their word-color-number association with the rest of our students, we would be more than happy to hear them at this time.

Well, it was interesting that you said "spirit or superconscious." Under the color, pink, I wrote spirit. *My spontaneous word was* spirit.

Your spontaneous word was *spirit*.

And spirit would be divine love.

What color did you put?

Pink.

Pink, yes.

Divine love. But I wrote spirit *before you said "spirit."*

Is that the first column, where you're supposed to have the word?

That was the color, pink.

The color was pink.

Yes. Yes.

I see. I see. And the word that you chose?

I chose upward.

Upward, yes. You chose the word *upward* and you chose the color pink. What was your number?

Six.

And the number was six. That's a very interesting relationship, as you can see, under the spontaneous reaction. Of course, we all know that six is the number of divine love. We also know that pink is divine love. And we notice that the conscious mind had written the word *upward*. So the association reveals itself. Anyone else care to share?

My subconscious word was serenity. *My color was red and my number was five.*

And your number was five. Well, now we find under your word that you had written *serenity*. We find that the relationship with your understanding, with your subconscious, with serenity is action. And we also find that your number was five, the number of faith. In other words, it is evident that the computer has computed that faith in action is your serenity. You understand, friends, this reveals things unto ourselves, if you stop and you consider it. Anyone else care to share with the class?

The word is join.

The word, the subconscious: *join.*

And the color is red.

The color is red.

And the number was eight.

And the number was eight.

Yes.

Yes. Well, the number, of course, of eight is also the number of double stability and infinite security. Red is the ancient color of action or healing and your subconscious computer released the word *join.* So it is self-evident that to join to your lasting or infinite security is through your own inner action. Obviously, the computer has accepted that as a truth. Do you understand?

Interesting.

Yes. Because, you see, friends, this is how the mind works. And what we're discussing in these classes is the Law of Association. Now another student has some words she would care to share with us.

The word is love. *The color, orange and the number, three.*

Yes. Well, we all know that the number three is the number of manifestation and that orange is the color of creation. And so we find, obviously, from what is revealed, that the love of creation is the individual's computed manifestation. So that, of course, reveals unto oneself that there is a strong love of creation—or God expressed through creation, may be better put—and that is the fullness or manifestation for the particular individual. Now anyone else?

I got love, *blue, and nine.*

Love, blue, and nine. What shade of blue?

A nice, soft blue.

Soft blue. Well, we find, of course, that the number nine is the number of totality. And that one finds their totality through love of the spiritual, which is, of course, the spiritual color. Now, you see, these things are very spontaneous or should be spontaneous. Because if they are spontaneous and they truly come— you see, if in any of these types of things that are given to help you to become aware, if it is not spontaneous, then the guard at the doorway to your subconscious comes up with a different word, you understand. So it is not going to reveal itself.

Well, I just got mark *and silver and nine.*

Mark, silver, and nine. Of course, nine is the number of totality and also of fulfillment. And you had the word *mark*: *m-a-r-k?*

Yes.

And silver is sterling character. Now when you get the word *mark*, is that associated with a personality?

No, I wrote different things down. I don't know why I thought of it, but I thought of The Mark of Zorro, *mark of sorrow, good marks in school, a dream, a mark of excellence.*

And you've got nine. What was your color?

Silver.

Nine and silver. Well, silver, of course, is sterling character. And it is evident that sterling character is very important to your computed mind. In other words, from that revelation, from your own inner being, character should be of great importance to you. Do you understand?

Wasn't that the superconscious, though, the color?

Absolutely, the color is the superconscious. But it is your relationship to mark and to the number of totality. See, it's the individual's relationship between the conscious mind, the subconscious mind, and the superconscious or the spirit. Now is there anyone else who cares to share?

You really got my curiosity up. I got think, red, *and six.*

Think, red, and six. *Think* was your word?

Yes.

And your color was red or the color of action. And your number was six: that's the number of divine love. Well, of course, that reveals that the act of thinking in divine love is of great importance to the particular individual. The relationship, you see, and the importance. For example, if the word is *think* and the color was red, well, that reveals the importance that one has placed upon the act of thought. Now consequently, one could say that the importance of the act of thought is computed to help one to find divine love. You understand? In other words, if the computer has computed that through the process of thinking, which is action, one will find divine love, then that is the path for the individual. Because that is what the individual's conscious, subconscious, and superconscious, through the laws of association, have computed. Anyone else?

Our father, *yellow, and two.*

Our father, yellow . . .

Just father.

Oh, I see. *Father*, yellow, and two. Well, of course, the yellow is the color of divine wisdom, and father is the symbol in the subconscious of God. Two is the duality or creation. That is indicative that the mind is seeking divine wisdom in creation. You understand? In other words, it's seeking to find God through the duality of creation. Anyone else wish to express?

I got freedom, *blue, and three.*

Freedom, blue, and three. Well, now, what color blue did you get?

Kind of a greenish blue.

A greenish blue. And *freedom*, greenish blue, and—what was your number? Three?

Yes.

Yes. Well, that means that mind has computed the way that it is going to find or manifest freedom is through its conscience and its understanding of spirit. In other words, you have found your God in your conscience. Do you understand?

Yes.

Now you might read and study many different things, but you have a very strong conscience in regard to spiritual matters. Anyone else, now, before we go on with the questions that were asked earlier?

All right. Now that little exercise, friends, has simply been given to you to help you to become aware of the minds that are governing your own lives through these laws of association. It's taking place all of the time.

Now we had a question in reference to will and the human intellect and feelings. Is that correct? Yes. Well, you're asking a question in reference to three states of being or three different minds. Number one: We have to deal with the mental body and what is known as the human intellect. Number two: We have to deal with the wellspring that is known as will. And number three: We have to deal with a body that is the feeling being. Now remember, we just got through speaking, earlier, that the feeling precedes the thought, for the feeling in one level of expression is the thought and the action on another dimension or another level. And so you want to know what is the relationship between your will, your intellect, and your feelings. Now by feelings, do you mean your emotions?

Your sense.

Your sense of feeling?

Your sense of feeling.

Yes, all right. Now let us go by example. Say that a person has a feeling, a sense of feeling, and we are now speaking of the clair-sensing, the clear-sensing, the clear feeling of our own spirit, all right? And this feeling comes up and wells up through the dimensions and it touches what is known as the human intellect, all right? Now the human intellect, of course, functions through duality, because it is a computer that accepts the right path, the wrong path; it accepts good, it accepts its so-called opposite. The human intellect is the computer of opposites. Now when a feeling comes from the spirit within ourselves and it touches this computer known as the human intellect, the human intellect, unless it has been trained to accept, you understand—

Is that where you use your will?

Yes, this is where will comes in. Unless the human intellect has been trained to accept the feelings from one's own spirit, what it does, it goes into what is known as dual decision or indecision. In other words, there are two decisions going in opposite directions and that's commonly referred to as indecision. Now the only way that I know of to change the computer, to get it to accept an inner feeling, is through the direct use of the will. And when a person, through concentration, directs the intellect to accept the inner spiritual feelings, without question—because, you see, to question is to doubt and to doubt is to question. Now that's the way the human intellect works. So it must be directed through the will to accept without question the inner feelings of one's own spirit.

What is the will?

What is the will? Do you mean the human will or the divine will? Because there are two types of will. There is the so-called human will, which is the false will that has based its determination upon computed facts in a lifetime. Now many people use that will as the will. That is not their spiritual or divine will.

That's a rebellious part.

That is correct. It is within all of us, you see. Now, for example, when a feeling comes up and you want to do something and your inner being knows, as far as you're concerned, that it's right for you, when it hits the intellect, it's divided. And that's where confusion sets in. This is where will must be exercised over the human intellect to accept, to accept without question. Now once the mind, the human intellect, has been trained to do that, you understand, once it's been trained to do that, there is a fuller expression of the Divine Spirit within us.

There is what?

A fuller expression of the Divine Spirit within us. Because, you see, the spirit and its flow are no longer, you understand, interfered with by what is known as the human intellect and the facts that it has computed over a lifetime. Now remember, friends, that today's facts are tomorrow's fiction. So what stability or security is there in a computer that one day has facts and the next day has it as fiction, only to have something else as facts? You won't find awareness and illumination in a computer that is designed by its very nature to keep changing. Do you understand?

No.

Well, perhaps I can put it another way. Two years ago, you thought a certain way with your human intellect.

Right.

And two years later, you find that you have changed certain facts that are in the human intellect.

That's right.

Now today you can accept some things that the human intellect absolutely refused two years ago. Is that correct?

Yes.

Yes. Now that human intellect that you have is the same basic type of computer that all human beings have. What I'm trying to say is very simple, friends. The moment that you permit the human intellect to govern your ship, your soul, and its destiny, then you're going to continue on the wheel of delusion. And this is why the statement goes, "When of thy mind"—human mind, the human intellect—"thou seekest to know the truth, on the wheel of delusion thou shalt traverse *[Discourse 1]*." Because the human intellect accepts and rejects constantly and it is not where awareness truly expresses itself.

Then, as you develop the sense of feeling, you'll be more alert to this.

The sense of feeling is already there. It is, in truth, not a matter of developing it: it is simply a matter of permitting it to express. It is a matter of stilling the so-called human intellect, which claims to know all the facts of what is right and what's wrong, what's acceptable and what's not acceptable, based entirely upon the experiences that it has had during this particular incarnation. In other words, we cannot expect the human intellect to know of life eternal, when it is not within the human intellect's purpose or within its nature as a computer to know that as a truth. The human intellect, my friends, cannot and does not know truth. The human intellect simply knows facts that are constantly changing, as the human intellect is expanding in its experiences and in its so-called knowledge. The human intellect cannot and does not know truth.

Talking about intellect, does this have any bearing on intellectuality? You mentioned that everyone has a human intellect. Do we come into this universe with a human intellect?

No.

Are most things that people think intellectual just part of their thinking program, something that they have read deeply into or not so deeply into? What is the human intellect?

When the soul enters form at the moment of conception, this brain that is created, this human intellect, is affected by the human intellect and its expression of both the mother and the father and the grandparents. In other words, the soul enters a mold, a part of which is known as the brain or the human intellect. Now the soul has merited that particular mold and that particular brain. Consequently, we find that some people have a stronger tendency toward intellectualizing things than other people. We find that some people are able to accept by an inner feeling, just an inner feeling that they have, different things without a constant questioning process.

Now it does not mean that the human intellect, which is designed to question, which is designed to store up information, which is designed to doubt—because by being designed to question, it's designed to do the opposite, you understand, and to doubt. Now that does not mean that we do not use the human intellect, because we all do, to some extent. But it does mean that in finding truth and spiritual awareness that we use the spirit. For it is the spirit, you understand, that is the awareness: it is not the mind. Now you can go on and on and on and on and on with the human intellect and the moment you try to mix the human intellect into spiritual awareness, you're going to find, sooner or later, that you have problems. Because, you see, the human intellect is going to accept one thing as truth one moment, only to reject it in the next moment. Because it cannot and is not designed to express truth. It is designed, my friends, to express facts. But facts are not truth.

That brings up a question. I have a sister and you brought up the point that the human intellect comes into the mold through the parents, the grandparents, and the lineage before. One child goes into spiritual thinking and the other child—I'm not saying my sister—goes into completely the opposite direction or they may have spiritual thinking, too, but they don't search. If this has to do with the parents, the grandparents, and what we have inherited or merited, how does that hold true?

Both are using the human intellect. The human intellect guides one into an inner search and spirituality. The human intellect also guides another into total materialism. But the human intellect is the vehicle which has guided them. Don't you see? And the human intellect is what has sent them on their journey into a multitude of experiences. But each soul is different. Now you can take two people and you can send them through college and they can both have a very high IQ. One may use that IQ and seek spiritual awakening, while the other may seek dire materialism. This has to do with the soul's merit system and what it has brought with it, you understand.

That's what I thought.

Yes. Absolutely and positively. And remember, friends, the more attention, which is the more energy, we give to the mind, the less we have to give to our spirit. Now I'm not saying that we should just open our mouths and be credulous and just accept things. We should learn to feel them. And when we feel them with our spirit, then we will know them.

Is that why it is better not to try to analyze spirituality or truth, but rather to make an acceptance? To start with acceptance instead of trying to piecemeal everything down or analyze it all out?

Well, the thing is that the mind is designed to serve the purpose of the mental world. And the spirit is designed to serve the
purpose of the spiritual world. And so when we mix the two, we
sometimes, ofttimes, get a hodgepodge, you see. It takes a mind
to know the mind; it takes a spirit to know the spirit. So if it is
the spirit that we are seeking, and I am sure that is what we
are all seeking, then let us place our attention upon that spirit,
that it may express itself and that we may have that feeling now.
Naturally, in our searching, we use the vehicle with which we
are most familiar. And obviously, most of us are most familiar
with the mental body, because we have not spent the time to
become familiar with the spirit and with the soul body and the
spiritual body. But as we spend more time and more attention,
which is more energy, on the spiritual, then we will be in a position to use the spiritual to guide our ship. Does that help with
your question?

Thank you.

*It just came to my mind, during your explanation, that we
call Spiritualism a science, a philosophy, and a religion. So the
science satisfies the intellectual seeking, whereas the feelings sat-
isfy the philosophical and the religious aspects.*

I would definitely say so. The science, for my understanding
and to my understanding, the science of Spiritualism serves a purpose in getting beyond the barrier of the mental. It serves that
purpose. But we must, of ourselves, go into those inner feelings.

*I don't want to belabor the point, but you mentioned a couple
of weeks ago that intelligence is a soul faculty.*

Intelligence is a soul faculty, but intelligence of a soul faculty is not the human intellect.

*It's an expression of the human intellect, I mean, of the intel-
ligence.*

It is an expression of the intelligence—it is some expression
of the intelligence, yes, limited, of course, by the intellect itself.

So the opening of the faculty of intelligence would not have any measurable influence on one's IQ?

Absolutely and positively not. Some of the greatest intelligent communication has come through people whose IQs are barely average.

May I ask a question about mental retardation? This is a condition, I assume, that someone merits. How long must it necessarily be with them? Can there be any reversal of that during this particular incarnation? Certainly somewhere along the way . . .

Oh, absolutely and positively. Now, by your statement, we do not mean to understand, however, that so-called mental retardation would stay with a person throughout this entire incarnation. Sometimes it does and sometimes it does not. That, of course, is entirely dependent upon the soul's merit in its evolutionary processes. Now in the world of spirit, I'm sure that you all realize that the mental retardation is an effect and not a cause; that the soul merited that particular type of limitation in this particular incarnation. But remember, friends, we've all merited some kind of limitation. After all, we have to have airplanes to fly, when we really shouldn't have to have them, you understand.

I'm sort of confused as to the difference between mind and brain.

Brain is the vehicle through which mind expresses itself. Now the brain goes back to the elements of nature; that's where it was composed. But we do take with us, of course, what is known as the mental body. The brain is simply the vehicle through which it expresses in a physical dimension.

I noticed you used them as though they were one and it confused me.

No. It is simply the vehicle through which the mind expresses itself. There is a mental body that's expressing itself through what is known, here, as the brain.

The mentally retarded have merited that condition in this incarnation.

All souls have merited their conditions.

Right. Through supplication on a spiritual level, may one intercede to perhaps alleviate that condition during this time?

If the soul has merited that relief. This is why, my dear friends, that some souls are very receptive to healing and some are not. This is according to what has been set into motion by the particular individualized soul.

If the intellect is not necessary to express spirituality, then would not someone mentally retarded have an advantage, rather than a limitation?

I did not mean to imply that the human intellect is not necessary to express spirituality. I don't believe that I made that statement. However, if I did, it was strictly in error. For while we are expressing here in this physical world and expressing through a brain, a physical being, then the human intellect, in order to communicate in this particular dimension, is necessary for expression. Now that expression—of course, all expression is an expression of our spirit. Some of it, you understand, is more—or let us say, some may feel that this is a good expression and that is an opposite expression, you understand. But all expression is the effect of the Divine Spirit, you see.

Now in reference to, seeming, what we call retardation, why do we call a person mentally retarded? We call a person mentally retarded because society has established certain rules and regulations and what they call the norm. Consequently, anyone that doesn't fit into what society, in any particular area, has dictated is normal, then they're abnormal. Now, to my knowledge, there is no divine dictate that says that a person who acts this way is normal and a person who acts that way is abnormal. This is what the mind or the human intellect dictates. It is not what the spirit dictates, to my understanding.

A week ago in Discourse 14, we read, "There is great truth in the statement that only through service will we find illumination." We've heard this for millions of years, I think. And another student brought up analyzing. Are we not analyzing the spiritual side of life? I mean, isn't there some merit to analyzing? So that we can get to a point where we can serve?

As long as a person needs to exercise the mental body and term that *analysis*, as long as that is needed for the individual, then analysis will continue. Now when awareness truly dawns in one's being, there is no longer need to analyze, because there is a true awakening. Now if we feel, you understand—if we think that we have reached that true awakening, by the very process of entertaining that in the human intellect or the mind, we lose the awareness. Do you understand? Because we have taken the spiritual and tried to get it into the human computer, the human intellect, where duality exists. The moment you express truth, you hear me, the moment the human intellect, which is causing my lips to move and a sound to come out, the moment that happens, you have the possibility of its opposite. The moment you speak a sentence, you have the potentiality and the possibility of speaking truth and falsehood at the same time, don't you understand? Because you are using the duality or creation to express. Does that help with your question?

Yes, it does. Thank you.

I don't want to feel as though I have just awakened to the final truth, but it dawned on me, while you were saying that, that we neither reject the analyzing side nor do we reject the other, but we must learn to just balance this on this very fine pinpoint, where they both serve, but neither dominates.

Absolutely and positively. And when we reach that balance— you see, what happens, it's just like—I know that many people interested in Spiritualism are interested in its science and its communication. Well, the moment that a person in their unfolding, the moment that they start to question the spiritual experience, if it is a spiritual experience, the moment they start to question it, they put it into the human intellect, into duality. Now this is simply what really happens in unfoldment. So they see a little light over there in the atmosphere. All right, the old human intellect gets hold of it and says, "Let's see, did I really see that light? Or did I trigger something inside of my head and cause myself to be under a type of self-hypnotic trance? Or was that a desire that I have suppressed and all of a sudden I saw that? And was I truly receptive to a spiritual dimension or is that something that someone sent me by thought transmission?" And the old mind goes on and on and on and on and on and on. And in the process, the true spiritual light is right in front of us and we can't possibly see it because we are so busy with the thoughts in the human intellect, that are whirling, that we can't see, because we have blinded ourselves to the spiritual dimension by overdirecting energy into the mental dimension.

Now the first thing that usually happens in unfoldment—one of those many things—is the person does have a little experience. Well, after they've had it, they need some encouragement and some support that they really did have that experience. Now why do we need that support, if we still need it? Well, it's very simple. The experience is new to us and the ego, the brain inside, says, "Well, I don't want to be deluded. I don't want to make a fool out of myself." Well, of course, when that happens, you've lost the spiritual. See? Instead of just going ahead, silently having your spiritual experiences, being grateful for the spiritual experiences that you have and not have the need to tell the whole universe because you don't need everybody's encouragement and support: you've got God's. And if you have God's, you and God become a majority. So what do you need everybody else's for?

You see, friends, it isn't our soul, it isn't our spirit, that needs anyone or anything to tell us how great we are and how much we're unfolding and how illumined we're becoming. You see, our soul doesn't need that; it has no need for that. Our spirit doesn't need it, because it already knows, you understand. It's our intellect that needs that, because it's our intellect that keeps doubting. You see, the reason that the intellect doubts is because, you see, the intellect questions and the intellect doubts. And as long as you keep your spiritual unfoldment in the dimension of the human intellect, you are going to keep going on with those kinds of experiences. And then life really isn't worth it. When it's so simple to sit back and say, "Well, this is the time for my spiritual experiences. I'll go ahead and have the experience of my spirit. It's wonderful and it's just beautiful. Fine, I won't open my big mouth to tell half of the world, because I don't need all their doubts and all their questions. Because if I get into that, then I'm not going to have this experience anymore, because my intellect is going to get triggered. And whenever I get any experience, I'm going to start all this questioning and all this doubting myself."

My friends, it's so simple, truly, just to learn to accept that people have different experiences and it is their divine right to do so. You don't need everybody to tell you how great you are. You don't even need them to tell you how wrong you are. I have plenty of that. But anyway, it serves its purpose. Don't you see, if it is truly spiritual, you do not need the human intellect blown up like a balloon so someone else can come along in the next minute and go *pop!* and it's totally deflated. Because then one moment you're encouraged and the next moment you're discouraged, because you don't let the Divine do its infinite, intelligent work. See? So in your unfoldment and on your particular paths, whatever they may be, remember this: it is your path. Be grateful it is your path and don't expect to find anybody else that has an identically same path. And if you will look at it that way and you will be grateful for what you already have, in that gratitude, you will even see more. Now we have time for a few more questions.

There was a question, however, concerning vibrations. Well, there has been much discussion about what vibrations really are, but perhaps this may help you. There is one of the minds in men that may be likened unto a tuning fork. And when that tuning fork is vibrating, there is an experience within the being, according to the vibration of this mind or this tuning fork. Now what one must realize is this: that that particular mind is known as the reactor. And it is the mind that most of us are using all of the time. We are reacting to stimuli from within and from without. And we are constantly doing this, seven days a week, twenty-four hours a day. That mind, known as the reactor, is the one that must be stilled before we can awaken to our own spirit. Now that reactor mind is not the conscious mind. It is not the human intellect. It isn't even the subconscious mind. But it is one of the minds that is within man: it is the reactor and it is also the mind known as vibration.

How many minds do we have?

Nine. Are there any other questions?

If there are nine minds, does each mind have its own kind of sight?

If you mean by "sight," that it is designed to serve a particular function or purpose, in that sense, yes.

Is the reactor mind a part of the vital body?

The reactor mind is the vital mind or the vital body.

Could the reactor mind be the ego?

No, the reactor mind is not the ego. No. It is the vital mind or the vital body. It also, of course, as all of us know, affects our health.

Is the brain, then, the vehicle for all these minds?

The brain is the vehicle for three of them.

The vital body is the one that the Russians have made their studies on, that can go out for nine minutes and be revitalized. Is this an automatic process or is it one that one could somehow train or teach to go out during the day?

It is an automatic process in the sense that without the rejuvenation of the vital body in the particular plane on which it enters, one would not long be in the physical body. It can, through certain processes, be trained, yes. Now we are not speaking of the astral body. We are not speaking of the spiritual body. We are not speaking of the soul body. We are speaking of the vital body, which is the vibrational body.

Is this the body that some healers bring up and work on?

Most healers work on bodies that are not the vital body, but there are some healers that do work on the vital body, although most are not aware of it. Yes. You see, my good friends, you must become aware of the body within before you become aware of the body without. And that takes a little effort and it takes a little time.

You mentioned that we have nine minds and nine bodies, is that correct?

That is correct.

I presume these bodies are related?

Yes, they are related.

If the superconscious is the odic, and the subconscious is the magnetic, and the conscious is the electric, what is the vital?

The vital body? Odic.

It's odic.

That is correct.

What are the nine minds?

They will be given according to the laws of what can be borne.

Is the vital body, then, the neutral? If it isn't magnetic or electric, then it's odic. The odic is neutral, is it not?

Yes.

Well, the vital body would be the . . .

Reactors are very neutral.

Well, that answers a lot. Thank you. In all my teachings and in all my class work, I have never heard of this. It's really quite a revelation and it's mind-staggering.

That that staggers the mind has the potentiality and the possibility, you understand, by staggering the mind to awaken the spirit.

This odic force or odic power is neutral and God is neutral. So this would be the spiritual body really, wouldn't it?

Is God an actor or a reactor?

Both.

Is it the sustaining power?

Yes, I would think it is.

Is creation the creator or is creation the created?

Created.

Then it's an effect.

Creation is an effect.

Then it's a reactor to an actor, isn't it?

Yes.

Friends, I see our time is past. Let's go have refreshments. Thank you very much.

JULY 5, 1973

CONSCIOUSNESS CLASS 21 ✎

Good evening, class. Before going into the reading of the discourses this evening, I should like to take a few moments in speaking to the class and on the studies that you have already received. Now I am aware that there appears to be, sometimes, a repetition of the same lesson. But we must consider, friends, that if a lesson is not perceived one way, then it must be given another way. Because until the lessons that we have to learn in life are perceived, they will continue to repeat themselves over and over and over again.

Now repetition serves a good purpose in that, sooner or later, when one is experiencing repetition of the same thought patterns or experiences, several things take place in the mental body. One of those things that takes place is a discouragement in the repetition of the lesson. And usually the first thing that happens to the mind is to continue to put the cause, of course, for it outside of ourselves. Now sooner or later, as the lessons continue to be repeated, we start to think of other causes that could be set into motion. And the day arrives, in time, with this repetition, that we awaken to the fact that it is an expression from within our own being. And that is when we are ready to make whatever necessary changes there are to change the habit patterns of thought inside of ourselves. Now we all know that we are controlled by certain attitudes. We are aware of that fact because that fact is a demonstrable one. And so it is that we seek to rise to other levels or states of consciousness, because we feel this discouragement and, ofttimes, disgust with the levels that we have been entertaining for so long.

Now a wise man once said that he who has patience may will what he wants. And so it is that wisdom lives in patience. The sadness of that particular statement is that very few of us are willing to exercise or to demonstrate the necessary patience to attain what we desire to attain. The length of time to any attainment that we are seeking is ever dependent upon the obstructions on the path that we have created to that particular attainment. Now if we have sought for thirty or forty years, or even five or ten years, for a particular fulfillment of any desire or any attainment and we have not yet received it, then what happens to us? We begin to accept what is known as defeat. We begin to say to ourselves that it is obviously not in the divine plan or divine order for me. That is not the wisest way of the fulfillment of one's attainment or of their desire. Because when we state that it evidently is not in order for me, what we are, in truth, doing, we are setting another law into motion.

Now there's a vast difference between that type of thinking and the type of thinking that releases it to the Divine Intelligence. Now when we want something and we release it to a divine plan, a divine order, and in divine time, we are not stating that it is not in order for us. We are simply removing the thought from the limitation of the mind and releasing it to a universal intelligence, so that it may be brought into our life as we rise to the state of consciousness where we can be receptive to it.

Now I know that we are all seeking to be more positive in our thinking. The great obstruction to being positive in our thoughts and in our attitudes is our unwillingness to express patience, which is a soul faculty. "All things come to he who is patient" is again and again demonstrated by many people throughout the world. But why is it that we have difficulty in expressing patience? Well, it's really quite simple. To express the soul faculty of patience is to remove the ego from its crown. And consequently, that is the difficulty in expressing patience. It is not the soul that doesn't have patience, because the soul faculty is patience, but it is the self, the house of the senses, that does not have patience. Because, you see, my friends, the house of the senses, known as the ego, does not have wisdom and wisdom lives in patience. So don't try to find patience in the house of the senses: it doesn't exist there. And if you feel that you have waited a lifetime for this or you have waited a lifetime for that, it simply means that you have kept the thought in the house of the senses and have not released it, in truth, to the Divine Intelligence, that it may come to you through your own soul faculties.

[Discourses 13 and 14 are read aloud by students.]

Now we'll go on with our questions this evening. If you will just be so kind as to raise your hands, I'll be happy to answer them to the best of my ability.

Yes, on page 40 of The Living Light, *the first paragraph* [Discourse 13], *I am somewhat confused as to what is meant by "invisible powers."*

Yes, in reference to page 40, in speaking of these invisible influences, they mean to say by "invisible," these influences that most people are not aware of, because they are not consciously aware of the things that are influencing them. And these influences are guiding our ship, our life. There are very few people in the world today that are aware of the patterns of mind. They are invisible to their sight because they have not made the effort to see them. That is what is referred to in that particular paragraph.

Knowing the Wise Man's feelings about the usage of words and his carefulness in using certain words, could I possibly have a discussion as to the meaning of subjective *and* objective?

Yes—

Also, can one be objective about one's subjectivity?

That's a very good question in reference to whether or not one can be objective about one's subjectivity. Now man is a triune being. And the only way of viewing and being truly objective is for man to become neutral in the sense of this neutrality of mind. This attitude rises our consciousness to the point of the superconscious, where we are able to see not only the subjective within our form, but also the objective within our form. This is what is referred to in reference to the electric, the magnetic, and the odic. And so it is that if man chooses to be objective and to see his objectivity, then man must awaken and express through the soul faculty which is known as reason.

Now reason will not only see the objective, but reason will see the subjective. For example, we cannot be objective and we cannot truly be subjective as long as our soul consciousness is expressing through either level, the objective or the subjective. We must, through a disassociation process—in other words, by disassociation we are moving our consciousness from the personal to the principle. We become more universal in our thought. Now as long as we have the person or personality consciousness, then we cannot truly be objective and we cannot truly be subjective. Do you understand? We must first consider the ways that are provided by the Divine Intelligence to become universal. We have to rise to a state of consciousness which is the universal consciousness. And when we rise to the universal consciousness, which takes us through what is known as the avenue of the superconscious, then we can truly be objective and we can truly be subjective. Does that help with your question?

It does somewhat. All my life I've always felt that subjective is here and objective is there. I didn't realize that you could be both.

Subjective and *objective* is the same as *action* and *reaction*. The moment something is objective, it becomes subjective and the moment that something is subjective, it becomes objective. It is the same Law of Creation that deals with action and reaction, positive and negative, etc. and etc. It has to do with one's state of consciousness. For example, in the process of expressing through what one calls an objective attitude of mind, in the very process, one is subjective—and vice versa. This is why we cannot find truth until we rise out of the duality of creation. We must rise above action and reaction in order to see truly what the law really is. We have to become inaction. We must always rise to the principle, to the point of the triangle in order to see its base clearly.

In other words, we must first be introspective before, let's see, how does that work—to be subjective is to be introspective, right?

That's what it means to many people.

But that's not the true meaning of it?

There is more than one meaning to the word *subjective*. But we must deal with what it means to the student who is asking the question.

I see.

Yes. And as long as it means that to you, then we will answer accordingly.

I'm having a great deal of difficulty trying to perceive the two.

Perhaps it is because you are—perhaps—still expressing on the base of the triangle, which is the duality law. And the duality, the Law of Creation or Duality, can cause a confusion if one does not pause in the duality and rise out of the Law of Creation to the point of principle where they can see clearly.

Now ofttimes it has been said before that "The letter of the law killeth, but the spirit of the law giveth life." The spirit of the law is the level of awareness, which is the true cause of the expression. As long as we study the expression, we cannot, in truth, find the real cause. As long as our minds are on the level of the effects and how it works, we cannot find the principle behind the "how it works." How it works, my friends, is an effect: it is not a cause. The conscious mind says, "If I learn how it works, then I have found the cause or the principle of it." That is not true, my dear students. When you find out how something works, you have an understanding, you hear, of the principle in expression. But you do not have an understanding of the principle itself. And so, I am sure, if you rise out of the Law of Duality that you will be able to find what is meaningful to you, between the objective and the subjective within yourself. Because they are, in truth, one and the same.

Is it true that if one does not have discipline, that they will lose sight of principle?

Without discipline, there is no principle.

I am very pleased that you touched on the ego in your discussion earlier. I wondered, even though you have talked about the ego in the past, if you could give us a more in-depth explanation for this drive for expression, why we have it, the path that it follows, and some of the emotions that it affects.

The nature of the Divine Spark, known as Infinite Intelligence or God, is an expansion principle. The Divinity, in its expression, expands. And in its expansion, it multiplies. And in its multiplication, it divides—or vice versa. And so this Divine Spirit or Principle that expresses through form is the drive itself: that *is* the drive. Now in the words of today, we would not call God ego. We wouldn't call the Infinite Intelligence ego. But we would understand this drive that is in all form. It is the Power itself that is driving and expanding itself in its expression.

Now in the human form, unless this drive or this energy is brought into some type of a balance in its expression, the first thing that happens is an awareness within the self, which is known as self-preservation: it's the first step in this expression. And unless this is brought under the soul faculties of reason, what happens is that the drive itself, being narrowed to one particular area of self-related experiences, expands out of proportion what is called the ego. Now when that happens, the mind entertains the thought that it is It. It no longer is capable of seeing that it is merely the vehicle of the expression of this Divine Power or Intelligence. And when that happens, we have an imbalance in the mental body. Consequently, we find ourselves in a great many different problems. Now it is just as dangerous and detrimental to annihilate the ego, or attempt to annihilate it, as it is to overexpand it. There has to be a balance.

Now, as we have spoken before, that all forms of life have a need to experience this energy or this Divine Intelligence, this Power, itself. There is that need within all forms in creation. Now unless we use some wisdom in the direction of this energy—if we narrow, through our own thinking, its expression—what happens to us, there is a greater demand by our mind for the experience of this energy. Say, for example, a man has perhaps five areas in which he feels fulfilled in life in expressing this intelligent energy. And unless he is able to fully express through those narrow five paths, there is a feeling in the emotional body of an unfulfillment. Consequently, the first thing that a person considers in spiritual unfoldment is broadening their horizons.

Now by "broadening the horizons," we mean to say, to entertain in thought the possibilities of experiencing this energy in more areas than the narrow, limited ones that we have set into motion. For example, some people can have this experience of joy or energy by going to the mountains. Some people may experience it by watching certain shows on television. Some people may experience it by going to a baseball game.

But you see, we have narrowed the expression of the Divine Intelligence to such a point that what is known as our ego, what it is truly doing, is demanding more and more attention, for energy follows attention. And so it is when you find people that seem to be expressing a great ego expression, that is a very sad situation, because it simply means that they are not experiencing God's divine joy, because they have limited, within their own thinking, the expression through which they will permit God to experience this joy, which is inside of ourselves. And that is where we have people who demand that this be done and demand that that be done and demand that each individual or each thing work according to whatever this computer has accepted. Because, you see, if that is the problem that we have, it is an ego problem: it's an imbalance. The proper wording is a *mental imbalance problem*, because that's truly what it is. And if the person has accepted that this is the way this should be done and that is the way that should be done and that is the way that should be done, what they experience, when everything is done according to what they have accepted in mind, they experience this joy. They experience God's love: this is what is truly taking place.

Now, they can experience, anyone can experience this divine love by broadening their horizon, don't you see? And then they will not have to demand that people act in a certain way at a certain time according to what their computer has programmed in their own subconscious. And so, my friends, if you would just make the daily effort to experience God's love in a broader way—our horizons are so narrowed and so limited by what we have programmed them to be that it seems the race is filled with a mental imbalance from the inability to express this divine love of God. Does that help with your question?

That's excellent. Thank you.

You're more than welcome.

It's very interesting about this broadening of horizons. When I call the office, I hear this and that—and right away a horizon is limitation to me. No matter where I go, as long as I can see a horizon. I'm wondering whether my thinking on that is in limitation—

When man, expressing through form, is no longer able to see a horizon or see the form through which he is expressing, then man will no longer be in form. Therefore, in the teaching we are trying to get them to broaden the narrow limits of their horizon, but not to miss the horizon. Because if we no longer view the horizon, my dear friends, we no longer have a goal. And when we no longer have a goal, we no longer have an expression of God's love to carry us on.

I have one more question, a basic, simple question. What is meant by the Living Light?

Yes. The question is asked, "What is meant by the Living Light?" The Light is the Divine Intelligence. And we accept that the Divine Infinite Intelligence is a living, demonstrable principle in all universes and in all places. And that is the true meaning of the Living Light. You see, if Light is Light, then it is the Divine. And if it is the Divine, then it is living. Does that help with your question?

Very much. Thank you.

You're more than welcome. Someone else have a question now?

I'm still working on the subconscious, but I have a couple of questions I'd like to ask. Do the same opportunities exist to converse with the superconscious that exist for conversations between the conscious and the subconscious?

Yes, the same opportunities exist, in reference to that question. Absolutely.

And can this be reached through meditation?

It is reached through meditation, which is a method by which a person may bring their conscious and subconscious minds into balance or harmony. When the base of the triangle is balanced, it sees its true home, which, in this particular discussion, would be the superconscious.

Is there any way to distinguish between telepathic communication and thoughts originating in the subconscious itself, because, certainly, this must be a source of much inaccuracy among psychics and mediums?

Indeed, it is a source of a great deal of discomfort and problems in communication. And the only way I know that a person may become aware of what thoughts are originating in the depths of the subconscious—now remember, friends, this is a very delicate thing that we are discussing, for the subconscious has many different levels of awareness. You have the subconscious area of the brain in which you have all the experiences recorded in your present soul incarnation. Then, you have the other division of the subconscious, in which you are a part of the whole subconsciousness of the race. Then, you have a part which is known as the solar consciousness. Then, you have a part which is known as the universal consciousness, etc., etc., etc. So the thing is for man to first become aware of the subconscious that is the part of the computer that is his particular, you understand, record of experiences since his soul's incarnation in form. And once becoming aware of that, then you can become aware of the other areas of the mind that are in the so-called subconscious.

Yes. Now there's an old saying that "There is nothing new under the sun" and, of course, that is very true. There is nothing new under the sun and "under the sun," what that means to say, in our understanding, is under the Light itself. There is nothing new to the Divine Intelligence, to the Infinite Intelligence; otherwise, the Infinite Intelligence would not be infinite and intelligent, you see. There is nothing new to God, to the Divine.

Is it our astral or is it our mental body that goes out on flights? And how is conscious awareness of these excursions affected?

Yes. The lady is asking the question, Is it our astral body or is it our mental body that takes flight or goes out on flights and has experiences? My friends, it is both. It is both. And how is an awareness of this accomplished? Well, it's very simple: when man, through daily concentration and meditation, through the sincere effort to find the kingdom of God within, when he finds the kingdom, he will find the kingdom's many mansions. And the many mansions, you understand, are the bodies through which the soul is expressing itself. And as the Bible stated, "In my Father's house are many mansions." This is why, my friends, you first seek the kingdom. Then you can move to find the different mansions which are in the kingdom. And so it is, through a daily effort, that man sincerely seeks to find what he calls God or the kingdom or the spirit within and stops seeking the individual mansions that are in the kingdom. Then, he will know through which body he is expressing at any given moment. Then, he will have conscious awareness of the so-called astral or mental flights. And he will even have awareness of soul flights, if he has a soul body in which to take a soul flight.

Now I have heard many times people say, "Well, last night, I had a wonderful soul flight and I went to the highest realms in the world of spirit." And I don't know how they got there. Because, you know, it's like an automobile, you see: if you want to physically move the body, you've got to have transportation to get it there. So if you want to go to New York with your physical body, you've got to move the physical body. Now if you want to go to a soul realm, well, you've got to have a soul body in which to get to a soul realm. Fortunately or unfortunately, not all of us have that completed yet. You understand. Does that help with your question?

Yes, it does.

Someone else had a question.

In keeping with an earlier question, regarding the various lev-els of the subconscious, can the so-called memory par excellence be likened to the divine subconscious, if there is such a thing?

Well, it could be likened unto, with this memory par excellence, it could be likened unto—remember, friends, I could not say that it is a divine subconscious in that sense, because the memory par excellence is a soul faculty. Remember, it is an individualized soul faculty. It is not a universal soul faculty. It is not the cosmos itself. It is the experiences that the individualized soul has experienced in its incarnations. And therefore, it could not be likened unto the Infinite Intelligence. No. No, it couldn't. But it could well be likened unto all of the experiences in all of the bodies and incarnations that the soul has gone through. That is the memory par excellence of which we are referring to.

Then, the individualized expression would be necessary for the manifestation of the memory par excellence?

Yes. Because you must realize, students, that the expansion of principle is at the cost, you understand, of the contraction of personality, and vice versa. The more that the soul expresses through personality, that contracts its expression through principle, because that is the law of the duality of creation or form. And so if we in our consciousness express more through principle, there's an expansion in that area; there is a positive and a definite contraction through the level of what is known as personality. And so it is in the spiritual unfoldment, the first thing that we teach is an education of the ego, which is a refinement and a contraction of its expression in order that the principle may expand and we can find the Divine Light of the spirit. Does that help with your question?

Is that the true meaning of giving?

That is the true meaning of giving. Giving is a returning to the Divinity, which is all one and one is all. And it is also the path to illumination, because it is through service that we become illumined. Because through service, my dear friends, the energy is released, you understand, more into the level of principle and less into the level of personality.

Keeping in mind the same train of thought, I was wondering why we must have expression through the form. Or why form? If, at one period of our evolution, male and female were as one, why was there form then?

Yes, there is form. In reference to Why does the Divine Intelligence require—if, indeed, it does require—form in order to express itself? In my understanding it is quite simple. Without form, my friends, there is no awareness. You see, it's like the atom. When you split the atom, there is an expression of what is known as power. And so it is when the formless enters form, there is what is known as awareness. You see, the awareness, my dear friends, comes through the Law of Creation, which is the Law of Duality. If you have nothing relative, then you have no awareness, because the awareness that you have, you are not aware that you have; and therefore you do not have it, because you cannot have that which you are not aware of. And so it is, it is through the creative principle of form itself and its duality that you have relativity. I mean, what can you be relative to if you are formless, whole and complete, and free, and you have nothing to be relative to? You have no awareness. And this is why we have awareness.

If, at one period, when we were as one, male and female in one body as one—

Yes. Yes, in the evolutionary process, that is the evolution.

Relative to this discussion, did they need form for this expression?

Yes, there was form. Yes. Yes. Whenever you have expression, friends, you have form. When you have no form, you have no expression. And when you have no expression, you have no awareness. There is no awareness without expression.

Well, then, the spoken word would be expression of form.

Indeed, it is. Every time you speak a word, a form takes place in the atmosphere. When the eyes are opened, you will see the forms of the words that you express. For example, he says here in this book [*The Living Light*], think thoughts of beauty and express words of beauty, because then beautiful things will take place, if your mind, your soul, and your heart are in harmony with the expression.

Now when I go over to spirit—many years from now, I hope—and I have a little more service—

My friends, remember, we are in spirit as much as we have opened the soul faculties—

No, when I trans—when I—

When you leave the physical body. Yes.

And all these forms, beautiful and otherwise, are there. How does one grow through these forms?

When there is no longer a need of the mental body for the experience, then they will no longer be with us. The forms, the children that we have created, stay with us as long as we remain their parents, as long as we have the need or the attachment to them. Now we can't say that, for example, we have created certain forms and then we decide when we get on the other side, "Oh, that's a horrible form. I no longer need that." It doesn't work that way. It works through laws that we have established through our own expression. Now, if we have a need inside of ourselves, for example, to experience God's love through attention and we have channeled that to a certain way, and that creates a certain form in the atmosphere, and we are not aware of that form until we leave the physical body and we find it's a form that is distasteful to us, for example, we don't just say, "I no longer need that," because that is not the way we make changes. Now if it were possible to do that, if it were possible to have that type of a magic wand, don't you see, all of us would be freed of all of our problems and of all of our disturbances this very instant. But there is no way that I have found that that is possible.

Growth is not a fast thing. It is a slow, gradual step up the eternal ladder of progression. The patterns that have been established by us are not outgrown overnight. Of course, the less we entertain them, you understand, then the less we need them. And the less we need them, the less we experience them. But that is a slow, gradual process. Slow steps are the only healthy steps and the only sure, sound steps for anyone to make.

Do all spirits who make the transition, who just go over, who had no understanding of this at all, do they see these forms?

Yes, they most certainly do. They do experience all of their children, their family, and their creations. It doesn't matter whether or not they had this understanding or they didn't. The laws are totally impartial and they do experience them and they do, in time, outgrow them, by no longer feeding them. By "feeding," I mean having the need of expressing the energy through that particular thought level. Yes.

I'm not sure I understand what it means to be of service: to be of service to God or to be of service on a human level, to become more selfless, or is it a combination of all?

When man chooses to serve what we call God, in the very process of that expression, he does become less self-conscious, less self-oriented. And when that takes place, then there is not only a broadening of one's horizon, but there is a great joy that takes place in experience within the depths of one's own soul. Yes.

Here in Discourse 13, it says, "The time has come when it is the greater goal that you must perceive for otherwise progression shall cleanse the path." Would you please explain what is meant by "progression shall cleanse the path"?

Yes. In reference to the statement in *The Living Light*, It is time that you perceive the greater goal or progression shall cleanse the path: now a person starting on the spiritual pathway, many things take place in their life. They are seeking something different than what they are used to experiencing. And by the very Law of Seeking, they set other laws into motion. And when that happens, they step on the path of progression. And when one steps on the path of spiritual progression, certain habit patterns, certain levels of awareness, they are, in the process, cleansed from the person's universe. Now sometimes a person is consciously aware of their goal, you understand, and they consciously make choices of, for example, no longer expressing a certain level of awareness. Certain patterns no longer entertain their thought because their goal is ever in front of them. Don't you see? However, there are those who are seeking a better way. And in the Law of Seeking, progression—the Law of Progression—will cleanse their path. Now, for example, they have not consciously decided, "Well, I'm no longer going to express through that level, that level, that level, and that level." Progression herself will automatically remove those levels. Does that help with your question?

Yes. Thank you.

I should like to know why, in certain individuals, conscience is strong or manifests itself overtly?

Do you mean "conscience" or "conscious"?

Conscience.

Conscience, yes.

And in others it seems to be lacking.

Yes, that's most understandable. And I'll be happy to share with you my understanding of that. It appears, you understand, that some of us feel that some people have a very awakened, so to speak, conscience. Others, it seems, have no conscience at all. That is your question, isn't it? The only way that we are going to be able to see the conscience of another is to become the person in question. Many people have a very awakened conscience, but it does not express itself in what we understand to be a conscience. For example, many of us express our conscience in society, that this is the right thing to do and that is the wrong thing to do; that it is not right to expect for another what one does not expect for oneself. Now we could call that a conscience. Would you not agree?

Yes.

Yes. Perhaps we could say the Golden Rule, that is a conscience. Well, now, my good friends, we must consider going a little deeper than that. We must consider that if we want to find the conscience of another, we must become their thoughts and we must become their very being. Then, we will be able to find that conscience. Perhaps it does not express in the ways that we feel are an expression of conscience. Perhaps it is expressing during their sleep and in their dreams. Perhaps it is expressing in the quiet moments of their own thoughts, but they are not programmed to express what we call conscience in the way that we have become programmed to express conscience. Now everyone has a conscience, because a conscience is that spiritual sensibility that lies within the soul, but it expresses in a multitude of different ways. We can look into the world at some politicians and say, "Well, they have no conscience at all." They may have one of the greatest consciences that man will ever know. It just is not being expressed in the way that we understand conscience to express itself. Does that help with your question?

Thank you very much.

I wanted to ask you, what is the moral responsibility of the individual that we say every Sunday from our Declaration of Principles?

The moral responsibility of all individuals is known by the individuals. And in this Association and under the understandings of the Living Light, it is not within the providence of those associated with Serenity to know what is a proper moral standard for any individual. Moral standards are a very individual expression of one's own soul and if we decide what is morally just for one, then what we have, in truth, done is expressed our level of awareness, which may or may not be right.

Now, in the teachings of the Living Light, we teach the divine merit system. We teach the laws of personal responsibility. We also teach that whatever happens to us is caused by us. Now if we feel that we are a very moral person and we feel that we have become associated with a person or persons that are immoral, then we must ask ourselves in all honesty, in truth, "What level in my being that I have not been aware of is expressing itself at this time?" Don't you see? Morals are a very individual thing and each one knows in their soul what their morals are.

Well, I meant, more or less, by our Declaration of Principles, where we say, I think it is the sixth or seventh principle in our— [At each church service, the congregation was invited to speak forth the Declaration of Principles of the National Spiritualist Association of Churches.]

"We believe in the moral responsibility of the individual."

Yes.

Do you not believe in your moral responsibility?

Why, certainly.

But do you not agree that, perhaps, you find your moral responsibility a little different than another's?

Naturally, but what does it mean as a mass group to say it each time?

Each one says it from their own level of awareness and each one knows by their own conscience what is their moral responsibility. The church, in and of itself, does not dictate what is the moral responsibility of any individual and the Spiritualism that we understand does not dictate the moral responsibility. The individuals themselves dictate their own moral responsibility. Does that help with that question?

To a degree. I think I am thinking personal responsibility probably more than moral responsibility.

Yes. Well, the personal responsibility, by its very statement, is personal. Yes. Remember that personal responsibility
is personal.

*I wasn't thinking of personal morals or anything like that. I
was thinking of the—*

Personal responsibility is known by the individual himself.

Thank you.

You're more than welcome.

*In relation to that answer, you said the individual himself
would dictate his own.*

That is correct.

By the very dictation, is not the individual limiting himself?

Now that's a very deep question. You must understand the
Law of Soul Incarnation. If a soul is incarnated into a society in
which its vehicles are brainwashed to a particular way of expression, then that is what the soul has merited by incarnation at
that particular time. You understand? Now the moral standards
of today are not the moral standards of yesterday. They keep
on changing, according to people's thoughts and etc. However,
if the soul has merited the incarnation and the experiences and
the dictates of a society with its morals in the twentieth century,
instead of experiencing the dictates and the moral standards in
the Victorian era, then, of course, that is the individual soul's
merit system. Those are the laws that it has set into motion and,
of course, the limitation, if you look at it in the ways of limitation, the limitation has been set into motion before we entered
the flesh. You understand? Does that help with your question?

*Well, yes, it does. However, could you not work through that
limitation?*

Well, that depends on how much control you have given to
society. Now, if in your computations and in what you have accepted in mind, that society is the governing factor in your life
and these are the basic standards of the society in which you
are living, then, of course, you, naturally, are going to accept

the dictates of that particular society. However, if you're a rebel, or whatever you would care to call it, and you want to express a little bit differently, then, of course, you, as an individual, must pay that price in the society that you have found your soul captured. Does that help with your question?

Thank you very much.

You're more than welcome.

Is all this that has been spoken what you could call the law of relativity?

Well, I wouldn't say it quite that way. Remember that man, by his very nature, is an identity being. And so we are constantly identifying. We identify with this group. We identify with that group. We identify with this society or we identify with that society. Now when a person identifies with any particular society, by the Law of Identity, they receive energy, of course, attention. Do you understand? In other words, they fit into that particular ballpark or that particular society. Now, if you decide to make a change, that means you will no longer be in harmony with that particular society. Is that intelligent to you? And when you are no longer in harmony with it, you are no longer receiving energy from it and you will suffer the consequences. Do you understand?

But it's all fairly relative, isn't it?

Well, if you want to look at it that way, absolutely. If you want to look at it in the way of relativity, everything is relative. Everything, don't you see. The only thing that is not relative is the Divine Void. That's not relative.

I hadn't raised my hand yet. There has been considerable mention, both prior to reading the discourse and in the discourse itself, regarding lessons being repeated. And it has been stated that "truth is taught through indirection, demonstration, and example [Discourse 18]." I would like to come down off the high thing and get down to a little practical thing here at the moment in the level at which I'm asking the question. When we are given examples through indirection and do not respond, what direction is the tendency for the lesson to take?

Well, now in reference to your question, I am sure that you understand that it varies according to the many levels of one soul's expression at any given time. If a lesson is given—and "truth is taught through indirection, demonstration, and example," however, is an integral part of the teachings of truth—and when the lesson is given in indirection and it is not perceived by the student, the question is asked, What is the normal path that it takes? The path that it takes, in and of itself, is not normal, because it is so varied. But I can say this: the principle of the teaching of the lesson is ever the same, ever the same. For example, if a child is taught that they have breakfast at a certain time, and one morning, they don't show up on time for breakfast, and if the parent has cleared the table and there is no breakfast there, that is one way of teaching the child. You understand? Now there's another way of teaching the child. If the child continues to not be at breakfast on time and the parent gets tired of taking the food away and having the experience, it is within the parent's choice, you understand, to change to a more direct method. And when the child is late to have the breakfast hot and waiting for them and to pour a little arsenic in it. *[The students laugh loudly.]* You see, the lesson will still be learned. And so it is, my good friends, you understand, that the lessons are taught in many different ways.

Thank you, friends. Let us go have refreshments.

JULY 12, 1973

INDEX

A

Absolute, 522

Absolute knowing, 287

Acceptance, 451, 528, 539, 540, 542

Acceptance of death, 275

Accident, 227, 339

Acting *versus* reacting, 255, 256, 552

Action, 80, 87, 126, 140, 166, 442, 536–538, 556

Acupuncture, 447

Adversity, 162, 205–206, 212, 230, 358, 407, 421

Affirmation, 491, 519

Age of communication, 226

Ages past, 3, 4

Air, 57, 76, 105, 226, 352

Air center, 264

All, 235

Allegorical form, 410

Allness, 215, 322

Allsoul, 3, 4, 46, 58, 61, 62, 93–94, 180, 233, 239, 246, 290, 292, 294, 318, 319, 337, 339–341, 370, 452

Analysis, 547

Analyzing, 379, 436

Anatomy, parts of, 33, 39, 55, 71, 77, 79–80, 85, 254, 264, 265, 292, 379, 428, 505, 506

Angels, 30, 425, 426

Angels of Light, 6, 143

Anger, 78, 87, 88, 217, 385

Animal instinct, 239, 243

Animal vibration, 243

Animals, 21, 238, 244, 245, 283, 406, 516

Annihilation, 558

Anxiety, 9

Application, 284, 314, 396

Appreciation, 51

Aquarian Age, 224, 226

Art, 417, 420

Art of giving, 27, 196, 197, 199, 409, 441, 497

Art of questioning, 424

Aspiration, 4, 26, 39, 81, 152, 188, 495, 504

Astral birth, 275

Astral body, 36, 57, 128, 162, 228, 302, 304, 338, 380, 451, 520, 521, 562

Astral dimension, 327, 357, 380

Astral experience, 520

Astral flights, 562

Astral realms, 254, 293, 294, 327, 375, 376, 507, 508, 521

Astral substance, 34, 157, 380, 521

Astral world, 7, 223, 356, 357, 377

Astrology, 226

Atlantis, 225

Attachment, 18, 35, 94, 126, 175, 186, 211, 212, 230, 262, 286, 319, 320, 346, 358, 360, 384, 407, 522, 523, 565

Attachments, refining, 234

Attainment, 553

Attention, 34, 51, 99, 232, 282, 375, 448, 492, 513–516, 529, 543, 559, 565, 571

Attitude, 124, 125, 554